Lecture Notes in Computer Science 6420

Commenced Publication in 1973
Founding and Former Series Editors:
Gerhard Goos, Juris Hartmanis, and Jan

Antonio Casimiro   Rogério de Lemos
Cristina Gacek (Eds.)

Architecting Dependable Systems VII

 Springer

Volume Editors

Antonio Casimiro
University of Lisbon
Faculty of Science
Campo Grande, Bloco C6, Piso 3
1749-016 Lisbon, Portugal
E-mail: casim@di.fc.ul.pt

Rogério de Lemos
University of Kent
School of Computing
Canterbury, Kent CT2 7NF, UK
E-mail: r.delemos@kent.ac.uk

Cristina Gacek
City University, London
Centre for Software Reliability
Northampton Square, London EC1V 0HB, UK
E-mail: cristina.gacek.1@city.ac.uk

Library of Congress Control Number: 2010939153

CR Subject Classification (1998): D.2, D.2.11, D.1, F.3, D.3, C.2.4

LNCS Sublibrary: SL 2 – Programming and Software Engineering

ISSN   0302-9743
ISBN-10   3-642-17244-X Springer Berlin Heidelberg New York
ISBN-13   978-3-642-17244-1 Springer Berlin Heidelberg New York

springer.com

© Springer-Verlag Berlin Heidelberg 2010
Printed in Germany

Typesetting: Camera-ready by author, data conversion by Scientific Publishing Services, Chennai, India
Printed on acid-free paper   06/3180

Foreword

Today, in all kinds of systems, reaching from tiny devices to large global infrastructures, software plays a central role. In addition, information technology supports us in many daily activities and we therefore rely on the provision of the software-based services that are required to fulfill them. Therefore, our society and daily life depend more and more on complex software and its proper operation.

In particular, areas such as safety-critical systems, the critical role of software, and the need for dependable software systems have long been recognized. However, today the need for dependable software is no longer restricted to such special areas but has become a problem that has to be taken into account for many complex software systems.

These complex software systems can only be built when we architect them using existing as well as newly engineered parts that provide the required overall capabilities as a combination of the capabilities of its parts. During the development and evolution of such complex software, the software architecture therefore plays a crucial role in defining the relations between these parts: It permits us to decompose the software into manageable parts and to compose the software from existing or adapted parts and thus enables the cost-effective engineering of software by multiple teams.

This book series addresses the question of how the interplay of software architecture and dependability has to be approached. The effort is driven by a very successful series of workshops that brought together the international communities working on dependability and software architecture. Six books have been published and this seventh volume continues this successful endeavor to report on results in this research direction combining both fields.

During the last few years, architecting dependable software systems has gained more importance in sectors such as commerce, government, and industry. Not only dependability but also security issues have to be addressed during the development and evolution of the architecture. Furthermore, the dependability and security requirements cannot be considered in isolation, as architecting such systems essentially means finding the right trade-off among these attributes and the various other requirements imposed on the system.

Therefore, the workshop series on Architecting Dependable Systems (WADS) has joined forces with the Workshop on the Role of Software Architecture for Testing and Analysis (ROSATEA) and the Workshop on Views on Designing Complex Architectures (VODCA) in form of the newly established International Symposium on Architecting Critical Systems (ISARCS) that took place for the first time in June 2010 in Prague in the Czech Republic under my guidance as Program Committee Chair.

In this seventh book on the subject this tendency is also already visible and we also have contributions that address security issues even though dependability clearly remains the main focus.

The book includes parts addressing mobile and ubiquitous systems, architecting systems, fault management as well as experience and vision.

In the mobile and ubiquitous systems part, there are contributions that approach self-healing pervasive computing systems and self-management of ad hoc networks as well as cooperative backup for mobile nodes.

Papers on the identification of requirements in so–called systems of systems and the interaction on requirements and architectural pattern are contained in the part on architecting systems. In addition, some contributions address architecting dependable service-oriented embedded systems as well as robustness and timeliness for aerospace systems.

The fault management part provides articles on architecting dependable systems capable of proactive fault management and online diagnosis of performance problems.

In the final part on experience and vision, several reports on experience and related visions are presented. This includes discussions on collaborative QoS, software assumptions and failure tolerance, dependability and reflective computing and validation.

The combination of the latest research results and more experience and visionary papers in the last part does not only provide a good coverage of the area but also gives a very inspiring outlook. It shows what we can expect to achieve and where the challenges may lie in our future journey for more dependable complex software.

September 2010   Holger Giese

Preface

This is the seventh book in a series on *Architecting Dependable Systems*. This series started eight years ago, and brings together issues related to software architectures and the dependability and security of systems. This book includes expanded and peer-reviewed papers based on the selected contributions of the Workshop on Architecting Dependable Systems (WADS), organized at the 2009 International Conference on Dependable Systems and Networks (DSN 2009), and a number of invited papers written by recognized experts in the area.

Identification of the system structure (i.e., architecture) early in its development process makes it easier for the developers to make crucial decisions about system properties and to justify them before moving to the design or implementation stages. Moreover, the architectural level views support abstracting away from details of the system, thus facilitating the understanding of broader system concerns. One of the benefits of a well-structured system is the reduction of its overall complexity, which in turn leads to a more dependable and secure system. System dependability is defined as the reliance that can be justifiably placed on the service delivered by the system, while security can be defined as protecting the system and certain information it contains from unauthorized access and handling. Both have become essential aspects of computer systems as everyday life increasingly depends on software. It is therefore a matter of concern that dependability and security issues are usually left until too late in the process of system development.

Making decisions and reasoning about structure happen at different levels of abstraction throughout the software development cycle. Reasoning about dependability at the architectural level has recently been in the focus of researchers and practitioners because of the complexity of emerging applications. From the perspective of software engineering, traditionally striving to build software systems that are fault-free, architectural consideration of dependability requires the acceptance of the fact that system models need to reflect that it is impossible to avoid or foresee all faults. This requires novel notations, methods and techniques providing the necessary support for reasoning about faults (including fault avoidance, fault tolerance, fault removal and fault forecasting) at the architectural level. Moreover, due to the inherent design trade-off between dependability and security attributes, security issues should also be taken into account at the architectural level.

This book comes as a result of bringing together the research communities of software architectures, dependability and security, and addresses issues that are currently relevant to improving the state of the art in architecting dependable and secure systems. The book consists of four parts: Mobile and Ubiquitous Systems, Architecting Systems, Fault Management, and Experience and Vision.

The first part of this book is entitled "Mobile and Ubiquitous Systems" and contains three papers. The first paper of this part, authored by T. Bourdenas, M. Sloman and E. C. Lupu, and entitled "Self-Healing for Pervasive Computing Systems" presents Starfish, a self-healing framework for wireless sensor networks that follows the

Self-Managed Cell architectural paradigm. It includes an embedded policy system that allows reconfiguration of individual nodes as well as remote execution of actions by handling access control to remote resources, and supports adaptation of nodes allowing deployment of new strategies at run-time inside the network. The case studies presented provide insight into the validity of the fault model adopted, and give preliminary results on the accuracy of detection techniques. D. Blough, G. Resta, P. Santi and M. Leoncini, in their paper "Self-Organization and Self-Maintenance of Mobile Ad Hoc Networks," provide a set of topology control protocols that are designed for dynamic and failure-prone networks, relying on the explicit coordination of neighboring nodes for resource efficiency. The proposed solutions also account for the fact that transmission power levels range over discrete values. Extensive simulation results illustrate the potential benefits of these new protocols. The paper "Data Backup for Mobile Nodes: A Cooperative Middleware and an Experimentation Platform" by M.-O. Killijian and M. Roy presents a middleware architecture dedicated to the provision of cooperative data backup on mobile nodes. The proposed middleware relies on the belief that for building fast and reliable applications and services in a ubiquitous environment, local cooperation with neighboring nodes is the approach to follow in order to build fast and reliable applications and services. In addition to the middleware, the authors also present a platform for its experimental evaluation.

Part 2 of the book is entitled "Architecting Systems" and includes four papers focusing on dependability issues while architecting systems. In their paper, entitled "Identification of Security Requirements in Systems of Systems by Functional Security Analysis," A. Fuchs and R. Rieke address the security requirements elicitation step for safety-critical systems of systems. They adopt a method tracing down functional dependencies over system component boundaries onto the origin of information as a functional flow graph. Such a graph is then used to derive sets of authenticity requirements for the given security and dependability objectives.

The second paper in this part, "Implementing Reliability: The Interaction of Requirements, Tactics and Architecture Patterns," is authored by N. B. Harrison and P. Avgeriou. In this paper, the authors address the issue of actually implementing the reliability tactics, as introduced by L. Bass et al.[1], while architecting systems. The work focuses on the main factors affecting how, where, and the difficulty involved in adopting reliability tactics. The information presented can guide architects in their choices of patterns and tactics to use. The third paper, by S. Brennan, S. Fritisch, Y. Liu, A. Sterritt, J. Fox, É. Linehan, C. Driver, R. Meier, V. Cahill, W. Harrison and S. Clarke, is entitled "A Framework for Flexible and Dependable Service-Oriented Embedded Systems." The paper presents a framework that enables dynamic service composition for service-oriented embedded systems, based on model-driven development techniques. The framework considers the implications of dynamic composition and reconfiguration on temporal domain properties, as well as adverse feature interactions resulting from the service assemblies. In the final paper of this part, "Architecting Robustness and Timeliness in a New Generation of Aerospace Systems," J. Rufino, J. Craveiro, and P. Verissimo describe the foundations of an architecture for robust temporal and spatial partitioning aimed at a new generation of spaceborne systems that include advanced dependability and timeliness adaptation/control mechanisms.

---

[1] L. Bass, P. Clements, R. Kazman, Software Architecture in Practice, Addison-Wesley, 2003.

The paper introduces a formal system model addressing temporal properties and enabling its verification, and it includes a prototype implementation to illustrate the approach.

Part 3 of the book is on "Fault Management" and includes two papers. The first paper written by F. Salfner and M. Malek, is entitled "Architecting Dependable Systems with Proactive Fault Management." The authors provide a comprehensive overview of research in proactive fault management and methods for online failure prediction, and then they introduce a model to assess the effects of proactive fault management on system dependability metrics. Finally, the paper includes an architectural blueprint to illustrate how proactive fault management can be incorporated into system architecture. K. Bare et al. contribute to this part of the book with the paper "ASDF: An Automated, Online Framework for Diagnosing Performance Problems." They focus on performance problems in large-scale distributed systems, by automating problem localization so as to narrow down performance problems to a specific node or set of nodes. The viability of the approach is illustrated by discussions on its application to Hadoop.

Part 4 of the book is on "Experience and Vision" and includes four papers. M. A. Hiltunen and R. D. Schlichting contribute to the book with the paper "Is Collaborative QoS the Solution to the SOA Dependability Dilemma?" The paper reviews the vision of SOAs, and discusses the characteristics that make them particularly challenging for dependability. It then discusses techniques that have been proposed for building dependable SOAs, and argues that any successful solution to implement dependability requires collaborative quality of service (QoS). In the second paper, entitled "Software Assumptions Failure Tolerance: Role, Strategies, and Visions," V. De Florio shares his vision on a suitable approach to facilitate the design of fully autonomically resilient software systems. The author considers that increasing software complexity can be tackled through architectural and structuring techniques, but keeping a holistic view for addressing the problem of assumption failures. The paper provides strategies to achieve assumption failure-tolerant systems and discusses some practical tools that may be used for this purpose. The third paper authored by J.-C. Fabre and entitled "Architecting Dependable Systems Using Reflective Computing: Lessons Learnt and Some Challenges," discusses how the separation of concerns supported by the reflection paradigm is of interest for practical dependable systems, focusing in particular on fault–tolerance mechanisms. Based on his past experience, the author presents his perception on the use of reflective computing by identifying some lessons learned and listing some key challenges that should be addressed in the future. The paper entitled "Architecting and Validating Dependable Systems: Experiences and Visions" by A. Bondavalli, A. Ceccarelli and P. Lollini discusses the evolution of the challenges in architecting and validating critical systems with respect to the systems' evolution from traditional embedded systems towards pervasive, dynamic and heterogeneous systems. The experience gained and the expected future trends are considered in the context of several research projects.

Architecting dependable systems is now a well-recognized area, attracting the interest and contributions of many researchers. We are certain that this book will prove valuable for both developers designing complex applications and researchers building techniques supporting this. We are grateful to many people that made this book possible. Our thanks go to the authors of the contributions for their excellent work, the

DSN 2009 WADS participants for their active involvement in the discussions. We would also like to thank Alfred Hofmann and his team from Springer for believing in the idea of a series of books on this important topic and for helping us to get it published. Last but not least, we greatly appreciate the efforts of our reviewers who have helped us in ensuring the high quality of the contributions. They are Paris Avgeriou, Douglas Blough, Andrea Bondavalli, Walter Cazzola, João Craveiro, Vincenzo De Florio, Leonardo B. de Oliveira, Felicita Di Giandomenico, Jean-Charles Fabre, Andreas Fuchs, Karl M. Goeschka, Swapna S. Gokhale, Neil Harrison, Matti Hiltunen, Paola Inverardi, Svilen Ivanov, Paolo Lollini, Emil C. Lupu, Miroslav Malek, Rene Meier, Edgar Nett, Roland Rieke, Roshanak Roshandel, Matthieu Roy, José Rufino, Paolo Santi, Rick Schlichting, Paulo Sousa, Massimo Tivoli, Jó Ueyama, Marco Vieira and several anonymous reviewers.

September 2010   Antonio Casimiro
                                                                                          Rogério de Lemos
                                                                                           Cristina Gacek

Table of Contents

Part 4. Experience and Vision

Self-healing for Pervasive Computing Systems

Themistoklis Bourdenas, Morris Sloman, and Emil C. Lupu

Department of Computing, Imperial College London, UK
{t.bourdenas07,m.sloman,e.c.lupu}@imperial.ac.uk
http://www.doc.ic.ac.uk/

Abstract. The development of small wireless sensors and smart-phones have facilitated new pervasive applications. These pervasive systems are expected to perform in a broad set of environments with different capabilities and resources. Application requirements may change dynamically requiring flexible adaptation. Sensing faults appear during their lifetime and as users are not expected to have technical skills, the system needs to be self-managing. We discuss the Self-Managed Cell as an architectural paradigm and describe some fundamental components to address distributed management of sensing faults as well as adaptation for wireless sensor nodes.

1 Introduction

The development of small wireless sensors and smart-phones, which include various sound, video, motion and location sensors, have facilitated realising new pervasive applications. These include health-care applications to monitor physiological parameters such as blood-pressure, heart-rate, temperature or ECG of at-risk patients as well as determining their activity; monitoring and controlling temperature, humidity and lighting levels in buildings; environmental monitoring and flood warning and even tracking wildlife movement. These pervasive systems are expected to perform in a vast number of environments, ranging from urban to rural, with different requirements and resources. They are often mobile, in harsh environments and application requirements may change dynamically requiring flexible adaptation. Users may be non-technical so the systems need to be self-managing. Some applications such as health-care and flood warning may be life-critical and devices may be inaccessible for repairs so self-healing with respect to faults and errors is important.

Pervasive computing system rely on Wireless Sensor Networks (WSNs) for receiving feedback from the environment they interact with. Sensor networks use devices, known as 'motes', that have limited processing and power resources. They have to cater for deterioration of sensor accuracy over time due to physical phenomena such as overheating or chemical fouling as well as external factors such as low battery levels or physical damage. The quality of wireless links may vary, particularly with mobile systems, and devices may completely fail.

Faults in pervasive systems occur more frequently than in traditional distributed systems due to exposure to the physical environment. Hence, provisions

A. Casimiro et al. (Eds.): Architecting Dependable Systems VII, LNCS 6420, pp. 1–25, 2010.
© Springer-Verlag Berlin Heidelberg 2010

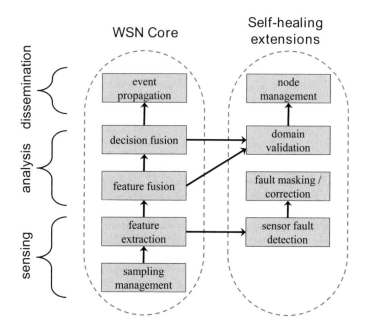

Fig. 1. Layered functional architecture of WSNs

for handling and recovering from faults must be an important design consideration. Frequent replacement of devices and manual recalibration are impractical and hinder the adoption and use by non-expert users with limited technical skills. The system has to be self-diagnosing and self-healing to maintain operational state and mask component failures from users.

Sensor networks are typically structured in three distinct layers as illustrated in figure 1. At the bottom is the *sensing* layer, e.g. room temperature sensing for air-conditioning control in a building. The middle layer is the *analysis*, where sensing events are processed refining observations for making decisions on the operating context. For instance, readings from different thermometers can be combined to determine a mean value, rate of change or event's boundaries. Furthermore, decisions in local areas can be composed for higher level reasoning of the environment. This process, called decision fusion, combines localised or low-level decisions with application-specific knowledge.

The top layer is the *dissemination* of decisions from the decision centres to the network. This, typically, involve orchestration of information available in different parts of the network. Faults in the architecture propagate upwards, where inaccuracy in readings at the bottom affect decision quality in higher layers. Therefore, errors have to be handled as close to their source as possible.

Pervasive systems should incorporate autonomic computing concepts to minimise required manual administration by end-users. The key attributes of autonomic systems are *self-configuration*, *self-healing*, *self-optimisation* and *self-protection* [11]. These attributes are not orthogonal as some depend on others. For instance, in order for a network to heal a defective component, it should be able to reconfigure itself and possibly optimise the use of its resources to allow for backup solutions.

This chapter will describe fundamental components that extend the Self-Managed Cell (SMC) architecture with fault management services on WSNs, focusing mostly on quality of sensor readings. This includes a taxonomy on sensor faults, statistical tools for correlating readings of relevant sensors that can be used to detect faults and a policy service for specifying and implementing adaptive behaviour within an SMC. An SMC, as described in our examples, consists of a set of wireless nodes as well as some terminal devices such as smart-phones.

We continue by introducing the Self-Managed Cell architecture and use of policy management as the control mechanism in autonomous environments. Section 2 presents Starfish, an embedded policy system, used to specify adaptation strategies in mote-based SMCs. Section 3 gives a formal definition of a fault handling framework for sensors and defines the fault classes we consider in the framework. In section 4 we describe self-healing service integration in the SMC architecture. Case studies are presented in section 5, while section 6 summarises related work. Finally, we conclude and discuss future work in section 7.

1.1   Self-Managed Cell Architecture

The Self-Managed Cell (SMC) is a structuring paradigm for autonomic management of pervasive systems [15]. It is a set of components, which forms an autonomous management domain that facilitates addition or removal of components, caters for error prone sensors, component failures and automatically adapts to the users' current activity or environment. It has a well-defined interface for interaction with other SMCs. A typical SMC could be the set of sensors and actuators plus smart-phone controller forming a body sensor network monitoring the health of a patient, the devices in an intelligent building, a group of autonomous vehicles collaborating on a search and rescue mission, or the routers and firewalls managed by an Internet Service Provider.

The SMC can be considered an architectural pattern that can be tailored on instantiation and that can be applied at different levels of scale. It includes a configurable set of services including a *Discovery Service* for discovering and authenticating new components as members of the cell, a *Policy Service* for specifying adaptive behaviour, an *Event Service* supporting publish-subscribe interactions between the services and components as well as context awareness, security, fault management etc. The cell maintains a set of *Managed Objects*, i.e. the components that carry out the tasks of the system. A remote SMC unit might be a *Managed Object*, itself, in a host SMC, thus composing complex structures and interactions. Figure 2 illustrates the architecture. The white elements are core SMC services and components, while grey elements are self-healing extensions that are discussed in this paper.

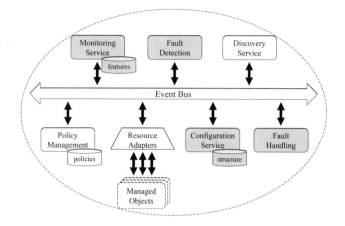

Fig. 2. A Self-Managed Cell with self-healing services (grey boxes)

def $\langle authpolicy \rangle$ $[+/-]$ **def** $\langle obligpolicy \rangle$
   subject $\langle role \rangle$ **on** $\langle event \rangle$
   target $\langle role \rangle$ **if** $\langle condition \rangle$
   if $\langle condition \rangle$ **do** $\langle action \rangle$
   action $\langle name \rangle$

(a)   (b)

Fig. 3. Syntax of (a) authorisation policy and (b) obligation policy

Policies are the control mechanism of the SMC that specify the behaviour of the entity. There are two types of policies; *obligation* policies, which are essentially Event-Condition-Action (ECA) rules expressing system behaviour in an event-driven model and *authorisation* policies, which define what resources or services can be accessed by remote SMCs. The policy notation is presented in figure 3.

Events in the system are generated by *Managed Objects* and are communicated to the *Policy Service* via the *Event Bus* of the SMC. Actions are operations exposed by *Managed Objects*. As *Managed Objects* can be remote resources, even different SMC units, communication occurs through local *Adapters* to abstract such details exposing simple interfaces for policies to operate on.

While the policy construct is the basic unit for defining behaviour, as the scale of running application increases, so does the need for higher-level constructs to manage their complexity. *Missions* are sets of policies that serve a specific task and are deployed as units on nodes. *Roles* are placeholders to which nodes with required capabilities are assigned when discovered. Thus, policies can be defined in terms of roles without statically binding nodes for defining interactions. This, further, enables role assignment to nodes at run-time. Missions can be associated with roles, i.e. the mission policies will be loaded into the node when it is assigned to the role. Similarly, modules required by a role can be associated with it.

2   The Starfish Framework

The *Starfish* platform [3] is an adaptation framework for WSNs that focuses on the self-healing aspects of the network. The framework's fundamental components are *Finger 2*; an embedded policy system for sensor nodes, *SML*; a module library to simplify programming of motes providing basic functions and tools used in sensing applications and *Starfish editor*; a client side graphical interface for managing policies, missions and roles on motes.

Starfish is, essentially, a realisation of the SMC architecture for sensor nodes, laying the infrastructure for management and adaptation within the network as well as deployment of self-healing strategies. The *Policy Service* is implemented by Finger 2, an embedded policy system for TinyOS 2.x.[1] *Starfish Modules* are the *Managed Objects* of the embedded SMC, while the event-based programming model of the TinyOS is utilised as the SMC *Event Bus* via which local services communicate. Policies invoke actions on modules and modules can generate events that trigger policies.

We focus on the the policy-based adaptation strategies for dealing with sensor faults and component failures, applying necessary reconfigurations. Modules can reside either locally or on a remote node and export *event* and *action* interfaces for policies. Communication with remote modules occurs transparently to the node, through local adapters.

2.1   Policy Management on Sensor Nodes

Finger 2 is an embedded policy system for motes. It is a scaled down version of the Ponder 2 [25] policy system. While Ponder 2 is able to run on mobile devices such as smart phones or gumstix, it requires a Java runtime environment that is not available on motes that typically have low computational and memory capabilities.

Consider a health-care body deployment scenario, where a nurse requires an update of a patient's ECG readings. Such a task can be expressed as a set of policies shown in figure 4. The nurse's device generates a *RequestUpdate* event and installs a new policy, *ECG_update*, on the patient's device. The action part of the policy is a remote invocation, where the nurse calls action *Install()* on patient's module *policy*. *ECG_update* is triggered every time a reading is available from the *sensor* module running on the patient's device. If the reporting sensor is of type ECG then the node uses its *network* module to send the value read back to the nurse, along with its local timestamp.

An authorisation policy permits nurses of grade 'staff nurse' to upload policies, if the patient's sensor has a battery level greater than 20%. In general, authorisation policies are used to protect nodes from incoming requests by other nodes. Remote interactions are subject to authorisation policy checks and may require authentication as described in [28]. Dynamic management of policies, i.e. loading, enabling or disabling policies at runtime, allows dynamic strategy

---

[1] http://www.tinyos.net/

```
def ECG_request
    on gui.RequestUpdate(patient, type)
    if network.IsAvail(patient) and type is ECG
    do patient.policy.Install(ECG_update)
```

On nurse's request for an ECG update, install 'ECG_update' on patient's endpoint.

```
def ECG_update
    on sensor.Reading(type, value)
    if type is ECG
    do network.Send(nurse, value, timer.Now())
```

On receiving of an ECG reading, send it to the nurse along with a local timestamp.

```
def allow_nurse_policy_install+
    subject nurse
    target patient
    if power.Level() > 20 and nurse.type is staff_nurse
    action policy.Install
```

Authorise access of 'policy.Install()' to a staff nurse given that the local power level is above 20%.

Fig. 4. Health-care scenario in policies

adaptation. Finger 2 runs on individual sensor nodes, instead of a remote sink outside the network, thus allowing an immediate, constrained form of dynamic reprogrammability.

Finger 2 Architecture. Figure 5 illustrates the high level architecture of Finger 2. Modules are unique instances in every node, i.e. only one *network* or *timer* instance exists per node, meaning that state is shared among policies that use them. Incoming events may either be internal, from devices on the node or external, from other nodes in the network. An external event is first checked by the *Authorisation Manager* to determine whether the source is allowed to emit events to the node. Events are eventually passed to the *Obligation Manager*, where they are uniformly handled by the *Event Manager* that looks up associated policies from the local repository.

Retrieved policies are forwarded to the embedded *Virtual Machine* for execution. Obligation policies, triggered by the event, are executed serially by the VM without any guarantee on the order of execution. The VM initially validates the condition part of each policy and executes the relevant actions if satisfied. Finger 2 modules provide two interfaces for policies, the *PredicateI* and *ActionI* respectively. For remote event invocations, the *Virtual Machine* consults the *Authorisation Manager* on whether the invoker is allowed to trigger the requested action. Thick black arrows in figure 5 represent the execution flow that has two starting points while thin solid arrows illustrate the interfaces between different components in the system. Finally, a dashed arrow indicates data access.

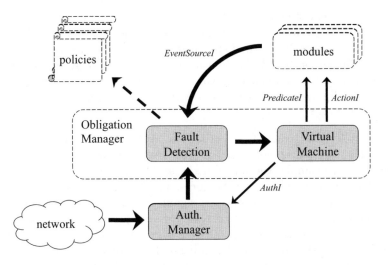

Fig. 5. Finger 2 architecture

Starfish Module Library. The Starfish Module Library (SML) for Finger 2 supports the most commonly used functions in WSN applications. These include sensor sampling, feature extraction, buffering, timers for scheduling of events and network primitives for exchange of messages among nodes. For instance, the *sensor* module provides the basic interface with the node's sensing devices, abstracting their details for the policy author. It provides a periodic sampling, *Sense()*, and immediate sampling, *Get()*, interfaces. Modules usually provide asynchronous interfaces for tasks that require an arbitrary amount of time for completion. Consequently, readings are not returned directly but through a *Reading()* event, when the value is available. The context variables of the event are the *type* of the sampled sensor (e.g. temperature, humidity, acceleration, etc.) and the sensor *value*. Context variables can be checked and used in the condition and action parts of an obligation policy.

The *feature* module includes feature extraction operations such as mean value, variance or correlation coefficient. A typical sensor application uses a few feature extraction techniques as close as possible to the sensing source to reduce the propagation cost of raw measurements from sensors in the network. Readings and features are stored using the *buffer* module that provides utility functions for storing data on the node. The *timer* module permits scheduling of events on the node, e.g. periodic transmission of data or calculation of an average of readings. Arithmetic, associative and logical operators used in conditions are implemented in respective modules. The *Network* and *serial* modules provide primitives for communication with other nodes or sending debugging and logging messages to the serial ports of the sensors.

The framework can be extended by adding new modules required in specific domains or for implementation of specialised algorithms. The design facilitates easy integration of new modules through simple interfaces.

Missions are sets of policies that accomplish a specific task. For instance, the transmission of the average temperature from a node to its cluster-head can be described as a combination of simple actions, described as policies, such as a periodic polling of on-board temperature, calculation of the average temperature value and finally, transmission of the message to the cluster-head using the radio. Aggregation of policies into missions assist their management and assignment to roles.

Roles simplify policy definition as they can abstractly describe participants in policies. They are placeholders that will be mapped to actual nodes at runtime. In the figure 4 example, the nurse in the authorisation policy is a role that a smart-phone, belonging to a specific nurse, may be assigned. Nodes are assigned initially some roles, however, these assignments can be modified at run-time provided the necessary modules, i.e. resources, are present on the node. Starfish provides modules to manage dynamic role assignment and mission deployment. When a role is assigned to a node, associated missions and policies are loaded (if not already there) and activated, while when a role is removed missions and policies are de-activated and may also be removed if memory space is an issue.

Configurations are the initial set of roles, missions and modules loaded on nodes. For instance a node may be assigned the roles of a data collector and cluster-head. New missions and policies can be loaded on nodes once they are deployed without disrupting their operation. Modules, which are essentially NesC[2] code, can not be modified after the initial configuration, due to the limitations of the operating system on uploading binary updates to motes. It would be feasible to extend Starfish to support such operation for other sensor environments that enable code-distribution and in-situ reprogramming [7].

3 Fault Classification

In this section we specify what we consider a self-healing framework for sensor reading faults and its requirements. Furthermore, we provide a taxonomy of the fault classes we consider.

3.1 Fault Framework

Values received from a sensing device are typically subject to transient or permanent faults that are present due to external environmental factors such as interference that distorts the observed attribute, electronic fouling of a sensor's circuitry, physical damage or deterioration of quality due to low energy levels on the node. Consequently, if we model the readings of a sensor that monitors an attribute as a random variable X, the input will be the *ground truth* plus a random *error factor*, as illustrated in equation 1.

$$X = g(X) + \sigma(X) \tag{1}$$

---

[2] http://nescc.sourceforge.net/

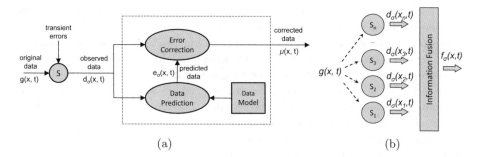

Fig. 6. (a) Model based error correction, (b) Information fusion process

The goal of a self-healing framework would be to minimise the *error factor*, $\sigma(X)$, in order for the sensor readings to be as close to the ground truth as possible. Thus, the reading from a sensor where the ground truth value is x at time instance t is an approximation function, $\mu(x, t)$, dependent on variables x and t.

The error component is affected by both *transient* and *permanent* faults on the sensors. A transient error is a random deviation from the reality that does not deteriorate the state of the sensor but only affects the input at the current time instance. A permanent error is an error that the sensor cannot recover from and has an effect on all subsequent readings unless corrective measures are taken.

A typical approach in the literature, to reduce the transient error component, is model-based correction [18], when observed attributes of the environment have a formal representation of their behaviour (i.e. a mathematical, probabilistic or heuristic rule-based model). Such systems provide an estimation of the input value based on a priori knowledge of the observed subject and temporal correlation of readings, thus constructing a prediction model.

Figure 6 (a) illustrates this approach, where transient errors in a sensor distort the ground truth. The observed value, $d_\sigma(x, t)$, is subject to errors. The estimated value of the system, $\mu(x, t))$ is a composition of the observed value and the expected value, $e_\sigma(x, t)$. Assuming a linear combination of the two values the *Error Correction* unit would produce and update parameters α and β in equation 2. The expected value is produced by the *Data Prediction* unit that uses the attribute's model and recently observed values to produce its estimation.

$$\mu(x, t) = \alpha d_\sigma(x, t) + \beta e_\sigma(x, t) \qquad (2)$$

In cases where multiple sensors are available, cooperation in a neighbourhood can be exploited to reduce errors. This process, shown in figure 6, is known as information fusion [8,27]. Observations from a group of sensors are aggregated in the fusion point, where they are combined to produce the estimated value. The fusion function depends on the type of sensors involved — there can be *homogeneous*, sensors of the same type that monitor the same attribute, or *heterogenous*, sensors of the same or different type that monitor different but correlated attributes.

In homogeneous groups the fusion function, $f_\sigma([x_i], t)$, is a form of consensus formula between participating nodes such as majority voting for discrete random variables or averaging for continuous random variables. Such schemes can be enhanced with weighted alternatives, where weights represent belief in the sensor's quality or degree of relevance to the attribute in question [19]. Homogeneous fusion is a case of *explicit* redundancy, where a defective sensor can be adequatelly replaced by others. In heterogeneous fusion, there is *implicit* redundancy, in which case losing a sensor cannot be entirely compensated for. Instead, remaining sensors produce a rough estimation of missing values and provide a potentially degraded but acceptable service.

Permanent, non fail-stop faults may manifest over time in sensors affecting their accuracy. Such faults are commonly referred to as *drift* or deviation from ground truth and are accumulative, i.e. the error increases over time worsening the effect of previous errors. For this class of faults collaborative on-line recalibration algorithms adapt to a deviating sensor by consulting co-located neighbours to adjust the parameters of its correction function $\Delta_\sigma(x, t)$. Consequently, the estimation function $\mu(x, t)$ of equation 2 can be extended as the linear combination of the four components discussed, shown in equation 3.

$$\mu(x, t) = \alpha d_\sigma(x, t) + \beta e_\sigma(x, t) + \gamma f_\sigma([x_i], t) + \delta \Delta_\sigma(x, t) \text{ where } i \in S \quad (3)$$

S is the set of nodes in the fusion group and the parameters α, β, γ and δ denote the relative importance in each function that affects the result.

A fault handling framework should allow deployment of such functions on the network nodes when necessary to maintain the quality of the monitoring service within acceptable levels. Deployment of these functions depends on the specific faults to be corrected. Hence, fault detection mechanisms for accurate identification of sensor state are required for different models of faults.

3.2   Fault Classes

We provide a taxonomy of faults occurring in sensors that will aid the elaboration of detection and recovery mechanisms. We have identified four classes of faults in [2], namely — *short, noise, constant* and *drift* faults. Table 1 summarises the characteristics and impact on the input for each class.

In general *short* faults are perceived as irregular spikes on the input signal, *noise* appears as an unstable signal, whereas *constant* faults are indicated by a flat signal. Finally, *drift* error is a gradual deviation of observed values from the ground truth. We formally define models for each class to help us elaborate their properties and the impact on the sensing application.

Short faults are present on the trace with a random probability, p. The affected data-points can be considered as the original reading multiplied by $[+/-]c$, which is the fault intensity parameter.

Noise faults are modeled as a Gaussian distribution with zero mean value, $\hat{\mu}$, and standard deviation σ. Similar noise models can be found in [26].

Table 1. Taxonomy of faults

Class	Definition	Impact
SHORT	momentary irregularity in the readings of a sensor	very small impact as long as spikes remain sparse, easily canceled out by simple filters
NOISE	prolonged increased variance on the reading values of sensors	impact depends on the signal-to-noise ratio, it can be smoothed using mean / median
CONSTANT	invariant repetition of an arbitrary value that may be relevant to the observed phenomenon	impact could be significant if value is relevant, otherwise it is similar to loosing the input of the sensor
DRIFT	typically smooth persisting deviation (e.g. linear) of the observed value from the ground truth	initially minor impact that is accumulated over time, eventually distorting readings

Constant faults are modeled as a persistent value v over a period of time t.
Drift errors are modeled as a permanent error that increases monotonically over time. We define drift as a linear function $f(t) = \alpha t + \beta$, where t is the time instance.

Modelling of faults allows us to study their properties and devise detection and prevention mechanisms. Modelling is also necessary to evaluate the accuracy of detection mechanisms. Unless we artificially inject faults on a sensor input we are unable to assert that the regions detected are actually faulty as we can not verify the ground truth. Injecting artificial errors enables precise identification of faulty regions and hence allows evaluation of detection mechanisms. This approach however raises the question of how accurately faults are modelled in comparison with faults found in real deployments. In the following sections, we provide accuracy results on detecting faults that follow our model as well as provide insight from real world traces that validates our assumptions on the modelling of these classes.

4   Self-healing Service in SMC

The Starfish platform converts a sensor node to an atomic self-managed unit itself, i.e. an SMC. Starfish modules are the *Managed Objects* of the platform and the *Event Bus* is the event system of TinyOS. A single mote can be considered to be a static SMC without a *Discovery Service*. Composition of such SMCs is achieved by using different architectural patterns to form more complex structures and collaborations in the network [23].

4.1   Fault Management Elements

A self-managed entity implies that it is able to self-heal, i.e. adapts to faults and errors before they start to deteriorate the provided service, or it can recover from a failure. Self-healing requires the combination of an adaptive framework with a set of detection and correction algorithms as defined in the previous section. The framework in this case is the SMC platform and the algorithms are deployed by policies. In this section we discuss such algorithms and how they can be deployed in SMCs. We extend the SMC architecture with self-healing services, as shown in figure 2 in section 1.1, and specialise them for the case of faults on sensing devices.

A *Monitoring Service* is the first step for self-healing as a feedback mechanism is necessary for the system in order to become aware of malfunctioning components. For the sensor node SMC monitoring involves features collected from sensors. A feature aggregation service is necessary in complex SMC structures where the cell is composed of several remote SMCs forming a unit. Policies allow control on features extracted and their collection methods using the SML modules described in section 2.1.

The *Fault Detection Service* operates on features collected by the *Monitoring Service* to validate input with defined models and identify misbehaving sensor and their fault class. The *Fault Handling Service* makes a decision for an appropriate strategy that will most effectively reduce the impact of the identified fault. Such strategies may involve isolating temporarily a defective sensor from the monitoring group of the pervasive application, substituting it with predictions of missing data or, using a collaborative approach, recalibrate the sensor to allow it remain an active monitoring unit.

The *Configuration Service* manages the structure of the SMC, its components and interactions with neighbouring or enclosing SMCs. It deploys decisions, made by the *Fault Handling Service* of the SMC, by manipulating local policies and distributing necessary updates to collaborators for reconfiguration of the network to a new structure.

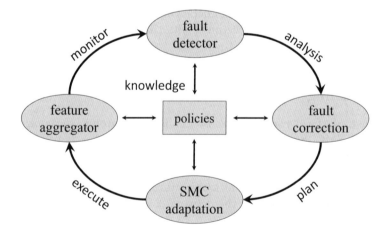

Fig. 7. Self-healing SMC feedback closed-loop

The four services described compose the closed feedback loop defined in the autonomic computing paradigm [11]. Figure 7 illustrates the association of these services with the components defined in the feedback loop. The *Feature Aggregator* is the *monitoring* phase of the loop collecting information on the system's condition. *Fault Detection* perform the *analysis* step of the loop diagnosing the state of the system. The *planning* step in the architecture is the *Fault Handling Service* that construct a process for adapting to or compensating for the effect of the malfunctioning entity of the SMC. Finally, *execution* of the proposed plan is performed by the *Configuration Service*, which modifies policies in local and remote SMCs to comply with the proposed plan.

Policies in SMC encapsulate the knowledge of the autonomic system, in essence the rules that encode the information specific to the application. Knowledge controls all steps in the feedback loop orchestrating components dictating their operation. In the rest of this section we present examples of of how knowledge can be described for the fault detection and reconfiguration of the network.

4.2   Fault Detection and Handling

Local Detectors can be used for all fault classes checking sensor features to validate their readings with respect to a model devised for the application. Such models can be tied to the application, setting hard thresholds, or more generic, where they apply general rules derived from fault class properties.

Short faults manifest themselves as an irrelevant sharp increase or decrease of the sensor's value. As a result, they can be filtered out by a pre-defined threshold. Alternatively the input can be compared with the last valid inputs, assuming that changes between consecutive readings of the monitored attribute will not be sharp. As *short* faults are instantaneous they can simply be discarded.

Such methods use heuristic thresholds tied to the application and the programmer's subjective perception of the attribute. Furthermore, fixed thresholds do not cope well with variable-state attributes (i.e. attributes that modify their behaviour over time) or unexpected behavioural changes. A more general approach, assuming that the input follows a Gaussian distribution, would be to consider *short* faults reading outside the $[\hat{\mu} - 3\sigma, \hat{\mu} + 3\sigma]$ range, where $\hat{\mu}$ is the mean value of the input and σ is the standard deviation of the input. In a normal distribution 99.7% of the values fall in this range.

Noise faults are prolonged fluctuation of the input signal that increases the observed variance, hence decreasing readings' quality. Consequently, a local monitor on the node can use a variance threshold, but again this approach is tied to the application. Additionally, it is not a very effective approach yielding a large number of false positives. This is especially apparent on variable-state attributes, where state transitions with faults can be easily confused.

Constant faults, contrary to *noise*, present zero variance on the input, thus a local monitor could identify them by looking for a flat signal. However, for attributes that have very slow and relatively stable values or a discrete number of states, identification based solely on a local monitor may not be effective confusing normal with erroneous behaviour.

Drift faults, contrary to the previous fault classes, do not have a significant effect on input's variance. Instead, the trend-line of readings is affected, gradually deviating from the ground truth. A local monitor can validate that the trend-line of an attribute follows an appropriately modelled pattern. Trend-lines can be calculated using linear regression analysis or roughly estimated by determining the line joining two suitable, distant data-points in the stored history. While the second approach is more susceptible to false positives it requires significantly less computation. The two approaches appear to perform comparably, from experimental results. Deviation from the model trend-line can be calculated using the slope ratio of the modelled and observed trends. Exceeding a threshold should trigger a drift alarm.

Local fault detectors inherently depend on the accuracy of modelling the monitored attributes, assuming that a priori knowledge exists. If this is not the case or the model is inaccurate, it can confuse the system decreasing overall quality. Moreover, local monitors are unable to handle unexpected behaviour and do not adapt to periodic attributes (e.g. temperature over a year period) or subjects that exhibit different states (e.g. accelerometer on a person standing or walking).

Homogeneous Collaboration can be used in cases where local monitors are inadequate and locality of sensors can be exploited by comparing their extracted features. In homogeneous setups (i.e. sensors monitoring the same attribute) direct comparison of features such as mean value or variance have a straightforward interdependency and can be easily associated among nodes.

Nodes can reason about their state, realising which sensors are more likely to be defective in their neighbourhood, e.g. using voting schemes. For instance, sensors can compare their input's variance, to identify whether high or very low variance are the result of normal behaviour or errors in the sensing device caused by *noise* or *constant* faults respectively. The key assumption in using homogeneous collaboration for fault detection is the fact that a phenomenon or event that manifests itself in an area affects all sensing devices within that area. Faults occurring in nodes are stochastically uncorrelated, thus with adequate redundancy in the network, the probability that the majority of sensors are defective becomes statistically insignificant.

Collaboration of sensors deployed in different nodes involves network communication raising the issue of information distribution in the network. A completely distributed communication approach, requires all nodes in a neighbourhood to exchange information with each other. Every node applies, respectively, the fault detection algorithms locally. The benefit of the approach is that it is decentralised with no central arbitration, being more resilient to failures of individual nodes. Moreover, decisions are made at the enforcement point avoiding extra routing of reconfiguration messages from evaluation point to the enforcement point.

The downside of a fully distributed approach is that, although, work is distributed fairly among all participating nodes, the overall energy requirements of the network significantly increase as every node must listen to its radio for incoming messages from neighbours. Active listening for incoming messages consumes significant amounts of energy preventing nodes to enter a low-power sleep mode. Power consumption deteriorates further in scenarios where the sensing radius of a node is greater than its communication range, requiring multi-hop communication protocols to disseminate information in its sensing neighbourhood. In such cases, the distributed approach does not scale well as the communication cost for a group of N nodes is $O(N^2)$ requiring every member of the group to communicate with every other member.

A hierarchical approach, using local leaders, helps alleviate most of these problems. Nodes are assigned to potentially overlapping clusters that elect a representative leader (cluster-head) that collects feature information from the group members. Clustering allows leaf nodes to enter a sleep mode when not sampling or transmitting data, significantly saving energy. However, it also introduces uneven consumption of energy in the network with regard to cluster-heads. Thus, leadership roles can be assigned to more powerful nodes with greater storage and processing capacity. Additionally, they create local single points of failure within the group. However, leader outages can be addressed with leader re-election schemes. Hierarchy inside the networks decreases the communication complexity, when sensing radius is greater than the communication radius. The worst case scenario remains $O(N^2)$, when every node has only one single-hop neighbour and the group forms a minimal connected graph. Nonetheless, the complexity of communication reduces to $O(Nlog_b(N))$ for an even distribution of nodes in the physical space, where the logarithm base is the average connectivity degree of nodes in the group.

Heterogeneous Collaboration allows sensors of different types to cooperate in detection of faults. Homogeneous collaboration assumes redundancy of sensors in the deployment but in certain scenarios such assumptions may not be practical or even feasible. For instance, there is a physical limit of sensors that can be deployed on a patient's body before they become obtrusive and hinder mobility.

In heterogeneous collaboration, algorithms try to utilise implicit redundancy of sensors to assert their normal operation. Implicit redundancy exists in the network by deploying sensors that monitor different attributes of a phenomenon that combined give insight on occurring events in the environment. Such attributes, though not directly comparable as in the case of homogeneous sensors, exhibit a degree of correlation allowing study of their interdependence. Consider an ambient deployment of thermometer and humidity sensors — although these attributes are not straightforwardly comparable we can determine their dependence by studying their correlation. Sensors of a 3D-accelerometer, though of the same type, are also not directly comparable, as they monitor three different attributes — acceleration in orthogonal axis. Nevertheless, input in all three axis is correlated when the device is worn by a patient to determine her movement.

Models of interdependency allow identification of anomalous behaviour in sensors and hint at potential classes of faults. One measure of dependency is the correlation coefficient that measures linear dependency between variables. The correlation coefficient between two random variables X and Y is defined in equation 4.

$$corr(X, Y) = \frac{E(XY) - E(X)E(Y)}{\sqrt{E(X^2) - E^2(X)}\sqrt{E(Y^2) - E^2(Y)}} \tag{4}$$

$E(X)$ denotes the mean value of the random variable X. Correlation coefficient is bound in the $[-1, 1]$ range. The closer the absolute value is to 1 the more correlated the random variables are, where a negative value indicates negative correlation. A value of 0 denotes that the variables are completely independent. This scale facilitates reasoning about the state of sensors when for example, signals that should be correlated become independent.

Communication patterns and information distribution in heterogeneous collaboration are similar to the case of homogeneous. However, algorithms employed in heterogeneous approaches tend to be more demanding in computation and storage requirement. Consequently, they are better suited for cluster based systems, where higher capacity nodes perform the analysis in the group.

4.3   Configuration Service

In figure 4, we have presented a short example on SMC interactions using policies. The *Configuration Service* can manipulate policies to deploy and dynamically adapt strategies relating to the *Fault Handling Service*, in mote SMCs.

Figure 8 demonstrates how adaptation can be expressed in policies. Policy 'AdaptOnTemperatureDrift' responds to an event from the *Fault Detection Service* and disables the temperature collector role on a faulty node. This is a call to a module of a remote SMC, thus, an appropriate authorisation policy is required installed at the target node. Furthermore, the policy instructs the *Configuration Service* to setup a recalibration process on the temperature sensor. The *Configuration Service* can reorganise the structure of the SMC by loading appropriate missions and roles to units for the completion of a task.

> **def** AdaptOnTemperatureDrift
>   **on** faultDetectionService.Detected(*fault, type, node*)
>   **if** *fault* **is** drift **and** *type* **is** temperature
>   **do** *node*.role.Disable(TemprCollect), configService.Setup(RecalibTemp)

On detection of thermometer's drift install the recalibration mission on the faulty node, disable its collection role and apply the missing data prediction in the SMC configuration service.

> **def** PredictRecalibrate
>   **on** faultHandlingService.Prediction(*node, type, value*)
>   **if** *type* **is** temperature
>   **do** *node*.faultService.Recalibrate(type, value, *node*.sensor.Get(type))

On prediction of a missing temperature value use it to recalibrate the faulty node by comparing it with its own reading.

Fig. 8. Policy re-configuration and adaptation example

The second policy 'PredictRecalibrate' is part of the 'RecalibTemp' adaptation that is applied on the SMC, located on the node that runs the *Fault Handling Service* and the prediction model of temperature readings. When a new prediction is made, the faulty node is requested to perform a comparison of the prediction with its temperature input in order to construct a drift model that will assist it to build a linear transformation that would adjust its consequent readings removing the effects of drift.

5   Case Studies

Case studies on real world deployments help us investigate the presence and effects of sensors faults in WSNs. We present in this section studies from ambient building monitoring as well as body networks for activity recognition. We investigate fault manifestation on real world traces and provide some insight on the effectiveness of detection algorithms discussed.

5.1   Ambient Monitoring

Motelab is a sensor test-bed,[3] deployed in the EECS building at Harvard University, running TinyOS 2.x. The test-bed included, at the time, 120 TMote Sky nodes equipped with temperature, humidity and light sensors. The nodes are deployed over three floors in pairs. Nodes are mains, not battery powered and have an ethernet connection that is only used for programming and monitoring. Nodes communicate through their 802.15.4 interfaces. Typically, there is one pair of nodes per room for each floor, while some larger rooms include a couple of pairs. We have used the test-bed to study behaviour of long running temperature and humidity sensors.

We ran a sampling program on Motelab for several sessions ranging from 1 to 7 hours. Motelab limits experiments to 30 minutes slots. Consequently, we run 30 minutes sessions with five minutes gaps. The trace was collected over a total period of 24 hours. Nodes sample every $30sec$ as temperature and humidity values do not exhibit sharp fluctuations. Consequently, a five-minute gap between sessions translates to 10 missing samples. We analysed the readings from collected sessions to identify properties of the monitored environment and investigate irregularities in the input.

The first observation is that sensors are not calibrated, as their readings do not correspond to realistic temperature or humidity values for working spaces, which are most of the monitored rooms. Furthermore, collocated nodes return significantly different values — ranging from 2^oC to 5^oC. Their relative sensing variations, however, follow similar trends denoting that they monitor the same events. This condition prohibits drawing conclusions between sensors in different rooms, e.g. to examine how temperature and humidity varies among offices. Nevertheless, pairs of collocated sensors can still be correlated to study their relative observations.

---

[3] http://motelab.eecs.harvard.edu/

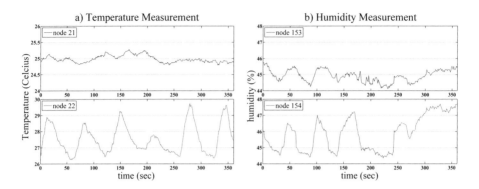

Fig. 9. Examples of sensor pair input irregularities

Temperature and humidity are physical properties that typically do not present sharp variations in their values in short time intervals. Especially, in a controlled, air-conditioned environment such as office space. This assumption has been verified from the experimental results, where sensors exhibit small value fluctuations in consequent readings. Given that sensors are deployed in adjacent pairs, sharing a common Stargate node through a serial cable, we expect the sensor readings from pairs to closely follow each other. Experimental findings have, again, confirmed this assumption for the majority of cases. Nonetheless, there have been occurrences where nodes present irregularities and deviate from their neighbouring measurements as illustrated in figure 9. We consider such anomalies indications of erroneous behaviour on nodes.

In figure 9 (a), node 22 temperature readings appear to record a periodic phenomenon, while its neighbour maintains relatively stable readings. In figure 9 (b) one node exhibits significantly higher amplitude in its reaction to environmental changes compared to the other one. Node 154 presents double scale amplitude compared to node 153 while monitoring the same events. In other cases, a sensor can become noisier than expected due to malfunction.

We confirm that there is correlation between the two sensors of different modalities on a node, as well as between same type sensors on adjacent nodes, by calculating their correlation coefficient. Figure 10 presents the probability density function (PDF) of correlation between sensors. We use a 60 samples window for calculating the correlation coefficient. Readings appear highly statistically correlated. In general, same type sensors observe physical properties in similar fashion. More than 80% of the humidity sensors present a correlation higher than 0.8. Temperature sensors appear to be slightly less correlated, with a coefficient of 0.7 for 80% of the node pairs.

When comparing temperature to humidity sensors we observe negatively correlation between the two properties, meaning that an increase in temperature generally corresponds to a decrease in humidity and vice versa. Around 65% of occurrences appeared to have a correlation value less than −0.8. The PDF

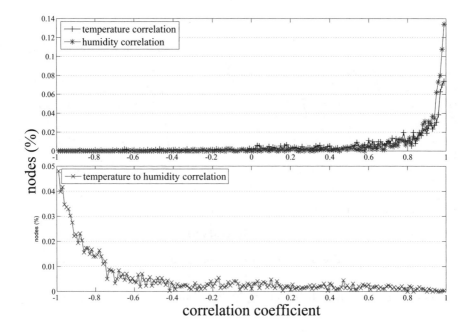

Fig. 10. Probability Density Function of sensor readings correlation in Motelab

graph again shows that there is a solid relation between measured environmental properties.

Victoria & Albert Museum in London has deployed a custom hardware WSN for monitoring temperature and humidity in exhibition rooms. Sensors are deployed in the surroundings as well as inside exhibit casings. Collected data consists of two years trace from 78 nodes, each equipped with a pair of thermometer and humidity monitor. We use this trace to examine faults that are found in real, long running deployments. Unfortunately, there is no automatic means for asserting manifestation of the faults in the trace. We have applied detection mechanisms and manually examined the traces to subjectively validate faulty instances.

We isolate cases where faults are apparent and verify that they follow one of the models we have defined, validating our initial class modelling. An example of drift manifestation is shown in figure 11, where two neighbouring nodes' temperature daily average readings are plotted for a period of 110 days. Node 127 is observed to consistently drift reaching a difference of $2^oC - 3^oC$ from node 128. Node 128 is a relatively fresh replacement (a couple of months), while on day 71 node 127 is also replaced by another physical node, maintaining the same node id. It is evident that after the node replacement the difference between the two sensors' readings is diminishing.

The drift in figure 11 presents a smooth linear deviation from the observations of node 128, which are assumed to be closer to reality. The difference between the

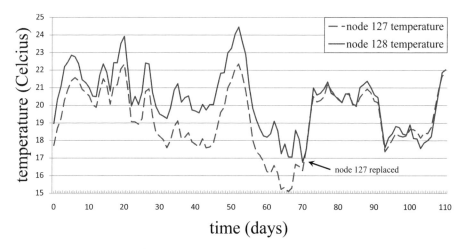

Fig. 11. Drift error in real world trace

two nodes fluctuates over the period of 70 days, but there is a definite increasing trend.

5.2   Activity Recognition

In [2], we present a study on two body area network deployments that monitor user activity. The first deployment uses an e-AR sensor, a BSN node [27] attached to the user's ear. while the second one uses a glove equipped with 19 accelerometers and one fibre optic sensor for evaluating a surgeon's skill through gesture recognition [12]. The traces of both the case studies were provided by the Institute of Biomedical Engineering, Imperial College London.

The e-AR node consists of three accelerometers in orthogonal axes. The experiment involves trace from twelve different individuals performing predefined activities in the following order: sitting, reading, eating, standing, tilting head, walking, sitting, slouching and lying on a sofa. Each activity is performed for a few tens of seconds up to a minute. In [20] the authors proposed a Bayesian network mixture model approach for their classification method. Further analysis of the trace is presented in [1,17], ambient sensors are used to collect image blobs for behaviour profiling.

The glove experiment uses accelerometers attached to the fingers and the palm as well as an optical sensor that measures bending of the wrist. The surgeon performs five activities sequentially, operating a tool tip; left/right traverse, open/close, up/down traverse, rotating the roticulator and rotating the tool tip anti-clockwise. The 20 sensors are attached to four different nodes that communicate wirelessly to a sink. Five individuals perform the activities in the trace, for the duration of a few seconds.

We study the impact each fault class has on activity recognition by injecting faults randomly in signals of the e-AR and glove traces and run detection

Table 2. Fault Detection Accuracy

detector	hit-rate	fall-out	delay (samples)
SHORT	99.54%	0.77%	0.00
NOISE (v)	98.33%	7.43%	8.41
NOISE (c)	100%	6.32%	143.53
DRIFT (r)	95.22%	19.47%	197.99
DRIFT (c)	78.22%	3.89%	346.31

algorithms discussed in section 4. In section 3.2, we justified why fault injection allows accuracy evaluation of fault detection mechanisms. For every BSN node, we inject a fault in one of its sensors. Table 2 briefly summarises the overall accuracy of detection methods per fault class. For space consideration, the table presents the average results for experiments that were run with different fault parameters. Evaluation of the *constant* fault detection is omitted, as in the case of accelerometer, detection is trivial due to the fluctuating nature of the accelerometer's signal.

The metrics used for the evaluation are the *hit-rate* of detected faults, where a hit indicates at least one alert is triggered during fault manifestation; the *fallout*, which is defined as the ratio of false positives to the sum of false positives and true negatives; and the time *delay* between the moment a fault appears and its detection moment. Time in the table is measured in samples, while nodes take 32 samples per second. The duration of an injected fault like *noise* or *drift* is 1200 samples.

The local detector for *short* faults proved to be very accurate, yielding very low false positives. The delay attribute is not relevant for *short* faults as they are instantaneous. Even though the experiments involve only accelerometer sensors (apart from the optical bend input) the network can be considered heterogeneous as sensors monitor different aspects of acceleration, i.e. different axis or different fingers in the glove case. Hence, we compare both homogeneous and heterogeneous collaboration detectors for *noise* and *drift* faults. In homogeneous collaboration we use the variance ratio (v) for *noise* faults and regression (r) for *drift*, while (c) in table 2 indicates the correlation coefficient method.

Both *noise* detection techniques have high hit-rates, however, the variance method gives a slightly increased number of false positives. Noisy areas, however, are detected faster using the variance feature. The increased delay in heterogeneous approach is attributed to the extended history of samples used for calculating the correlation coefficient. Consequently, the feature adapts slower to new behaviour. We used a history of 200 samples in the experiments. The history size is a trade-off between detection delay and the number of false positives.

The regression technique for *drift* faults has a higher hit-rate compared to correlation, but at a cost of high fall-out. As expected, further analysis of the results indicated that the *drift* cases that escaped detection from the heterogeneous method are those that have a very smooth deviation from ground truth, thus with lower impact. The high detection delay of the *drift* errors, that appears in both approaches, is tolerable, as the effects at the beginning of drift appearance are marginal.

Regression analysis for detecting the input's trend is a computationally intensive process. An alternative is using a very rough estimation by calculating the slope of the line passing over two data-points. This approach yielded slightly degraded results compared to regression, but is comparable, considering the computation gains. It should be noted that the correlation coefficient only captures linear correlation between random variables thus a different approach such as entropy or mutual information can present higher accuracy on detection.

6   Related Work

Related work in the area involves management architectures in WSNs and fault detection/handling mechanisms. In both cases, solutions are categorised as *centralised* or *distributed*, where neighbourhood collaboration is utilised. *Centralised* solutions suffer on scaling — the sink is a single point of failure and a concentration point for messages. In multi-hop deployments, the nodes around the sink suffer significantly from high traffic as they need to relay messages from the rest of the network, causing an increase in their power consumption. Furthermore, multi-hop routing to the sink adds significant (possibly unbounded) delays for message delivery, which may prove inappropriate for applications where event propagation time is critical, such as health-care. A hybrid, *hierarchical* approach, that assigns local managers inside the network, pushes decision making closer to affected node and reduces traffic towards the sink.

Management frameworks, such as [22,21], focus on the network and node level and cater for fail-stop faults involving connectivity and energy depletion of nodes. There are two monitoring models for such approaches; *active*, where queries are periodically injected in the network and *passive*, where detected issues are reported to the leader placed outside the network to perform operations for network reconfiguration. The global state collected in the sink, typically, includes routing tables, node connectivity and energy maps of nodes.

Network re-configuration implies an adaptation infrastructure in the network. Node re-programming is an approach that has been studied, however, dissemination of binary images to nodes is a process that requires increased bandwidth and rebooting of nodes. Such issues have been examined in [10,13,16]. Maté [14] is a different approach on code updates, being an embedded virtual machine for TinyOS with a configurable instruction set. Scripts are significantly smaller and easier to transmit compared to binary images, however, operational overhead of a VM on nodes can be substantial.

Facts [24] is a rule-based system based on facts, i.e. local or remote data in a node. Rules, which are similar to the Finger 2 obligation policies, are triggered when a fact is modified (c.f. events) and evaluate boolean conditions related to other facts that need to be satisfied in order for the rule to perform a function. Functions are the equivalent of actions in Finger 2 and can modify facts or can interact with sensors or actuators via the node operating system. Facts are a data-centric declarative approach and their overall approach follows the expert-systems paradigm. The examples given in the paper focus on conserving energy by powering-down some nodes in the network and it is not clear that they can cater for self-adaptation, i.e. rules that can modify available rulesets and change the behaviour of a node in the network. Policies provide an event driven description of behaviour. We argue that the event-driven approach is closer to the nature of sensor systems and their operating systems, thus a more natural way of defining behaviour and adaptation for the administrator.

Neighbourhood collaboration has been used for fault tolerant binary decisions or event detection, i.e. whether an event has occurred. An example of such approach is [9]. In [5,6] the authors propose collaborative neighbourhoods for bounds identification of event regions, tolerating faulty local decisions. Redflag [26] is a framework that takes into account accuracy faults that appear on sensors and tries to introduce quality metrics for readings as well as link status across the network. It provides services for validating readings as well as node and link status reporting. The services can be partially customized by tuning specific parameters, but it does not provide for handling of errors other than isolation. Finally, [4] attempts to tackle the issue of in-situ collaborative recalibration using neighbourhood readings.

7   Conclusion

We have presented Starfish, a self-healing framework that follows the Self-Managed Cell architectural paradigm. Starfish is an instantiation of an SMC for wireless sensor networks. It includes Finger 2, an embedded policy system, that allows reconfiguration on individual nodes as well as remote execution of actions, handling access control to remote resources. It supports adaptation on nodes allowing deployment of new strategies at run-time inside the network.

We have, further, provided a formal definition of faults found on sensors and define a fault-handling framework including services that are implemented as module libraries for Finger 2. These services use features extracted from sensor readings to analyse the state of the sensing devices and validate their correctness. Many approaches in the literature assume homogeneous sensor redundancy in a constrained area. While this assumption can be valid for a class of applications there are scenarios where this is not practical or economically sound. Using correlation metrics on different sensor inputs, we try to maintain high fault-detection accuracy with implicit redundancy of sensors avoiding dense deployment of sensing devices that observe the same attribute.

The case studies presented provide some insight on the validity of our fault models and give preliminary results on the accuracy of detection techniques. We intend to extend the investigation of correlation between monitored attributes to refine detection mechanisms by distinguishing events and behavioural changes from faults on sensors. Autonomic healing and recalibration of sensing devices inside the network, also, requires further investigation.

References

1. Atallah, L., ElHelw, M., Pansiot, J., Stoyanov, D., Wang, L., Lo, B., Yang, G.Z.: Behaviour profiling with ambient and wearable sensing. In: IFMBE Proc. of 4th Int. Workshop on Wearable and Implantable Body Sensor Networks (BSN 2007), vol. 13, pp. 133–138. Springer Science, Heidelberg (2007)
2. Bourdenas, T., Sloman, M.: Towards self-healing in wireless sensor networks. In: 6th Int. Workshop on Wearable and Implantable Body Sensor Networks, pp. 15–20. IEEE, Berkeley (2009)
3. Bourdenas, T., Sloman, M.: Starfish: Policy driven self-management in wireless sensor networks. In: ACM ICSE Workshop on Software Engineering for Adaptive and Self-Managing Systems (SEAMS 2010), Cape Town, South Africa, pp. 75–84 (2010)
4. Bychkovskiy, V., Megerian, S., Estrin, D., Potkonjak, M.: A collaborative approach to in-place sensor calibration. In: Zhao, F., Guibas, L.J. (eds.) IPSN 2003. LNCS, vol. 2634, pp. 301–316. Springer, Heidelberg (2003)
5. Chen, J., Kher, S., Somani, A.: Distributed fault detection of wireless sensor networks. In: Workshop on Dependability Issues in Wireless Ad-hoc Networks and Sensor Networks (DIWANS), Los Angeles, USA, pp. 65–72. ACM, New York (2006)
6. Ding, M., Chen, D., Xing, K., Cheng, X.: Localized fault-tolerant event boundary detection in sensor networks. In: IEEE International Conference on Computer Communications (INFOCOM 2005), Miami, USA, pp. 902–913 (2005)
7. Dunkels, A., Gronvall, B., Voigt, T.: Contiki-a lightweight and flexible operating system for tiny networked sensors. In: 29th IEEE Int. Conference on Local Computer Networks (LCN 2004), pp. 455–462 (2004)
8. Hall, D.L., Llinas, J.: Handbook on Multisensor Data Fusion. CRC Press, Boca Raton (2001)
9. Hsin, C., Liu, M.: Self-monitoring of wireless sensor networks. Computer Communications 29(4), 462–478 (2005)
10. Hui, J.W., Culler, D.: The dynamic behavior of a data dissemination protocol for network programming at scale. In: Proceedings of the 2rd International Conference on Embedded Networked Sensor Systems, SenSys 2004, Baltimore, MD, USA, pp. 81–94 (2004)
11. Kephart, J.O., Chess, D.M.: The vision of autonomic computing. Computer 36, 41–50 (2003)
12. King, R., Lo, B., Darzi, A., Yang, G.Z.: Hand gesture recognition with body sensor networks. In: IEE Proc. of 2nd. Int. Workshop on Wearable and Implantable Body Sensor Networks, London, pp. 92–95 (April 2005)
13. Kulkarni, S.S., Wang, K.: Mnp: Multihop network reprogramming service for sensor networks. In: International Conference on Distributed Computing Systems (ICDCS), Columbus, USA, pp. 7–16 (2005)
14. Levis, P., Culler, D.: Mate: A tiny virtual machine for sensor networks. ACM SIGARCH Computer Architecture News 30(5), 85–95 (2002)
15. Lupu, E.C., Dulay, N., Sloman, M.S., Sventek, J., Heeps, S., Strowes, S., Twidle, K., Keoh, S.-L., Schaeffer-Filho, A.: Amuse: autonomic management of ubiquitous e-health systems. Concurrency and Computation: Practice and Experience 22(3), 277–295 (2007)
16. Marron, P.J., Lachenmann, A., Minder, D., Gauger, M., Saukh, O., Rothermel, K.: Management and configuration issues for sensor networks. International Journal of Network Management 15(4), 235–253 (2005)

17. McIlwraith, D.G., Pansiot, J., Thiemjarus, S., Lo, B.P.L., Yang, G.Z.: Probabilistic decision level fusion for real-time correlation of ambient and wearable sensors. In: Proc. of the 5th International Workshop on Body Sensor Networks (BSN), Hong Kong, China (2008)

18. Mukhopadhyay, S., Panigrahi, D., Dey, S.: Model based error correction for wireless sensor networks. In: Proc. of the First IEEE Communications Society Conference on Sensor and Ad Hoc Communications and Networks (SECON), pp. 575–584. IEEE Computer Society, Los Alamitos (2004)

19. Ould-Ahmed-Vall, E., Riley, G.F., Heck, B.: Distributed faulttolerance for event detection using heterogeneous wireless sensor networks. Georgia Tech/CERCS, Tech. Rep. GIT-CERCS-06-09 (2006)

20. Pansiot, J., Stoyanov, D., McIlwraith, D., Lo, B.P.L., Yang, G.Z.: Ambient and wearable sensor fusion for activity recognition in healthcare monitoring systems. In: Proc. of the 4th International Workshop on Body Sensor Networks (BSN), Aachen, Germany (2007)

21. Ramanathan, N., Chang, K., Kapur, R., Girod, L., Kohler, E., Estrin, D.: Sympathy for the sensor network debugger. In: Proceedings of the 3rd International Conference on Embedded Networked Sensor Systems, SenSys 2005, San Diego, USA, pp. 255–267 (2005)

22. Ruiz, L.B., Siqueira, I.G., Oliveira, L.B., Wong, H.C., Nogueira, J.M.S., Loureiro, A.A.F.: Fault management in event-driven wireless sensor networks. In: Proceedings of the 7th ACM International Symposium on Modeling, Analysis and Simulation of Wireless and Mobile Systems, MSWiM 2004, Venice, Italy, pp. 149–156 (2004)

23. Schaeffer-Filho, A., Lupu, E., Sloman, M.: Realising Management and Composition of Self-Managed Cells in Pervasive Healthcare. In: 3rd International Conference on Pervasive Computing Technologies for Healthcare, London, U.K (2009)

24. Terfloth, K., Wittenburg, G., Schiller, J.: Facts-a rule-based middleware architecture for wireless sensor networks. In: Proc. of the 1st Int. Conf. on Communication System Software and Middleware, COMSWARE (2006)

25. Twidle, K., Lupu, E., Sloman, M., Dulay, N.: Ponder2: A policy system for autonomous pervasive environments. In: IEEE Fifth International Conference on Autonomic and Autonomous Systems (ICAS 2005), Valencia, Spain, pp. 330–335 (2009)

26. Urteaga, I., Barnhart, K., Han, Q.: Redflag a run-time distributed, flexible, lightweight, and generic fault detection service for data-driven wireless sensor applications. In: Proceedings of the 2009 IEEE International Conference on Pervasive Computing and Communications, PerCom 2009 (2009)

27. Yang, G.-Z.: Body Sensor Networks. Springer, London (2006)

28. Zhu, Y., Sloman, M., Lupu, E.C., Keoh, S.L.: Vesta: A secure and autonomic system for pervasive healthcare. In: 3rd International Conference on Pervasive Computing Technologies for Healthcare (Pervasive Health 2009), London (2009)

Self Organization and Self Maintenance of Mobile Ad Hoc Networks through Dynamic Topology Control

Douglas M. Blough[1], Giovanni Resta[2], Paolo Santi[2], and Mauro Leoncini[3]

[1] School of ECE, Georgia Tech, Atlanta, GA, USA
[2] Istituto di Informatica e Telematica del CNR, Pisa, Italy
[3] Università di Modena e Reggio Emilia, Italy

Abstract. One way in which wireless nodes can organize themselves into an ad hoc network is to execute a topology control protocol, which is designed to build a network satisfying specific properties. A number of basic topology control protocols exist and have been extensively analyzed. Unfortunately, most of these protocols are designed primarily for static networks and the protocol designers simply advise that the protocols should be repeated periodically to deal with failures, mobility, and other sources of dynamism. However, continuously maintaining a network topology with basic connectivity properties is a fundamental requirement for overall network dependability. Current approaches consider failures only as an afterthought or take a static fault tolerance approach, which results in extremely high energy usage and low throughput. In addition, most of the existing topology control protocols assume that transmission power is a continuous variable and, therefore, nodes can choose an arbitrary power value between some minimum and maximum powers. However, wireless network interfaces with dynamic transmission power control permit the power to be set to one of a discrete number of possible values. This simple restriction complicates the design of the topology control protocol substantially. In this paper, we present a set of topology control protocols, which work with discrete power levels and for which we specify a version that deals specifically with dynamic networks that experience failures, mobility, and other dynamic conditions. Our protocols are also novel in the sense that they are the first to consider explicit coordination between neighboring nodes, which results in more efficient power settings. In this paper, we present the design of these topology control protocols, and we report on extensive simulations to evaluate them and compare their performance against existing protocols. The results demonstrate that our protocols produce very similar topologies as the best protocols that assume power is a continuous variable, while having very low communication cost and seamlessly handling failures and mobility.

Keywords: Wireless multihop networks, topology control, dynamic networks, fault tolerance.

1 Introduction

The topology control problem in wireless ad hoc networks is to choose the transmission power of each node in such a way that energy consumption is reduced and some

A. Casimiro et al. (Eds.): Architecting Dependable Systems VII, LNCS 6420, pp. 26–52, 2010.

property of the communication graph (typically, connectivity) is maintained. Besides reducing energy consumption, topology control increases the capacity of the network, due to reduced contention to access the wireless channel. In fact, in [9] it has been shown that it is more convenient, from the network capacity point of view, to send packets along several short hops rather than using long hops[1]. Given the limited availability of both energy and capacity in ad hoc networks, topology control is thus considered a major building block of forthcoming wireless networks.

Ideally, a topology control protocol should be asynchronous, fully distributed, fault-tolerant, and localized (i.e., nodes should base their decisions only on information provided by their neighbors). Furthermore, it should rely on information that does not require additional hardware on the nodes, e.g. to determine directional or location information. A final requirement of a good topology control protocol is that it generates a connected and relatively sparse communication graph. These latter features, besides reducing the expected contentions at the MAC layer, ease the task of finding routes between nodes.

Most existing topology control protocols focus on initial construction of a good topology. These protocols concentrate on static network environments where one-time topology construction is sufficient, but do not explicitly consider how to maintain a good topology as network conditions change. Sources of dynamism in ad hoc networks include mobility, failures, and dynamic joins of nodes. One approach, designed primarily to deal with node failures, is to construct an initial topology that is highly redundant and can therefore tolerate some dynamic changes without impairing basic network properties such as connectivity. However, this approach is not sufficient to deal with highly dynamic environments such as those arising from node mobility. In addition, due to the high level of redundancy in the initial construction, these topologies are inefficient in that they force nodes to use higher transmission powers than necessary at a given time to withstand potential future changes. The higher than necessary transmission powers result in higher energy consumption by nodes, which reduces network lifetime, and increased interference in the network, which degrades network performance. Thus, these static approaches favor short-term dependability at the expense of longer-term network survivability, while at the same time incurring very serious performance costs.

In this paper, we propose a new approach to topology maintenance, which dynamically adjusts the topology on an as needed basis in response to network changes. Our approach considers failures, and other sources of dynamism, as an inherent feature in the network and explicitly considers how to maintain a good topology while operating the protocol in a stable and efficient manner. Thus, we do not simply propose to reexecute a static protocol periodically, which would result in a very high overhead. Rather, we maintain local network conditions within a certain range and take explicit local steps to maintain those conditions only when they fall out of the specified range. This allows us to maintain global network properties in the presence of failures, while executing maintenance operations locally and only when sufficient changes have occurred to warrant topology adjustment. In our protocols, we also assume the use of discrete transmission power levels, an assumption that holds true in all existing

---

[1] This does not necessarily hold true in worst-case distributions of nodes and for a particular choice of the contention measure, see [5].

network interface cards with dynamic transmission power adjustment (a basic requirement for topology control). We also consider explicit coordination between nodes to optimize the topology, rather than having each node optimize its own conditions. In Section 8, we do a thorough evaluation of our protocols, which validates their essential features, namely that they produce good quality topologies with low energy cost and interference while seamlessly and efficiently handling highly dynamic network conditions.

2 Related Work

The topology control problem [22] has been deeply investigated in the literature in recent years, including theoretical studies aimed at characterizing optimal topologies according to some performance metric (see, e.g., [19,21,25]), and more practical approaches presenting distributed, localized topology control protocols, sometimes with proven performance bounds with respect to optimal [2,3,8,10,15,18,20,27,28]. Included in this work is our original k-Neighbors approach [2,3], upon which this current work builds. Some papers [4,5] also addressed the topology control problem with the goal of reducing interference, instead of energy consumption as traditionally done in the topology control literature. In this section, we discuss the topology control approaches most relevant to this paper, namely those explicitly designed to address fault-tolerance and/or node mobility.

Fault-tolerant topology control has been addressed in some recent papers. Typically, fault-tolerance is achieved by requiring some level of redundancy in the constructed topology, e.g., k-connectivity (for some $k > 1$) of the communication graph instead of simple connectivity. For instance, in [1], the authors generalize the CBTC protocol of [27] to construct k-connected topologies in a three-dimensional setting. A distributed algorithm based on localized construction of k-spanning sub-graphs is presented in [16], while [17] mainly focuses on characterizing the critical transmission range for k-connectivity. Other studies essentially extend topology optimization problems to the case of k-connectivity, e.g. [6], which deals with heterogeneous networks, and [25], which focuses on the optimal k-connected topologies for all-to-one and one-to-all communications. However, all of these approaches use static redundancy, which produces denser topologies with higher transmission powers, and correspondingly more interference. Thus, the topologies generated by these protocols suffer both from high energy usage and low throughput, since many studies have shown that wireless multi-hop network performance is interference limited. Despite the higher overheads associated with static redundancy protocols, none of them are guaranteed to maintain connectivity for mobile networks. Thus, the benefits gained from the high overheads are not at all clear. Our alternative approach, proposed herein, dynamically adjusts the topology on an as needed basis to maintain certain properties while failures and node mobility are occurring.

Relatively few papers have been explicitly concerned not only with construction of the network topology, but also with its maintenance in presence of dynamic network conditions due to, e.g., node mobility, failures, and new nodes joining the network. In [27], the authors describe a procedure to reconfigure the network topology built by

CBTC in presence of node join/leaves. However, no evaluation of the procedure's overhead nor its capability to maintain a good topology is carried out. Most of the dynamic events discussed in [27] require the protocol to be completely reexecuted by at least one node, which incurs substantial cost in environments with moderate to high dynamism. In [26], the authors present a distributed algorithm for building a k-connected topology in a three-dimensional network, and describe a procedure for updating the topology in presence of dynamic network conditions. However, again there is no evaluation of the performance of the protocol under dynamic conditions.

To the best of our knowledge, the only papers that explicitly deal with topology control in presence of node mobility are [18] and [21]. In [18], the authors introduce the notion of *contention index*, and show through simulation that capacity of a mobile network shows a high degree of correlation with the contention index independently of node speed. Then, they present a localized, distributed protocol called MobileGrid aimed at keeping the contention index of each node close to the optimal value. However, while properties of the contention index have been evaluated in a mobile setting, the overall MobileGrid protocol has been evaluated only in stationary networks. In [21], the authors present two simple neighborhood-based protocols and evaluate their performance in both static and mobile settings. However, the paper only evaluates the throughput and average delay experienced when a set of random flows are created in the network, with and without topology control. Although throughput and delay of a set of random flows are an indirect indication of the quality of the underlying network topology, an explicit evaluation of important network properties such as connectivity, average node degree, and energy cost is missing in [21]. Thus, the one presented in this paper is, to the best of our knowledge, the first distributed topology control approach whose performance (expressed in terms of connectivity, average degree, and energy cost of the constructed topologies) is extensively evaluated in both stationary and mobile networks. In addition, the protocols of [18,21] both suffer from a technical flaw, which is described in detail in the next section.

In addition to dealing with dynamic networks, the topology control protocols we present herein are based on selection of a discrete and finite set of transmission power levels. The idea of using level-based power changes was introduced in [20], and further developed in [12], neither of which considers dynamic networks. The protocols proposed in [12,20] change the transmission power on a per-packet basis: the network nodes exchange messages at different power levels in order to build the routing tables (one for each level); the information contained in these tables is then used by the nodes to set the appropriate transmission power when sending messages. Since the topology of the network is not changed by these protocols, we call this approach *power control*, instead of topology control. Nevertheless, the assumption that transmission power can only be set to certain predetermined values, which our protocols, as well as those of [12,20], adopt is coherent with all existing wireless networking cards that have power control capability. Thus, this feature is essential to a practical topology control approach.

A final novel aspect of the work described in this paper is an "unselfish" version of our topology control protocol, in which nodes try to coordinate their power increases in order to "minimize" the overall local power consumption. To our knowledge, this is the first protocol to consider explicit coordination between nodes. In summary, our protocols are the first to be evaluated thoroughly in dynamic settings, the first to consider discrete power levels without the use of per packet power control, and the first to consider explicit coordination between nodes.

3 Preliminaries and Working Assumptions

The protocols presented in this paper are based on the following assumptions:

- nodes can transmit messages at different power levels, denoted $p_0, \ldots, p_{max}$, which are the same for all nodes,
- message loss is handled at the MAC layer, e.g. through a retransmission mechanism, and
- the wireless medium is *symmetric*, i.e., if node v can receive a message sent by node u at power p_i, then u is able to receive a message sent by v using the same power p_i.

The second assumption is very similar to the assumption of an abstract MAC layer, recently proposed by Kuhn, Lynch, and Newport [13]. The third assumption, namely that the wireless medium is symmetric, is not essential. In fact, this assumption is not used in the dynamic version of the protocol presented in Section 7. In this section, we adopt this assumption in order to simplify the presentation of the static version of the protocol. However, the static version could easily be augmented to exchange neighbor lists (as is done in the dynamic protocol version) instead of simple power levels (see static protocol reported in Figure 1). With this augmentation, the symmetric medium assumption can be removed. This change, while complicating the protocol specification, would not increase the *number* of messages exchanged but would incur an increase in the size of each message.

For the sake of brevity, in the following we will say that a node is *at level i* if its current transmission power is set to p_i. Also, we will let A_i denote the radio coverage area of a given node at level i, $i = 0, \ldots, max$. Note that the assumptions above only guarantee that $A_i \subseteq A_{i+1}$, without imposing any particular shape to the surface covered by a node at level i. In particular, the surface is not necessarily circular, as is assumed in many papers.

Let $G = (N, E)$ be the directed graph denoting the communication links in the network, where N is the set of nodes, with $|N| = n$, and $E = \{(u, v): v$ is within u's transmission range at the current power level$\}$ is the (directed) edge set. Clearly, as the nodes may be at different levels, $(u, v) \in E$ does not imply $(v, u) \in E$.

For every node u in the network, we define the following neighbor sets:

- the *incoming neighbor set*, denoted $N_i(u)$, where $N_i(u) = \{v \in N : (v, u) \in E\}$.
- the *outgoing neighbor set*, denoted $N_o(u)$, where $N_o(u) = \{v \in N : (u, v) \in E\}$.
- the *symmetric neighbor set*, denoted $N_s(u)$, where $N_s(u) = N_i(u) \bigcap N_o(u) = \{v \in N : (v, u) \in E$ and $(u, v) \in E\}$.

Clearly, the neighbor sets of node u change as u's level and the levels of nodes in its vicinity vary. The ultimate goal of our topology control protocols is to cause $N_s(u)$ to contain k (or slightly more than k) nodes, where k is an appropriately chosen parameter[2]. Motivations for our interest in the number of *symmetric* neighbors of a node can be found in [2].

Note that, when a node u changes its level, only the set $N_o(u)$ can vary, i.e. a node has only partial control of its set of symmetric neighbors. Furthermore, the only neighbor set that a node can directly measure is $N_i(u)$, which is not impacted by an increase in u's power level. Thus, to increase the sizes of $N_i(u)$ and $N_s(u)$, some nodes in the vicinity of u must increase their transmission powers. This fact points out a flaw in some existing neighborhood-based protocols, which do not use explicit control messages.

Consider, for example, the MobileGrid protocol of Liu and Li [18]. MobileGrid is based on a parameter called the *contention index* (*CI*). The goal of MobileGrid is to achieve an "optimal" value of *CI* at each node. For any given node u, *CI* is defined as the number of nodes within u's transmission range (including u). However, *CI* is estimated as the number of nodes whose messages can be overheard by u. Using our terminology, *CI* at node u is defined in terms of $N_o(u)$, but it is estimated in terms of $N_i(u)$. If the estimated *CI* is too low at node u, the protocol prescribes that u's transmission power be increased. This may increase the number of nodes within u's transmission range, but it definitely does not increase the estimated value of *CI* and might actually decrease it due to other nodes' responses to u's increase. Since the estimated *CI* does not increase, u will increase its power level again at the next period and it is possible that this repeats until u reaches the maximum power.

Another neighborhood-based protocol which does not use explicit control messages is the LINT/LILT protocol of Ramanathan and Rosales-Hain [21]. However, in [21], the authors assume that a symmetric set of neighboring nodes is available as a result of the underlying routing protocol, which is left unspecified. In a certain sense, the problem incurred by MobileGrid is thus overlooked.

In order to avoid the problem mentioned above, our neighbor-based protocols make use of explicit control messages.

4   Basic Protocol for Static Networks

Our neighborhood-based topology control with power levels (NTC-PL) protocol implements the following idea. By circulating short control messages, nodes can let neighbors know their current power level. Based upon this information, and knowing its own level, a node can determine its symmetric neighborhood. If the number of symmetric neighbors is too low, a node can then send one or more control messages (of a different type) and trigger a power level increase in nearby nodes that are potential neighbors. This process continues until there are at least k symmetric neighbors or the node reaches the maximum power setting. In Section 6, we will discuss how to set the value of the fundamental parameter k.

The protocol uses two types of control messages: *beacon* and *help* messages. Both types of messages contain the sender's ID and current power level. Beacon messages are used to inform current (outgoing) neighbors of the power level of the sender, so that their symmetric neighbor sets can be properly updated. On the contrary, help messages

---

[2] This requirement will be loosened in the mobile version of the protocol.

are used to trigger some of the receivers to increase their transmission power level, so that the symmetric neighbor count of the help sender is (possibly) increased.

Initially, all nodes set their powers to level 0, and send a beacon message. After node u has sent this initial message, it waits for a certain stabilization time T_0, during which it only performs interrupt handling routines in response to the messages received by other nodes. The main goal of these routines, which are described in detail below, is to update u's symmetric neighbor set. After time T_0, node u checks whether it has at least k symmetric neighbors. If so, it becomes *inactive*, and from this point on it participates in the protocol by simply responding (if necessary) to the control messages sent by other nodes. Otherwise, it remains *active*, and it enters the *Increase Symmetric Neighbors* (ISN) phase. During the ISN phase, node u sends help messages at increasing power levels, with the purpose of increasing the size of its symmetric neighbor set. This process is repeated until $|N_s(u)| \geq k$, or the maximum transmission power level is reached. The routines that are executed upon the reception of control messages are described next.

When node u receives a beacon message (v, l_v), it first checks whether $v \in N_i(u)$. If so, u has already received a control message from v, and the current beacon is simply ignored. Otherwise, u stores in a local variable $l_v(u)$ the level l_v, which represents the minimum power level needed for u to reach node v[3]. Furthermore, node u includes v in its list of incoming neighbors and, if $l_u \geq l_v$ (here, l_u denotes u's current power level), also in the list of symmetric neighbors.

When node u receives a help message (v, l_v), it checks whether this is the first control message received by v. If so, it sets the $l_v(u)$ variable and the set of incoming and symmetric neighbors as described above. Furthermore, node u compares its power level to l_v and, if $l_u < l_v$, it increases its power level to l_v, so that v's symmetric neighbor set will eventually be increased in size. As a side effect, node v is included in $N_s(u)$. In increasing its power from level l_u to l_v, node u sends a sequence of beacons, one at each power level from $l_u + 1$ to l_v. By doing so, we guarantee that when the variable $l_u(y)$ is set at node y, it actually stores the minimum power required for y to reach node u.

If the help message (v, l_v) is not the first control message from v that is received by u, then $v \in N_i(u)$, and node u knows the minimum power level needed to reach v (which is stored in the variable $l_v(u)$). Thus, node u simply checks whether $v \in N_s(u)$; if so, u is already a symmetric neighbor of v, and the help request from v is ignored. Otherwise, $l_u < l_v$, and the power level of u is increased to $l_v(u)$ (which is the minimum level needed to render u and v symmetric neighbors), using the same step by step power increase procedure described above.

A pseudo-code description of the NTC-PL protocol is shown in Figure 1. In order to improve readability, we drop the u from the variables $l_x(u)$, $N_s(u)$, and $N_i(u)$. Finally, we recall that when a node is at level i, all the messages are sent at power p_i.

It is easy to see that the protocol terminates in finite time. Moreover, the following theorem shows that there exist values of the waiting times T_l such that the protocol correctly determines a symmetric communication graph, which has the following property: the power setting of a node is always the minimum necessary for it to have k

---

[3] Here, the symmetry assumption of the wireless medium is used.

- Main:
  - set $l = 0$, $N_i = N_s = \{\}$;
  - send beacon (u, l);
  - set $h = 0$; /* Remark: remember the level before sleeping */
  - wait (for a stabilization time) T_0;
  - repeat
    - if $|N_s| \geq k$ exit; /* ... and starts operating */
    - set $l = h + 1$;   /* Go up one level (if no power increase has been forced by interrupt handling routines) */
    - send help message (u, l);
    - set $h = l$; /* Remark: (again) remember the level before waiting */
    - wait T_l;
  - until $l = max$
  - start node operations;
- Upon receiving a beacon message (v, λ):
  - if $v \notin N_i$
    - $l_v = \lambda$;
    - $N_i = N_i \bigcup \{v\}$;
    - if $l \geq l_v$ then $N_s = N_s \bigcup \{v\}$;
- Upon receiving a help message (v, λ):
  - if $v \in N_i$ and $v \notin N_s$ stepwise-increase$(l + 1, l_v)$;
  - if $v \notin N_i$
    - $l_v = \lambda$;
    - $N_i = N_i \bigcup \{v\}$;
    - if $l < l_v$ stepwise-increase$(l + 1, l_v)$;
      else $N_s = N_s \bigcup \{v\}$;
- Procedure stepwise-increase (i, f);
  - for $h = i, \ldots, f$, do:
    - set $l = h$;
    - send beacon (u, l);
    - $N_s = N_s \bigcup \{z\}$, for any $z \in N_i$ s.t. $l = l_z$;

Fig. 1. Algorithm NTC-PL performed by node u

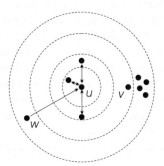

Fig. 2. Example in which the "unselfish" behavior of node u generates a more energy efficient local solution

symmetric neighbors, except when one of its in-neighbors requires help in achieving its own symmetric neighbor requirement.

Theorem 1. *The NTC-PL protocol satisfies the following properties:*

(a) the total number of control messages exchanged is $O(n \cdot max)$;

moreover, there exist values T_l, $l = 0, \ldots, max$, of the waiting times such that:

(b) at the end of the protocol execution, node $u \in N_s(v)$ if and only if node $v \in N_s(u)$;
(c) node u sends the help message at level i only if the number of nodes in A_{i-1} is smaller than k, $i < max$.

Proof: By code inspection, it is easy to see that a node (either active or inactive) sends at most one beacon and one help message per level. Hence, the total number of control messages sent is at most $2n(max + 1)$, which proves (a).

If the waiting times T_l are sufficiently large, all the messages triggered by a help request sent by node u are received by u before the node checks its neighbor count again. This implies that: (1) if node v becomes symmetric neighbor of u in response to the help message, then u will include v in its symmetric neighbors set after the stabilization time, and (b) is proved; (2) denoting with n_{i-1} the number of nodes in the coverage area A_{i-1} centered at u, node u will have symmetric neighbors count at least n_{i-1} after sending the help message at power $i-1$ and waiting for the stabilization time; thus, node u sends the help message at power i only if $n_{i-1} < k$, and (c) is proved. ∎

5 Protocol Variation with Unselfish Behavior

The NTC-PL protocol presented in the previous Section leaves room for some optimization. A first simple optimization is the following. Suppose that there is a node u having fewer than k neighbors in its A_{max} vicinity, and such that the surface $A_{max} - A_j$ centered at u is empty, for some $j < max$. This circumstance can be easily detected: all that is required is one additional variable $b(u)$ storing the last level at which u has added to its symmetric neighbor set. When node u eventually sets its level to max, and verifies that $|N_s(u)|$ is still less than k, it can safely backtrack to power level $b(u)$.

A second and more serious opportunity for optimization is motivated by the observation that a help message in the NTC-PL protocol causes *all* nodes that receive it to become symmetric neighbors of the sender, if they are not already. This mechanism might be quite inefficient, forcing unnecessary power increases in the vicinity of the help sender. For example, suppose the surface A_{i-1} of node u contains $k - 1$ nodes, and that the surface $A_i - A_{i-1}$ contains $c > 1$ potential symmetric neighbors. In this case, NTC-PL would force all the nodes in $A_i - A_{i-1}$ to increase their power levels, increasing u's symmetric neighbor set size to $k + c - 1$. On the other hand, a single power increase among the nodes in $A_i - A_{i-1}$ would have been sufficient for u to meet its requirement on $N_s(u)$.

Another potential inefficiency of NTC-PL is illustrated in Figure 2. Suppose $k = 4$ and the transmission powers of nodes u, v, and w are set to levels 2, 1, and 4, respectively. Assume also that $|N_s(v)| \geq 4$ and $|N_s(w)| \geq 4$. Finally, suppose that the levels correspond to the following transmission power settings: 1mW, 5mW, 20mW, 30mW, 50mW, and 100mW (these are the power levels used in the Cisco Aironet card [7]). Now, node u has at least two choices for reaching the desired number of neighbors:

- "selfish" behavior: since $|N_s(u)| < 4$, send a help request at level 2, thus forcing node v to increase its power level;
- "unselfish" behavior: use the information stored in $N_i(u)$, which lists w, and increase the level to $l_w(u)$.

In case of selfish behavior, which corresponds to the basic protocol implementation, the overall power increase in the vicinity of u is 10mW+25mW, due to node u stepping up one level and v two levels. In case of unselfish behavior, the increase is 30mW, due to u stepping up two levels. Hence, from a total energy standpoint, unselfishness is preferable in this case. Note that the opposite conclusion would be drawn if the node powers in Figure 2 were all scaled up by one level. In that case, the power increases would change to 50mW (20mW+30mW) for the selfish approach and 70mW for the unselfish one.

This example, with its opposite conclusions depending on the node power levels, along with the NTC-PL inefficiency described above, motivates the design of an "unselfish" variation of the basic protocol, which we call NTC-PLU.

Suppose node u has ended its $(i-1)$th round and still has fewer than k symmetric neighbors. Its behavior is now modified according to the following rules.

- Instead of sending a help control message at level i, which would trigger blind power increases, node u sends an *enquiry* control message, carrying the same data as the help request.
- In response to an enquiry, a node at level less than i does not immediately step up; rather, it sends a *reply* control message at (temporary) level i, whose purpose is to let u know that it is a potential helper. The reply message contains the sender's ID and current power level. By gathering this information from all the potential helpers, node u is able to identify the locally "optimal" solution in its vicinity.
- Node u schedules one of several possible actions, whose aim is to satisfy the constraint on the symmetric neighbor set (or to get closer to it) at the minimum energy cost: (i) simply increase u's current power, if there are enough elements in $N_i(u) - N_s(u)$ to reach the threshold k; (ii) send a generalized help (i.e., the old-style help request); (iii) send a *selective* help, asking a subset of the nodes in A_i to increase their power levels.

Note that in NTC-PLU some nodes perform temporary power increases, thus partially impairing our periodic approach to topology control. However, these changes in the power level occur only during the network setup phase, and not during the network operational time, as is the case with per-packet topology control.

Selective help requests call for a decision in order to choose the target nodes. This can be done by again using energy considerations, and ties can be broken randomly. In any case, we remark that, because of full asynchrony and in absence of a global coordination, a solution which is locally optimal at a certain time might become sub-optimal later (e.g., because a certain node in the u's vicinity would have increased its transmission power later, in response to another help message). Unfortunately, predicting transmission power increases is impossible in practice, and the optimizations performed by NTC-PLU can be regarded only as *heuristics*.

With respect to NTC-PL, NTC-PLU allows a finer control of the symmetric neighbor set, so a better energy efficiency is expected. On the other hand, NTC-PLU in general exchanges more control messages as compared to NTC-PL, due to up to three phases of interaction (enquiry–reply–help) between nodes. Thus, simulation can help us to understand the relative performances of the two protocols.

Before ending this section, we remark that the optimizations based on the well-known triangular inequality described in [2] can be applied to the final communication graphs produced by both NTC-PL and NTC-PLU. In order to apply these optimizations, which are aimed at identifying edges in the communication graph that can be pruned without impairing connectivity and symmetry, it is sufficient that every node, at the end of the protocol execution, sends a message containing its list of symmetric neighbors.

6   Setting the Value of k

The desired number of symmetric neighbors k is clearly a fundamental parameter of our protocols: small values of k are likely to induce disconnected communication graphs, while large values force the majority of the nodes to end protocol execution at larger than necessary levels. In this section, we characterize the "ideal" value of k both analytically and through simulation.

Note that, the problem of determining the ideal number of neighbors has already been studied in [2]. However, in [2] the focus was on the number of nodes a node could reach, rather than on symmetric neighbors. Moreover, the protocol in [2] was distance based, and it was assumed that each node could set its transmission range to any value between 0 and the maximum range. As a consequence, it was possible to set the nodes' ranges so that each node had exactly k (outgoing) neighbors. Here we are interested in symmetric neighbors and have the availability of only a small number of power settings, which makes it infeasible to obtain exactly k neighbors in all cases. Nonetheless, the results in [2] (which in turn depends on a fundamental theorem in [29]) can be used to prove the following theorem, which holds under the assumption that the radio coverage area is circular.

Theorem 2. *Let n nodes be placed uniformly at random in $[0, 1]^2$ and assume that maximum power is sufficient for each node to reach at least k other nodes. Let L_k be the actual communication graph generated by NTC-PL with parameter k, and let L_k^- be the graph obtained by L_k by removing the asymmetric links. If $k \in \Theta(\log n)$, then L_k^- is connected w.h.p.*[4]

Proof: By property (c) of Theorem 1 and the above assumption on maximum power, every node u at the end of the protocol execution has a power level sufficient to reach at least its k closest neighbors. This means that L_k is a super-graph of the k-closest neighbors graph G_k, and also that L_k^- is a super-graph of the symmetric sub-graph G_k^- of G_k. Hence, the proof follows immediately by the fact that, as proven in Theorem 2

---

[4] W.h.p. means with probability converging to 1 as the number n of network nodes goes to infinity.

of [2], $k \in \Theta(\log n)$ implies that graph G_k^-, which is a sub-graph of L_k^-, is connected w.h.p. ∎

It can be seen that the same result of Theorem 2 holds also for the communication graph generated by NTC-PLU.

Note that the result stated in Theorem 2 holds under the assumption of perfectly circular coverage region, which is hardly met in practical scenarios. Yet, recent works [14,24] support the conjecture that the same asymptotic result on the value of k holds also in a cost-based connection model, which is shown in [24] to closely resemble log-normal shadowing propagation (i.e., irregular coverage regions).

The characterization of the ideal value of k given in Theorem 2 is of theoretical interest, but it cannot be used in practice. Thus, we have evaluated the value of k to be used in the NTC-PL and NTC-PLU protocols by simulation. For different values of n, we have performed 1000 experiments with increasing values of k, recording the percentage of connected graphs generated at the end of the protocol execution. The ideal value of k, which will be used in the subsequent set of simulations aimed at evaluating the performance of our protocols, is the minimum value such that at least 98% of the graphs generated by the NTC-PL protocol are connected. Note that, in general, the graphs generated by NTC-PL and NTC-PLU are different, so different values of k could be used. We have verified through our experiments that the graphs generated by NTC-PLU are relatively less connected than those generated by NTC-PL with the same value of k. However, with the value of k chosen (which guarantees at least 98% of connectivity with NTC-PL), also the graphs generated by NTC-PLU show good connectivity on the average. For this reason, in the simulations reported in Section 8, we have used the same value of k in both protocols.

Table 1. Ideal value of k for different values of n

n	k	n	k
50	6	300	4
100	5	350	4
150	4	400	4
200	4	450	4
250	4	500	4

The ideal values of k for different values of n are reported in Table 1. The value of $k = 4$ provides at least 98% connectivity for values of n in the range 150–500, while higher values of k are needed for smaller networks. Note that these values are considerably smaller than those needed by the k-NEIGH protocol of [2]. As discussed above, this is due to the fact that, on the average, several symmetric edges are added by NTC-PL and NTC-PLU with respect to the minimum value of k required.

7   Protocol Variation for Dynamic Networks

In this section, we present a protocol variation for dynamic networks, which handles mobility, failures, and dynamic joining of nodes. The principal complicating factor in dealing with dynamic networks for neighborhood-based protocols is the inherently transient nature of the neighbor set of a node. Due to this, we can not hope to calculate N_s exactly but only to estimate it. Consider, for example, when a node in $N_s(u)$ moves out of range of u. There is an unavoidable delay before this event is detected and, during this time, $N_s(u)$ is not accurate. One must also be careful not to adjust power levels too quickly when topology changes occur, lest the protocol exhibit unstable behavior.

Based on the discussion above, our version of NTC-PL for dynamic networks is based on the following two key ideas. First, in order to estimate N_s, nodes periodically send beacon messages containing their estimated N_i sets at their current power levels. If node u hears a beacon from node v and $u \in N_i(v)$, then u and v are symmetric neighbors. Second, instead of trying to maintain $|N_s|$ at a value of exactly k, we set low and high water marks on $|N_s|$, denoted by k_{low} and k_{high}, respectively. A node initiates steps to increase its neighbor set size only when its estimated $|N_s|$ falls below k_{low} and tries to decrease its neighbor set size only when the estimated $|N_s|$ exceeds k_{high}. These basic ideas are sufficient to deal with all sources of dynamism, which include mobility, node failures, and node joins. Note also that these mechanisms no longer rely on the assumption of a symmetric wireless medium and, hence, we remove that assumption for this section.

The details of our procedure for estimating N_s are given in Figure 3. When a node is first powered up, it initiates this procedure, which is described next. Nodes send beacon messages containing their N_i sets every T seconds, where T is a user-specified parameter that provides a trade off between protocol overhead and delay in detecting changes to the neighbor set. Whenever a node u receives a message (beacon or otherwise) from node v, u adds v to its N_i set. When u receives a beacon message from v, u also adds v to its N_s set if u appears in the N_i set of v that is contained in the beacon message. Also when receiving a beacon message from v, u sets a timer to expire in T seconds. If the timer expires before u receives another beacon from v, then v is no longer an in-neighbor (nor a symmetric neighbor) of u.

The remainder of the protocol sets forth the actions to be taken when the size of N_s falls below k_{low} or exceeds k_{high}. Figure 4 shows the procedure for increasing $|N_s|$, while Figure 5 shows how a decrease in $|N_s|$ is achieved.

There are two main differences in how $|N_s|$ is increased in the dynamic case (Figure 4) compared to the static version of NTC-PL. First, a node's N_i set is included with its help message. This is to allow nodes that receive help messages to use the most recent information to determine if the sender is a symmetric neighbor given that the N_s set is only an estimate of the actual symmetric neighbor set. The second, and more important, difference is that nodes which respond to help messages increase their power level by only one setting in the dynamic case, whereas in the static case they increase their power to match that of the sender. Since this does not guarantee that responders will be heard by the help requester, its N_s set might not be increased by this response. This is the reason that help requesters send help messages multiple times at the same power level.

While re-sending help messages at the same power level might seem inefficient, the simulation results of Section 8.3 demonstrate that the message overhead of the dynamic protocol is extremely low. This is due to the use of low and high water marks

Main:

$l = 0; N_i \leftarrow \emptyset; N_s \leftarrow \emptyset$
every T seconds do
    send beacon message (u, l, N_i)

Upon receiving an ordinary (non-beacon) message from node v:

$N_i \leftarrow N_i \cup \{v\}$
if Timer$_v = 0$ then set Timer$_v$ to expire in T seconds

Upon receiving a beacon message $(v, l_v, N_i(v))$:

$N_i \leftarrow N_i \cup \{v\}$
if $u \in N_i(v)$ then $N_s \leftarrow N_s \cup \{v\}$
if $|N_s| > k_{\text{high}}$ then call decrease_neighbors()
set Timer$_v$ to expire in T seconds

Upon expiration of Timer$_v$:

$N_i \leftarrow N_i - \{v\}; N_s \leftarrow N_s - \{v\}$
if $|N_s| < k_{\text{low}}$ then call increase_neighbors()

Fig. 3. Procedure for estimating N_s performed by node u

increase_neighbors()

while $(|N_s| < k_{\text{low}})$ and $(l < max)$ do
    count $\leftarrow 0$
    while $(|N_s| < k_{\text{low}})$ and (count $< l$) do
        send help message (u, l, N_i)
        wait T_l
        count $\leftarrow$ count+1
    if $(|N_s| < k_{\text{low}})$ then $l \leftarrow l + 1$

Upon receiving a help message $(v, l_v, N_i(v))$:

$N_i \leftarrow N_i \cup \{v\}$
if $(u \notin N_i(v))$ then
    if $(l < l_v)$ then $l \leftarrow l + 1$
    send beacon message (u, l, N_i)
if $u \in N_i(v)$ then $N_s \leftarrow N_s \cup \{v\}$

Fig. 4. Procedure for increasing N_s performed by node u

on k, which are quite effective at limiting the frequency of protocol execution, making minor inefficiencies during protocol execution much less important. The primary motivation behind repetitive help messages at the same power level is to avoid the following scenario, which can occur in networks with mobility. A node requires a high power level while communicating in a sparse part of the network and then moves to a denser part where nodes are communicating with much lower power levels. Since the node sends its help message at its current power level, the basic NTC-PL protocol would decrease_neighbors()

    while ($l > 0$) and ($|N_s| > k_{high}$) do
        send a check_reduce message (u, l)
        wait T_l
        if stop message received then exit
        otherwise $l \leftarrow l - 1$
    if $|N_s| < k_{low}$ then $l \leftarrow l + 1$

Upon receiving a check_reduce message (v, l_v):

    if ($v \in N_s$) and ($|N_s| = k_{low}$) and ($l \geq l_v$)
        then send stop message to v

Fig. 5. Procedure for decreasing N_s performed by node u

potentially cause many nodes in the dense part of the network to switch to very high power levels, which is clearly wasteful of energy. The procedure in Figure 4, while using more control messages and time, produces more graceful changes in power levels and avoids unnecessary large increases in power by many nodes.

The need to decrease the number of neighbors (Figure 5) arises with mobility and/or dynamic node joins, because the basic NTC-PL protocol ensures that nodes' power levels are set as small as possible. For example, with mobility, a node could require a high power level in one area but that level could produce far more neighbors than necessary when it moves to a new area. The ability to decrease levels is therefore required. We must be cautious when power levels are decreased, however, lest we leave another node with too few neighbors causing it to initiate a round of help messages and possibly leading to circular behavior. Thus, before we allow a node to reduce its level, we force it to send a "check reduce" message to its current neighbors to make sure that the reduction will not leave any node with too few neighbors. If any node that hears a check reduce message from v has v as a symmetric neighbor, has the minimum number of symmetric neighbors currently, and is in danger of not hearing v if v's power level is reduced, then it sends a stop message to v. If v hears at least one stop message, then it does not reduce its power level.

One remaining question is how to choose k_{low} and k_{high}. The main considerations are as follows. k_{low} should be set high enough to maintain the desired connectivity property. For a given k_{low}, k_{high} determines the width of the allowable k range, which influences protocol stability and message overhead. If the k range is quite wide, the protocol will not be triggered often and it will have low overhead and exhibit stable behavior. On the other hand, a wide k range, will produce a higher average k, which means higher node degrees and energy costs. Thus, k_{high} should be set to the smallest value that maintains stable protocol behavior and reasonable overhead. In Section 8.3, we carefully evaluate the choices of these parameters through simulation.

Similar to the dynamic version of our protocol, the LINT protocol of [21] tries to maintain the symmetric neighbor set size between low and high water marks. However, LINT suffers from the same problem pointed out earlier with the MobileGrid protocol of [18]. In LINT, nodes simply increase their transmission range when the number of neighbors is too low. The problem is that increasing a node's transmission range is not guaranteed to increase its neighbor set size and might even lower it. LINT does not do the type of local coordination that is part of our protocols and is necessary to ensure that actions taken by nodes have the desired effect (increasing or decreasing the neighbor set size). Thus, *our dynamic protocol is the first that can guarantee a lower bound on the symmetric neighbor set size of a node in a dynamic environment.* Furthermore, it includes the ability to decrease neighbor set sizes and to ensure that larger-than-necessary transmission power adjustments do not occur, two features that are not necessary in the static version of the protocol.

8 Simulations

In this section, we report the result of simulations we have performed to evaluate the performances of our protocols, both on static networks and on dynamic networks.

The performances of the various protocols are compared with respect to the following metrics:

– total *energy cost*, defined as the sum of the power levels of all nodes: at the end of protocol execution for the static protocols and as a function of time for the dynamic protocol
– average *logical* and *physical* node degrees. The logical degree of node u is its degree in the communication graph, while the physical degree is the number of nodes in the radio coverage area of u. Due to the removal of asymmetric links and to optimizations, the physical degree is usually larger than the logical degree.
– the average number of messages per node : sent during phase 1^5 for the static protocols and as a function of time for the dynamic protocol
– for the dynamic protocol only, the average percentage of nodes that are in the largest connected component (LCC) of the communication graph

The energy cost gives an idea of the energy efficiency of the topology generated by the protocol, while the node degree (especially the physical degree) gives a measure of the expected number of collisions at the MAC layer, and thus, of the expected impact on network capacity [9]. The average LCC size is used to evaluate network connectivity in the dynamic case. Note that no protocol can guarantee the network is fully connected at all times in that case. Thus, we strive to maintain as many nodes as possible in the largest connected component.

8.1 Simulation Results for Static Networks: Minimum Density

Besides the NTC-PL and NTC-PLU protocols, we have evaluated the performance of the CBTC protocol of [27], which is the best known static topology control protocol. We have adapted CBTC to take into account the transmission power level actually available; i.e., the transmission power level of any node at the end of CBTC execution is rounded up to the next power level available.

For the three topology control protocols considered, we implemented both the basic version (called phase 1 in the following), and the optimization that can be carried out

---

^{5} We recall that phase 2 requires one further message per node sent in both protocols.

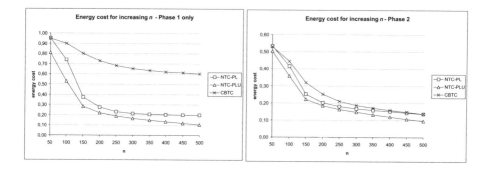

Fig. 6. Energy cost of the NTC-PL, NTC-PLU and CBTC protocols as the network size increases, before (left) and after (right) optimization. The energy cost is normalized with respect to the case of no topology control, where all the nodes transmit at maximum power.

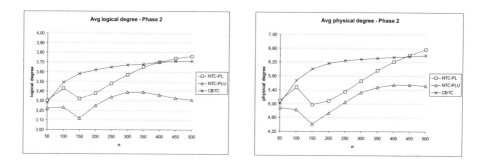

Fig. 7. Average logical (left) and physical (right) node degree after the optimization phase

on the communication graph generated after phase 1 (see [2,27] for details on the optimization phase). The optimization phase of the various protocols is called phase 2 in the following.

In the first set of simulations, we have considered networks of increasing size, while maintaining the node density at the minimum level required to guarantee connectivity w.h.p. when all nodes transmit at maximum power.

We have considered the transmission power levels specified in the data sheets of the Cisco Aironet 350 card [7], namely 1mW, 5 mW, 20mW, 30mW, 50mW, and 100mW. As reported in the data sheets, the transmission range at maximum power is about 244 meters. According to this data, and assuming a distance-power gradient of $\alpha = 2$, we have determined the transmission range at the other power levels, which are 173m, 134m, 109m, 55m and 24m, respectively. This setting of the transmission range resembles a simple free space wireless channel model.

We have considered a simulation area of 1 square kilometer. According to the data reported in [23], the minimum number of nodes to be deployed in the simulation area in order to generate a communication graph which is connected w.h.p. when all the nodes transmit at maximum power is about 100. We have then increased the number of nodes in steps of 50, up to 500, scaling the simulation area in such a way that the node

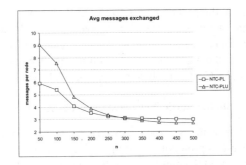

Fig. 8. Average number of message per node sent during phase 1 of the NTC-PL and NTC-PLU protocols

density remains the minimum necessary for connectivity at maximum power. We have also considered smaller networks, composed of 50 nodes.

The results of this set of simulations are reported in Figures 6–8, and are averaged over 1000 runs. From the figures, it is seen that:

- both NTC-PL and NTC-PLU clearly outperform CBTC in terms of energy cost when optimizations are not implemented. The relative savings achieved by our protocols increase with the network size, and they can be as high as 67% (NTC-PL) and 77% (NTC-PLU).
- when optimizations are implemented, our protocols still perform better than CBTC in terms of energy cost. However, in this case the relative gain in performance is less significant. The relative improvement of NTC-PL with respect to CBTC can be as high as 21% (when $n = 150$), but tends to be less significant as n increases. On the contrary, the improvement achieved by NTC-PLU with respect to CBTC tends to increase with n, and can be as high as 30% when $n = 500$. The energy savings achieved by our protocols with respect to the case of no topology control increase with n, and can be as high as 86% for NTC-PL, and as high as 91% for NTC-PLU.
- concerning the logical and physical node degree of the communication graph, NTC-PLU performs clearly better than the other protocols, especially in terms of physical degree (which is the one that determines the expected impact on network capacity). The average physical degree when NTC-PLU is used is as much as 26% smaller than that generated by CBTC, and as much as 12% smaller than that generated by NTC-PL. With respect to the case of no topology control, NTC-PLU reduces the average physical node degree by about 75%.
- NTC-PLU always perform better than NTC-PL, with respect to both energy cost and node degree. In terms of communication overhead, NTC-PLU exchanges more messages than NTC-PL when the network size is small. However, when the network size increases, the situation is reversed: for $n \geq 300$, NTC-PLU generates fewer messages than NTC-PL. Although, when being executed at a particular node, NTC-PLU generates more messages at a given power level than NTC-PL, NTC-PLU will terminate earlier than NTC-PL in their searches for the proper power level in some cases. For example, a node executing NTC-PLU will terminate its protocol execution when it knows that increasing its own power to a certain level is

sufficient to achieve the proper symmetric neighborhood size and that doing so is more efficient than stepping through more power levels and sending help messages at each of those levels. For larger networks, the benefits of this early termination appear to outweigh the higher per level communication costs. Thus, when the network size is large, NTC-PLU performs better than NTC-PL in all respects.

8.2   Simulation Results for Static Networks: Increasing Density

In the second set of experiments, we have evaluated the effect of node density on the performance of the various protocols. Starting with the minimum density scenario for $n = 100$, we have increased the number of nodes up to $n = 400$ while leaving the side s of the simulation area unchanged (1 kilometer in all cases).

The results of this set of simulations, which are not reported herein, are practically identical to those obtained in the minimum density scenario. In other words, for a given value of n, the performance of NTC-PL, NTC-PLU and CBTC does not change with the side of the deployment region, i.e., with the node density. This is due to the fact that the protocols considered rely on relative, rather than absolute, location information. In case of NTC-PL and NTC-PLU, the information considered is relative distance, while in case of CBTC it is relative angular displacement.

We believe this result is quite interesting, since it shows that *it is only the size n of the network that determines the performances achieved by the various protocols*, in terms of both energy savings and increase in network capacity.

8.3   Simulation Results for Dynamic Networks

The simulation set-up for dynamic networks is as follows. We focus on mobility as the source of dynamism, because this produces a much more dynamic situation than would typically occur with node failures and joins. The mobility model we consider is the widely-used random waypoint model [11]. We use the same size deployment region (1 square km) and the same transmission power levels as in the static network simulations. The number of nodes is 100. The pause time for the random waypoint model is set to zero, to produce the most dynamic possible network. We consider both a low speed scenario and a high speed scenario. Node velocity is set to 1 m/sec in the low speed case and 15 m/sec in the high speed case. Nodes send beacon messages once every second in the dynamic protocol.

One of the main issues to evaluate is how to set the lower and upper thresholds (k_{low} and k_{high}) on neighborhood size. We carry out two sets of experiments to evaluate this. In the first set of experiments, we gradually increase both k_{low} and the width of the range. We refer to these as the $k=x$-$2x$ experiments, because we set k_{low} to 5, 6, 7, and 8, and set k_{high} to twice k_{low} in each case. In the second set of experiments, we fix k_{low} to 5 and we narrow the range by gradually reducing k_{high}. We refer to these as the $k=5$-x experiments.

Figures 9 and 10 show the results for the $k=x$-$2x$ experiments, at low speeds and high speeds, respectively. We first describe the low speed results (Figure 9). With each of the different ranges of k values, the protocol is able to maintain more than 90% of the nodes in the network within the largest connected component (LCC). The LCC size varies

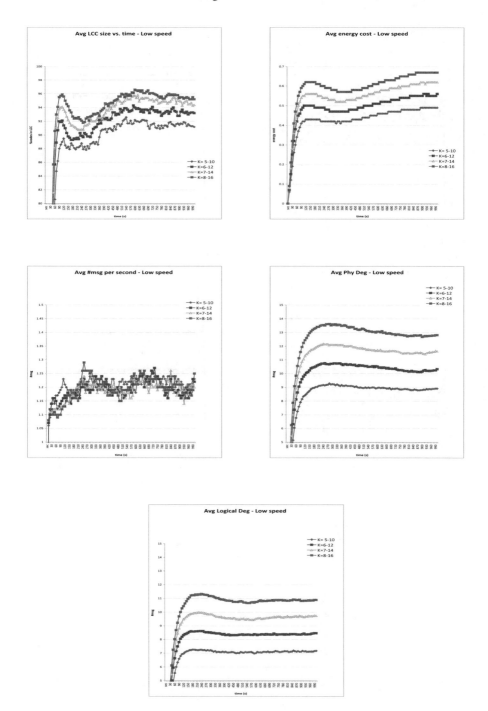

Fig. 9. Dynamic protocol performance: low speed nodes, different neighborhood size ranges

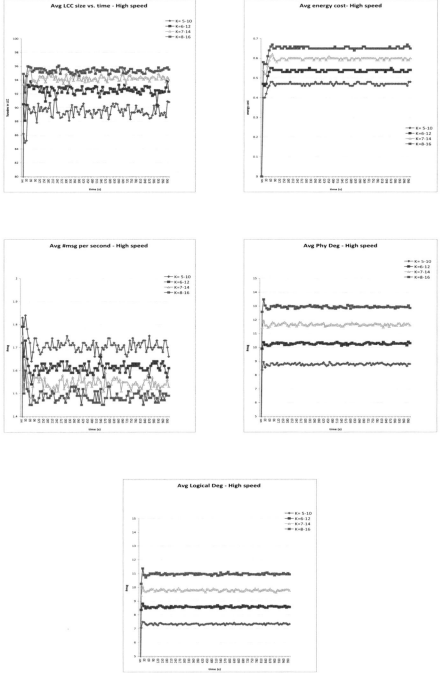

Fig. 10. Dynamic protocol performance: high speed nodes, different neighborhood size ranges

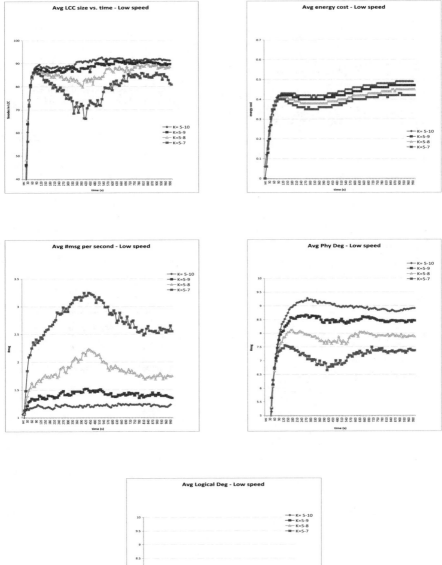

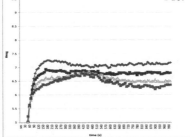

Fig. 11. Dynamic protocol performance: low speed nodes, different neighborhood size upper thresholds

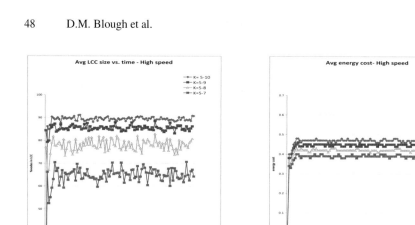

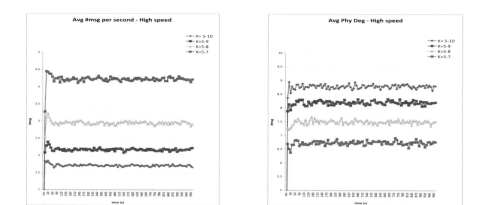

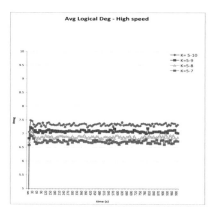

Fig. 12. Dynamic protocol performance: high speed nodes, different neighborhood size upper thresholds

from about 92% for k=5-10 up to about 96% for k=8-16. The protocol achieves this while still producing substantial energy savings. The energy cost varies from about 50% of the maximum power energy cost for k=5-10, up to around 68% of the maximum for k=8-16. It can also be seen that having a range of neighborhood sizes within which no protocol execution is triggered is very effective at keeping the overhead of the protocol low. Only around 1.2 messages per second per node are sent by the protocol for each of the neighborhood ranges. In terms of the density of the topologies that are produced, we see that the logical degrees fall in the middle of the neighborhood range, tending slightly toward the lower threshold. There is a steady increase in logical degree as the lower threshold of the neighborhood range is increased. Physical degree follows the same trends, but is slightly higher. Overall, the protocol with a neighborhood range of k=5-10 performs quite well, achieving better than 90% of nodes in the LCC with energy cost about 50% of the maximum power setting, a logical degree of 7, and a physical degree of 9, while only exchanging 1.2 messages per second per node.

In looking at the high speed results (Figure 10), we see that the protocol performance is very similar to the low speed results in terms of energy cost, logical degree, and physical degree. The main differences are that there is more variation in the LCC size and the message cost is higher. The variation in LCC size can be attributed to multiple neighborhood changes occurring before the protocol can finish adjusting to the first change. This situation can temporarily cause some local connectivity losses that are repaired with a short delay. These variations are most noticeable for the narrowest neighborhood range (k=5-10), and are hardly noticeable for the widest range (k=8-16). Since, at a higher speed, more neighborhood changes occur per unit of time, we would expect message cost to increase. Nevertheless, the cost is still quite low, ranging from 1.5 messages per second up to 1.7 messages per second. Although LCC size is slightly degraded compared to the low speed case, the narrowest range is still able to achieve around 90% of the nodes in the LCC and the wider ranges are still above 90%.

Figures 11 and 12 show the results for the k=5-x experiments, at low speeds and high speeds, respectively. Again, we focus on the low speed results (Figure 11) first. As the neighborhood range becomes narrower, we expect that the protocol will be triggered more often and so the message cost will increase. Also, since the lower threshold of the range remains fixed, as the range becomes narrower, we should see a reduction in logical and physical degree. The results do indeed illustrate these general trends. It is interesting to see that when we narrow the range from k=5-10 to k=5-9, we achieve almost the same LCC size, so there is little impact on the quality of the topology in terms of connectivity. There are also noticeable benefits in terms of degree: average logical degree and average physical degree are both reduced by 0.5, which is about a 7% reduction. There is a smaller benefit in terms of energy cost (about 4%). These benefits come at a relatively small increase in message cost, from about 1.25 messages per second to about 1.4 messages per second (an 11% increase). This indicates that some narrowing of the neighborhood range is beneficial. However, when the range is narrowed further (the k=5-8 and k=5-7 cases), the results degrade substantially. The protocol takes a long time to converge to a stable LCC size and the message cost is substantially increased, particularly during the transient phase while the LCC size is converging. While the k=5-8 results do eventually reach a good state, the transient period is quite long. We believe this is due to the random waypoint mobility model, which has a steady state node distribution that concentrates most of the nodes in the center of the region. The protocol appears to work well with a narrow neighborhood range once this concentration effect has occurred but poorly prior to that. Since this is just an artifact of the mobility model, we do not recommend using the narrower neighborhood ranges in general settings.

For the high speed case (Figure 12), there is a noticeable drop-off in LCC size when going from k=5-10 to k=5-9. However, if slightly lower than 90% LCC size can be tolerated, the k=5-9 range has similar benefits in terms of degrees and energy to what it achieved in the low speed case. In contrast to the low speed case, we do not see the long convergence times for the k=5-8 and k=5-7 neighborhood ranges. We attribute this to the faster convergence of the random waypoint model to its steady state node distribution due to the higher speed of the nodes. Both of the narrower neighborhood ranges perform fairly poorly here in terms of LCC size and so are probably not suitable regardless of their better convergence behavior.

9   Discussion

In this paper, we have presented topology control protocols that use a discrete number of transmission power levels, as opposed to assuming that the power level can be set to an arbitrary value in a given range. The protocols implement a neighborhood based approach to topology control in which a node uses its number k of nearest neighbors to route in/out traffic. We have shown by means of extensive simulations that the protocols are effective in reducing the energy cost, comparing favorably with the well known CBTC protocol of Wattenhofer, et al. [27]. We have also proposed and thoroughly evaluated a variation of our base protocol, which is designed for dynamic networks that experience failures, mobility, and other dynamic conditions. Our results show that this dynamic protocol can effectively establish and maintain topologies with low degrees and good connectivity properties in highly dynamic environments, while incurring very low message overheads.

Our protocols rely on appropriate selection of neighborhood size parameters: k in the case of static networks and the range $[k_{low}, k_{high}]$ in the dynamic network case. Our simulation results provide a starting point for selection of these parameters in actual networks. We recommend starting with a fairly conservative choice, e.g. $k = 5$ for static networks of medium to large size, $k = 6$ for small static networks, a range of $[5, 10]$ for moderately dynamic networks, and a range of $[6, 12]$ for highly dynamic networks. These parameters can then be gradually adjusted over time to minimize overhead and energy consumption while maintaining desired network properties.

A final issue worth discussion is the discovery that, when nodes coordinate their transmission power decisions, an unselfish topology control protocol performs better than a selfish one. Thus, to optimize the overall topology, it is necessary to ensure that nodes are acting for the common good and not in their own self-interests. Designing schemes which can provide rewards to nodes that faithfully execute an unselfish protocol is an interesting topic for future research.

References

1. Bahramgiri, M., Hajiaghayi, M., Mirrokni, V.S.: Fault-tolerant and 3-Dimensional Distributed Topology Control Algorithms in Wireless Multi-hop Networks. Wireless Networks 12(2), 179–188 (2006)
2. Blough, D.M., Leoncini, M., Resta, G., Santi, P.: The k-NEIGH Protocol for Symmetric Topology Control in Ad Hoc Networks. In: Proc. ACM MobiHoc 2003, pp. 141–152 (June 2003)
3. Blough, D.M., Leoncini, M., Resta, G., Santi, P.: The k-Neighbors Approach to Interference Bounded and Symmetric Topology Control in Ad Hoc Networks. IEEE Trans. on Mobile Computing 5(9), 1267–1282 (2006)
4. Blough, D.M., Leoncini, M., Resta, G., Santi, P.: Topology Control with Better Radio Models: Implications for Energy and Multi-Hop Interference. Performance Evaluation 64(5), 379–398 (2007)
5. Burkhart, M., von Rickenbach, P., Wattenhofer, R., Zollinger, A.: Does Topology Control Reduce Interference. In: Proc. ACM Mobicom 2004, pp. 9–19 (2004)
6. Cardei, M., Yang, S., Wu, J.: Fault-Tolerant Topology Control for Heterogeneous Wireless Sensor Networks. In: Proc. IEEE Int. Conference on Mobile Ad Hoc and Sensor Systems (MASS), pp. 1–9 (2007)
7. Cisco Aironet 350 data sheets,
   http://www.cisco.com/en/US/products/hw/wireless
8. Dyer, M., Beutel, J., Thiele, L.: S-XTC: A Signal-Strength Based Topology Control Algorithm for Sensor Networks. In: Proc. IEEE Int. Symp. on Autonomous Decentralized Systems (ISADS), pp. 508–518 (2007)
9. Gupta, P., Kumar, P.R.: The Capacity of Wireless Networks. IEEE Trans. Information Theory 46(2), 388–404 (2000)
10. Huang, Z., Shen, C., Srisathapornphat, C., Jaikaeo, C.: Topology Control for Ad Hoc Networks with Directional Antennas. In: Proc. IEEE Int. Conference on Computer Communications and Networks, pp. 16–21 (2002)
11. Johnson, D., Maltz, D.: Dynamic Source Routing in Ad Hoc Wireless Networks. In: Mobile Computing, pp. 153–181. Kluwer Academic Publishers, Dordrecht (1996)
12. Kawadia, V., Kumar, P.R.: Power Control and Clustering in Ad Hoc Networks. In: Proc. IEEE Infocom 2003 (2003)
13. Kuhn, F., Lynch, N., Newport, C.: The Abstract MAC Layer. In: Keidar, I. (ed.) DISC 2009. LNCS, vol. 5805, pp. 48–62. Springer, Heidelberg (2009)
14. Kuhn, F., Wattenhofer, R., Zollinger, A.: Ad Hoc Networks beyond Unit Disk Graphs. Wireless Networks 14, 715–729 (2008)
15. Li, L., Halpern, J.H., Bahl, P., Wang, Y., Wattenhofer, R.: A Cone-Based Distributed Topology Control Algorithm for Wireless Multi-hop Networks. IEEE/ACM Trans. on Networking 13(1) (2005)
16. Li, N., Hou, J.C.: FLSS: A Fault-Tolerant Topology Control Algorithm for Wireless Sensor Networks. In: Proc. ACM Int. Conference on Mobile Computing and Networking (Mobicom), pp. 275–286 (2004)
17. Li, X.-Y., Wan, P.-J., Wang, Y., Yi, C.-W.: Fault-Tolerant Deployment and Topology Control in Wireless Networks. In: Proc. ACM Int. Symp. on Mobile Ad Hoc Networking and Computing (MobiHoc), pp. 117–128 (2003)
18. Liu, J., Li, B.: MobileGrid: Capacity-aware Topology Control in Mobile Ad Hoc Networks. In: Proc. IEEE Int. Conference on Computer Communications and Networks, pp. 570–574 (2002)

19. Lloyd, E., Liu, R., Marather, M.V., Ramanathan, R., Ravi, S.S.: Algorithmic Aspects of Topology Control Problems for Ad Hoc Networks. Mobile Networks and Applications 10(1-2), 19–34 (2005)
20. Narayanaswamy, S., Kawadia, V., Sreenivas, R.S., Kumar, P.R.: Power Control in Ad Hoc Networks: Theory, Architecture, Algorithm and Implementation of the COMPOW Protocol. In: Proc. European Wireless 2002, pp. 156–162 (2002)
21. Ramanathan, R., Rosales-Hain, R.: Topology Control of Multihop Wireless Networks using Transmit Power Adjustment. In: Proc. IEEE Infocom 2000, pp. 404–413 (2000)
22. Santi, P.: Topology Control in Wireless Ad Hoc and Sensor Networks. John Wiley and Sons, Chichester (2005)
23. Santi, P., Blough, D.M.: The Critical Transmitting Range for Connectivity in Sparse Wireless Ad Hoc Networks. IEEE Transactions on Mobile Computing 2(1), 1–15 (2003)
24. Scheideler, C., Richa, A., Santi, P.: An $O(logn)$ Dominating Set Protocol for Wireless Ad Hoc Networks under the Physical Interference Model. In: Proc. ACM MobiHoc, pp. 91–100 (2008)
25. Wang, F., Thai, M.T., Li, Y., Cheng, X., Du, D.: Fault-Tolerant Topology Control for All-to-One and One-to-All Communication in Wireless Networks. IEEE Trans. on Mobile Computing 7(3), 322–331 (2008)
26. Wang, Y., Cao, L., Dahlberg, T.A., Li, F., Shi, X.: Self-Organizing Fault-Tolerant Topology Control in Large-Scale Three-Dimensional Wireless Networks. ACM Trans. on Autonomous and Adaptive Systems 4(3) (2009)
27. Wattenhofer, R., Li, L., Bahl, P., Wang, Y.: Distributed Topology Control for Power Efficient Operation in Multihop Wireless Ad Hoc Networks. In: Proc. IEEE Infocom 2001, pp. 1388–1397 (2001)
28. Wattenhofer, R., Zollinger, A.: XTC: A Practical Topology Control Algorithm for Ad-Hoc Networks. In: Proc. Int. Workshop on Algorithms for Wireless, Mobile, Ad Hoc and Sensor Networks, WMAN (2004)
29. Xue, F., Kumar, P.R.: The Number of Neighbors Needed for Connectivity of Wireless Networks. Wireless Networks 10, 169–181 (2004)

Data Backup for Mobile Nodes:
A Cooperative Middleware and
an Experimentation Platform*

Marc-Olivier Killijian and Matthieu Roy

CNRS, LAAS, 7 avenue du colonel Roche, F-31077 Toulouse, France
Université de Toulouse, UPS, INSA, INP, ISAE, LAAS, F-31077 Toulouse, France
`name.surname@laas.fr`
`http://theresumeexperience.blogspot.com/`

Abstract. In this paper, we present a middleware for dependable mobile systems and an experimentation platform for its evaluation. Our middleware is based on three original building blocks: a Proximity Map, a Trust and Cooperation Oracle, and a Cooperative Data Backup service. A Distributed Black-box application is used as an illustrative application of our architecture, and is evaluated on top of our mobile experimental platform.

1 Problem Statement

Finding the proper abstractions to design middleware for the provision of dependable distributed applications on mobile devices remains a big challenge [1]. The number of mobile communicating devices one can meet in every-day life is dramatically increasing: mobile phones, PDAs, handheld GPS, laptops and notebooks, portable music and video players. Those devices benefit from an amazing number of sensors and communication interfaces. The interconnection of these systems does not only result in a huge distributed system. New technical and scientific challenges emerge due to the mobility of users and of their devices, or due to the massive scale of uncontrolled devices that constantly connect and disconnect, fail, etc. To handle those systems' dynamics, cooperation-based approaches à la peer-to-peer seem attractive. An important question is thus to know if and how can we design a sound middleware that offers useful building blocks for this type of system. Another crucial question is to study how we can correctly evaluate those highly mobile and dynamic systems.

This paper addresses these two questions: we present a *middleware architecture* dedicated to the provision of cooperative data backup on mobile nodes and

---

* This work was partially supported by the Laboratoire d'Analyse et d'Architecture des Systèmes (LAAS) under the ARUM internal project, French National Center for Scientific Research (CNRS), by the MoSAIC project (ACI S&I, French national program for Security and Informatics), the European Hidenets project (EU-IST-FP6-26979), and the European ReSIST network of excellence (EU-IST-FP6-26764).

A. Casimiro et al. (Eds.): Architecting Dependable Systems VII, LNCS 6420, pp. 53–73, 2010.

a *platform* for its experimental evaluation. This architecture is exemplified by implementing a Distributed Black-Box (DBB) application which provides a virtual device, whose semantics is similar to avionics black-boxes, that track cars' history in a way that can be replayed in the event of a car accident. This application ensures information is securely stored using replication mechanisms, by means of exchanging positions between cars. Our implementation is based on three original services: a *Proximity Map*, a *Trust and Cooperation Oracle*, and a *Cooperative Data Backup*.

This DBB application is a good illustration of the use of the various middleware services and applications that users can benefit from thanks to mobile communicating devices, such as in the automobile context with car-to-car communication. As a "classical" black-box, its aim is to record critical data, such as engine / vehicle speed, brake status, throttle position, or the state of the driver's seat belt switch. As a "smart" black-box, it can also be used for extending the recorded information with contextual information concerning the neighboring vehicles, and ideally the various vehicles that were involved in a given accident. Indeed, information stored by the application leverages vehicle-based parameters and communication-induced information.

The proposed architecture is based on four main middleware building blocks, namely a Networking service, a Proximity Map, a Trust and Cooperation Oracle, and a Cooperative Data Backup service. This architecture and the DBB application will be described in Section 2. This distributed architecture being targeted to mobile nodes (automobiles), it has been implemented and evaluated on top of a mobile robot platform described in section 3. Finally, we conclude this paper and give some further trails of research in Section 4.

2   Architecture and System Model

The work presented in this section was conducted in the course of the Hidenets project. Hidenets (HIghly DEpendable ip-based NETworks and Services) was a specific targeted research project funded by the European Union under the Information Society Sixth Framework Programme. The aim of Hidenets was to develop and analyze end-to-end resilience solutions for distributed applications and mobility-aware services in ubiquitous communication scenarios.

The overall architecture used in this work is depicted on Fig. 1. The mobile platform, the hardware and other experimental settings will be described later in Section 3. This architecture is a partial implementation of the Hidenets architecture and has been detailed in the projects deliverables, see e.g. [2] or [3]. Apart from standard hardware-related services (networking, localization...), we propose three new building blocks, targeted for mobile systems, that are described in the following subsections. The rationale of these building blocks is as follows:

Proximity map. Before being able to backup data, a mobile node has first to discover its neighbors and the resources and services they offer. The proximity

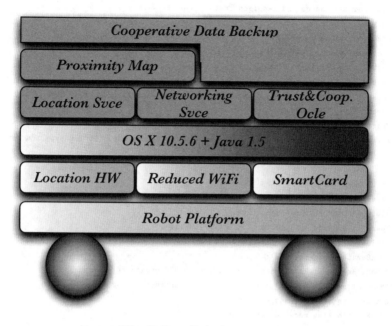

Fig. 1. Overall Architecture

map represents the local knowledge a node has about its vicinity. This can vary according to wideness (the number of communication hops represented on the map) and according to accuracy (how often is the map updated). Notice that, in this work, the aim of the proximity map is twofold: it is used to know which nodes can be used for cooperation, and is also used as a source of data to be backed up by the distributed black-box application, as we shall see later.

Trust and cooperation oracle. In order to interact with a priori unknown neighbors for critical services (e.g., collaborative backup), a node has to evaluate the level of trust it can assign to each of its neighbors. The purpose of the trust and cooperation oracle is to evaluate this level of trust and to incite nodes to cooperate with one another.

Cooperative data backup. The provision of a cooperative backup service at the middleware level is the major contribution of the architecture described in this paper. This service acts as a peer-to-peer storage resource sharing service for backup and restoration of critical data. There are four main tasks to achieve when considering cooperative data backup : (1) discovering storage resources in the vicinity, (2) negotiating a contract with the neighboring cars for the use of their resources, (3) handling a set of data chunks to backup and assigning these chunks to the negotiated resources according to some data encoding scheme and with respect to desired properties like dependability, privacy, confidentiality, and finally (4) taking care of the recovery phase, i.e., the data restoration algorithm.

```
// A node produces, sends and receives instances of Packet
class Packet {
    // size of payload is bounded
    protected byte[] payload;
    protected Node destinationNode;
    protected Node sourceNode;
    // Packets are typed, i.e., a client can request to receive packets of type "PMAP"
    protected String typeOfPacket;
    // There are actually several versions of the constructor
    Packet(byte[] message, Node destinationNode,  Node sourceNode,  String typeOfPacket);
}


class NetworkService {
    // NetworkService implements the singleton pattern,
    // i.e. only one instance is active
    // There is thus no constructor for NetworkService,
    // getInstance returns a reference to the unique instance of the NetworkService
    NetworkService getInstance();
    void basicBroadcast(Packet msg); // Performs a UDP broadcast of msg
    boolean unicast(Packet msg); // Performs a TCP unicast of msg
    Packet receive(String messageType);
        // Non-blocking receive operation,
        // if no message of type messageType in the queue, it returns null
}
```

Fig. 2. Adhoc Networking API

2.1   Communication and Network Layer

Since Java provides no specific support for ad hoc networking[1], we implemented a specific package for handling multiple WiFi interfaces. This package supports both UDP broadcasting and TCP unicasting. It handles indexing, choping and unchoping of arbitrary size messages and deals with typed messages. As we are only interested in local interactions within an entity's neighborhood, our network layer implements one-hop interactions only, and does not address the problem of routing in an ad-hoc network.

The package API is provided in Fig. 2. There are basically three important methods: basicBroadcast, unicast and receive. It is worth noticing that messages are typed by a string. This is very useful when several services can concurrently access the network service. They can use one or several types each and this way, won't consume other services messages. For example, the Proximity Map and the Trust and Cooperation Oracle, both described in the following sections, produce messages with, respectively, the PMAP and the TCO types. When the Proximity Map calls the receive method, it receives messages of type PMAP only, even if there are TCO-typed messages in the queue. Those TCO typed messages thus remain in

---

[1] There was a working group concerned with adhoc networking for Java. They produced a preliminary draft entitled "JSR-259 Ad Hoc Networking API" in 2006, but this draft didn't evolve since and no actual implementation was produced.

the queue until the Trust and Cooperation Oracle calls the `receive` method requesting a TCO-type message.

The rationale of having both broadcasting and unicasting available is simple. In a cooperative ad-hoc network, nodes need to interact with their neighbors which they do not a priori know. They can thus broadcast services advertisement or discovery requests in order to explore their vicinity. Once they acquired enough knowledge about the resources available in their network vicinity, they can use point-to-point communication, i.e. unicast, to access those resources. We believe that this is the only way cooperative services can be implemented on top of mobile adhoc networks and deal with nodes mobility and failures.

2.2 Localization and Proximity Map

In many applications dedicated to mobile nodes, and especially for cooperation-based applications, a node needs to interact with its neighbors. Furthermore, the quality of service that may be provided by a given component can vary according to the vicinity, e.g. the quantity of neighbors, their density, etc. It is then necessary to formalize this view of the vicinity into a more abstract representation. This is the purpose of the *Proximity Map* building block, that provides an abstraction of the physically attainable network of entities. The aim of this building block is to provide applications with information aggregated from both localization and networking layers.

Indeed, the goal of the proximity map is to gather physical information about nodes in the vicinity. When using its proximity map, a given node has a view of the nodes in its vicinity (defined as being the nodes which are reachable within H hops), their location information, and the freshness of the pieces of information.

This problem has similarities with neighbor discovery protocols for ad-hoc routing algorithms, that can be divided into proactive schemes and reactive schemes. In a reactive scheme, information about routing is constructed on demand, i.e., as soon as a message has to be sent to a previously unknown destination. In a proactive scheme, the entity periodically sends messages on the network to look for new neighbors, and to verify the availability and reachability of already discovered neighbors. Since we are only interested in local interactions, and due to the fact that the set of entities is large and unknown to participants, we designed the proximity map as a proactive service.

Intuitively each node periodically beacons its proximity map to its 1-hop neighbors, and collects similar information from its direct neighbors. When merging these pieces of information, it is able to update its proximity map with new nodes that appeared as neighbors of neighbors, nodes which have moved, nodes whose connectivity changed, etc. The preliminary ideas about the proximity map can be found in [4]. To implement the proximity map, we use location-stamped beacons[2]. Each node keeps a map of its knowledge of the location and connectivity of other nodes, which is represented as a graph as shown in Fig. 3. This

---

[2] In addition to the location of the node, beacons could also include other useful information about the sending node's radio coverage, its battery life, etc.

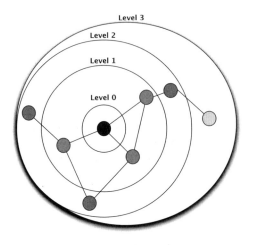

Fig. 3. The Proximity Map Knowledge

graph is regularly updated when the node receives a beacon and is also regularly sent to the node's neighbors in its beacons.

Map construction: The pseudo-code of the Proximity Map protocol is given in Fig. 4. Here is the intuition behind it :

1. First, the node only knows its own location, it creates a proximity map `knowledge` and set itself as the root element of the graph.
2. The protocol is run every D time units, it thus loops and sleeps so as to emulate a periodic thread.
3. It updates its position and broadcasts its knowledge to neighbors,
4. Then, the node receives its neighbors' Proximity Maps, and fusions them with its own.
5. After collecting all its neighbors information, it prunes its Proximity Map to a maximum of H hops.
6. Then it performs the failure detection, i.e. removes nodes that are too old.

Map accuracy: Map accuracy can be evaluated with respect to two criteria:

- *timing*: is the map synchronized with reality or does it carry old connectivity and positioning information?
- *failure*: are the nodes present in a Proximity Map still alive and connected?

Timing issues are quite simple. First let's say that we call level 0 information about the node itself, level 1 information about its 1 hop neighbors, and level n information about its n hops neighbors. Then, quite intuitively, we can say that if beacons are sent every D time units, then level L information is $(L \times D)$ time units old. Because high-level knowledge is older and because having the knowledge of the whole network is unnecessary, the maximum level of knowledge is bounded. The Proximity Map algorithm is pro-active and enables a node to

```
// First we initialize knowledge
knowledge = new ProximityMapStorage();
// At the beginning, we only know our own position
knowledge.setRootElement( myPosition );

// Loop forever
do {
  // Sleep D time units
  sleep(D);

  // Update our own position
  knowledge.changeRootElement( myPosition );

  //Send our PMAP to neighbors
  basicBroadcast(PMAP);

  // And also to receive the PMAPS and to integrate them
  while (there are PMAPs to be handled) {
    ProximityMap fromNeighbor = NetworkService.receivePMAP();
    if (fromNeighbor is not from myself) {

      // Extract information and add it to my own PMAP
      knowledge.addToPMAP(fromNeighbor);
    }
  }

  // Prune my PMAP so that it longest path does not exceed H
  knowledge.prune(H);

  // Perform failure detection, i.e. remove nodes whose information is too old
  for each node in knowledge {
    if ( (node.timestamp - currentTime) > failureDeltaTime ) {
      remove node from knowledge;
}}} while(true);
```

Fig. 4. The Proximity Map Algorithm

know the other nodes physically present within the area if H is sufficiently large. When H is not large enough, or the coverage obtained is not sufficient, a reactive protocol may be used to complete location information further than H hops.

In the absence of fault, at any time after $(H \times D)$ time units, a node knows the location and coverage of its H hops neighbors. It should however be noted that at any time t, every node in the network has a different view of the connectivity since its level 1 information is D time units old, its level n is $n \times D$ time units old, etc.

At the moment, the bound H is determined statically according to the application, the density of the network and other environment parameters. An interesting future work would be to modify this protocol to have a dynamic H parameter that can be statically initialized and adapted at runtime according to the environment variation and to the application needs. It is worth noting that increasing H has important consequences on both the network load and on the memory footprint of the proximity map. However, in some application scenarios, for example when the network density is low and when node connections get low, it would be quite beneficial to have a deeper knowledge of the network. An idea worth experimenting would be to adjust H while keeping the memory footprint constant, i.e. exploring the network while there is some free memory for the protocol and garbage collecting the older nodes when freeing memory is necessary.

Regarding faults and failures, it is interesting to notice that the Proximity Map protocol is intrinsically resilient to faults. Indeed, let us first consider *crash failures*: when a node fails, it stops sending beacons and thus it will be removed from its neighbors' Proximity Maps after they didn't receive information about it for $failureDeltaTime$ time units. So a node that is n hops from a failed node (with $n < H$)will remove the failed node from its map after $failureDeltaTime + n \times D$. Now, if we consider *intermittent faults*, for example a bad position given by the GPS device or even a proximity map containing bad information, since beacons are sent every D time units, the faulty information will vanish and be replaced by the fresh and correct information. If we suppose that the faulty beacon is sent only once (i.e. the duration of the intermittent fault is less than D time units), the effects on the global system will last at most $min(H \times D, failureDeltaTime)$: either the furthest node stays at H hops and will receive fresh information after $H \times D$, or it will come closer and will get it sooner or even it will go further and henceforth never receive fresh information but will remove the failed node from its Proximity Map after $failureDeltaTime$ time units.

When building the Proximity Map, and in general in our whole architecture, we disregarded Byzantine behaviors because they should be avoided by the next building block: the Trust and Cooperation Oracle. However, it is interesting to note that given the intrinsic redundancy of the positioning and network connectivity among the various nodes of the network, it is relatively easy to imagine a byzantine-resilient version of the Proximity Map. Indeed, when a node i receives a beacon from a node j, i can check if the position advertised by j is consistent with the views of its neighbors. Of course, this holds only when there is no collusion between i's neighbors. However, this Byzantine-resilient version of the Proximity Map is future work, in the next section we present and discuss another approach for dealing with non cooperative, rationale, but also Byzantine nodes.

2.3   Trust and Cooperation Oracle

The trust and cooperation oracle (TCO) is our second building block for cooperative services. A cooperative service emerges from the cooperation of entities that are generally unknown to one another. Therefore, these entities have no a priori trust relationship and may thus be reluctant to cooperate. In cooperative systems without cooperation incentives, entities tend to behave in a rational way in order to maximize their own benefit from the system. The goal of the trust and cooperation oracle is therefore to evaluate locally the level of trust of neighboring entities and to manage cooperation incentives [5].

```
class TCO {
  // TCO implements the singleton pattern,
  // i.e. only one instance is active
  // There is thus no constructor for TCO,
  // getInstance returns a reference to the unique instance of the TCO
  TCO getInstance();

  // Main method for TCO, it returns the trust the nodes have in another node
  float trustLevel(NodeID n);
}
```

Fig. 5. Trust and Cooperation Oracle API

Synergy is the desired positive effect of cooperation, i.e., that the accrued benefits are greater than the sum of the benefits that could be achieved without cooperation. However synergy can only be achieved if nodes do cooperate rather than pursuing some individual short-term strategy, i.e. being rational[3]. Therefore, cooperative systems need to have cooperation incentives and rationality disincentives. There are several approaches to this, some are based on microeconomy and some others are based on trust. Typically, for micro-economic approaches, a node has to spend "money" for using a service and earns "money" for servicing other nodes. Regarding trust, a common approach is to use the notion of reputation, a level representing the level of trust that may be placed on a node, which can be computed locally by a single node, or collectively and transitively by a set of nodes. Another approach based on the notion of trust relies on the use of trusted hardware, e.g. a smart-card. Whatever the most appropriate approach in a given context, the TCO leverages this information by providing a single interface with simple semantics. Given a node identifier n, it returns the probability that this node n cooperates correctly for the next interaction, as shown in Fig. 5.

When the various entities participating in a cooperative service belong to the same administrative domain, or to a limited number of domains, the question of trust establishment can be answered in a simple manner. For example, if we consider the case of a single administrative domain such as an enterprise, we can make the assumption that any node within the enterprise is going to cooperate. The problem of the trust establishment is thus reduced to the question of identifying the nodes which are part of the enterprise. When multiple, but limited, administrative domains are involved, the question can sometimes be simplified in a similar manner.

In an automotive context, we consider that there are a limited number of different middleware providers. We can also state that it is at least unusual and potentially dangerous for vehicle owners to modify the software their vehicle is running, and that software updates are relatively rare. As a result, there are only a few different legacy middleware versions. We can thus consider that the

---

[3] A rational node always tries to maximize its benefits from the system, i.e. it behaves selfishly.

middleware is certified, i.e., a trusted authority within the infrastructure domain can generate and distribute certificates. These certificates can be verified in the ad-hoc domain by a trusted hardware, e.g. in the Hidenets platform a smart-card. In this setting the concept of trust can be seen as all-or-nothing: when the certificate is verified, the middleware is legitimate, full trust is granted; on the other hand, when the certificate cannot be verified, this means that the middleware was modified and henceforth no trust can be given to the node.

In other application domains, such as cooperative backup of personal data stored on mobile devices such as smartphones for example, such a black or white notion of trust is not acceptable. Indeed, in such open settings, where many heterogeneous hardware and software cohabit, trust should rather be established based on the behavior of the nodes and their users than on the middleware legacy. The interested reader will find several approaches to deal with trust establishment, such as in [6] or in [5]. These different approaches can obviously be used to realize the Trust and Cooperation Oracle API and return a more balanced vision of trust, i.e. varying between 0 and 1.

2.4   Cooperative Data Backup Service

The cooperative backup service aims to improve the dependability of data stored by participating nodes by providing them with mechanisms to tolerate hardware or software faults, including permanent faults such as loss, theft, or physical damage. To tolerate permanent faults, the service must provide mechanisms to store the users' data on alternate storage nodes using the available communication means. The problem of cooperative backup of critical data can be divided in three steps: i) discovering storage resources in the vicinity (this step is performed using the proximity map service), ii) negotiating a contract with the neighboring nodes for the use of their resources (this step uses the trust and cooperation oracle), and iii) handling a set of data chunks to backup and assigning these chunks to the negotiated resources according to a data encoding scheme and with respect to desired properties of dependability, privacy, availability and confidentiality. The service is also in charge of the recovery phase, i.e., the data restoration algorithm.

The Cooperative Data Backup service provision is designed using the following principles:

- A client of the service provides a data stream to be backed up to the `backup` operation with a unique identifier for the stream.
- The stream passes through a series of chopping and indexing operations in order to produce a set of small (meta-) data chunks to be backed up (more details can be found in [7]).
- A backup thread runs periodically, it processes the block buffer, queries the Proximity Map service and the Trust and Cooperation Oracle in order to produce a potential contributors list. Then it places data blocks on contributors according to given placement and replication strategies, as described in [7] and [8].

```
void run() { // This is the main loop method
  loop { // It serves client requests and processes network messages
    sleep(D); // Sleeps D time units
    handleRestoration(); // Handles client restoration requests
    receiveCBPackets(); // Processes CooperativeBackup messages
    backupData(); // And processes client backup requests
}}
void handleRestoration() {
  for all blockID in missingBlocks {
    // We first try to find all locally-available requests
    if blockID is found locally {
      store the corresponding block in replyStorage;
      remove blockID from missingBlocks
    } else { // if the block has not been found locally then send a request for it
      Net.basicBroadcast(request for blockID, "CooperativeBackup");
}}}
void receiveCBPackets() {
  while there are packets typed "CooperativeBackup" to be handled {
    if source of packet is trusted enough by the TCO {
      if packet is a storage request {
        unpack the block contained in p and store it locally under blockID
      } else if packet p is a restoration request {
        unpack the blockID requested in p
        search in the local storage for blockID
        if the block was found, unicast it to the sender of the request
      } else { // it is then a reply to a restoration requested
        unpack the blockID and the block data sent in p
        store block locally with blockID
        remove blockID from missingBlocks
}}}}
void backupData() {
  // Example: straightforward backup policy: each block is distributed only once
  Build the list of nodes candidates for backup, using ProximityMap and TCO
  while (there are blocks to backup in backupStore and there are candidates) {
    for each candidate taken in a randomized order {
      unicast a storage request for the next block in backupStore to the candidate
      if the unicast was successful, remove the block from the backupStore;
    }
    rebuild the candidates list
}}
```

Fig. 6. Cooperative Data Backup Algorithm

When the client wants to restore data, it can either submit the unique identi-fier of the stream to the asynchronous restore operation and then poll it period-ically, or it can directly call the synchronous restore operation that will return when the data has been successfully restored. To that means, a periodic thread handles the restoration waiting queue: it looks for given IDs, unpacks the received blocks and potentially adds new identifiers to the waiting queue according to the decoding operation on received data chunks (i.e. data or meta-data).

Fig. 6 gives the pseudo-code for both cooperative backup. A periodic thread handles restoration requests, then processes network packets and then handles backup requests. Restoration first looks locally if the requested block is found, if it is not the case it broadcasts a request looking for the block (by sending its unique block ID). Processing network messages involves dealing with three type of messages: 1-Storage requests, 2-Restoration requests and 3-Restoration replies. Of course only the messages sent by trusted sources (by the TCO) are processed. Handling backup requests implies implementing a particular backup strategy, i.e. placing each block a certain number of times on the nodes available in the vicinity (and trusted by the TCO).

In [8], we discuss various backup strategies and we provide an analytical evaluation of the storage cost and dependability of these strategies as a function of a few parameters such as: α the rate of peers' encounters, β the rate of infrastructure connectivity (to perform backup using the Internet), and of course λ the failure rate. Basically, we showed that the cooperative backup approach is beneficial (i.e., yields data dependability an order of magnitude higher than without cooperative backup) only when $\frac{\beta}{\lambda} > 2$ and $\frac{\alpha}{\beta} > 10$. We demonstrated that cooperative backup can decrease the probability of data loss by a factor that can be as large as the ad hoc to Internet connectivity ratio $\frac{\alpha}{\beta}$.

```
class CooperativeBackup {
    // CooperativeBackup implements the singleton pattern,
    // i.e. only one instance is active
    // There is thus no constructor for CooperativeBackup,
    // getInstance returns a reference to the unique instance of the CooperativeBackup
    CooperativeBackup getInstance();

    // submitBackupData feeds the CooperativeBackup with data to be backed up
    //  the data can be later restored by providing its unique identifier UUID
    public void submitBackupData(byte data[], UUID key );

    // submitRestore requests the restoration of the data identified by uid
    // the data will be available later through a call to restore
    public void submitRestore(UUID uid);

    // restore returns the data identified by uid if the data has been restored
    //  and returns null otherwise
    public byte[] restore(UUID uid);
}
```

Fig. 7. Cooperative Data Backup API

The Cooperative Data Backup Service API is given in Fig. 7. This service is very simple to use. First, the client of the service needs to get an instance of the service through a call to getInstance. Then it can send backup and restoration requests through *submitBackupData* and *submitRestore* respectively. The client can get the restored data back, later on, using the *restore* method. This method, as the other two methods, is non-blocking and returns *null* if the data is not restored yet. With the Cooperative Data Backup Service, data is identified through a unique identifier (we used the Java's UUID in the implementation). This means that clients of the service have to compute (and remember) these identifiers. This is classically obtained by constructing a directory containing all the identifiers of the backed up data and by backing up this directory using a static identifier, that one can easily remember, such as the node MAC address for example.

2.5   The Distributed Black-Box Application

Using the above described services, we implemented a Distributed Black-Box application. In a few words, this application backs up a stream of data for every car that consists of a periodic sampling of a car's proximity map. The cooperative backup service is used to replicate these streams among neighboring cars, or to an infrastructure when connectivity permits it. The stream of any participant (be it crashed or not) can then be restored either from neighboring devices (cars in ad-hoc mode), or from the infrastructure. In more details, the application maintains a Black-box view of the car vicinity. This view contains the car position, its proximity map pruned to a maximum of 10 hops, a timestamp. This view is serialized and submitted to the Cooperative Data Backup Service using a unique identifier that consists in the concatenation of the car license plate number and the current time. When a car crashes and its Black-box view needs to be reconstructed, one has to submit the crashed car license plate number and the time interval in which one is interested. For example, if an accident happened to a specific car on the 1st of july around noon, one can want to get the Black-box views of the car "02 ARUM 31", between "1st July 2010 - 12:05" and "1st July 2010 - 12:15". The Distributed Black-Box application will try to restore all the Black-box views corresponding to this pattern. After these requests propagate through the network, and when the corresponding replies begin to arrive, the restoration client can travel back in time and try to understand what happened to the crashed car.

3   The ARUM Experimental Platform

To the best of our knowledge, little research has been done on the evaluation of resilience in ubiquitous systems. Most of the literature in this domain concerns evaluation of users experience and human-computer interfaces. However, some work is also looking at defining appropriate metrics for the evaluation of distributed applications running on ubiquitous systems [9,10]. [11] is looking at a general approach to evaluate ubiquitous systems. In this paper, the authors argue that quantitative measurements should be complemented with qualitative evaluation. Their argument is that there is a number of problems for which evaluation cannot be easily quantified. Thus an evaluation should be conducted using an hybrid quantitative/qualitative strategy.

It is clear that the area of resilient computing has proposed a number of contributions concerning the evaluation of distributed systems and this paper will not survey this domain. Analytical evaluation is probably the most popular technique, such as within Assert [12] in the avionics application domain. More recently, experimental evaluation started to gain attention. The approach taken is often based on dependability benchmarking, for example DBench [13] addresses dependability benchmarking of operating systems.

In the ubiquitous and mobile computing area, evaluation of resilient mechanisms remains an open problem. In most cases, the proposed algorithms are evaluated and validated using network simulators [14,15]. Since simulators use a model of physical components, such as wireless network cards and location systems, this raises concerns on the coverage of the assumptions that underlie the simulation [16]. Little work concerning the evaluation of algorithms in a realistic mobile experimental environment is available. However, related work is discussed in Section 3.4.

3.1   Scalability

The above mentioned lack of a realistic mobile experimental environment calls for the development of a realistic platform, at a laboratory scale, to evaluate and validate fault-tolerance algorithms (in particular the services described in Section 2) targeting systems comprising a large number of communicating mobile devices equipped with various sensors and actuators. The goal is to have an experimentation platform allowing for reproducible experiments (including mobility aspects) that will complement validation through simulation. As we will see, an important issue within this platform is related to changes of scale so as to emulate many various systems.

In the ARUM[4] project, we are developing an experimental evaluation platform composed of both fixed and mobile devices [17,18,19]. Technically speaking, each mobile device is composed of some programmable mobile hardware able to carry the device itself, a lightweight processing unit equipped with one or several wireless network interfaces and a positioning device. The fixed counterpart of the platform contains the corresponding fixed infrastructure: an indoor positioning system, wireless communication support, as well as some fixed servers. Our platform is set up in a room of approximately $100m^2$ where mobile devices can move around. By changing scale, we can emulate systems of different sizes. Hardware modeling of this type of system requires a reduction or increase of scale to be able to conduct experiments within the laboratory. To obtain a realistic environment, all services must be modified according to the same scale factor.

---

[4] ARUM stands for an Approach for the Resilience of Ubiquitous Mobile systems. It is an internal project funded by the Laboratoire d'Analyse et d'Architecture des Systèmes (LAAS).

For example, if we consider a Vehicular Ad-hoc NETwork (VANET) experiment, a typical GPS in a moving car is accurate to within $5 - 20m$. So, for our $100m^2$ indoor environment to be a scaled down representation of a $250000m^2$ outdoor environment (that represent a scale reduction factor of 50 for distances), the indoor positioning accuracy needs to be at least $10 - 40cm$. The following table summarizes the required change in scale for all peripherals of a node.

Device	Real Accuracy	Scaled Accuracy
Wireless	range: $100m$	range: $2m$
GPS	$5m$	$10cm$
Node size	a few meters	a few decimeters
Node speed	a few m/s	$< 1m/s$

3.2   Technological Aspects

Positioning. Several technologies are currently available for indoor location [20], mostly based either on scene analysis (e.g. using motion capture systems) or on triangularization (of RF and ultrasound [21] or wireless communication interfaces [22]). In this section, we describe the various systems we used, and analyze both their positive and negative aspects.

To reach our desired level of accuracy for indoor positioning, we first used a dedicated motion capture technology that tracks objects based on real-time analysis of images captured by infra-red cameras. The Cortex[5] system is able to localize objects at the millimeter scale, which is more than enough for the VANET setting. This technology uses a set of infrared cameras, placed around the room, that track infrared-visible tags. All cameras are connected to a server that computes, based on all cameras images, the position of every tag in the system. We equipped our small robots with such tags, and the computers on the robots connect to the server to get their positioning information. Although the precision attained was more than enough for our needs, the system has some drawbacks: the whole system is very expensive (in the order of $100k$€), calibration is a tedious task, and infrared signals cannot cross obstacles such as humans.

To overcome these limitations, we are currently developing a new localization system, based on two different technologies that have complementary advantages. The first one is based on infrared cameras, as for Cortex, but the system is reversed: cameras are on-board, and locate themselves by tracking statically placed infrared-visible tags. This system is coupled with an Ultra-Wide-Band-based localization system, Ubisense. Ultra-Wide-Band-based localization (UWB) is performed by 4 sensors, placed in the room at each corner, that listen for signals sent by small tags that emit impulses in a wide spectrum. Such impulses can traverse human bodies and small obstacles, so the whole system is robust to external perturbation, but, from our preliminary measurements, attainable precision is less than $10cm$.

---

[5] http://www.motionanalysis.com

We thus advocate that the coupling of these two technologies will result in a localization system with desirable properties: it is relatively cheap, it is robust to external perturbations such as obstacles, and has most of the time a precision about the order of a centimeter.

Mobility. Another important question is how to make the devices actually mobile. Obviously, when conducting experiments, a human operator cannot be behind each device, so mobility has to be automated. This is why we considered the use of simple small robot platforms in order to carry around the platform devices. The task of these robots is to "implement" the mobility of the nodes. The carried devices communicate with the robot through a serial port. This way they can control the mobility, i.e. the trajectory, the stops and continuations, the fault-injection, etc.

A node in the system is implemented using a laptop computer, that includes all hardware devices and the software under testing, that is carried by a simple robotic platform, the Lynxmotion 4WD rover. A 4WD rover is able to carry a full node during a few hours, running at a maximum speed of $1m.s^{-1}$, which is consistent with our assumptions.

To have reproducible patterns of mobility, the rover embarks a dedicated software that moves the robot using two different schemes. Both designs allow for testing different algorithms using the same mobility pattern, and for testing the same algorithm with different mobility scenarios.

In the simple scheme, a robot is following a black line on the floor. This solution is easy to implement but imposes that the operator "draws" the circuit for every different mobility pattern.

The second scheme couples a predefined mobility pattern with the positioning service and ensures a given node moves according to the predefined pattern, programmed by the operator. This solution is more flexible: each node has its own mobility pattern specified for each experiment.

Communication. The last and most important design issue for the platform concerns wireless communications. Indeed, the communication range of the participants (mobile nodes and infrastructure access-points) has to be scaled down according to the experiment being conducted. For example, with a VANET experiment, a typical automobile has a wireless communication range of a few hundred meters, say $200m$. With a scale reduction factor fixed at 50, the mobile devices communication range has to be limited to $4m$. However, to cope with other experiments and other scale reduction factors, this communication range should ideally be variable.

A satisfying solution consists in using, for this purpose, signal attenuators placed between the WiFi network interfaces and their antennas. An attenuator is an electronic device that reduces the amplitude or power of a signal without appreciably distorting its waveform. Attenuators are passive devices made from resistors. The degree of attenuation may be fixed, continuously adjustable, or incrementally adjustable. In our case, the attenuators are used to reduce the signal received by the network interface. The necessary capacity of the attenuators

Fig. 8. The ARUM platform

depends on many parameters such as the power of the WiFi interfaces and the efficiency of the antennas, but also on the speed of the robot movements, the room environment, etc.

3.3 Application Scenario

As can be seen on Fig 1, the middleware described in this article is running on top of Apple OS X.5.6 and Java 1.5. The hardware (Macbook with additional WiFi interface and some localization hardware) is carried by a Lynxmotion 4WD rover. The resulting platform can be seen on Fig. 8. We currently own four fully equipped robots. We were thus able to emulate the Distributed Black-Box in a setting with three cooperating cars and a police coming after an accident has taken place. During the first part of the scenario, the three cars backup each others' Black-Box data for each other, then one of the cars looses control and leaves the circuit track to crash in a wall. After the accident has been reported, including the ID of the crashed car and the approximated time of the accident, the police enters the scene and requests restoration of the black box data for a given period of time that surrounds the accident. Once the data is successfully restored, the police is then able to replay the film of the accident, and to identify the other involved cars if there are any. A movie of this scenario is available at `http://homepages.laas.fr/mroy/hidenets/`

3.4 Related Work

Relatively little work concerning the evaluation of algorithms in a realistic mobile experimental environment is available. Most of the available platforms are based on wired emulation of wireless networks [23]. Wired wireless emulators such as EMPOWER [24], and EMWIN [25] use a centralized emulation layer and rely on switching equipment to disseminate messages to "mobile" nodes. Non-centralized wireless testbed emulators such as SEAWIND [26] or SWOON [27] rely on a wired configurable testbed similar to Emulab [28]. These testbed emulators make use of various link shaping techniques to approximate a wireless link. Typically, a special node is used for one or more links that need to be emulated. The quality of the emulation can suffer since these testbeds utilize switching equipment and multiple nodes to propagate messages. Both Mobile Emulab [29] and MiNT [30] use robots to emulate mobility of wireless nodes. The mobile version of Emulab embarks Motes to emulate a wireless sensor network; wireless experiments are carried at the building scale. Similarly to our platform, MiNT uses signal attenuators to reduce the space needed for experiments [31]. However, in order to reduce MiNT's node cost, the positioning subsystem is based on simple web-cams and henceforth is not precise.

3.5 Mobility Issues

Building a platform for evaluating mobile systems was clearly a challenge, as illustrated by the small number of other available platforms that implement real mobility. But placing laptops on wheels is not enough to evaluate distributed mobile applications in meaningful mobile configurations. The way the nodes move, both from their own perspective, but also according to other nodes movement, is a very interesting scientific issue that needed to be addressed. We believe that the usual mobility models used for the evaluation of mobile systems are not satisfactory. A mobility model dictates how the nodes, once distributed in the space, move. A mobility model involves the nodes' locations, velocities and accelerations over time. The topology and movement of nodes are key factors in the performance of the system under study. Because the mobility of the nodes directly impacts the performance of the protocol, if the mobility model does not reflect realistically the environment under study, the result may not reflect the performance of the system in the reality. The majority of existing mobility models for ad hoc networks do not provide realistic movement scenarios [32]. We are currently working on the use of real mobility traces from various sources in order to build more realistic mobility models to use in our analytical and experimental evaluation. The production and usage of such real-life mobility traces also raise a lot of privacy concerns that we recently began to address, see e.g. [33].

4   Conclusion

In this paper, we presented a middleware for building resilient cooperative mobile systems. This middleware is based on our belief that in an ubiquitous environment, with many fixed and mobile communicating nodes that do not know each other a priori, local cooperation with neighboring nodes is the approach to follow in order to build fast and reliable applications and services. This calls for network and middleware layers that encourages the application to first discover available services in the vicinity, then evaluate trustiness of available resources, and finally interact with those services. This is the purpose and the philosophy behind the design of the Network and communication layer, the Proximity Map, and the Trust and Cooperation Oracle. Another important aspect of ubiquitous and mobile computing models is the fact that communication can be ephemeral. This is the reason why we designed a Cooperative Data Backup Service: a node can leverage the ephemeral encounters it makes in order to replicate and disseminate its critical data. We have shown that using these building blocks, it is very easy to build a resilient cooperative application: a Distributed Black-box that reliably stores critical data.

Up to now, most of the algorithms and protocols for mobile systems were evaluated using simulators and analytical techniques in the best cases. We advocate that these evaluation techniques do not capture all the complexity inherent to a ubiquitous and mobile computing environments. Hence, we developed a platform based on (1) mobile robots, (2) scaled-down wireless communication interfaces, and (3) extremely precise localization, in order to perform realistic experimental evaluation of mobile services and applications.

We used with success this platform to run and evaluate the middleware building blocks, and the Distributed Black-box application presented in this paper. This raised a lot of technical questions but also many design issues. Indeed, the middleware building blocks were profoundly influenced by the fact that it was implemented for real-life use, using real (i.e. not simulated) hardware and that the whole hardware platform was really mobile. Both the middleware and the platform influenced each other in a kind of virtuous circle. Both of them will be reused in other settings, to build and to evaluate other resilient architectures and other mobile cooperative applications.

References

1. Roy, M., Bonnet, F., Querzoni, L., Bonomi, S., Killijian, M.-O., Powell, D.: Georegisters: An abstraction for spatial-based distributed computing. In: OPODIS 2008. LNCS, vol. 5401, pp. 534–537. Springer, Heidelberg (2008)
2. Arlat, J., Kaâniche, M. (eds.): Hidenets. revised reference model. deliverable nr. d1.2, LAAS-CNRS. Contract Report nr. 07456 (September 2007)
3. Casimiro, A., et al.: Resilient architecture (final version). LAAS-CNRS, Tech. Rep. 08068 (December 2008), http://www.di.fc.ul.pt/tech-reports/07-19.pdf
4. Killijian, M.-O., Cunningham, R., Meier, R., Mazare, L., Cahill, V.: Towards group communication for mobile participants. In: Proceedings of Principles of Mobile Computing (POMC), pp. 75–82 (2001)
5. Courtès, L., Killijian, M.-O., Powell, D.: Security rationale for a cooperative backup service for mobile devices. In: Bondavalli, A., Brasileiro, F., Rajsbaum, S. (eds.) LADC 2007. LNCS, vol. 4746, pp. 212–230. Springer, Heidelberg (2007)
6. Nouha, O., Yves, R.: Cooperation incentive schemes. Institut Eurecom, France, Tech. Rep. EURECOM+2026 (September 2006)
7. Courtes, L., Killijian, M.-O., Powell, D.: Storage tradeoffs in a collaborative backup service for mobile devices. In: European Dependable Computing Conference (EDCC), pp. 129–138 (2006)

8. Courtes, L., Hamouda, O., Kaaniche, M., Killijian, M.-O., Powell, D.: Dependability evaluation of cooperative backup strategies for mobile devices. In: Pacific Rim Dependable Computing, pp. 139–146 (2007)
9. Basu, P., Ke, W., Little, T.D.C.: Metrics for performance evaluation of distributed application execution in ubiquitous computing environments. In: Workshop on Evaluation Methodologies for Ubiquitous Computing at Ubicomp 2001 (2001), http://zing.ncsl.nist.gov/ubicomp01/
10. Castro, P., Chen, A., Kremenek, T., Muntz, R.: Evaluating distibuted query processing systems for ubiquitous computing. In: Workshop on Evaluation Methodologies for Ubiquitous Computing at Ubicomp 2001 (2001), http://zing.ncsl.nist.gov/ubicomp01/
11. Burnett, M., Rainsford, C.P.: A hybrid evaluation approach for ubiquitous computing environments. In: Workshop on Evaluation Methodologies for Ubiquitous Computing at Ubicomp 2001 (2001), http://zing.ncsl.nist.gov/ubicomp01/
12. Arlat, J., Barone, M.R., Crouzet, Y., Fabre, J.-C., Kaaniche, M., Kanoun, K., Mazzini, S., Nazzarelli, M.R., Powell, D., Roy, M., Rugina, A.E., Waeselynck, H.: Dependability needs and preliminary solutions concerning evaluation, testing and wrapping. LAAS, Toulouse, Tech. Rep. 05424 (2005)
13. Kanoun, K., Madeira, H., Moreira, F., Cin, M., Garcia, J.: Dbench - dependability benchmarking. In: Dal Cin, M., Kaâniche, M., Pataricza, A. (eds.) EDCC 2005. LNCS, vol. 3463. Springer, Heidelberg (2005)
14. Das, S.R., Castañeda, R., Yan, J.: Simulation-based performance evaluation of routing protocols for mobile ad hoc networks. Mob. Netw. Appl. 5(3), 179–189 (2000)
15. Hamida, E.B., Chelius, G., Gorce, J.M.: On the complexity of an accurate and precise performance evaluation of wireless networks using simulations. In: 11th ACM-IEEE Int. Symp. on Modeling, Analysis and Simulation of Wireless and Mobile Systems, MSWIM (2008)
16. Cavin, D., Sasson, Y., Schiper, A.: On the accuracy of manet simulators. In: Proceedings of the Second ACM International Workshop on Principles of Mobile Computing, POMC 2002, pp. 38–43. ACM Press, New York (2002)
17. Killijian, M.-O., Rivière, N., Roy, M.: Experimental evaluation of resilience for ubiquitous mobile systems. In: Proc. of UbiComp, Workshop on Ubiquitous Systems Evaluation (USE), pp. 283–287 (2007)
18. Killijian, M.-O., Roy, M.: Brief announcement: a platform for experimenting with mobile algorithms in a laboratory. In: Tirthapura, S., Alvisi, L. (eds.) PODC, pp. 316–317. ACM, New York (2009)
19. Killijian, M.-O., Roy, M., Severac, G., Zanon, C.: Data backup for mobile nodes: a cooperative middleware and experimentation platform. In: Proc. of the Workshop on Architecting Dependable Systems of the IEEE International Conference on Dependable Systems and Networks (DSN 2009), Lisboa, Portugal (2009)
20. Hightower, J., Borriello, G.: A survey and taxonomy of location systems for ubiquitous computing (2001), http://citeseer.ist.psu.edu/hightower01survey.html
21. Smith, A., Balakrishnan, H., Goraczko, M., Priyantha, N.B.: Tracking Moving Devices with the Cricket Location System. In: 2nd International Conference on Mobile Systems, Applications and Services (Mobisys 2004), Boston, MA (June 2004)
22. Correal, N.S., Kyperountas, S., Shi, Q., Welborn, M.: An uwb relative location system. In: Proc. of IEEE Conference on Ultra Wideband Systems and Technologies (November 2003)

23. Havey, D., Chertov, R., Almeroth, K.: Wired wireless broadcast emulation. In: 5th International workshop on Wireless Network Measurements, WiNMee (2009)

24. Zheng, P., Ni, L.M.: Empower: A network emulator for wireline and wireless networks. In: Proceedings of IEEE InfoCom. IEEE Computer and Communications Societies (2003)

25. Zheng, P., Ni, L.M.: Emwin: Emulating a mobile wireless network using a wired network. In: Proceedings of the 5th ACM International Workshop on Wireless Mobile Multimedia, pp. 64–71. ACM Press, New York (2002)

26. Kojo, M., Gurtov, A., Manner, J., Sarolahti, P., Alanko, T., Raatikainen, K.: Seawind: a wireless network emulator. In: Proceedings of 11th GI/ITG Conference on Measuring, Modelling and Evaluation of Computer and Communication Systems (2001)

27. Huang, Y.L., Tygar, J.D., Lin, H.Y., Yeh, L.Y., Tsai, H.Y., Sklower, K., Shieh, S.P., Wu, C.C., Lu, P.H., Chien, S.Y., Lin, Z.S., Hsu, L.W., Hsu, C.W., Hsu, C.T., Wu, Y.C., Leong, M.S.: Swoon: a testbed for secure wireless overlay networks. In: Proceedings of the Conference on Cyber Security Experimentation and Test, CSET 2008, pp. 1–6. USENIX Association, Berkeley (2008)

28. White, B., Lepreau, J., Stoller, L., Ricci, R., Guruprasad, S., Newbold, M., Hibler, M., Barb, C., Joglekar, A.: An integrated experimental environment for distributed systems and networks. In: Proc. of the Fifth Symposium on Operating Systems Design and Implementation, pp. 255–270. USENIX Association, Boston (December 2002)

29. Johnson, D., Stack, T., Fish, R., Flickinger, D.M., Stoller, L., Ricci, R., Lepreau, J.: Mobile emulab: A robotic wireless and sensor network testbed. In: INFOCOM. IEEE, Los Alamitos (2006)

30. Chiueh, T.-c., Krishnan, R., De, P., Chiang, J.-H.: A networked robot system for wireless network emulation. In: Proceedings of the 1st International Conference on Robot Communication and Coordination, RoboComm 2007, pp. 1–8. IEEE Press, Piscataway (2007)

31. De, P., Raniwala, A., Sharma, S., cker Chiueh, T.: Mint: a miniaturized network testbed for mobile wireless research. In: INFOCOM, pp. 2731–2742. IEEE, Los Alamitos (2005)

32. Musolesi, M., Mascolo, C.: Mobility models for systems evaluation. In: State of the Art on Middleware for Network Eccentric and Mobile Applications (MINEMA), Springer, Heidelberg (2009)

33. Gambs, S., Killijian, M.-O., del Prado Cortez, M.N.: Gepeto: A geoprivacy-enhancing toolkit. In: AINA Workshops, pp. 1071–1076. IEEE Computer Society, Los Alamitos (2010)

Identification of Security Requirements in Systems of Systems by Functional Security Analysis

Andreas Fuchs and Roland Rieke

Fraunhofer Institute for Secure Information Technology (SIT)
Rheinstrasse 75, 64295 Darmstadt, Germany
{andreas.fuchs,roland.rieke}@sit.fraunhofer.de

Abstract. Cooperating systems typically base decisions on information from their own components as well as on input from other systems. Safety critical decisions based on cooperative reasoning however raise severe concerns to security issues. Here, we address the security requirements elicitation step in the security engineering process for such systems of systems. The method comprises the tracing down of functional dependencies over system component boundaries right onto the origin of information as a functional flow graph. Based on this graph, we systematically deduce comprehensive sets of formally defined authenticity requirements for the given security and dependability objectives. The proposed method thereby avoids premature assumptions on the security architecture's structure as well as the means by which it is realised. Furthermore, a tool-assisted approach that follows the presented methodology is described.

Keywords: security requirements elicitation, systems of systems security engineering, security analysis for vehicular communication systems.

1 Introduction

Architecting novel mobile systems of systems (SoS) poses new challenges to getting the dependability and specifically the security requirements right as early as possible in the system design process. Security engineering is one important aspect of dependability [1]. The security engineering process addresses issues such as how to identify and mitigate risks resulting from connectivity and how to integrate security into a target architecture [2]. Security requirements need to be explicit, precise, adequate, non-conflicting with other requirements and complete [13].

A typical application area for mobile SoS are vehicular communication systems in which vehicles and roadside units communicate in ad hoc manner to exchange information such as safety warnings and traffic information. As a cooperative approach, vehicular communication systems can be more effective in avoiding accidents and traffic congestion than current technologies where each

A. Casimiro et al. (Eds.): Architecting Dependable Systems VII, LNCS 6420, pp. 74–96, 2010.

vehicle tries to solve these problems individually. However, introducing dependence of possibly safety-critical decisions in a vehicle on information from other systems, such as other vehicles or roadside units, raises severe concerns to security issues. Security is an enabling technology in this emerging field because without security some applications within those SoS would not be possible at all. In some cases security is the main concern of the architecture [22].

The first step in the design of an architecture for a novel system of systems is the requirements engineering process. With respect to security requirements this process typically covers at least the following activities [17,16,15]

- the identification of the target of evaluation and the principal security goals and the elicitation of artifacts (e.g. use case and threat scenarios) as well as risk assessment
- the actual security requirements elicitation process
- a requirements categorisation and prioritisation, followed by requirements inspection

In this paper we address the security requirements elicitation step in this process. We present a model-based approach to systematically identify security requirements for system architectures to be designed for cooperative applications in a SoS context. Our contribution comprises the following distinctive features.

Identification of a Consistent and Complete Set of Authenticity Requirements. We base our method on the following general assumption about the overall security goal with respect to authenticity requirements:

> *For every safety-critical action in a system of systems, all information that is used in the reasoning process that leads to this action has to be authentic.*

To achieve this, we first derive a functional model of a system by identification of atomic actions and functional dependencies in a use case description. From this model we generate a dependency graph with the safety-critical function under consideration as root and the origins of decision relevant information as leaves. Based on this graph, we deduce a set of authenticity requirements that is comprehensive and defines the maximal set of authenticity requirements from the given functional dependencies.

Security Mechanism Independence. The most common problem with security requirements is, that they tend to be replaced with security-specific architectural constraints that may unnecessarily constrain the choice of the most appropriate security mechanisms [4].

In our approach we avoid to break down the overall security requirements to requirements for specific components or communication channels prematurely. So the requirements identified by this approach are independent of decisions not only on concrete security enforcement mechanisms to use, but also on the structure, such as hop-by-hop versus end-to-end security measures.

Throughout this paper we use the following terminology taken from [1]: A *system* is an entity that interacts with other entities, i.e., other systems. These other systems are the *environment* of the given system. A *system boundary* is the common frontier between the system and its environment. Such a system itself is composed of *components*, where each component is yet another system. Furthermore, in [1] the *dependence* of system A on system B represents the extent to which system A's dependability is affected by that of system B. Our work though focuses on purely functional aspects of dependence and omits quantitative reasoning. For the approach proposed, we describe the *function* of such a system by a *functional model* and treat the components as atomic and thus we do not make preliminary assumptions regarding their inner structure. Rather, the adaption to a concrete architecture is considered to be a task within a follow-up refinement and engineering process.

The subsequent paper is structured as follows. Section 2 gives an overview of the related work on security engineering and requirements identification methodologies. In Sect. 3 we introduce a scenario from the automotive domain that will serve as use case throughout the rest of this text. Section 4 introduces the proposed approach to requirements identification, exemplified by application on the given use case. Section 5 presents an tool-assisted methodology that follows this approach utilising the scenario. Finally, the paper ends with conclusions and an outlook in Sect. 6.

2   Related Work

The development of new security relevant systems that interact to build new SoS requires the integration of a security engineering process in the earliest stages of the development life-cycle. This is specifically important in the development of systems where security is the enabling technology that makes new applications possible. There are several common approaches that may be taken, depending on the system architect's background.

In order to design a secure of vehicular communication system, an architect with a background in Mobile Adhoc Networks (MANETs) would probably first define the data origin authentication [27] of the transmitted message. In a next step he may reason about the trustworthiness of the transmitting system. An architect with a background in Trusted Computing [7] would first require for the transmitting vehicle to attest for its behaviour [25]. Advanced experts may use the Trusted Platform Module (TPM) techniques of sealing, binding, key restrictions and TPM-CertifyKey to validate the trustworthiness and bind the transmitted data to this key [24]. A distributed software architect may first start to define the trust zones. This would imply that some computational means of composing slippery wheels with temperature and position happen in an untrusted domain. Results may be the timestamped signing of the sensor data and a composition of these data at the receiving vehicle.

This shall only illustrate a few different approaches that might be taken in a security engineering process for new SoS. Very different types of security requirements are the outcome. Some of these leave attack vectors open, such as the manipulation of the sending or receiving vehicle's internal communication and computation.

Another conclusion that can be derived from these examples is related to premature assumptions about the implementation. Whilst in one case the vehicle is seen as a single computational unit that can be trusted, in another case it has to attest for its behaviour when sending out warnings. The trust zone based analysis of the same use cases however requires for a direct communication link and cryptography between the sensors and the receiving vehicle and the composition of data is moved to the receiver side. A direct result of falsely defined system boundaries typically are security requirements that are formulated against internal subsystems rather than the system at stake itself, To overcome these problems several methods for security requirements elicitation have been proposed.

A comprehensive concept for an overall security requirements engineering process is described in detail in [16]. The authors propose a 9 step approach called SQUARE (Security Quality Engineering Methodology). The elicitation of the security requirements is one important step in the SQUARE process. In [15] several concrete methods to carry out this step are compared. These methods are based on misuse cases (MC), soft systems methodology (SSM), quality function deployment (QFD), controlled requirements expression (CORE), issue-based information systems (IBIS), joint application development (JAD), feature-oriented domain analysis (FODA), critical discourse analysis (CDA) as well as accelerated requirements method (ARM). A comparative rating based on 9 different criteria is also given but none of these criteria measures the completeness of the security requirements elicited by the different methods.

A similar approach based on the integration of Common Criteria (ISO/IEC 15408) called SREP (Security Requirements Engineering Process) is described in [17]. However the concrete techniques that carry out the security requirements elicitation process are given only very broadly. A threat driven method is proposed but is not described in detail.

In [13] anti-goals derived from negated security goals are used to systematically construct threat trees by refinement of these anti-goals. Security requirements are then obtained as countermeasures. This method aims to produce more complete requirements than other methods based on misuse cases. The refinement steps in this method can be performed informally or formally.

In [4] different kinds of security requirements are identified and informal guidelines are listed that have proven useful when eliciting concrete security requirements. The author emphasises that there has to be a clear distinction between security requirements and security mechanisms.

In [9] it is proposed to use Jackson's problem diagrams to determine security requirements which are given as constraints on functional requirements. Though this approach presents a methodology to derive security requirements from security goals, it does not explain the actual refinements process, which leaves open, the degree of coverage of requirements, depending only on expert knowledge.

In [10,11,12] Hatebur et al. describe a security engineering process based on security problem frames and concretised security problem frames. The two kinds of frames constitute patterns for analysing security problems and associated solution approaches. They are arranged in a pattern system with formal preconditions and postconditions for the frames which makes dependencies between them explicit. A method to use this pattern system to analyse a given security problem and find solution approaches is described. The focus of [10] is on anonymity, while [11] focusses on confidential data transmission, and [12] addresses accountability by logging and the steps of the process.

In [14] actor dependency analysis is used to identify attackers and potential threats in order to identify security requirements. The so called i^* approach facilitates the analysis of security requirements within the social context of relevant actors. In [6] a formal framework is presented for modelling and analysis of security and trust requirements at an organisational level. Both of these approaches target organisational relations among agents rather than functional dependence. Those approaches might be utilised complementary to the one presented in this paper, as the output of organisational relations analysis may be an input to our functional security analysis.

Though all of the approaches may lead to a sufficient level of security for the designed architecture, there is no obvious means by which they can be compared regarding the security requirements that they fulfil. The choice of the appropriate abstraction level and system boundaries constitutes a rather big challenge to SoS architecture design, especially with respect to SoS applications like the one presented here.

The method described in Sect. 4 in this paper is based on the work presented in [5], whereas the tool-assisted methodology that builds on this approach presented in Sect. 5 is a new contribution of this work. We are targeting here the identification of a consistent and complete set of authenticity requirements. For an analysis of privacy-related requirements with respect to vehicular communication systems please refer to [26].

3　Vehicular Communication Systems Scenario

The derivation of security requirements in general, especially the derivation of authenticity requirements represents an essential building block for system design. With an increase in the severity of safety-relevant systems' failures the demand increases for a systematic approach of requirements derivation with a maximum coverage. Also during the derivation of security requirements, no pre-assumptions should be made about possible implementations. We will further motivate this with respect to the requirements derivation process with an example from the field of vehicle-to-vehicle communications.

3.1　Example Use Cases

In order to illustrate our approach we use a scenario taken from the project EVITA (E-Safety Vehicle Intrusion Protected Applications) [23]. The scenario is based on an evaluation of security relevant use cases for vehicular communication systems in which vehicles and roadside units communicate in an ad hoc manner to exchange information such as safety warnings and traffic information. Optionally, local danger warning information can also be provided to in-vehicular safety concepts for further processing.

Our example system consists of vehicles $V_1, \ldots, V_n$. Each V_i has its driver D_i and is equipped with an Electronic Stability Protection (ESP) sensor ESP_i and a Global Positioning System (GPS) sensor GPS_i. Within each vehicle's on-board network, the scenario involves a communication unit (CU) CU_i for sending and receiving messages. Furthermore, a connection to a Human Machine Interface (HMI) HMI_i is required for displaying the warning message, e.g. via audio signals or on a display. Furthermore, the example system includes a roadside unit (RSU) that can send cooperative awareness messages cam. For simplicity reasons we assume that the same information is provided by all roadside units in the system, so we can abstract from the individual entity. Our vehicle-to-vehicle scenario is based on the following use cases:

Use case 1. A roadside unit broadcasts a cooperative awareness message.

Use case 2. A vehicle's ESP sensor recognises that the ground is very slippery when accelerating in combination with a low temperature. In order to warn successive vehicles about a possibly icy road, the vehicle uses its communication unit to send out information about this danger including the GPS position data indicating where the danger was detected.

Use case 3. A vehicle receives a cooperative awareness message, such as a warning about an icy road at a certain position, from a roadside unit or another vehicle. It compares the information to its own position and heading and signals the driver a warning if the dangerous area lies up front.

Use case 4. A vehicle receives a cooperative awareness message. It compares the information to its own position and heading and retransmits the warning, given that the position of this occurrence is not too far away.

For local danger warning applications, at least two entities are involved, namely the vehicle receiving a critical warning message and the entity sending such a message. The entity that sends out the message can be another vehicle, a roadside unit or traffic light, or an infrastructure based server. The scenario uses the actions described in table 1.

4   Functional Security Analysis

The approach described in the following can be decomposed into three basic steps. The first one is the derivation of the functional model from the use case descriptions in terms of an action oriented system. In a second step the system at stake is defined and possible instantiations of the first functional model are elaborated. In a third and final step, the actual requirements are derived in a systematic way, resulting in a consistent and complete set of security requirements.

Table 1. Actions for the example system

Action	Explanation
$send(\text{cam(pos)})$	A roadside unit broadcasts a cooperative awareness message cam concerning a danger at position pos.
$sense(ESP_i, \text{sW})$	The ESP sensor of vehicle V_i senses slippery wheels (sW).
$pos(GPS_i, \text{pos})$	The GPS sensor of vehicle V_i computes its position.
$send(CU_i, \text{cam(pos)})$	The communication unit CU_i of vehicle V_i sends a cooperative awareness message cam concerning the assumed danger based on the slippery wheels measurement for position pos.
$rec(CU_i, \text{cam(pos)})$	The communication unit CU_i of vehicle V_i receives a cooperative awareness message cam for position pos from another vehicle or a roadside unit.
$fwd(CU_i, \text{cam(pos)})$	The communication unit CU_i of vehicle V_i forwards a cooperative awareness message cam for position pos.
$show(HMI_i, \text{warn})$	The human machine interface HMI_i of Vehicle V_i shows its driver a warning warn with respect to the relative position.

4.1   Functional Model

Information flow between systems and system components is highly complex, especially given that a system can evolve via the replacement of its components. Consequently, an important aspect of security evaluation is the analysis of the potential information flows. We use the analysis of the potential information flows to derive the dependencies for the functional model.

For the description of the functional model from the use cases an action-oriented approach is chosen. The approach is based on the work from [18]. For reasons of simplicity and readability the formal description of the model is omitted here and a graphical representation is used to illustrate the behaviour of the evaluation target.

A functional model can be derived from a use case description by identifying the atomic actions in the use case description. These actions are set into relation by defining the functional flow among them. This action oriented approach considers possible sequences of actions (control flow) and information flow (input/output) between interdependent actions.

In the case of highly distributed systems and especially a distributed system of distributed systems, it is very common that use cases do not cover a complete functional cycle throughout the whole system under investigation. Rather only certain components of the system are described regarding their behaviour. This must be kept in mind when deriving the functional model. In order to clarify this distinction, functional models that describe only parts of the overall system behaviour will be called *functional component model*.

Figures 1(a) and 1(b) show functional component models for a roadside unit and a vehicle respectively. These models are derived from the example use cases given in Sect. 3.1. The functional flow arrows outside of the vehicle's boundaries

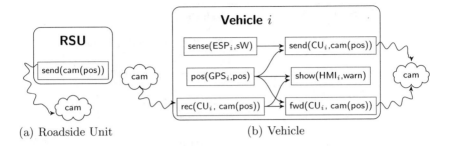

Fig. 1. Functional component models

refer to functional flows between different instances of the component, whilst internal flow arrows refer to flows within the same instance of the component. For the given example, the external flows represent data transmission of one system to another, whilst the internal flows represent communication within a single system.

4.2   System of Systems Instances

Based on the functional component model, one may now start to reason about the overall system of systems which consists of a number of instances of the functional components. The synthesis of the internal flow between the actions within the component instances and the external flow between systems (in this case vehicles and roadside units) builds the global system of systems behaviour. In order to model instances of the global system of systems, all structurally different combinations of component instances shall be considered. Isomorphic combinations can be neglected. Finally, all possible instances may be regrouped and the system's boundary actions (denoting the actions that are triggered by or influence the system environment) have to be identified. These will be the basis for the security requirements definition in the next step.

   In Fig. 2 an example for a possible SoS instance combining use cases 1 and 3 comprising a roadside unit and a vehicle is presented. In this SoS instance vehicle V_w receives cooperative awareness message from a RSU.

4.3   Functional Security Requirements Identification

The set of possible instantiations of the functional component model is used in a next step to derive security requirements. First, the boundary actions of the system model instances are determined. Let the term *boundary action* refer to the actions that form the interaction of the internals of the system with the outside world. These are actions that are either triggered by occurrences outside of the system or actions that involve changes to the outside of the system.

   With the boundary actions being identified, one may now follow the functional graph backwards. Beginning with the boundary actions by which the system takes influence on the outside, we may propagate backwards along the functional

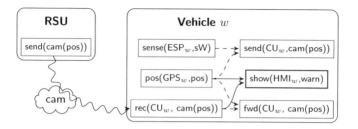

Fig. 2. Vehicle w receives warning from RSU

flow. These backwards references basically describe the functional dependencies of actions among each other. From the functional dependency graph we may now identify the end points - the boundary actions that trigger the system behaviour that depends on them. Between these and the corresponding starting points, the requirement exists that without such an action happening as input to the system, the corresponding output action must not happen as well. From this we formulate the security goal of the system at stake:

Whenever a certain output action happens, the input actions that presumably led to it must actually have happened.

Example 1 (Boundary Actions and Dependencies). In the SoS instance in Fig. 2 we are interested to identify the authenticity requirements for the boundary action $show(HMI_w, \text{warn})$. Following backwards along the functional flow we derive that the output action $show(HMI_w, \text{warn})$ is depending on the input actions $pos(GPS_w, \text{pos})$ of vehicle w and $send(\text{cam(pos)})$ of the RSU.

These dependencies shall now be enriched by additional parameters. In particular, it shall be identified which is the entity that must be assured of the respective authenticity requirements. With these additional parameters set, we may utilise the following definition of authenticity from the formal framework of Fraunhofer SIT [8] to specify the identified requirements.

Definition 1. $auth(a, b, P)$: *Whenever an action b happens, it must be authentic for an Agent P that in any course of events that seem possible to him, a certain action a has happened (for a formal definition see [8]).*

Example 2 (Derive Requirements from Dependencies). For the dependencies in Example 1 this leads to the following authenticity requirements with respect to the action $show(HMI_w, \text{warn})$:

- It must be authentic for the driver of vehicle w that the relative position of the danger he/she is warned about is based on correct position information of his/her vehicle. Formally: $auth(pos(GPS_w, \text{pos}), show(HMI_w, \text{warn}), D_w)$
- It must be authentic for the driver of vehicle w that the roadside unit issued the warning. Formally: $auth(send(\text{cam(pos)}), show(HMI_w, \text{warn}), D_w)$

It shall be noted that the requirements elicitation process in this case utilises positive formulations of how the system should behave, rather than preventing a certain malicious behaviour. Also it has to be stressed that this approach guarantees for the system / component architect to be free regarding the choice of concepts during the security engineering process.

This manual analysis may reveal that certain functional dependencies are presented only for performance reasons. This can be valuable input for the architects as well, and sometimes reveals premature decisions about mechanisms that were already done during the use case definition phase.

This approach cannot prevent the specification of circular dependencies among systems' actions but usually this is avoided for well-defined use cases. This actually originates from the fact that every action represents a progress in time. Accordingly an infinite loop among actions in the system would indicate that the system described will not terminate. The requirements derivation process will however highlight every functional dependency that is described within the use cases. Accordingly, when the use case description incorporates more than the sheer safety related functional description, additional requirements may arise. Therefore, the requirements have to be evaluated towards their meaning for the system's safety. Whilst one can be assured not to have missed any safety relevant requirement, this is a critical task because misjudging a requirement's relevance would induce security holes. Once an exhaustive list of security requirements is identified, a requirements categorisation and prioritisation process can evaluate them according to a maximum acceptable risk strategy.

4.4   Formalisation

Formally, the functional flow among actions can be interpreted as an ordering relation ζ_i on the set of actions Σ_i in a certain system instance i. To derive the requirements the reflexive transitive closure ζ_i^* is constructed. In the following we assume that the functional flow graph is sequential and free of loops, as every action can only depend on past actions. Accordingly, the relation is anti-symmetric. ζ_i^* is a partial order on Σ_i, with the maximal elements max_i corresponding to the outgoing boundary actions and the minimal elements min_i corresponding to the incoming boundary actions. After restricting ζ_i^* to these elements $\chi_i = \{(x, y) \in \Sigma_i \times \Sigma_i \mid (x, y) \in \zeta_i^* \wedge x \in min_i \wedge y \in max_i\}$ this new relation represents the authenticity requirements for the corresponding system instance: *For all $x, y \in \Sigma_i$ with $(x, y) \in \chi_i$: $auth(x, y, stakeholder(y))$* is a requirement. Accordingly the union of all these requirements for the different instances poses the set of requirements for the whole system. This set can be reduced by eliminating duplicate requirements or by use of first-order predicates for a parameterised notation of similar requirements.

Example 3 (Formal Derivation of Authenticity Requirements). For the given system model instances, we may now identify the authenticity requirements for the action $show(HMI_w, warn)$ using the actions and abbreviations defined in table 1. Graphically, this could be done by reversing the arrows and removing the dotted arrows and boxes.

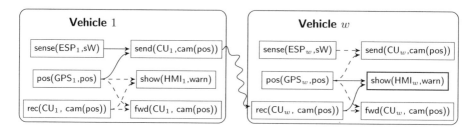

Fig. 3. Vehicle w receives a warning from vehicle 1

Figure 3 shows an example for a possible SoS instance combining use cases 2 and 3 comprising two vehicles. In this SoS instance vehicle V_w receives cooperative awareness message from vehicle V_1. Formally, for the SoS instance depicted in Fig. 3, we can analyse:

$$
\begin{aligned}
\zeta_1 =\{&(sense(ESP_1, \mathrm{sW}), send(CU_1, \mathrm{cam(pos)})), \\
&(pos(GPS_1, \mathrm{pos}), send(CU_1, \mathrm{cam(pos)})), \\
&(send(CU_1, \mathrm{cam(pos)}), rec(CU_w, \mathrm{cam(pos)})), \\
&(pos(GPS_w, \mathrm{pos}), show(HMI_w, \mathrm{warn})), \\
&(rec(CU_w, \mathrm{cam(pos)}), show(HMI_w, \mathrm{warn}))\} \\
\zeta_1^* =&\zeta_1 \cup \{(x, x) \mid x \in \Sigma\} \cup \{ \\
&(sense(ESP_1, \mathrm{sW}), rec(CU_w, \mathrm{cam(pos)})), \\
&(sense(ESP_1, \mathrm{sW}), show(HMI_w, \mathrm{warn})), \\
&(pos(GPS_1, \mathrm{pos}), rec(CU_w, \mathrm{cam(pos)})), \\
&(pos(GPS_1, \mathrm{pos}), show(HMI_w, \mathrm{warn})), \\
&(send(CU_1, \mathrm{cam(pos)}), show(HMI_w, \mathrm{warn}))\} \\
\chi_1 =\{&(sense(ESP_1, \mathrm{sW}), show(HMI_w, \mathrm{warn})), \\
&(pos(GPS_1, \mathrm{pos}), show(HMI_w, \mathrm{warn})), \\
&(pos(GPS_w, \mathrm{pos}), show(HMI_w, \mathrm{warn}))\}
\end{aligned}
$$

For further analysis we consider a possible SoS instance combining use cases 2, 3 and 4 comprising three vehicles as shown in Fig. 4. In this SoS instance vehicle V_2 forwards warnings from vehicle V_1 to vehicle V_w.

An analysis of the SoS instance with 3 vehicles as depicted in Fig. 4 will result in:

$$
\chi_2 = \chi_1 \cup \{(pos(GPS_2, \mathrm{pos}), show(HMI_w, \mathrm{warn}))\}
$$

In the given SoS model the forwarding of a message is restricted by a *position based forwarding policy* with respect to the distance from the danger that is being warned about and the time of issue of the danger sensing. We could therefore assume a maximal number of system instances involved general enough to cover

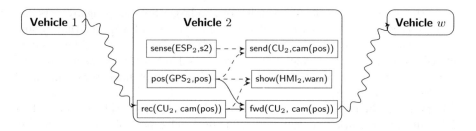

Fig. 4. Vehicle 2 forwards warnings (vehicles 1, 2 and w are instances from Fig. 1)

all these cases, e.g. by utilising a description in a parameterised way. An analysis for an SoS instance with i vehicles will result in:

$$\chi_i = \chi_{i-1} \cup \{(pos(GPS_i, \text{pos}), show(HMI_w, \text{warn}))\}$$

The first three elements in each χ_i will obviously always be the same in all instances of the example. The rest of the elements can be expressed in terms of first-order predicates. This leads to the following authenticity requirements for all possible system instances for the action $show(HMI_w, \text{warn})$:

$$auth(pos(GPS_w, \text{pos}), show(HMI_w, \text{warn}), D_w) \tag{1}$$

$$auth(pos(GPS_1, \text{pos}), show(HMI_w, \text{warn}), D_w) \tag{2}$$

$$auth(sense(ESP_1, \text{sW}), show(HMI_w, \text{warn}), D_w) \tag{3}$$

$$\forall x \in V_{forward} : auth(pos(GPS_x, \text{pos}), show(HMI_w, \text{warn}), D_w) \tag{4}$$

$V_{forward}$ denotes the set of vehicles per system instance, that forward the warning message.

As mentioned above, the resulting requirements have to be evaluated regarding their meaning for the functional safety of the system. For the first three requirements the argumentation is very straight forward regarding why they have to be fulfilled:

1. It must be authentic for the driver that the relative position of the danger he/she is warned about is based on correct position information of his/her vehicle.
2. It must be authentic for the driver that the position of the danger he/she is warned about is based on correct position information of the vehicle issuing the warning.
3. It must be authentic for the driver that the danger he/she is warned about is based on correct sensor data.

The last requirement (4) however must be further evaluated. Studying the use case, we see that this functional dependency originates from the position based forwarding policy. This policy is introduced for performance reasons, such that bandwidth is saved by not flooding the whole network. Braking this requirement would therefore result either in a smaller or in a larger broadcasting area. As bad as those cases may be, they cannot cause the warning of a driver that should not be warned. Therefore we do not consider requirement (4) to be a safety related authenticity requirement. It can be considered a requirement regarding availability by preventing the denial of a service or unintended consumption of bandwidth.

In practice, the method described here has been applied in the project EVITA [23] to derive authenticity requirements for the development of a new automotive on-board architecture utilising vehicle-to-vehicle and vehicle-to-infrastructure communication. A total of 29 authenticity requirements have been elicited by means of a system model comprising 38 component boundary actions with 16 system boundary actions comprising 9 maximal and 7 minimal elements.

5   Tool-Assisted Requirements Identification

The method for deriving authenticity requirements as described in the previous section relies on manual identification and processing only. In this section we will give an example on how to use the capabilities of existing tools, such as the SH verification tool [20] in order to facilitate the process especially for larger models.

As the previous section explained, the basis for the systematic identification of authenticity requirements for a given system is the relations between maxima and minima of the partial order of functional dependence. In this approach we first identified the direct relations of adjacent actions, then built the reflexive transitive closure and finally extracted those relations from this set that exist between maxima and minima of this partial order.

The tool-assisted approach will proceed in reverse order. First we will identify the maxima and minima of the partial order – without deriving the actual partial order – and then we will identify combinations of maxima and minima that are related by functional dependence. This approach will be illustrated with a simple example first, to provide the general idea and then with a more complex example, in order to demonstrate the application of abstraction techniques to cover the analysis of non-trivial systems.

5.1   Formal Modelling Technique

In order to analyse the system behaviour with tool support, an appropriate formal representation has to be chosen. In our approach, we choose an operational finite state model of the behaviour of the given vehicular communication scenario that is based on *Asynchronous Product Automata (APA)*, a flexible operational specification concept for cooperating systems [20]. An APA consists of a family of so called *elementary automata* communicating by common components of their state (shared memory). We now introduce the formal modelling techniques used, and illustrate the usage by our collaboration example.

Definition 2 (Asynchronous Product Automaton (APA))
An Asynchronous Product Automaton *consists of*

- *a family of* state sets $Z_s, s \in \mathbb{S}$,
- *a family of* elementary automata $(\Phi_t, \Delta_t), t \in \mathbb{T}$ *and*
- *a neighbourhood relation* $N : \mathbb{T} \to \mathfrak{P}(\mathbb{S})$.

$\mathbb{S}$ *and* $\mathbb{T}$ *are index sets with the names of state components and of elementary automata and* $\mathfrak{P}(\mathbb{S})$ *is the power set of* $\mathbb{S}$.
For each elementary automaton (Φ_t, Δ_t) *with* Alphabet Φ_t, *its* state transition relation *is*

$$\Delta_t \subseteq \bigtimes_{s \in N(t)} (Z_s) \times \Phi_t \times \bigtimes_{s \in N(t)} (Z_s).$$

For each element of Φ_t *the state transition relation* Δ_t *defines state transitions that change only the state components in* $N(t)$. *An APA's (global) states are elements of* $\bigtimes_{s \in \mathbb{S}} (Z_s)$. *To avoid pathological cases it is generally assumed that* $N(t) \neq \emptyset$ *for all* $t \in \mathbb{T}$.
Each APA has one initial state $q_0 = (q_{0s})_{s \in \mathbb{S}} \in \bigtimes_{s \in \mathbb{S}} (Z_s)$.
In total, an APA $\mathbb{A}$ *is defined by*

$$\mathbb{A} = ((Z_s)_{s \in \mathbb{S}}, (\Phi_t, \Delta_t)_{t \in \mathbb{T}}, N, q_0).$$

An elementary automaton (Φ_t, Δ_t) *is* activated *in a state* $p = (p_s)_{s \in \mathbb{S}} \in \bigtimes_{s \in \mathbb{S}} (Z_s)$ *as to an* interpretation $i \in \Phi_t$, *if there are* $(q_s)_{s \in N(t)} \in \bigtimes_{s \in N(t)} (Z_s)$ *with* $((p_s)_{s \in N(t)}, i, (q_s)_{s \in N(t)}) \in \Delta_t$.
An activated elementary automaton (Φ_t, Δ_t) *can execute a state transition and produce a successor state*

$$q = (q_r)_{r \in \mathbb{S}} \in \bigtimes_{s \in \mathbb{S}} (Z_s), \ if$$

$$q_r = p_r \ for \ r \in \mathbb{S} \setminus N(t) \ and \ ((p_s)_{s \in N(t)}, i, (q_s)_{s \in N(t)}) \in \Delta_t.$$

The corresponding state transition is $(p, (t, i), q)$.

For the following analysis by model checking and abstraction we use a reduced version of the functional component model of a vehicle that corresponds to the functional model illustrated in Fig. 1(b) but does not contain the *forward* action.

Example 4 (Finite State Model of the Collaboration Components). The vehicle component model described in Sect. 4.1 is specified for the proposed analysis method using the following *APA state components* for each of the vehicles:

$$\mathbb{S}_i = \{esp_i, gps_i, hmi_i, bus_i, net\}, \text{ with}$$
$$Z_{esp_i} = \mathfrak{P}(\{sW\}),$$
$$Z_{gps_i} = \mathfrak{P}(\{pos1, pos2, pos3, pos4\}),$$
$$Z_{hmi_i} = \mathfrak{P}(\{warn\}),$$
$$Z_{bus_i} = \mathfrak{P}(Z_{esp} \cup Z_{gps} \cup Z_{hmi})) \text{ and}$$
$$Z_{net} = \mathfrak{P}(\{cam\} \times \{V_1, V_2, V_3, V_4\} \times Z_{gps}).$$

The *inputs* to the vehicle model are represented by the state components esp_i and gps_i. esp_i represents input measurements taken by the ESP sensor. A pending data set here will trigger the *sense* action for slippery wheels. gps_i represents the derivation of GPS position information. Pending data here will trigger the *pos* action for retrieving the current position of the vehicle.

The *outputs* of the vehicle model are represented by the state component hmi_i that represents the HMI interface's display, showing (warning) information to the driver. The *show* action will push information to this medium.

Internally the vehicle component has an additional state component bus_i representing its internal communication bus. It is filled with information from the *rec*, *sense* and *pos* action and read by the *send* and *forward* action.

Finally, *net* is a shared state component between all the vehicles that represents the wireless communication medium. A pending message here will trigger the *rec* action of the component. The actions *send* and *forward* will push a message into this medium.

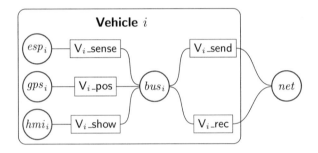

Fig. 5. APA model of a vehicle

The *elementary automata* $\mathbb{T}_i = \{V_{i\text{-}pos}, V_{i\text{-}sense}, V_{i\text{-}rec}, V_{i\text{-}send}, V_{i\text{-}show}\}$ represent the possible actions that the systems can take. These specifications are represented in the data structures and initial configuration of the state components in the APA model. Elementary automata and state components of the APA model of a vehicle are depicted in Fig. 5. The lines in Fig. 5 between state components and elementary automata represent the neighbourhood relation.

The state transition relation for the APA model of a vehicle is given by:

$$\Delta_{V_{i\text{-}sense}} = \{((esp_i, bus_i), (esp), (esp_i \setminus \{esp\}, bus_i \cup \{esp\}))$$
$$\in (Z_{esp_i} \times Z_{bus_i}) \times ESP \times (Z_{esp_i} \times Z_{bus_i}) \mid esp \in esp_i\}$$
$$\Delta_{V_{i\text{-}pos}} = \{((gps_i, bus_i), (gps), (gps_i \setminus \{gps\}, bus_i \cup \{gps\})$$
$$\in (Z_{gps_i} \times Z_{bus_i}) \times GPS \times (Z_{gps_i} \times Z_{bus_i}) \mid gps \in gps_i\}$$

$$\Delta_{V_i\_send} = \{((bus_i, net), (esp, gps, msg), (bus_i \setminus \{esp, gps\}, net \cup \{msg\}))$$
$$\in (Z_{bus_i} \times Z_{net}) \times (ESP \times GPS \times NET) \times (Z_{bus_i} \times Z_{net}) \mid$$
$$esp \in bus_i \wedge gps \in bus_i \wedge msg = (\text{cam}, gps)\}$$

$$\Delta_{V_i\_rec} = \{((net, bus_i), (msg, gps, \text{warn}), (net \setminus \{msg\}, bus_i \setminus \{gps\} \cup \{\text{warn}\}))$$
$$\in (Z_{net} \times Z_{bus}) \times (NET \times GPS \times HMI) \times (Z_{net} \times Z_{bus_i}) \mid$$
$$msg \in net \wedge gps \in bus_i \wedge distance(msg, gps) < \text{range}\}$$

$$\Delta_{V_i\_show} = \{((bus_i, hmi_i), (\text{warn}), (bus_i \setminus \{\text{warn}\}, hmi \cup \{\text{warn}\}))$$
$$\in (Z_{bus_i} \times Z_{hmi_i}) \times HMI \times (Z_{bus_i} \times Z_{hmi_i}) \mid \text{warn} \in bus_i\}$$

The model is parameterised by i except for the shared state component net.

5.2   Formal Representation of System of Systems Instances

The SoS instance that we investigate first includes two vehicle components that are assumed to be within the wireless transmission range similar to the example given in Fig. 3. In this SoS instance vehicle V_2 receives cooperative awareness message from vehicle V_1. Therefore the net components are mapped together, such that outputs of each one of the vehicles are input for the other vehicle. The rest of the inputs (Sensors and GPSs) as well as outputs (displays) are not internal parts of the system but filled and read by the systems environment. It should be noted that timing behaviour is not included in the model, because we solely want to retrieve functional dependencies. As we want to instantiate V_1 to perform use Case 2 and V_2 to perform use Case 3, we set

- V_1's sensor input to a measurement of slippery wheels sW,
- V_1's GPS input to some position pos1 that is within warning range of V_2 and
- V_2's GPS input to some position pos2 that is within warning range of V_1.

Example 5 (Finite State Model of an SoS Instance with 2 Vehicles)
The state components for this instance are

$$\mathbb{S} = \{esp_1, pos_1, bus_1, hmi_1, esp_2, pos_2, bus_2, hmi_2, net\}$$

and the set of elementary automata is

$$\mathbb{T} = \{V_1\_sense, V_1\_pos, V_1\_send, V_1\_rec, V_1\_show,$$
$$V_2\_sense, V_2\_pos, V_2\_send, V_2\_rec, V_2\_show\}.$$

The neighbourhood relation $N(t)$ can be read directly from the graphical illustration in Fig. 6. The initial state for our simulation is defined as:

$$q_0 = (q_{0\_esp_1}, q_{0\_gps_1}, q_{0\_bus_1}, q_{0\_hmi_1}, q_{0\_esp_2}, q_{0\_gps_2}, q_{0\_bus_2}, q_{0\_hmi_2}, q_{0\_net})$$
$$= (\{\text{sW}\}, \{\text{pos1}\}, \emptyset, \emptyset, \emptyset, \{\text{pos2}\}, \emptyset, \emptyset, \emptyset).$$

For example $(q_0, (V_1\_sense, \text{sW}), (\emptyset, \{\text{pos1}\}, \{\text{sW}\}, \emptyset, \emptyset, \{\text{pos2}\}, \emptyset, \emptyset, \emptyset))$ is a state transition of this SoS instance.

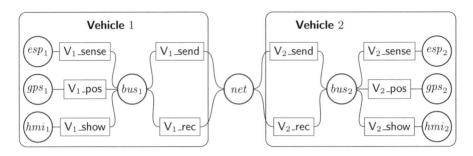

Fig. 6. APA model of a SoS instance with 2 vehicles

5.3   Computation of System of Systems Behaviour

Formally, the behaviour of our operational APA model of the vehicular communication system is described by a reachability graph. In the literature this is sometimes also referred to as labelled transition system (LTS).

Definition 3 (Reachability graph)
The behaviour of an APA is represented by all possible coherent sequences of state transitions starting with initial state q_0. The sequence $(q_0, (t_1, i_1), q_1)$ $(q_1, (t_2, i_2), q_2) \ldots (q_{n-1}, (t_n, i_n), q_n)$ with $i_k \in \Phi_{t_k}$ represents one possible sequence of actions of an APA.

State transitions $(p, (t, i), q)$ may be interpreted as labelled edges of a directed graph whose nodes are the states of an APA: $(p, (t, i), q)$ is the edge leading from p to q and labelled by (t, i). The subgraph reachable from the node q_0 is called the reachability graph of an APA.

We used the *Simple Homomorphism (SH) verification tool* [20] to analyse the functional component model for different concrete instantiations of the model. The tool has been developed at the *Fraunhofer-Institute for Secure Information Technology*. The applied specification method based on Asynchronous Product Automata is supported by this tool. The tool manages the components of the model, allows to select alternative parts of the specification and automatically *glues* together the selected components to generate a combined model of the APA specification. It provides components for the complete cycle from formal specification to exhaustive validation as well as visualisation and inspection of computed reachability graphs and minimal automata. The tool provides an editor to define homomorphisms on action languages, it computes corresponding minimal automata [3] for the homomorphic images and checks simplicity of the homomorphisms. If it is required to inspect some or all paths of the graph to check for the violation of a security property, as it is usually the case for liveness properties, then the tool's temporal logic component can be used. Temporal logic formulae can also be checked on the abstract behaviour (under a simple homomorphism). The method for checking approximate satisfaction of properties fits exactly to the built-in simple homomorphism check [20].

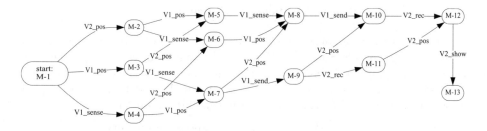

Fig. 7. Reachability graph of SoS instance with two vehicles in the SH verification tool

Computation of SoS Instance's Behaviour. Starting with the analysis, we define a representation of the component behaviour in preamble language of the SH verification tool according to the use cases. Then for a first simple example, we instantiated it twice – with a warning vehicle V_1 and a vehicle that receives the warning V_2, similar to Fig. 6. After an initial state is selected, the reachability graph is automatically computed by the SH verification tool. Fig. 7 shows the reachability graph resulting from the analysis of the model instance in Fig. 6. Please note that the tool prints the state q_0 as M-1.

5.4 Evaluating the Functional Dependence Relation

Starting from the model of the system components and their instantiations the reachability analysis provides a graph with serialised traces of actions in the system. In order to identify the *minima* of such a system, we look at the initial state *M-1* of the reachability graph. Every action that leaves the initial state on any of the traces is obviously a minimum, because it does not functionally depend on any other action to have occurred before. In order to identify the *maxima* we investigate those actions leading to the dead state from any trace. These actions do not trigger any further action after they have been performed.

Example 6 (The SH verification tool's result for Example 5)
The minima of this analysis: The corresponding maxima:

M–1
V1_sense M–4   M–12 V2_show
V1_pos M–3   M–13+
V2_pos M–2   +++ dead +++

Since we now have identified the maxima and minima of the partial order of functionally dependent actions, we must evaluate which of these maxima have a functional dependence relation. For this simple example, it can easily be seen from the reachability graph, that the maximum only occurs after all the minima have occurred in each of the traces, i.e. the maximum depends on all the identified minima. Accordingly, the simple example has the following set of requirements: $auth(V_1\text{-}sense, V_2\text{-}show, D_2)$, $auth(V_1\text{-}pos, V_2\text{-}show, D_2)$, $auth(V_2\text{-}pos, V_2\text{-}show, D_2)$.

5.5   Abstraction Based Verification Concept

In order to further demonstrate our approach for a more complex scenario, a second example of a SoS instance that includes four vehicles – two pairs of two vehicles, each pair within communication range but out of range from the other pair, performing the same scenario each (V_1 warns V_2 and V_3 warns V_4) – can be seen in Fig. 8 with the corresponding reachability graph in Fig. 9.

The minima of this analysis:

M–1
V1_sense M–7
V3_sense M–6
V1_pos M–5
V2_pos M–4
V3_pos M–3
V4_pos M–2

The corresponding maxima:

M–168 V2_show
M–167 V4_show
M–169+
+++ dead +++

Obviously, the reachability graph in Fig. 9 that is generated from the complex scenario cannot be evaluated directly. However the technique of abstraction can help us to identify if a given maximum functionally depends on a given minimum.

Behaviour abstraction of an APA can be formalised by language homomorphisms, more precisely by alphabetic language homomorphisms $h : \Sigma^* \to \Sigma'^*$. By these homomorphisms certain transitions are ignored and others are renamed,

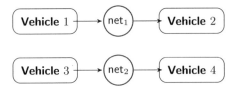

Fig. 8. Model for SoS instance with four vehicles

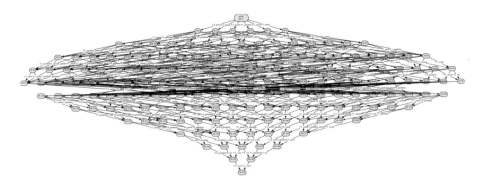

Fig. 9. Reachability graph of SoS instance with four vehicles in the SH verification tool

which may have the effect, that different transitions are identified with one another. A mapping $h : \Sigma^* \to \Sigma'^*$ is called a language homomorphism if $h(\varepsilon) = \varepsilon$ and $h(yz) = h(y)h(z)$ for each $y, z \in \Sigma^*$. It is called alphabetic, if $h(\Sigma) \subset \Sigma' \cup \{\varepsilon\}$.

In order to analyse dependencies for each pair of maximum and minimum in the graph in Fig. 9, we can now define alphabetic language homomorphisms that will map every action except the given pairs of maximum and minimum to ε. The computed abstract representations then provide a visualisation focussing on the two actions, helping us to see directly, if the given maximum can occur independent of the given minimum or if it depends on the minimum's prior occurrence.

Example 7. The minimal automaton computed from the reachability graph under the homomorphism that preserves V_1_sense and V_2_show is depicted in Fig. 10. This graph indicates a functional dependence relation between the given maximum and minimum.

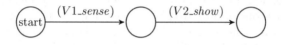

Fig. 10. Minimal automaton with maximum and minimum

The homomorphism preserving V_1_sense and V_4_show will result in the graph depicted in Fig. 11 that indicates the given maximum and minimum not to have a functional dependence relation.

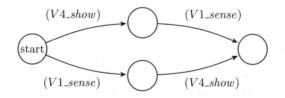

Fig. 11. Minimal automaton with independent maximum and minimum

Following this approach, testing each of the maxima with each of the minima for functional dependence, the complex scenario has the following set of requirements (with the stakeholder of V_4 to be driver D_4 of course):

$auth(V_1\_sense, V_2\_show, D_2)$, $auth(V_1\_pos, V_2\_show, D_2)$,
$auth(V_2\_pos, V_2\_show, D_2)$, $auth(V_3\_sense, V_4\_show, D_4)$,
$auth(V_3\_pos, V_4\_show, D_4)$, $auth(V_4\_pos, V_4\_show, D_4)$.

6   Conclusion

The presented approach for deriving safety-critical authenticity requirements in SoS solves several issues compared to existing approaches. It incorporates a clear scheme that will ensure a consistent and complete set of security requirements. Also it is based directly on the functional analysis, ensuring the safety of the system at stake. The systematic approach that incorporates formal semantics leads directly to the formal validation of security, as it is required by certain evaluation assurance levels of Common Criteria (ISO/IEC 15408). Furthermore the difficulties of designing SoS are specifically targeted.

Starting from this set of very high-level requirements, the security engineering process may proceed. This will include decisions regarding the mechanisms to be included. Accordingly the requirements have to be refined to more concrete requirements in this process. The design and refinement process may reveal further requirements regarding the internals of the system that have to be addressed as well.

Future work may include the derivation of confidentiality requirements in a similar way as was presented here. Though this will require for different security goals, as confidentiality is not related to safety in a similar way, but rather to privacy. Non-Repudiation may also be a target that should be approached in cooperation with lawyers in order to find the relevant security goals. Furthermore, the refinement throughout the design process should be evaluated regarding possibility of formalising it in schemes with respect to the security requirements refinement process.

For the tool-assisted method in Sect. 5, traditional model checking techniques allow a verification of SoS behaviour only for systems with very few components. We are developing an abstraction based approach to extend our current tool supported verification techniques to such families of systems that are usually parameterised by a number of replicated identical components. In [19] we demonstrated our technique by an exemplary verification of security and liveness properties of a simple parameterised collaboration scenario. In [21] we defined uniform parameterisations of phase based cooperations in terms of formal language theory. For such systems of cooperations a kind of self-similarity is formalised. Based on deterministic computations in shuffle automata a sufficient condition for self-similarity is given. Under certain regularity restrictions this condition can be verified by a semi-algorithm. For verification purposes, so called uniformly parameterised safety properties are defined. Such properties can be used to express privacy policies as well as security and dependability requirements. It is shown, how the parameterised problem of verifying such a property is reduced by self-similarity to a finite state problem.

Acknowledgments. Andreas Fuchs developed the work presented here in the context of the project EVITA (ID 224275) being co-funded by the European Commission within the Seventh Framework Programme. Roland Rieke developed the work presented here in the context of the projects Alliance Digital Product Flow (ADiWa) (ID 01IA08006F) and VOGUE (ID 01IS09032A) which are both funded by the German Federal Ministry of Education and Research.

References

1. Avizienis, A., Laprie, J.C., Randell, B., Landwehr, C.E.: Basic concepts and taxonomy of dependable and secure computing. IEEE Trans. Dependable Sec. Comput. 1(1), 11–33 (2004)
2. Bodeau, D.J.: System-of-Systems Security Engineering. In: Proc. of the 10th Annual Computer Security Applications Conference, Orlando, Florida, pp. 228–235. IEEE Computer Society, Los Alamitos (1994)
3. Eilenberg, S.: Automata, Languages and Machines, vol. A. Academic Press, New York (1974)
4. Firesmith, D.: Engineering security requirements. Journal of Object Technology 2(1), 53–68 (2003)
5. Fuchs, A., Rieke, R.: Identification of authenticity requirements in systems of systems by functional security analysis. In: Proceedings of the 2009 IEEE/IFIP Conference on Dependable Systems and Networks Workshop on Architecting Dependable Systems (WADS 2009), Supplementary Volume (2009),
   http://sit.sit.fraunhofer.de/smv/publications/
6. Giorgini, P., Massacci, F., Mylopoulos, J., Zannone, N.: Requirements engineering meets trust management: Model, methodology, and reasoning. In: Jensen, C., Poslad, S., Dimitrakos, T. (eds.) iTrust 2004. LNCS, vol. 2995, pp. 176–190. Springer, Heidelberg (2004)
7. Group, T.C.: TCG TPM Specification 1.2 revision 103 (2006),
   http://www.trustedcomputing.org
8. Gürgens, S., Ochsenschläger, P., Rudolph, C.: Authenticity and provability - a formal framework. In: Davida, G.I., Frankel, Y., Rees, O. (eds.) InfraSec 2002. LNCS, vol. 2437, pp. 227–245. Springer, Heidelberg (2002)
9. Haley, C.B., Laney, R.C., Moffett, J.D., Nuseibeh, B.: Security requirements engineering: A framework for representation and analysis. IEEE Trans. Software Eng. 34(1), 133–153 (2008)
10. Hatebur, D., Heisel, M., Schmidt, H.: A security engineering process based on patterns. In: Proceedings of the International Workshop on Secure Systems Methodologies using Patterns (SPatterns), DEXA 2007, pp. 734–738. IEEE Computer Society, Los Alamitos (2007), http://www.ieee.org/
11. Hatebur, D., Heisel, M., Schmidt, H.: A pattern system for security requirements engineering. In: Proceedings of the International Conference on Availability, Reliability and Security (AReS), pp. 356–365. IEEE, Los Alamitos (2007),
   http://www.ieee.org/
12. Hatebur, D., Heisel, M., Schmidt, H.: Analysis and component-based realization of security requirements. In: Proceedings of the International Conference on Availability, Reliability and Security (AReS), pp. 195–203. IEEE Computer Society Press, Los Alamitos (2008), http://www.ieee.org/
13. van Lamsweerde, A.: Elaborating security requirements by construction of intentional anti-models. In: Proceedings of the 26th International Conference on Software Engineering, ICSE 2004, pp. 148–157. IEEE Computer Society, Los Alamitos (2004)
14. Liu, L., Yu, E., Mylopoulos, J.: Analyzing security requirements as relationships among strategic actors. In: 2nd Symposium on Requirements Engineering for Information Security, SREIS 2002 (2002)
15. Mead, N.R.: How To Compare the Security Quality Requirements Engineering (SQUARE) Method with Other Methods. Tech. Rep. CMU/SEI-2007-TN-021, Software Engineering Institute, Carnegie Mellon University, Pittsburgh, PA (2007)

16. Mead, N.R., Hough, E.D.: Security requirements engineering for software systems: Case studies in support of software engineering education. In: Proceedings of the 19th Conference on Software Engineering Education & Training, CSEET 2006, pp. 149–158. IEEE Computer Society, Washington (2006)

17. Mellado, D., Fernández-Medina, E., Piattini, M.: A common criteria based security requirements engineering process for the development of secure information systems. Comput. Stand. Interfaces 29(2), 244–253 (2007)

18. Ochsenschläger, P., Repp, J., Rieke, R.: Abstraction and composition – a verification method for co-operating systems. Journal of Experimental and Theoretical Artificial Intelligence 12, 447–459 (2000),
http://sit.sit.fraunhofer.de/smv/publications/; copyright: ©2000, American Association for Artificial Intelligence, All rights reserved,
http://www.aaai.org

19. Ochsenschläger, P., Rieke, R.: Abstraction based verification of a parameterised policy controlled system. In: International Conference "Mathematical Methods, Models and Architectures for Computer Networks Security" (MMM-ACNS-7). CCIS, vol. 1, Springer, Heidelberg (2007),
http://sit.sit.fraunhofer.de/smv/publications/

20. Ochsenschläger, P., Repp, J., Rieke, R., Nitsche, U.: The SH-Verification Tool Abstraction-Based Verification of Co-operating Systems. Formal Aspects of Computing, The International Journal of Formal Method 11, 1–24 (1999)

21. Ochsenschläger, P., Rieke, R.: Uniform parameterisation of phase based cooperations. Tech. Rep. SIT-TR-2010/1, Fraunhofer SIT (2010),
http://sit.sit.fraunhofer.de/smv/publications/

22. Papadimitratos, P., Buttyan, L., Hubaux, J.P., Kargl, F., Kung, A., Raya, M.: Architecture for Secure and Private Vehicular Communications. In: IEEE International Conference on ITS Telecommunications (ITST), pp. 1–6. Sophia Antipolis, France (June 2007)

23. Ruddle, A., Ward, D., Weyl, B., Idrees, S., Roudier, Y., Friedewald, M., Leimbach, T., Fuchs, A., Grgens, S., Henniger, O., Rieke, R., Ritscher, M., Broberg, H., Apvrille, L., Pacalet, R., Pedroza, G.: Security requirements for automotive on-board networks based on dark-side scenarios. EVITA Deliverable D2.3, EVITA project (2009), http://evita-project.org/deliverables.html

24. Sadeghi, A.R., Stüble, C.: Property-based attestation for computing platforms: caring about properties, not mechanisms. In: Proceedings of the 2004 Workshop on New Security Paradigms, NSPW 2004, pp. 67–77. ACM, New York (2004)

25. Sailer, R., Zhang, X., Jaeger, T., van Doorn, L.: Design and implementation of a TCG-based integrity measurement architecture. In: Proceedings of the 13th USENIX Security Symposium. USENIX Association (2004)

26. Schaub, F., Ma, Z., Kargl, F.: Privacy requirements in vehicular communication systems. In: IEEE International Conference on Privacy, Security, Risk, and Trust (PASSAT 2009), Symposium on Secure Computing (SecureCom 2009), Vancouver, Canada (August 2009),
http://doi.ieeecomputersociety.org/10.1109/CSE.2009.135

27. Shirey, R.: Internet Security Glossary, Version 2. RFC 4949 (Informational) (August 2007), http://www.ietf.org/rfc/rfc4949.txt

Implementing Reliability: The Interaction of Requirements, Tactics and Architecture Patterns

Neil B. Harrison[1,2] and Paris Avgeriou[1]

[1] Department of Mathematics and Computing Science, University of Groningen,
Groningen, The Netherlands
[2] Department of Computer Science, Utah Valley University, Orem, Utah, USA
harrisne@uvsc.edu, paris@cs.rug.nl

Abstract. An important way that the reliability of a software system is enhanced is through the implementation of specific run-time measures called runtime tactics. Because reliability is a system-wide property, tactic implementations affect the software structure and behavior at the system, or architectural level. For a given architecture, different tactics may be a better or worse fit for the architecture, depending on the requirements and how the architecture patterns used must change to accommodate the tactic: different tactics may be a better or worse fit for the architecture. We found three important factors that influence the implementation of reliability tactics. One is the nature of the tactic, which indicates whether the tactic influences all components of the architecture or just a subset of them. The second is the interaction between architecture patterns and tactics: specific tactics and patterns are inherently compatible or incompatible. The third is the reliability requirements which influence which tactics to use and where they should be implemented. Together, these factors affect how, where, and the difficulty of implementing reliability tactics. This information can be used by architects and developers to help make decisions about which patterns and tactics to use, and can also assist these users in learning what modifications and additions to the patterns are needed.

1 Introduction

Software reliability has been defined in ISO 9126 as "The capability of the software product to maintain a specified level of performance when used under specified conditions." [1]. This standard states three key components of reliability: fault tolerance, recoverability, and maturity, including availability. Fault tolerance is, "The capability of the software product to maintain a specified level of performance in cases of software faults or of infringement of its specified interface." Recoverability is, "The capability of the software product to re-establish a specified level of performance and recover the data directly affected in the case of a failure." Maturity is "The capability of the software product to avoid failure as a result of faults in the software." Availability is "The capability of the software product to be in a state to perform a required function at a given point in time, under stated conditions of use" [1]. Software that is highly reliable must exhibit all these characteristics.

A. Casimiro et al. (Eds.): Architecting Dependable Systems VII, LNCS 6420, pp. 97–122, 2010.

Designing and implementing highly reliable software is very challenging. Besides the fact that the software to make a system reliable is very exacting, it can affect much of the system, and require a significant amount of software: over half of the millions of lines of code written for the 5ESS® Switching System were devoted to error handling. Fortunately, software designers have come up with numerous measures to improve software reliability, based on extensive experience. These measures are implemented in the software, and are designed to help make the software tolerant to faults. These faults include, but are not limited to hardware failures, errors in data, or bugs in the code itself. Many of these measures are well understood and have been documented. Utas [3] describes many such measures, as does Hanmer [4]; both are based on extensive experience in designing and developing carrier-grade telecommunication systems. Hanmer and Utas refer to these as reliability patterns. Some similar measures have been described by Bass et al [2] and called "tactics." For the sake of clarity and simplicity, we call all these measures tactics. The tactics identified by Bass et al [2] address the aforementioned components of reliability as follows: how to detect faults (addressing fault tolerance and maturity), how to prepare for recovering from faults (addressing availability and recoverability), how to recover after a fault (addressing recoverability), and how to prevent faults from causing failures (addressing fault tolerance and maturity).

However, even with the knowledge of the reliability tactics, one must still design and implement them in the system being developed. The difficulty of doing so depends in part on the nature of the tactic to be implemented. The implementation of some tactics requires some code to be written in nearly every component of the system architecture, while other tactics may be implemented with only limited impact. It depends on the tactic.

A given tactic also has different interactions with different architectural structures. Several architectural structures are commonly used, and are called architecture patterns [5] or architectural styles [6, 7]. The compatibility between several common architecture patterns and several common reliability tactics has been investigated [8]. The information about their compatibility is highly useful, because it may help us avoid tactics (or patterns) that are incompatible with the patterns (or tactics) being used. Of course, the harder it is to implement a tactic, the more error-prone the implementation is likely to be. The compatibility information is so far limited to one-to-one relationships: the compatibility of a single tactic with a single architecture pattern. But nearly all commercial systems are complex: they contain multiple architecture patterns (see [9]), and use multiple reliability tactics (see [10]).

But this is not all: every system is different, and has different constraints. Constraints, such as functional, non-functional, and business requirements, earlier design decisions and physical limitations, also affect the structure and behavior of the system. In this paper, we are particularly interested in requirements related to reliability: they are closely tied to the reliability tactics and the architecture patterns. This leads to the key question for this work:

How do the nature of tactics, software architecture patterns, and requirements interact with each other to influence the achievement of reliability in a software architecture?

We have tried to answer this question through a typical research cycle of grounded theory consisting of the following: we first looked at the tactics themselves, we then investigated the interaction between tactics and the pattern structures and finally we looked into an actual system design which included reliability requirements. We found three general ways that the nature of tactics influences the architecture. We found regular ways that multiple architecture patterns interact with tactics. And we found that requirements affect the tactics in two general ways. To fully understand the tactic impact, selection and implementation, one must consider all these factors.

The main contribution of this work is that it provides information into how these factors influence the implementation of tactics, which is indicative of the effort needed as well as difficulty in implementation and future system maintenance. This information can be used to make architectural tradeoff decisions, as well as in development planning. This knowledge is important when one designs even moderately complex software architectures (two or more patterns) that must be reliable.

In the following sections, we describe how tactics are implemented in complex systems. In section 2, we give background and describe the challenge of implementing tactics in complex systems. Section 3 describes the three factors that influence how and where tactics are implemented. Throughout sections 2 and 3, we use a running example of an airline booking system. In section 4, we describe how the information can be used in a practical setting, and how it fits with typical software architecture processes. We provide a case study and other validation in section 5. Section 6 describes related work, and section 7 describes future work.

2   Background: Architecture Tactics and Patterns

Designing the architecture of a software system consists of designing the structure and behavior of the system. This comprises making decisions about the software elements, the externally visible properties of those elements, and the relationships among them (from [2]). One of the key challenges of software architecture is to make decisions that satisfy not only the functional requirements of the system, but also the nonfunctional requirements, or quality attributes. One of the most important quality attributes is often reliability. Architectural decisions may support each other, but often conflict each other; thus tradeoffs are a common aspect of architecting. Two of the most important types of decisions are those concerning how to meet quality attributes (architecture tactics), and decisions about the overall structure and behavior (architecture patterns). These are discussed in turn below.

Let us consider a system to book airline tickets, which will be used as a running example. The system has multiple simultaneous users, distributed geographically. Two of the most important requirements related to reliability are as follows:

1.   Availability: the system must always be available for use; the consequences are potentially significant loss of revenue. After all, if a customer can't access the reservation system, he or she will turn to a competitor.
2.   Data integrity: data must be correctly recorded, and must be accurately recovered as necessary. Transactions must be completed accurately.

(Note that these are not the only reliability requirements on such a system, but are the two we will consider in this example.) A tactic is a design decision that is intended to improve one specific design concern of a quality attribute. The tactics concerning reliability are especially important. For example, a reliability design concern is how to detect whether a component is unable to perform its function, so that it can be restarted. One tactic to implement this design concern is "Heartbeat": each component must send periodic heartbeat messages to a central controller (or, alternatively, to other components.) If a heartbeat message is not received from a component after a specified period, the component is assumed to be no longer sane and must be restarted.

Many tactics have been identified [2], including several important reliability tactics. Other tactics have also been identified, although they might not specifically be referred to as tactics. (See [3] and [4], for example).

Some tactics are related to each other in that they improve the same reliability concern; Bass et al refer to these as "design concerns." In some cases, such tactics are alternatives to each other. For example, detecting faulty processing is a design concern. The tactics to address this design concern are Ping-Echo, Heartbeat, and Exceptions. Ping-Echo and Heartbeat are alternatives to each other.

In the airline reservation system, we analyze different types of faults that the system may experience. These include:

- Bugs in software, including infinite loops, deadlock, and livelock, can cause software components to hang. Such problems can make the system unavailable.
- Hardware failures or software bugs can cause data integrity errors – it may be impossible to write data, or reads may produce corrupt data. This affects the correctness of the processing.
- There are numerous ways and places that communication between the client component and the main processor may fail. If these fail at the wrong time during the completion of a transaction, the transaction may be incorrect; e.g., the main server completes the transaction, but the user client does not receive confirmation. The user thinks the transaction was not completed and tries again, ending up purchasing two tickets.

(Again, this is a sample only). In response to these modes of failure, we design measures to deal with them. These include measures to detect and report faults, recover from them, or prevent the faults from disrupting the system. Some of these measures are:

- Ping-Echo: In order to detect failed or unresponsive components so they can be restarted, a component sends out a periodic ping request to other components which must be answered within a certain timeframe.
- Raising Exceptions: Each component must detect certain types of error conditions and raise exceptions. (Handling the exceptions is of course also necessary, and other tactics are used to handle exceptions.)
- Active or passive redundancy: In order to minimize single points of failure, components are duplicated, with various different methods to ensure synchronization between a failing component and its duplicate coming online to replace it.
- Transactions and checkpoint/rollback: Create atomic transactions that are recorded atomically, and ways to undo them if necessary.

Software patterns offer solutions to recurring problems in software design and implementation. A pattern describes a problem and the context of the problem, and an associated generic solution to the problem. Patterns have been used to document solutions to software problems. The best known software patterns describe solutions to object-oriented (OO) design problems [11], but patterns have been used in many aspects of software design, coding, and development [12].

Architecture patterns are patterns that describe proven architectural solutions to common system designs. They lay out the high-level structure and behavior of the system. They seek to satisfy multiple functional and non-functional requirements of the system. Several common architecture patterns have been developed, and are documented so that they can be widely used [5, 13, 14]. In this paper, we concern ourselves with architecture patterns and their relationship to reliability; for the remainder of this paper, all references to "patterns" refer to software architecture patterns.

One of the most common architecture patterns in the Layers pattern. The layered architecture consists of multiple hierarchical layers of functionality, each layer providing services to the layer above it, and serving as a client to the layer below [6]. In many systems, the lower layers are hidden from all except the adjacent higher layer.

The airline booking system's architecture is shown in the following diagram.

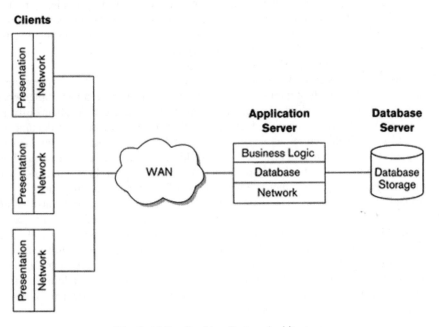

Fig. 1. Airline Booking System Architecture

We can see the following patterns in the architecture:

1. Client-Server: The application server and database server are the server side, with multiple clients.
2. Layers: The application server exhibits a layered architecture.

3. Presentation Abstraction Control (PAC): The clients use the PAC pattern. Each client has a presentation component, which interacts with an abstraction of the system, and controlled by the business logic in the server.
4. Shared Repository: This pattern is quite speculative, as it is not clear whether accesses to the database are shared or not. For the purposes of this study, we err on the side of more complexity, and consider that the pattern is present.

3   Factors That Influence Tactic Implementation

There are three factors involved with the impact of tactics on a multi-pattern architecture. We summarize them as follows:

1. Tactics have a natural tendency to fall into one of three categories of impact on the components of the system. These categories are based on how broadly the tactic impacts the system, i.e. whether the tactics impact all or some of the system components. Most of the tactics affect only some of the components of the system. In this case, the key question becomes, "Which components are affected?" This is important, because implementation may be easy in some components (a good fit), and hard in others (high impact; a bad fit). Naturally, we want to implement a tactic in the easiest (low impact) way possible, but are there no guidelines for where it is easy or hard. Even if you know which components easily accommodate a tactic, that doesn't mean that you can automatically pick the easy spot. As noted above, this is influenced chiefly by the reliability requirements.
2. Previous decisions about the system become constraints to which the system must conform. Although all previous decisions may affect the selection and implementation of tactics, we are chiefly concerned in this work with decisions about software architecture patterns – mainly which architecture patterns to use. The documentation of many architecture patterns note whether there are particular problems with implementing certain reliability tactics.   This helps answer the question about guidelines for where a tactic's implementation is easy or hard. In architectures with multiple patterns, you can then see where tactics fit well in the architecture.
3. Reliability requirements: There are two aspects of reliability requirements that are important. First, a requirement specifies a certain property of reliability to be achieved, such as high availability. This helps direct the selection of particular tactics to be used. The second aspect is that a reliability requirement must indicate what part(s) of the application it applies to. For example, a requirement of high availability specifies that it concerns call processing (not system administration). This directs where a component is to be implemented, namely in the part of the architecture that does call processing.

The next three subsections describe the factors in detail.

3.1   The Nature of Tactics

Section 2 has described how given tactic impacts a given pattern; additional detail is found in [8]. If a pattern is part of a multi-pattern architecture, the magnitude of the impact may change, but the nature of the impact of the tactic on the pattern does not change. For example, a common tactic for assessing the health of processes is "Ping-Echo." The nature of the impact is that processes must receive ping messages and respond to them. A multi-pattern architecture generally has more processes than a single-pattern architecture; thus more processes are impacted by the Ping-Echo tactic (all processes must receive and respond). Therefore, the magnitude of the impact of the Ping-Echo tactic is larger (than in a single pattern architecture), but the nature of the impact – the way that processes are modified – does not change.

The impact of a tactic on the individual patterns sets up the possible range of impact of the tactic on the entire system. In other words, we look at the impact of the tactic on the individual patterns in the system; the aggregate impact of the tactic on the system is generally no worse (greater) than the greatest impact on an individual pattern, and the impact is generally no better (less) than the smallest impact on any individual pattern.

Let us consider why. First, let us consider the best case: the tactic must be implemented somewhere in the system; the place with the least impact would be the pattern with the least impact; it can't be less than that. Even if one were to implement part of the tactic in one pattern and part in a different pattern, the amount of implementation can't go down; it's essential complexity (see [16]).

The worst case would be that the tactic must be implemented in all the patterns in the system. If the tactic is implemented in all patterns, it impacts each one, and the overall impact would approach the impact of the greatest impact on an individual pattern. This gives us a typical upper bound. For example, raising exceptions is typically required of all components of a system; therefore, it affects all the components of every pattern in the system. Therefore, each pattern feels the full impact of this tactic.

Let us now take a higher level view than detailed impact on individual patterns. We examine the impact of a tactic on the components of an architecture as a whole. In particular, we are interested in whether or not a tactic impacts a component. We find that there are three general categories of interaction of a tactic with the architectural components of a system. With one exception (the second category), we do not consider the details of that interaction, or how that interaction is accomplished. The categories are as follows:

1. **A tactic impacts all of the components** in the architecture. For example, a tactic for fault detection is Exception Raising. All components must implement Exception Raising.
2. **A tactic impacts all of the components** in the architecture, and one of the functions required by the tactic is that there is a **central coordinating component** that controls the other components in some way. (This is the exception about details of interaction that is mentioned above). For example, in the Ping-Echo tactic, a central process periodically sends requests to processes requesting that they verify their health.
3. **A tactic is implemented using just some of the components** in the architecture, leaving the remainder of the components unaffected. Which specific components are used depends on where the tactic is to be implemented, which is determined by the specific reliability requirements. For example, systems where the correctness of certain calculations are critical may employ the Voting tactic. In voting, the calculation is performed by three or more different components, each developed

independently of the others. In this case, only the component that performs the calculation and its calling component are affected; all other components have no other changes.

We analyzed all the reliability tactics given in [2] and found that each tactic can be classified in one of the three above categories. We also analyzed several tactics from [3] and [4], and also found this to be true. Our evidence suggests that these categories are sufficient to classify all reliability tactics. Due to space limitations, we focus only on the tactics from [2].

A few words of explanation are in order. First, architectures are composed of connectors and components, as well as behavior. However we consider only components for simplicity. Also, based on previous experience [8], we expect that connectors work the same way as components. A thorough exploration of connectors and behavior is a subject of future work.

Second, one might wonder why the second category (impact all components, with a central controller) is a separate category from the first, after all, it is a special case of the first. The controlling component has strong architectural implications – a controller must communicate with all other components. If an architecture already has such a controller, it is often easy to incorporate the tactic, and may even be trivial. For example, the Broker pattern has such a component. On the other hand, if the architecture has no such component, adding it is usually very disruptive to the architecture. Therefore, it is useful to consider this category separately from the first.

In the airline reservation system, let us consider the tactic we identified. The tactics we identified fall into the following categories:

1. Ping-Echo: This requires that each component must respond to the ping messages. In addition, one component must initiate the ping messages, and manage the responses. (Category 2: impacts all components, plus a central component). (Another possible option is to dispense with a central controller, and have a scheme where components are responsible for monitoring each other's health.) It appears that the most natural central component is the application server, (see figure 2). Or because the application server may itself be composed of multiple software components (not shown), it may a component within the application server.

2. Exception Raising: Generally, Exception Raising should be done consistently across the application, which means that each component must raise exceptions as well as respond to other exceptions. (Category 1: There is no explicit central component, but all exceptions must be appropriately handled. This may hint at a central "handler of last resort", but it really depends on the tactics chosen to handle the exceptions). There are two special considerations: first, who should the database component report exceptions to? Clearly, exceptions should be reported to the component that can correctly handle the fault; in this case, it is likely the application server component. Second, should the client presentation components also report exceptions to the application server? It is more likely that the exceptions be raised and handled locally.

3. Active Redundancy: A single component can manage the redundant components. Some systems are entirely redundant, while others may have a few critical components that are redundant; perhaps the data store or communication infrastructure components. Which components must be duplicated depends on the system

requirements (Category 3). The obvious candidates for redundancy are the application server and the database. In order to maintain availability, the application server should be replicated, and active redundancy appears to be a viable choice. Because information from the database is necessary to make a reservation, the database should also be available at all times, and should be replicated.

4. Passive Redundancy: This impacts more than one component, because the passive component must receive state updates from the active. It is likely that the modifications can be confined to a few components though. (Category 3, impacts some components; who is duplicated depends on the requirements; same rationale as for Active Redundancy). Passive redundancy may be an alternative to active redundancy for the application server. Due to the fact that database actions are transactional in nature, passive redundancy may be a more natural choice for replicating the database than active redundancy. Note that regardless of the choice of redundancy type, one should try to design it so that it is invisible to other components; i.e., it should be entirely transparent to the clients.

5. Transactions: Processing is bundled into transactions which can be undone all at once, if necessary. Transactions make checkpointing and rollback easier. It affects those components that deal with the details of the transactions. (Category 3: impacts some components. The requirements help shape which components deal with transactions). Any database actions are naturally transaction-oriented; this is a good fit, and can be done entirely within the database component. However, a purchase is also a natural transaction, and the notion of transactions therefore must permeate the design of the application server, as well as the clients themselves. Here we see how the notion of a transaction is driven by the requirements, which in turn affects how and which components are affected.

6. Checkpoint/Rollback: Likely to affect all components that deal with the data/transactions/state that must be checkpointed and rolled back. This impacts some or all of the components that are directly involved with the state of the data being processed. (Category 3, because not all components are directly involved in the state of the system). This is a natural fit with transactions, and the impact follows the same pattern: database transactions can be checkpointed and rolled back entirely within the database components; rolling back of user purchases affects all components.

For each tactic, this information helps us understand the components needed for implementing it. Of course, this must be placed in the context of the architecture of the system, including the patterns used.

3.2 The Impact on Multiple Patterns

Because tactics are realized within the architecture, tactics have some effect on the architecture and the architecture patterns used. While the purpose of a tactic is to focus on a single design concern of reliability, the impact may be broad, affecting many or even all of the components of the architecture.

We have studied the impact of implementing tactics on patterns and in the case where the pattern provides the structures needed by the tactics , we found that the impact can be minimal. On the other hand, the impact can be great if the pattern's structures must be substantially modified, or if many different structures must be added. We described five levels of impact as follows:

1. Good Fit (+ +): The structure of the pattern is highly compatible with the structural needs of the tactic.
2. Minor Changes (+): The tactic can be implemented with few changes to the structure of the pattern, which are minor and more importantly, are consistent with the pattern. Behavior changes are minor.
3. Neutral (~): The pattern and the tactic are basically orthogonal. The tactic is implemented independently of the pattern, and receives neither help nor hindrance from it.
4. Significant Changes (-): The changes needed are more significant. They generally involve adding a few components that are not similar to the pattern, and/or moderately modifying the existing components.
5. Poor Fit (- -): Significant changes are required to the pattern in order to implement the tactic. They consist of the addition of several components, major changes to existing structure and behavior, and/or more minor changes, but to many components.

These levels describe the amount of impact on the architecture; full descriptions are given in [8]. One may also consider this to be a rough indicator of the difficulty of adding a given tactic, although we do not make any specifications of difficulty or expected effort.

In [8] we analyzed how a given reliability tactic is implemented in a given architecture pattern. We see that the tactic can require the architect to modify components and connectors, and possibly even create additional components and connectors. However, industrial systems are quite complex, involving multiple architecture patterns. Therefore, we must consider implementing tactics in this larger context.

In a study of the architectures of 47 industrial software projects, we found that 37 used more than one architecture pattern [15]. Most had two, three, or four patterns. The most we saw in a single architecture was eight. Therefore, it is not sufficient to consider the impact of a tactic on a single pattern, but we must consider the potential impact on all the patterns in the architecture.

There are several possibilities of how a tactic might interact with an architecture that contains multiple architecture patterns. A possibility on the one side is that the tactic interacts with all the patterns in the architecture. On the other extreme, the tactic might need to interact with only one of the architecture patterns. Clearly, the second possibility has a smaller impact on the architecture than the first. Therefore, for a given tactic and a given system, the challenge is to determine how many of the patterns are impacted, and in what way the tactic implementation affects them.

The impact of tactics on multiple patterns is shaped by the category of tactic, as described previously. As the pattern category differentiates the tactics on their impact on components, and patterns embody components, we see how tactic categories relate to multiple pattern impacts. They are as follows:

1. If the tactic impacts all components, then it must be implemented in all the patterns. The magnitude of impact will tend to be at or near the magnitude of the "worst" pattern in the system. For example, the tactic "raising exceptions" requires that every component either raise exceptions or have a good reason not to. Thus this tactic affects every component of every architecture pattern.
2. If the tactic impacts all components and requires a central controller, then the impact on the system will often be better than the impact of the "worst" pattern. The

reason is that high impact on the "worst" pattern may well be because one needs to add a central component (and all the associated connectors). However, if there is another pattern in the architecture that has a central component, then the tactic will probably be able to take advantage of it and can be implemented in that pattern. In fact, the necessary connectors will also probably be in place. Thus the impact on the system may be near the impact on the pattern with the central component. This impact can be quite low. So, in this case it depends on which patterns are present in the system. For example, during an architecture review of a distributed time-tracking system, we found that the designers had neglected to sufficiently handle cases where a client loses connectivity with the server. A heartbeat was added which (in this case) required that each component periodically generate a heartbeat message, as well as a central component to handle the heartbeat messages and detect unresponsive components. The system included the Broker and Layers patterns, and the central component was a natural fit with the broker component of the Broker pattern.

3. If the tactic impacts some of the components, one would certainly want to implement the tactic in the pattern with the smallest impact. However, depending on the requirements of the application, this may not always be possible. We discuss this in the next section. However, this gives a starting point for considering impact; a best case scenario. For example, in a space exploration simulation game, we explored the need to recover from erroneous input by using transactions and rollback. The system included both the Layers and Active Repository patterns. The designers could consider which of the patterns would be a best fit for these tactics, but the key consideration was the application itself – what exactly needed to be rolled back in the event of an error. In this application, the fact that games were dynamic indicated that transactions and rolling back were more appropriately implemented in the Layers pattern.

The following table summarizes the nature of the impacts:

Table 1. Impact Categories' Impact on Multiple Patterns

Tactic Impact Category	Impact on Patterns' Components	Impact Tendency
All components	All components in all the patterns are affected	Impact is that of the pattern with the greatest ("worst") impact
All components, plus central controller	All components in all the patterns affected; placement of central controller is significant	If a pattern supports a central controller, impact is less than the "worst" pattern
Some components	May be possible to implement in a single pattern	Ideally, impact is that of the "best" pattern. But requirements play a major role here.

This gives us a basic understanding how a given tactic will be implemented in the patterns of an architecture. It also gives us a basic idea of the magnitude of impact on the architecture caused by the tactic. However, this information is as yet insufficient to fully understand how a tactic will be implemented in the architecture. We need more information, specifically about the purpose of a given tactic in the system. We need to consult the requirements of the system; the other major factor.

In the airline reservation system, let us consider the impact of the tactics we identified on the patterns in the system. Remember the four patterns identified were Client-Server (CS), Layers (L), Presentation Abstraction Control (PAC), and Shared Repository (SR).

1. Ping-Echo: Impact: CS: +, L: +, PAC: ~, SR: ~. Since this tactic impacts all components, plus a central component, the overall impact should be neutral or better. Analysis: All components must be notified and respond. CS components have the necessary communication paths built in, and the Server component is a natural central component. Therefore this tactic is compatible with the patterns, but is not an ideal match (overall impact: +).
2. Exceptions: Impact: CS: ~, L: ++, PAC: ~, SR: ++. Since this tactic impacts all components, the overall impact tends to be the most severe of the patterns; in this case neutral.
3. Active Redundancy: Impact: CS: +, L: +, PAC: +, SR: ++. We see that this tactic is compatible with all the patterns. Since it impacts some components, the overall compatibility is good, and if the tactic can be confined to the SR pattern, the overall compatibility could be very good.
4. Passive Redundancy: Impact: CS: +, L: +, PAC: ~, SR: ++. The impact is similar to Active Redundancy, except for PAC, which is not as compatible. Does the fact that this tactic is not as good a fit with PAC as Active Redundancy push us toward Active Redundancy? Not necessarily. If the redundancy is implemented in components that do not interface with the PAC components, it doesn't matter.
5. Transactions: Impact: CS: ++, L: ++, PAC: +, SR: ++. This tactic is a good fit with all the patterns except PAC, where there are issues of keeping multiple presentations in synch. Since this tactic impacts some components depending on the requirements of the system, we may be able to implement it away from the PAC components.
6. Checkpoint/Rollback: CS: ++, L: ++, PAC: -, SR: ++. This is very similar to Transactions except that keeping multiple transactions in synch is likely more involved because of rollbacks. The analysis is the same, though.

3.3 The Role of System Reliability Requirements

The above general descriptions of impact are a starting point for understanding how a tactic impacts a system architecture. In addition, the system's reliability requirements that trigger the selection of the tactics play a major role in the impact of the tactics. Certain system requirements may cause a tactic to be implemented in certain components; that is, in certain architecture patterns. This can override any attempt to implement the tactic where it would be easiest to implement. Therefore, decisions about how (and where in the architecture) to implement tactics are driven not just by the architectural structure, but also by the system reliability requirements. This then demands that the detailed requirements be analyzed as part of the reliability architecting process.

System reliability requirements shape the implementation and impact of reliability tactics in two important ways. The first way is that reliability requirements influence which design concerns are to be satisfied by tactics. In particular, different ways in which faults affect the system are identified and the actions taken in response are decided in order to meet the requirements. For example, consider a telecommunications system that must be highly available to process calls – 99.999% of the time. In order to meet this requirement, architects identify that components may fail due to hardware or software failures. In order to meet the availability requirement, all components must run nonstop; therefore, failed components must be detected and restarted quickly.   The design concern is timely detection of failed components. A tactic that implements this design concern might be Heartbeat.

The second way that requirements affect the impact of reliability tactics is that they often specify which part of the system a tactic applies to. For instance, in the example above, high availability applies to call processing only. Therefore, any components that are involved in call processing must implement their portion of the Heartbeat tactic. However, other components, such as those dealing with provisioning, system administration, or billing, will likely not be subject to the Heartbeat tactic.

The process of architecting is highly iterative and quite intuitive. Therefore, one doesn't necessarily determine all the reliability requirements first, etc. In fact, the requirements, architecture decisions, and tactical decisions are done in different orders, piecemeal, and basically together. So a decision to use a tactic, combined with a reliability requirement, might dictate the selection of a particular pattern that fits the tactic well. Or a tactic might be selected over a different alternative because it fits with a pattern that has already been selected. So the process is very fluid; we have found that consideration of architecture and the selection and design of reliability tactics often happen simultaneously [17].

Consideration of each of these factors helps complete the picture of how and where a tactic will be implemented in the architecture, as well as which tactics to use (if not already determined). The result is that the architecture is more complete: the architecture patterns are now modified to accommodate the implementation of the tactics.

Let us consider the tactics in the airline reservation system that are category 3 – they impact some components based on the requirements of the system.

1. Availability: in considering Active or Passive Redundancy to help achieve high availability, one must decide which critical components must be replicated. The critical functionality to be replicated is the business logic, which is found in the Layers pattern, so the overall impact is that of Redundancy on Layers. Since the impact of both redundancy tactics on the Layers patterns is positive, it helps us understand that from an architecture viewpoint, it doesn't matter which redundancy tactic we select in this application.

2. In order to achieve data integrity, we consider using Transactions and Checkpoint/Rollback: Both tactics are a very good fit for all the patterns except PAC. So the question becomes whether transactions and rolling back can be defined below the level of the user interface. This is very likely – user interaction can be designed so that actions are encapsulated in transactions, and rolling back to previous states

or data should be transparent to the user. This information guides us to design the user interaction along lines of transactions and gives us motivation for doing so.

4 Use in the Architecture Design Process

One of the major challenges in developing reliable systems is that decisions about implementing reliability must be made early; it is exceedingly difficult to retrofit reliability into an established architecture if it was not planned for. Yet the implications of architectural reliability decisions may not be understood, resulting in design and implementation difficulties later on. The information about how requirements, tactics and architecture patterns interact can help ameliorate these difficulties, or at least anticipate some of them. The information can be used during the architecture design process to consider tradeoffs in tactic selection, to refine and re-negotiate requirements, and to a lesser extent, in pattern selection or modification. The impact information is not intended to be used to generate specific effort estimates; it does not have sufficient detail or specificity.

In this chapter, we do not propose a specific architecture design process for incorporating reliability tactics into an architecture. Instead, we describe how the information about how requirements, tactics and architecture patterns interact can fit in a general model of architectural design [18]. The main activities in the model are architectural analysis, architectural synthesis, and architectural evaluation. The output of architectural analysis is architecturally significant requirements, the output of architectural synthesis is candidate architectural solutions, while architectural evaluation assess the candidate solutions with respect to the requirements.

The first activity, architectural analysis, is focused on understanding the architecturally significant requirements. This includes refining reliability requirements and identifying the associated design concerns. For example, if high availability of the system is a requirement, an associated design concern may be replication. A key question is which part of the system must run nonstop, as that will determine where the candidate tactics must be implemented. We might also ask whether the system may have momentary interruptions, which would allow a passively redundant solution rather than an active redundancy. The answers to these questions help clarify the requirements, and will be used (later) as tactics are selected and decisions made about where the tactics should be implemented.

The architectural synthesis activity is typically where tactics and patterns are considered. The design concerns point us to certain tactics; for example the replication design concern leads us to consider Active Redundancy, Passive Redundancy, and Spare. The candidate tactics and requirements are major drivers for pattern selection. This implies a certain amount of iteration among architectural analysis and synthesis, as the architecturally significant requirements and candidate patterns are iteratively refined. The information about the impact of tactics on multiple patterns can be used here to optimize the required effort from the combination of patterns and tactics. Candidate patterns and tactics are major pieces of candidate architecture solutions.

The architectural evaluation activity is to determine whether the proposed architectural solutions fulfill the architecturally significant requirements. The additional information about tactics' categories of interaction as well as the detailed reliability requirements can enhance the ability of architects to effectively evaluate candidate architectural solutions.

The following figure shows the architecture design activities as described by Hofmeister et al. It is annotated with the activities related to requirements, tactics and patterns, and their interactions. These are shown by the numerals attached to activities and data flows, and are described at the bottom of the figure.

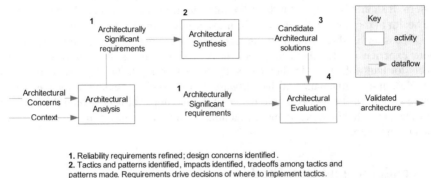

1. Reliability requirements refined; design concerns identified.
2. Tactics and patterns identified, impacts identified, tradeoffs among tactics and patterns made. Requirements drive decisions of where to implement tactics.
3. Candidate solutions include tactic and pattern information, with impact information
4. Requirements and nature of tactics can help evaluate solutions

Fig. 2. Architecture design activities from [18], with pattern and tactic activities

The following are two examples of how the tactic and pattern information is used in the architectural synthesis and evaluation activities to improve the quality of the architecture.

The activity was architectural synthesis, and the system performed automated sequential manipulation of paper. The key reliability requirements included that the papers had to be processed correctly, and that any machine malfunctions did not cause further problems (fault tolerance). Key tactics used included transactions, ping-echo, and exception raising. The main pattern was Pipes and Filters (P&F), which supported the sequential (and configurable) nature of the paper processing. Another prominent pattern was Model View Controller (MVC), which provided the user interaction with the system. The main challenge was that the reliability tactics all were poor fits for the P&F pattern. However, they all were able to take advantage of the controller component of the MVC pattern, which communicated with each of the components of the P&F pattern.

Discussion: reliability tactics and architectural patterns are generally considered simultaneously, so one might ask which came first. Did the architects tentatively select the patterns first, and then used their components in designing the reliability tactics, or did they see the need for a controlling component for the tactics, and then added the MVC pattern on top of that component? It is almost certainly some of both: the highly iterative nature of architectural design means that many ideas are considered and tried as the architects work to create an architecture. Regardless, the information about how tactics and patterns fit together help shape the architecture.

In the second example, the activity was an architectural evaluation, performed just as development was getting underway. The system was a distributed time tracking system. The key reliability requirements were data accuracy and availability, although availability was not critical – the consequences of downtime were not catastrophic. Key patterns were Client-Server and Layers (on the server); Broker was identified during the evaluation as a desirable extension to Client-Server. The review uncovered that the architects had not fully considered all the ramifications of faults, and as a result, the Heartbeat tactic was added. Impact on the three patterns showed that it was the best fit in the Broker pattern, which added to the motivation to adopt the Broker pattern. It should be noted that the reliability requirements indicated the need to know the health of the remote clients, which fit exactly with the Broker pattern.

Discussion: In this case, the designers were somewhat inexperienced in reliability; more experienced designers may well have designed the system more comprehensively for fault tolerance. In such cases, the reviews serve to highlight potential issues with design or maintenance of the software. For example, a review of the paper processing system in the first example revealed the incompatibility between the P&F pattern and the reliability tactics as a potential trouble spot during future maintenance and enhancement.

5   Validation and Case Study

Validation of this work has three parts that correspond to the three factors discussed in section 3: the nature of tactics, the impact on multiple patterns and the role of requirements. We began by analyzing the reliability tactics to determine how many components in a given architecture they affect (some or all). This confirmed the three categories of tactics interaction with components, described above. The second part was to verify and refine the impact categories of tactics on multiple patterns, by considering the tactics applied to common pairs of architecture patterns. The third part was a case study that considered a real architecture where we identified its architecture patterns, and analyzed how the reliability requirements influence the selection and implementation of tactics.

5.1   Tactic Impact on Architectures

We analyzed all the reliability tactics from Bass [2]. For each tactic, we analyzed how it should be implemented: what functionality is needed, and what components and connectors are needed to implement that functionality. We determined whether the tactic's implementation must be in all components, or just some of the components.

We began by identifying how (in general terms) the tactic should work, and what components and connectors are needed. This was done by studying the tactic descriptions [mainly in 2, 3, and 4]. We then considered how the tactic would be implemented in a system. Would the tactic require that all major components of a system take part in implementing the tactic, or could the tactic be implemented in a subset of a system's components? In each case, we found that a tactic was clearly in one or the other category.

For the tactics that required implementation in all components, we also examined the tactic to see whether a central controlling component was a part of the tactic. We found that these tactics could be categorized into either needing a central component or not. Ping-Echo requires a central controlling component. Raising Exceptions does not (note that handling the exceptions is separate from raising them, and would be done using whatever tactics are most appropriate for the type of exception). The tactic "Heartbeat" requires implementation in all components, and may or may not employ a central controlling component. Aguilera et al describe the use of a heartbeat with no central controller in [19].

For the tactics that impact some components, we considered which components would be affected. The ideal model is that the tactic should be implemented in the pattern where it is the best fit – where the impact is the lowest. However, we found that the components where a tactic should be implemented depended on what part of the system needed the associated reliability. For example, there are several replication tactics (Active Redundancy, Passive Redundancy, and Spare). In order to decide in which pattern to implement the redundancy, one must decide which part of the system needs to be replicated. This would be dictated by the requirements of the system, namely what critical functions must run nonstop. We found that in every case where a tactic is implemented in some components, we could not say definitively where the tactic should be implemented, because it would provide that reliability feature to a particular part of the system. Instead, the answer was always, "It depends on the requirements to state which part of the system must have this reliability feature."

We found that each tactic fits into one of the three categories, as shown in the table below. (The categories, as described earlier are 1 – all components, 2 – all components with a central component, and 3 – some components).

Table 3. Categories of Impact of Common Reliability Tactics

Design Concern	Tactic	Impact Category
Tactics for Fault Detection		
	Ping-Echo	2
	Heartbeat	1 or 2
	Exceptions	1
Fault Recovery -- Preparation		
	Voting	3
	Active Redundancy	3
	Passive Redundancy	3
	Spare	3
Recovery -- Reintroduction		
	Shadow	3
	State Resynchronization	3
	Checkpoint/Rollback	3
Fault Prevention		
	Removal From Service	3
	Transactions	3
	Process Monitor	3

We see that most of these tactics impact some of the components. We also see that the tactics' categories appear to be generally consistent within design concerns. We have not studied other reliability tactics (from Utas [3], Hanmer [4], or other sources) enough to know whether these trends are consistent; this is noted as future work.

5.2 Impact of Tactics on Pairs of Patterns

To begin to validate the information about how tactics impact multiple-pattern architectures, we considered the impact of each tactic on common pairs of patterns. Future work is warranted to extend this to pattern triplets and beyond; however, in our analysis of the airline booking system (the running example), we found that the relationship among pairs applied sequentially appears to be the same as analyzing multiple patterns together. In our earlier work we showed that virtually all significant systems contain multiple architecture patterns [15], and that the most common pairs of architecture patterns identified were the following:

1. Broker – Layers
2. Layers – Shared Repository
3. Pipes and Filters – Blackboard
4. Client-Server – Presentation Abstraction Control
5. Layers – Presentation Abstraction Control
6. Layers – Model View Controller

We analyzed how each tactic would be implemented in a system consisting of each one of the aforementioned pairs of patterns. We determined whether the impact category (see Section 3.2) was valid and whether the nature and magnitude of the impact supported the descriptions given above. This analysis helped form and validate the categories and the nature of the impact of the tactics in each category. A summary of the impact is shown in table 3. In the following table, the type of impact of the tactic is given with the tactic name. In the boxes, the two impact ratings in parentheses are the ratings of the two patterns, respectively. The other rating is the composite rating. In many cases, the rating shows a range, or is given as "likely" or "close to." These are cases where the requirements play a major role in where the tactic should be implemented, and this affects the impact on the architecture.

We note that tactics that are category 3 (some components) normally have impact that ranges between the impacts of the two patterns; the impact depends on the reliability requirements. However, in cases where the impact of the two patterns is the same, there would be no difference so we do not see a range of impact. We see this in several of the tactics in the table.

In the table we see that the Broker-Layers pattern pair is most compatible with the tactics. In fact, only one tactic has worse than a positive impact. The Broker-Layers pair is also the most common pair we found. This is more that good fortune: architecture patterns are usually at least partly selected based on the tactics that are selected (see [2]). We can surmise that one reason for selecting the Broker and Layers patterns is to accommodate one or more of these tactics.

Table 4. Impact of Tactics on Pairs of Patterns

Patterns / Tactics	Layers – Broker	Layers – Shared Rep	P&F – Blackboard	C-S – PAC	Layers – PAC	Layers – MVC
Ping-Echo (all, central)	(+, ++) ++	(+, ~) ~	(--, ~) Likely -	(+, ~) Close to +	(+, ~) ~ or better	(+, ~) ~
Heartbeat (all, central or not)	(+, ++) ++	(+, ~) ~	(--, ~) Likely -	(+, ~) Close to +	(+, ~) ~ or better	(+, ~) ~
Exceptions (all)	(++, +) +	(++, ++) ++	(--, --) --	(~, ~) ~	(++, ~) ~	(++, ~) ~
Voting (some)	(+, ++) + or better	(+, ~) Likely +	(++, +) Likely ++	(+, +) +	(+, +) +	(+, +) +
Act. Red. (some)	(+, ++) up to ++	(+, ++) likely ++	(++, +) + to ++	(+, +) +	(+, +) +	(+, +) +
Pass. Red. (some)	(+, ++) up to ++	(+, ++) likely ++	(-, ~) Likely ~	(+, -) Likely ~	(+, -) Close to +	(+, -) Close to +
Spare (some)	(~, ++) up to ++	(~, -) up to ~	(+, ~) Likely +	(+, ~) ~ to +	(~, ~) ~	(~. -) Likely ~
Shadow (some)	(+, ++) + or better	(+, ~) likely +	(+, -) - to +	(+, +) +	(+, +) +	(+, -) Close to +
State Resync (s)	(+, ++) +	(+, ++) + to ++	(--, +) Close to --	(+, -) Close to +	(+, -) Close to +	(+, ~) Close to +
Checkpoint Rollback (some)	(++, ++) ++	(++, ++) ++	(--, --) --	(++, -) Close to ++	(++, -) Closer to ++	(++, +) Close to ++
Rmve from Service (s)	(~, ~) ~	(~, ~) ~	(-, -) -	(~, ~) ~	(~, ~) ~	(~, ~) ~
Transactions (some)	(++, ++) ++	(~, ~) ~	(-, --) Close to -	(++, +) Close to +	(++, +) Close to ++	(++, ~) Close to ++
Process Monitor (s)	(++, ++) ++	(~, ~) ~	(-, -) -	(~, ~) ~	(~, ~) ~	(~, ~) ~

5.3 Case Study: Review of an Architecture

We performed an architectural review of a system. As part of this review, we identified the patterns in the architecture, the tactics used to achieve high reliability, and
how the tactics and patterns interacted. The data from this review should support or
refute the following questions:

1. Do the reliability tactics used impact multiple patterns?
2. Do the tactics impact the patterns in the tree ways described?
3. How do the failure modes impact where tactics are implemented?

The system we reviewed is proprietary, so details that identify the company, exactly
what the system processes, and the exact architecture cannot be given. A general
description of the system is as follows: It provides customized sequential processing
of certain types of physical materials. It is in effect, an automated assembly line, with
sequential stages, performing actions on the materials. The system includes custom
hardware modules, controlled by software within each module, as well as central
control of the entire assembly line.

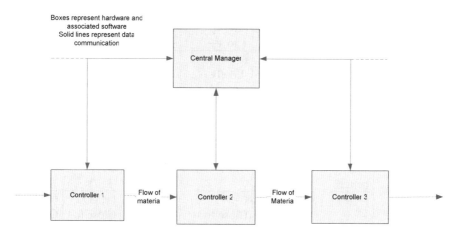

Fig. 2. Generalized architecture of assembly processing system

The system has important reliability requirements. The most important are that the
assembly must be done correctly – they must guarantee that no finished product has
been assembled incorrectly. A closely related requirement is that no finished product
may have any damaged parts. Another important requirement is that the system must
have high throughput; however, this does not imply that high availability is required.

Important failure modes, as well as the measures (tactics) adopted by the system to
deal with them included the following:

1. A hardware module ceases to function because of a hardware or software malfunction. In order to detect this, the designers used a Ping-Echo, with a central controller.
   Corrective action included notification of upstream modules to suspend work, but allowed downstream modules to complete processing. This is roughly analogous to the

tactic, "Fail to a Stable State", described by Utas [3]. Repairing the unit was a manual operation, so an alert was issued to the user.

2. Materials may be damaged by processing, or may arrive already damaged. In any case, a module may receive damaged materials. The modules have no way of automatically discarding damaged materials, so the corrective actions are the same as number 1. The difference is in detection: a module can detect damaged materials and use the "Raise Exceptions" tactic to inform the central controller.

3. If the communication link between the central controller and a processing module fails, the module may not be able to respond to commands such as suspending processing, nor can it report faults such as damaged materials. In this case, it appears to the central control that the module is not responsive, so it treats it as number 1, above.

4. The result of suspending processing can result in materials being not completed, or perhaps being completed incorrectly. The system must be designed so this does not happen. In order to prevent this problem, the processing of materials was divided into discrete units that could be completed independently; these units can be considered to be transactions of work.

The architects used the following tactics to achieve their reliability goals: Ping-Echo, Raising Exceptions, Fail to a Stable State, and Transactions. The key feature of the architecture was a set of independent hardware modules, arranged in sequence to process the materials. Their operation was coordinated by a central coordinator, which included a user interface. The architecture used numerous patterns, notably Model-View-Controller (the View was the user interface, the central controller was the Controller, and the processing modules together were the Model), Pipes and Filters (the Filters were the processing modules), Layers (within each processing module), and State-Driven (the system taken together).

Let us see how each tactic supports or refutes the earlier questions.

1. Ping-Echo must be implemented in the processing modules, but requires a coordinator. It does impact multiple patterns: each filter in Pipes and Filters must implement it; within each, at the highest layer in the Layers pattern; the State-Driven system must be aware of it, and the Controller in Model-View-Controller coordinates the pings.

2. Exceptions are raised by the Pipes and Filters, and the Layers within them. Any components involved with the system state would raise exceptions if there are any issues with state. Since the Filters are also the Model, they raise exceptions, but more to the point, the Controller must have some mechanism for catching the exceptions. So all patterns are affected.

3. Fail to a Stable State was not listed in the main analysis of the tactics, but it clearly impacts the Model-View-Controller, the Filters, and the State-Driven patterns.

4. Transactions impact the Filters and perhaps the Layers within them. Since the concern is the unfinished work within the Filters, it may be possible for the Filters to handle this tactic without involving other patterns – for example, the controller may simply have to issue a "resume" command, and the Filters complete the transactions in progress.

The impact of the tactics used on the architecture is shown in the following table. This table shows the impact of the tactics on the individual patterns, and the overall impact, along with an explanation.

Table 5. Impact of tactics on individual patterns and overall architecture

	Pipes & Fiters	Layers	MVC	State-Driven	Overall
Ping-Echo	- - (each Filter must respond, needs central cntl)	+ (good fit)	~	~ (States and pings orthogonal	- - (each Filter must respond; MVC provides cntl)
Raise Exceptions	- (each Filter must raise exceptions	++ (also is natural fit for handling)	~	+ (also good fit for handling)	- (all components must implement, including Filters
Fail to Stable State	+ (Filters can simply stop processing)	++ (Layers can catch lower level errors)	+ (States mainly in Model)	++ (a natural fit)	+ (all components affected, including Model and Filters)
Transactions	~ (Can help to divide work)	++ (good fit)	~	++ (a natural fit)	++ (implemented in State: in Model and Filters with few changes to them)

This shows us two characteristics of implementing tactics in the architecture. First, we see that some tactics might be implemented where there is a good fit with the patterns in the architecture. We see this with the following tactics: Transactions, and Fail to a Stable State. Of course, this depends on the types of failures and how they must be handled according to the requirements.

The second characteristic is that some tactics require that all the components of the software implement the behavior of the tactic; this is the case with these tactics: Exceptions and Ping-Echo. The impact of this characteristic is particularly striking in the case of Ping-Echo: in order for the filters to implement it, they had to establish direct communication with a central component, as well as implement mechanisms to respond to the ping messages in a timely manner. This caused a significant deviation from the standard Ping-Echo pattern.

This case study shows an example of each of the three types of impact of tactics described earlier. It shows how these tactics impact an architecture consisting of multiple tactics.

6 Related Work

The reliability tactics originally described by Bass et al [2] have been explored in more depth. Several of the tactics have been further specified, resulting in new sets of more specific tactics [22]. For example, the tactic called "Raising Exceptions" has been subdivided into tactics of "Error Codes" and "Exception Classes." While we have not examined these newer tactics in depth, we expect that these tactics have the same characteristics as their "parent" tactics, and have the same architectural impact. For example, the two exception tactics cited above are alternate ways of implementing raising exceptions below the level of the architecture; the architectural constructs for both are the same.

Tekinerdogan et al discuss using failure scenarios in software architecture reliability analysis as a way of identifying candidate tactics for improving the systems' reliability [23]. This identifies what must be implemented; this work adds information about how such tactics can be incorporated into the architecture, and the impact on the architecture of doing so.

Reliability is an important topic in software architecture evaluations; important issues identified during architecture reviews and evaluations are often associated with reliability (see 24, 25, 26, 27]). A part of assessing the risk of reliability issues, one should consider the impact of impacting their fixes – the tactics. This work helps architects understand the impact, and can thus help architects make more informed decisions during reviews.

Significant work has been done to analyze and predict reliability of systems based on the software architecture [28]. Approaches include using reasoning frameworks to do so [29, 30]. On the other hand, this work focuses on the impact on the architecture of measures taken to improve reliability. These are compatible; both should be considered when analyzing an architecture for reliability. A general reasoning framework for designing architectures to achieve quality attribute requirements has been proposed by Bachmann et al [31]. In this model, the impact of tactics on the architecture can be one of the inputs to the reasoning framework.

7 Future Work

We have studied a few of the tactics found in [3] and [4]; initial analysis supports the tactic categories and impacts shown here. All these tactics, as well as others found, should be studied. Producing a catalog of known reliability tactics along with their impacts would be useful. Such a catalog will need widespread input, as well as continuous updating.

We have observed that the categories of impact for the tactics tend to be similar for patterns that address the same design concern. (The design concern of fault detection has two in category 1 and one in category 2, but all affect all the components). It may be that the design concern influences or even dictates the tactic's impact category. However, only the Bass tactics are classified by design concerns. In order to determine whether this is a general rule, one must first classify other reliability tactics by design concern. Nonetheless, this appears to be potentially interesting, and we intend to study it further.

Some patterns and reliability tactics fit particularly well together, and may indeed be commonly used. We would like to investigate architectures to see whether some combinations of patterns and reliability tactics are common. These may form a set of "reliable architecture patterns;" variants of architecture patterns especially for highly reliable systems.

One very interesting consequence of implementing the tactics is that since it involves changing the architecture, some changes may actually change the pattern composition of the architecture. An architecture pattern may be added. In certain cases, an existing pattern may even change to a different pattern. Obviously, the transformation of one pattern to another can happen only where patterns are similar. We have seen two examples of this type of transformation in architectures we have evaluated. We intend to study this further in order to understand its architectural implications.

Further study should be done to examine the impact of reliability tactics on each other, and on other quality attributes, such as performance. Work has been done on tradeoff analysis as part of architectural analysis [10, 31]. Studies of reliability tactic interaction can provide specific information as input to such tradeoff analyses.

8   Conclusions

Measures taken to improve reliability (reliability tactics) are implemented in the context of three factors that influence its impact on the architecture of the system:

- The reliability requirements, which strongly influence which tactics are to be used, and what part of the system they apply to.
- Characteristics of the tactics themselves, namely whether the tactic has a natural tendency to be applied to all components of the system, or just a selected part.
- Constraints from other requirements and from design decisions. In particular, the architecture patterns used are important factors, because architecture patterns are commonly used, and the tactics impact them in regular and known ways.

Taken together, these factors create a picture of the impact of tactics on non-trivial architectures; those that involve multiple architecture patterns. This is of practical application, as most industrial systems use multiple patterns in their architectures. Architects can leverage this information to understand the potential impact of tactics on an existing or proposed architecture. They can use this to help make tradeoffs concerning the architecture and reliability tactics being used.

We have examined how reliability tactics would affect a real architecture, and found that the factors described above affect the impact of the tactics on the architecture as expected. We have also proposed how the investigation of the impact of tactics can be incorporated into typical software architecting processes. We recommend that this information be used during architecture of highly reliable software systems.

References

1. International Standards Organization, Information Technology – Software Product Quality – Part 1: Quality Model, ISO/IEC FDIS 9126-1
2. Bass, L., Clements, P., Kazman, R.: Software Architecture in Practice. Addison-Wesley, Reading (2003)

3. Utas, G.: Robust Communications Software: Extreme Availability, Reliability and Scalability for Carrier-Grade Systems. Wiley, Chichester (2005)
4. Hanmer, R.: Patterns for Fault Tolerant Software. Wiley Software Patterns Series. Wiley, Chichester (2007)
5. Buschmann, F., et al.: Pattern-Oriented Software Architecture: A System of Patterns. Wiley, Chichester (1996)
6. Shaw, M., Garlan, D.: Software Architecture: Perspectives on an Emerging Discipline. Addison-Wesley, Reading (1996)
7. Shaw, M.: Toward Higher-Level Abstractions for Software Systems. In: Tercer Simposio Internacional del Conocimiento y su Ingerieria, pp. 55–61 (October 1988); Reprinted in Data and Knowledge Engineering 5, 19–28 (1990)
8. Harrison, N., Avgeriou, P.: Incorporating Fault Tolerance Techniques in Software Architecture Patterns. In: International Workshop on Software Engineering for Resilient Systems (SERENE 2008), Newcastle upon Tyne, UK, November 17-19, ACM Press, New York (2008)
9. Harrison, N.B., Avgeriou, P.: Leveraging Architecture Patterns to Satisfy Quality Attributes. In: Oquendo, F. (ed.) ECSA 2007. LNCS, vol. 4758, pp. 263–270. Springer, Heidelberg (2007)
10. Wood, W.G.: A Practical Example of Applying Attribute-Driven Design (ADD), Version 2.0, Technical Report CMU/SEI-2007-TR-005, Software Engineering Institute (2007)
11. Gamma, E., Helm, R., Johnson, R., Vlissides, J.: Design Patterns: Elements of Reusable Object-Oriented Software. Addison-Wesley, Reading (1995)
12. Harrison, N., Avgeriou, P., Zdun, U.: Architecture Patterns as Mechanisms for Capturing Architectural Decisions. IEEE Software 24(4) (2007)
13. Schmidt, D., Stal, M., Rohnert, H., Buschmann, F.: Pattern-Oriented Software Architecture: Patterns for Concurrent and Distributed Objects. Wiley, Chichester (2000)
14. Avgeriou, P., Zdun, U.: Architectural Patterns Revisited – a Pattern Language. In: 10th European Conference on Pattern Languages of Programs, EuroPLoP (2005)
15. Harrison, N., Avgeriou, P.: Analysis of Architecture Pattern Usage in Legacy System Architecture Documentation. In: 7th Working IEEE/IFIP Conference on Software Architecture (WICSA), Vancouver, February 18-22, pp. 147–156 (2008)
16. Brooks, F.P.: No Silver Bullet—Essence and Accident in Software Engineering. IEEE Computer 20(4), 10–19 (1987)
17. Harrison, N., Avgeriou, P., Zdun, U.: Focus Group Report: Capturing Architectural Knowledge with Architectural Patterns. In: 11th European Conference on Pattern Languages of Programs (EuroPLoP 2006), Irsee, Germany (2006)
18. Hofmeister, C., Kruchten, P., Nord, R.L., Obbink, H., Ran, A., America, P.: Generalizing a Model of Software Architecture Design from Five Industrial Approaches. In: 5th Working IEEE/IFIP Conference on Software Architecture (WICSA), November 06 - 10, pp. 77–88. IEEE Computer Society, Los Alamitos (2005)
19. Aguilera, M.K., Chen, W., Toueg, S.: Using the Heartbeat Failure Detector for Quiescent Reliable Communication and Consensus in Partitionable Networks. Theoretical Computer Science, special issue on distributed algorithms 220(1), 3–30 (1999)
20. Rozanski, N., Woods, E.: Software Systems Architecture. Addison-Wesley, Reading (2005)
21. Booch, G.: Handbook of Software Architecture: Gallery, http://www.handbookofsoftwarearchitecture.com/index.jsp?page=Blog (accessed February 4, 2010)

22. Scott, J., Kazman, R.: Realizing and Refining Architectural Tactics: availability, Technical Report CMU/SEI-2009-TR-006, Software Engineering Institute (2009)
23. Tekinerdogan, B., Sozer, H., Aksit, M.: Software architecture reliability analysis using failure scenarios. J. Syst. Softw. 81(4), 558–575 (2008), http://dx.doi.org/10.1016/j.jss.2007.10.029
24. Bass, L., et al.: Risk Themes Discovered Through Architecture Evaluations, Technical Report CMU/SEI-2006-TR-012, 2006, Software Engineering Institute (2006)
25. Abowd, G., et al.: Recommended Best industrial Practice for Software Architecture Evaluation, Technical Report CMU/SEI-96-TR-025, Software Engineering Institute (1997)
26. Maranzano, J., et al.: Architecture Reviews: Practice and Experience. IEEE Software 22(2), 34–43 (2005)
27. Clements, P., Kazman, R., Klein, M.: Evaluating Software Architectures: Methods and Case Studies. Addison-Wesley, Reading (2002)
28. Gokhale, S.S.: Architecture-Based Software Reliability Analysis: Overview and Limitations. IEEE Trans. Dependable Secur. Comput. 4(1), 32–40 (2007), http://dx.doi.org/10.1109/TDSC.2007.4
29. Im, T., McGregor, J.D.: Toward a reasoning framework for dependability. In: DSN 2008 Workshop on Architecting Dependable Systems (2008)
30. Bass, L., et al.: Reasoning Frameworks, Technical Report CMU/SEI-2005-TR-007, Software Engineering Institute (2005)
31. Bachmann, F., et al.: Designing software architectures to achieve quality attribute requirements. IEE Proceedings 152(4), 153–165 (2005)

A Framework for Flexible and Dependable Service-Oriented Embedded Systems

Shane Brennan, Serena Fritsch, Yu Liu, Ashley Sterritt, Jorge Fox,
Éamonn Linehan, Cormac Driver, René Meier⋆, Vinny Cahill,
William Harrison, and Siobhán Clarke

Lero - The Irish Software Engineering Research Centre
Distributed Systems Group
School of Computer Science and Statistics
Trinity College Dublin, Ireland
{firstname.lastname}@cs.tcd.ie

Abstract. The continued development and deployment of distributed,
real-time embedded systems technologies in recent years has resulted in a
multitude of ecosystems in which service-oriented embedded systems can
now be realised. Such ecosystems are often exposed to dynamic changes
in user requirements, environmental conditions and network topologies
that require service-oriented embedded systems to evolve at runtime.
This paper presents a framework for service-oriented embedded systems that can dynamically adapt to changing conditions at runtime.
Supported by model-driven development techniques, the framework facilitates lightweight dynamic service composition in embedded systems
while predicting the temporal nature of unforeseen service assemblies
and coping with adverse feature interactions following dynamic service
composition. This minimises the complexity of evolving software where
services are deployed dynamically and ultimately, enables flexible and
dependable service-oriented embedded systems.

Keywords: Service-Oriented Architectures, Dynamic Adaptation, Predictable Reconfiguration, Predictable Feature Interaction, Embedded
Systems.

1   Introduction

Technologies for distributed, real-time embedded (DRE) systems have evolved
significantly in recent years in terms of both capability and accessibility. As
a result, sophisticated yet affordable hardware devices and wireless networking
protocols are now widely available and exploitable. These technological advances
enable progression from standalone, static systems to ecosystems comprising cooperative systems that can be dynamically adapted at runtime. For example,
this situation is illustrated in the context of automotive ecosystems by the augmentation of existing in-car systems, such as, collision avoidance and parking

---

⋆ Corresponding author.

A. Casimiro et al. (Eds.): Architecting Dependable Systems VII, LNCS 6420, pp. 123–145, 2010.

assistance with cooperative, dynamic services, such as, forward collision warning, adaptive cruise control and inter-jurisdiction electronic tolling. Such systems may be adapted dynamically when upgraded components become available or, as in the case of the tolling service, when a vehicle enters a new jurisdiction with alternative tolling technology.

While the possibility of dynamic service deployment and evolution in such ecosystems opens up an exciting range of application development opportunities, it also poses a number of complex engineering challenges. These challenges include facilitating timely, lightweight dynamic service composition, predicting the temporal behaviour of unforeseen service assemblies and preventing adverse feature interactions following dynamic service composition. In addition to addressing these core challenges it is also necessary to minimise the complexity of these advanced systems and to support heterogeneous deployment environments without spending a prohibitively expensive amount of effort on platform-specific reimplementation.

In this paper we present a framework for flexible and dependable service-oriented embedded systems. The overarching aim of our framework is to provide for greater flexibility in distributed, real-time embedded systems through support for dynamic service adaptation in a predictable manner. Model-driven and transformation-based development techniques allow for lightweight and re-usable dynamic service composition while predictive timing analysis combined with predictive feature interaction analysis ensures the validity of dynamically composed services.

The remainder of this paper is structured as follows. Section 2 identifies the key challenges that must be addressed in order to make dynamically-adaptable service-oriented embedded systems a reality. Section 3 introduces our framework and outlines how these challenges have been met. Section 4 presents related work and Section 5 concludes this paper.

2   Challenges

This section introduces the main challenges that must be addressed in our vision for flexible and dependable service-oriented embedded computing. The four core challenges are discussed in turn, starting with the wider software engineering challenges that emerge when developing dependable, dynamic service-oriented embedded systems.

2.1   Integration into Heterogeneous Target Environments and Managing Complexity Arising from Crosscutting Concerns

Emerging service-oriented embedded ecosystems compose a wide variety of distributed, real-time embedded systems, technologies and services. Integration into such heterogeneous target environments describes systems and services capable of being deployed on different, though related, platforms in an ecosystem with minimal change requirements. In this sense, Lampert and Koenig [27] define heterogeneous systems as those systems "consisting of multiple microprocessor types and operating systems." In our case of service-oriented embedded ecosystems, this definition is extended to include the complexities of communication media as an important trait in heterogeneity. The notion of platform consists of hardware, including microprocessors, controllers, sensors, and actuators, communication elements, and basic services, such as middleware, that allow software systems to operate on a particular hardware. Platforms represent software or hardware frameworks that allow software to be operational, i.e., to be able to run, such as: hardware architectures, middleware, and component models. Examples of platforms are Java, .Net, operating systems and platforms for mobile devices. Suites of application programming interfaces are also regarded as software platforms. As a result of this heterogeneity, service-oriented embedded ecosystems typically entail a range of deployment platforms that often necessitate multiple platform specific implementations of individual systems even though a specific service is conceptually a single-system solution. Traditional development of platform-specific versions of services is tedious and time consuming, leading to increasing costs and reduced time to market. Novel programming architectures and models that facilitate development and deployment of service-oriented embedded systems specifically in heterogeneous target environments are a key challenge for our vision of flexible and dependable service-oriented embedded computing becoming a reality.

The increasing complexity of distributed, real-time embedded systems impacts on the ease with which easily comprehensible system models can be created using standard system modelling techniques. DRE system models are typically required to represent non-functional Quality of Service (QoS) concerns relating to, for example, time and performance, that have system-wide impact [41]. Such concerns are considered crosscutting because they affect the structure and behaviour of functional concerns and cannot be cleanly decomposed. The presence of crosscutting concerns in a system results in the tangling of behaviours that represent distinct concerns in themselves and may impact negatively on system complexity. It is therefore a further challenge to support the design of modularised system models that promote clarity in design.

2.2 Dynamic Software Architecture Modification

A dynamic software architecture facilitates systems that can react to events at runtime [2]. Dynamic software architectures allow us to build dynamically adaptable systems by supporting the modification of a system's architecture at runtime. Possible modifications include structural adaptations that change the system configuration graph, for example, the creation of new and the deletion of existing components and connectors, as well as functional adaptations where components are replaced. Further, even more challenging changes are those that modify the behaviour of components and ultimately services. Such behavioral adaptation beyond traditional component reconfiguration or replacement typically supported by current approaches to dynamic adaptation represents a further challenge when maintaining system integrity while adapting systems in a timely manner.

In order to preserve system integrity during adaptation, the affected parts of a running system must be brought into a change-safe state before the change is executed [42]. Addressing this issue is more difficult when dealing with unanticipated system changes. Changes must be advertised to the existing system and it must be ensured that the new bindings are correct. Establishing new bindings might not be straightforward for components with new behavior and, as a result, different interfaces. A component's internal state must be preserved and transferred to its replacement. Changes might imply adaptation to multiple components. Ideally, such adaptation is applied in a batch transaction to all components. However, this might not be possible due to system deadlines that must be met and hence, changes might have to be applied in stages instead.

In general, DRE systems inherently have deadlines that must be met, especially when dynamic architecture modifications are being applied and any runtime changes must aim to minimize service disruptions.

2.3   Predictive Timing Analysis of Adaptable Software

In order to meet deadlines in the presence of dynamic adaptation it is essential to accurately predict the execution time of software (and components) based on the implementation of the software and on the characteristics of the target execution environment. An accurate execution time prediction facilitates efficient scheduling of computational tasks, efficient resource utilisation and reduced interference between concurrently executing processes. These non-functional parameters provide important metrics to determine the overall suitability of a piece of software for a given task, and can provide feedback to the dynamic adaptation process at runtime. This challenge we identify as predictable timing analysis.

Software timeliness is difficult to predict since the entire system (of which the software is a constituent part) contributes to the overall execution time value. Current timing analysis methods are either static or dynamic estimation processes. Static timing analysis evaluates the performance of the software in isolation, before deployment, using a combination of formal analysis techniques, mathematical models, hardware simulation and low-level software analysis. Dynamic timing analysis builds a predictive model from historic component execution data. However, both approaches are insufficient for dynamically adaptable systems, since the future software makeup is unknown at deployment time and any historic timing-measurement data is invalidated once an adaptation occurs. A new approach to timing analysis is required that supports dynamically adaptable software.

2.4   Predicting Adverse Feature Interaction in Adaptable Software

Service-oriented embedded systems enable development of applications in which many services collaborate and/or adapt based on contextual changes according to user needs. Feature interaction describes the situation in which the combination of two or more services (or components) that perform correctly in isolation results in unexpected and possibly adverse behaviour. Such adverse feature interaction may result from services exchanging information explicitly, or from implicit service interactions through shared resources. Traditional approaches for detecting and resolving adverse feature interaction rely largely on design-time techniques based on coordinating the service provider's development activities. Services in service-oriented embedded ecosystems are often supplied by a vast range of independent providers, rendering such approaches infeasible, especially when services are adapted dynamically at runtime. A main challenge is therefore to identify, predict and ultimately preclude adverse feature interaction in service-oriented embedded systems that dynamically adapt in a dependable manner.

3   Flexible and Dependable Service-Oriented Embedded Systems

This section presents our framework for flexible and dependable service-oriented embedded systems. The overall framework architecture is introduced followed by a detailed outline, with a special focus on how the challenges identified above have been met, of our model-driven approach to adaptation control and prediction.

In our framework for flexible and dependable service-oriented embedded systems, services are considered as software entities that provide a coordinating role in software systems, regardless of the specifics of their respective implementations. Depending on the level of abstraction of services, they may also be considered as interaction patterns [25] that, nevertheless, represent a notion of coordination. A salient characteristic of services is their ability to integrate with other services and their capability, typically in an integrated form, to represent features of software. As a result, it is fundamental for our framework to support services that can be composed, that these compositions of service components can be deployed and ultimately, adapted dynamically at runtime.

As illustrated in Fig. 1, the proposed framework is layered and separates adaptation management elements both at the functional as well as the deployment level. Our layered development approach supports a Modeling and Composition Layer as well as a Transformation Layer. Some of the previously identified challenges, including identification of crosscutting concerns, are addressed in the Modeling and Composition Layer. These concerns are captured in a platform independent aspect-oriented modeling language that abstracts away much of the platform specific complexity. Designs expressed in this modeling language are transformed through a model-to-model transformation that composes concerns to form a composed platform independent model.

This composed model is then transformed to a platform specific model in the Transformation Layer. In this layer, target platforms are described by platform models, capturing information, such as, bindings to underlying operating system libraries, microprocessor instruction sets, and native data types. This platform model also contains the component model of our framework, which adds support for runtime adaptation to platform specific models from which source code can be synthesised. The resulting system consists of components that can be

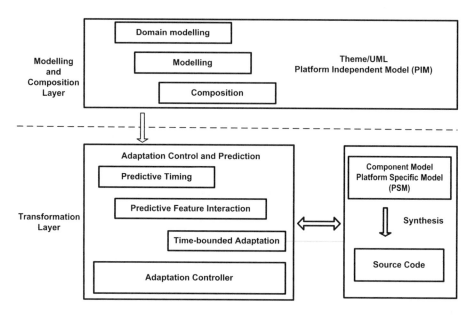

Fig. 1. Layered architecture for flexible and dependable service-oriented embedded systems

dynamically adapted at runtime through Adaptation Control and Prediction. Both, our model-driven approach and our approach to Adaptation Control and Prediction are described in detail below.

3.1   Model-Driven Theme/UML

In order to address the challenge of supporting deployment to heterogeneous target environments we adopt the model-driven engineering paradigm. Model-Driven Engineering (MDE) focuses developer attention on the specification of generic solutions at the model level through languages, such as UML, and facilitates subsequent progression from these generic models to working systems through automatic model-to-model and model-to-text transformations. The MDE principles of specifying abstract solutions and providing automatic transformations have the benefit of addressing issues surrounding platform heterogeneity and code quality [20]. However, the increasing complexity of distributed, real-time embedded systems impacts on the ease with which adequate system models can be created using standard system modelling techniques. Therefore, in order to support the development of complex software for heterogeneous target environments it is useful to be able to modularise distinct functional and non-functional concerns. This is performed at the Modelling and Composition Layer in Fig. 1, providing the input for the service model.

This modularisation is achieved using the aspect-oriented modelling language, Theme/ UML [9]. Theme/UML is an extension to UML that supports fine-grained decomposition and composition of both functional and non-functional concerns, including those that are crosscutting. Separated functional concerns are designed using standard UML to model each concern individually, with Theme/UML composition techniques addressing overlaps. As illustrated in Fig. 2, Model-Driven Theme/UML is provided as a set of tools with a supporting development process that facilitates modularised design and subsequent model composition and synthesis to source code [8,11]. The tool suite and process supports development of software and hardware designs for heterogeneous distributed, real-time embedded platforms by offering synthesis to a range of languages, including functional languages such as C.

The model-driven Theme/UML process contains three phases. The first phase involves system modelling via specification of base concerns, aspect concerns and composition relationships in Theme/UML. This is facilitated by a UML profile for Theme/UML, facilitating the development of Theme/UML models in any UML 2.0 compliant UML editor. The second phase involves composition of the models to produce a composed, platform-independent standard UML view of the system. Composition is achieved using a custom Eclipse plug-in, that takes the XMI produced during the modelling phase as input and processes it based on knowledge of the Theme/UML composition metamodel. The transformation phase includes both model-to-model transformations to support the transition to platform-specific models and a model-to-text transformation to synthesise source code.

In order to assess the applicability of Model-Driven Theme/UML to distributed, real-time embedded system development we conducted a case study involving the design and implementation of an artificial pacemaker [12]. The case study illustrates how Model-Driven Theme/UML facilitates separation of concerns in design, allowing specific requirements to be reasoned about in isolation. This separation of concerns was shown to help preserve key system properties such as comprehensibility, extensibility and reliability. However, the case study revealed a number of limitations of the UML-based modelling approach. Embedded systems are typically realised as a combination of both hardware and software. Whereas UML has proved its suitability to modeling software components, it has limited support for representing hardware concepts such as concurrency, timeliness and the physical properties of continuous functioning embedded systems.

In addition, recent advances in design automation and semiconductor manufacturing have resulted in the potential to build increasingly complex embedded systems that consequently require increasingly complex verification environments. These verification environments are constructed using domain specific languages that contain concepts that cannot be easily represented in standard UML. An analysis of the challenges in modelling these environments using Theme/UML has identified a number of limitations [16]. Specifically, temporal concerns, runtime constrained composition, constraints and type extension can not be easily modelled.

To address this limitation, a metamodel for the e hardware verification language was developed that can be used as part of the existing model-driven

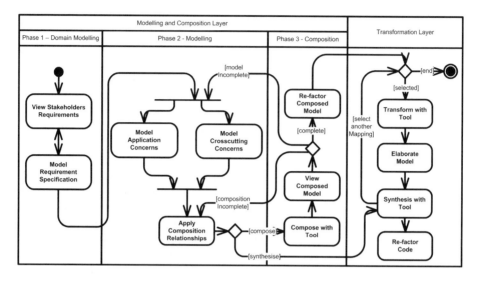

Fig. 2. The Model-Driven Theme/UML process

engineering toolset for embedded systems development [28]. The meta-model is implemented as an extension to UML, incorporating aspect-oriented constructs from Theme/UML and design and verification constructs from for Modeling and Analysis of Real-time and Embedded systems (MARTE) [32] to help engineers organise code in a way that makes it easy to deal with the concerns they care about in a verification environment. A limitation of the current e profile is how close it is to the code level, requiring engineers to first have a good knowledge of the e verification language. The extraction of verification features and constructs that are common to all verification languages into a higher level platform independent model will facilitate the design of verification testbenches at a higher level of abstraction and will eliminate the implementation and verification language specific features that are present in the current e UML profile. Current work is developing this abstract metamodel and extending the model-driven process we have defined for the construction of embedded system software to include verification.

The ability of the toolset to successfully manage complexity of both hardware and software components of distributed real-time embedded systems through the use of models at multiple levels of abstraction allow the challenges associated with dynamically adapting systems at runtime to be isolated to platform specific models that are generated automatically and from which source code can be synthesised.

3.2 Achieving Time-Bounded Adaptation with TimeAdapt

In order to achieve a dynamic software architecture we developed a component model and an adaptation manager that supports runtime adaptation. As shown in Fig. 3 the adaptation mechanism, called TimeAdapt, enables adaptations on the component model. The component model is obtained by transforming the Platform Independent Model (PIM) into a Platform Specific Model (PSM). The running system is then synthesised from the platform specific model. This model transformation is illustrated in Fig. 1.

The component model enables dynamically adaptive systems by supporting the following types of adaptation actions [24]: component service usage adaptation, component service updates and system configuration adaptations.

In our model, components can be dynamically linked to other components that provide the same service. The model can also be used to replace older implementations with new versions that might introduce additional behaviour and interfaces. In the case of component failure or removal, existing linked components are notified and references are updated as appropriate. During periods of adaptation, updated estimates of the execution time behaviour of the component model are forecast using an embedded predictive timing model, known as TimePredict.

For minimal service disruption during adaptations, changes to components are executed locally when possible. The likely effect these proposed adaptations will have on timing behaviour are first generated using TimePredict, and then evaluated by the Adaptation Controller based on the policies of the Reconfiguration Selection. Should the timeliness of the software be predicted to degrade sufficiently, the Adaptation Controller can decline or roll-back the adaptation.

The integrity of the system in view of the integrity of runtime changes is ensured by means of a lock-based approach. The lock-based approach guarantees that no ongoing communication between components can occur while adaptations are underway. In addition, the run-time adaptation logic is separated from the business logic so that a component developer can be oblivious to the complexity of the actual execution of a runtime change. This reduction in complexity follows from our model-driven approach. Equally important, a scheduler for runtime change operations ensures the timeliness of the underlying application. Adaptations are performed by means of reconfiguration techniques. Runtime changes are allocated according to their relative priorities. The scheduler also determines whether a given run-time adaptation can be executed within the specified time bound, following the results from the predictive timing device. And finally the Adaptation Controller coordinates with Feature Predict to avoid introducing changes that might alter systems dependability. After verifying both timing and feature interaction issues the Adaptation Controller requests TimeAdapt to implement the required changes in the system.

Although dynamic reconfiguration does not require a system shut down, it does have a certain impact on the running of a system. Service-based embedded systems impose additional constraints on dynamic software reconfiguration due to their need to react to many events, such as changes the operating status, user commands, and messages from other systems. These events typically compete with an ongoing dynamic reconfiguration process. As a result, the demands on the timeliness of such events impact the timeliness requirements of the reconfiguration process. In particular, the completion of a reconfiguration process might

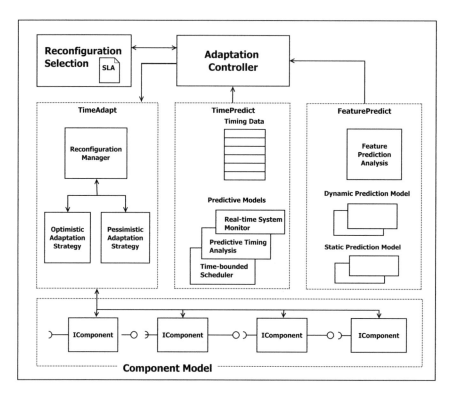

Fig. 3. Adaptation control and prediction

not always be feasible due to time constraints imposed by the arrival of events. TimeAdapt is a novel time-adaptive reconfiguration model for service-based embedded systems. Our time-adaptive reconfiguration model allows the dynamic adaptation of an ongoing reconfiguration sequence to dynamic time bounds, imposed by events occurring during adaptation. TimeAdapt dynamically adapts an ongoing reconfiguration to the time deadline of an occurring event by dynamically determining how many of the remaining reconfiguration actions can be executed within this time bound. This ensures that arriving events are processed appropriately and concurrently with an ongoing reconfiguration. TimeAdapt proposes adaptation execution within soft time bounds that is inspired by job scheduling in priority-driven real-time systems, so called deadline-aware scheduling. Depending on the current system configuration, a given event deadline and a remaining reconfiguration sequence, TimeAdapt's scheduling mechanism determines how much of the adaptation, i.e., the reconfiguration actions, can be scheduled and executed within a given deadline. This implies that the overall reconfiguration itself may be executed only partially to meet a given response deadline.

To ensure that structural dependency relationships between components are maintained in the presence of partially executed reconfigurations, TimeAdapt requires the partitioning of the reconfiguration sequence into sub-sequences that need to be executed atomically and sub-sequences that are safe to be interrupted. This partitioning starts with the reconfiguration specification. Such specifications can be manually specified or generated from the Modelling and Composition Layer. Based on the dependency relationships of the underlying configuration, the reconfiguration actions in this specification are partitioned into sub-sequences. Reconfigurations are conceived as soft real-time tasks with an associated release time and a time-bound or soft deadline. The overall worst-case execution time of a given reconfiguration sequence is obtained as the sum of all worst-case times of its contained reconfiguration actions. At reconfiguration runtime, the scheduling mechanism decides, whether to schedule the next reconfiguration action or to process an occurring event, based on the estimated duration of a reconfiguration sequence. If scheduled for execution, the sub-sequence is executed as a non-preemptive real-time task with the highest priority in the system. This ensures that sub-sequences are executed atomically and cannot be interrupted by other (system) tasks.

Our reconfiguration model has been designed to support systems with soft real-time requirements for their event deadlines, where missed deadlines are undesirable but tolerable. The ratio of deadlines met depends on the nature of the event deadline, as well as on the execution times of sub-sequences. Shorter deadlines are, naturally, more likely to be missed, as TimeAdapt enforces the completion of ongoing sub-sequences to ensure valid and safe system configurations.

Fig. 4(a) illustrates the basic principle of TimeAdapt by means of a reconfiguration sequence comprised of three reconfiguration sub-sequences, or actions a_1, a_2, a_3, which are to be executed sequentially. a_1 takes 2 time units to execute, whereas a_2, and a_3 take 1 time unit to execute. Fig. 4(a), 4(b), 4(c), 4(d), and 4(e) illustrate our approach when an event e occurs during an ongoing reconfiguration. In Fig. 4(b), 4(c), and 4(d), indicated by an arrow, the event occurs before any reconfiguration action is executed, whereas in Fig. 4(e) the event occurs during the execution of reconfiguration action a_1. In Fig. 4(b) the given event processing deadline t_d (latest start time) is longer than the overall reconfiguration sequence execution time, and hence all actions can be executed in sequence and without re-scheduling. In Fig. 4(c) t_d can fit the first reconfiguration action within its deadline. However, the remaining reconfiguration actions are only executed, after the event has been processed. In Fig. 4(d), the given deadline td is so short that no reconfiguration action fits the deadline. Hence, the event is immediately processed and the reconfiguration actions are executed after the event has been processed. Finally, Fig. 4(e) illustrates a scenario where a short event deadline conflicts with an ongoing reconfiguration action resulting in the event being processed after its deadline has passed.

The initial results of experiments evaluating TimeAdapt based on reconfiguration scenarios deployed on Java SunSpots embedded platforms are promising. These results (which we expect to publish in more detail shortly) show that

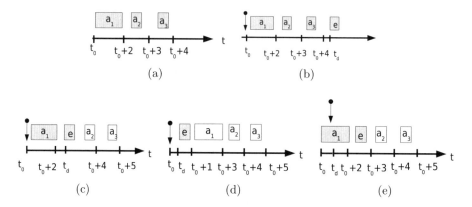

Fig. 4. The TimeAdapt reconfiguration model

TimeAdapt achieves a ratio of deadlines met that is 31% to 90% higher (depending on deadlines and event arrival rates) compared to reconfiguration approaches that do not consider incoming events. Furthermore, they demonstrate that even in the presence of arriving events, our reconfiguration model ensures the completion of a reconfiguration, in contrast to approaches that suffer from possible reconfiguration starvation where reconfiguration completion may be delayed indefinitely due to continuously arriving events.

TimeAdapt builds upon a component model that is based on the UML 2.0 architecture metamodel. Primitive components can be seen as blackboxes, providing and requiring services through their interfaces and containing executable code. Connectors are explicit entities that model the connections between two primitive components. They can be dynamically changed during runtime. Composite components contain other components, either primitive or composite, and hence, lead to a hierarchy of components. Dynamic reconfiguration actions are executed on composite components if they implement a reconfiguration interface. This interface defines the methods to add, remove and replace (sub-components) and to change bindings. The composite component takes care of the correct and oblivious execution of the reconfiguration action. For example, in case of a replace reconfiguration action, the component will be replaced and all connections to this component will be updated accordingly.

3.3   Predicting Timeliness in a Running Assembly with TimePredict

We use a statistical-based predictive model to support run-time timing analysis of dynamically reconfigurable software. Outlined in Fig. 3, TimePredict adjusts the scope of its evaluation, and the confidence of its estimates, based on the amount of time accorded to it during the adaptation cycle. The execution time behaviour of the software, especially, immediately after a functional adaptation, provides a qualitative metric to measure the effect of adapations on software behaviour.

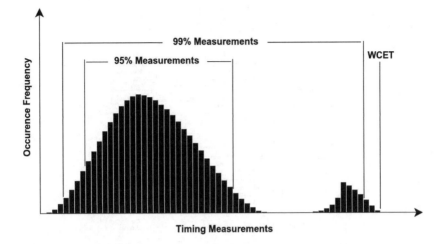

Fig. 5. A hypothetical distribution of timing values with prediction bounds

The acceptable operational limits of the software can be explored, allowing developers to build software capable of meeting dynamic QoS requirements in a changeable operating context. Adaptations, when they occur, may be required to complete quickly, and return the system to full working order within a given time bound. Since timing analysis can be part of the post-adaptation process or even concurrent with an adaptation process, it seems reasonable that any calculations to refresh the predicted timing behaviour should also adhere to a completion deadline.

Software execution times are typically influenced by external factors, such as, user inputs, processor caching and look-ahead, internal systems interrupts, communications latencies, and the execution history of the software at a particular instant. These influences result in small-scale variation within the execution times of even the most basic software. Fig. 5 illustrates an example of the typical frequency distribution of execution times, often with one or more 'peaks' caused by different execution paths and their attendant timing behaviours. The level of confidence in predicting the execution time behaviour of software is therefore providing ranges within which the next execution time is likely to fall. Fig. 5 shows the 95% and 99% bounds, i.e., the ranges where respectively 95% and 99% of the previously observed timing measurements have been observed. The absolute Worst-Case Execution Time (WCET) is another metric that is difficult to predict empirically, since it rarely (or never) occurs in practice. WCET estimation focuses on providing an over pessimistic time-bound to capture this value.

TimePredict provides a time-bounded estimate, that can be executed concurrently, or immediately following a functional adaptation. Using a statistical approach, we provide average-case and worst-case execution time bounds, each with an associated statistical level of confidence. This model, as part of

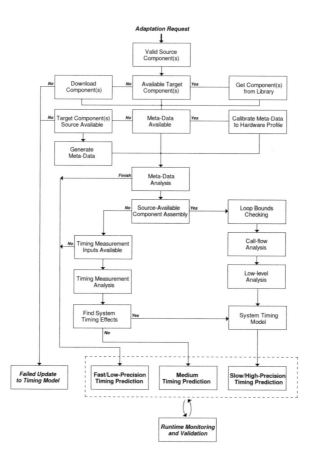

Fig. 6. Flowchart showing incremental timing analysis process

predictive timing, informs the Adaptation Controller of the likely execution time behaviour of proposed adaptations. Where available, timing meta-data describing the behaviour of individual component is used as input into the predictive process, reducing the effort required to establish the likely timing behaviour, and the time required to produce an updated estimate.

Timing meta-data, essentially providing a summary of previously observed execution time measurements for a particular component, is first verified within the predictive model, using a measurement-based approach. Where there is disagreement, for example, where the metadata was generated under a different system or load conditions, our predictive model corrects the estimate to illlustrate the true run-time behaviour of the software. Using a combination of linear regression modelling (average-case) and extreme-value models (worst-case) two bounded timing estimates can be produced, describing the central tendency of the software execution time, and likely extreme variation in timing behaviour respectively.

The next step is to incorporate information about the current system-level operating parameters as inputs into a more detailed predictive timing model. We evaluate the effects of system load, resource consumption levels, and interrupts on the timing behaviour of software, with a view towards providing a point estimate of future 'interference' to timing behaviour based on the currently prevailing operating conditions. Static system descriptors, such as, OS type, memory/disc size, CPU speed and swap size, provide a profile by which a system can be identified. Dynamic descriptors, such as, system loads, resource consumption levels, process queue, size etc., augment this profile with live performance metrics. We construct a series of system profiles, each with a well-described (statistical) relationship between workload levels and timing performance, for a number of systems. These profiles are used as reference guides within the predictive timing model, to catalogue the risk of disturbance to software timing behaviour due to abnormal system loads. This information is used to evaluate timing constraints as well as the impact of changes to systems performance. Our approach incorporates system profiles, (component) timing metadata, and measurement based timing estimation into an adaptive timing model, i.e., a model that can modify its performance to meet criteria, such as deadlines, without adversely compromising the accuracy of its timing predictions. This is achieved using incremental analysis levels, ranging from quick estimates, through to more thorough (re)evaluation of the software as illustrated in Fig. 6.

This incremental timing analysis allows a trade-off between the precision of the expected estimate with the time available in which to generate the (new) estimate after an adaptation occurs in the software. By increasing or decreasing the number of data points making up the timing estimate, we can change the execution time of the predictive method itself, albeit with a change in the level of confidence associated with the estimate.

As our approach utilizes a statistical model to predict software timeliness, an estimate is generated from a statistical model of the observed timing behaviour of the software during execution. Since estimates are inferred from observational data, rather than from an exhaustive formal analysis techniques, the probability of the estimate being inaccurate, i.e., the estimated timing bounds being violated, are closely related to the goodness of fit of the statistical model to the data, the likely cost of incorrectly estimating the execution time, and the acceptable levels of pessimism within the timing estimate. An ideal timing estimate would be always correct, and provide timing bounds that are sufficient to always encapsulate the execution time of the software, and no more.

However, in real-world situations, we must find a balance between accepting the (very small) possibility of being in error occasionally, and providing meaningful non-pessimistic timing estimates. When providing a statistical guarantee of worst-case timeliness, we can only say that, on average, the worst-case value we describe will not be exceeded at more than the specified rate. For example, a WCET bound with a stated 99% level of confidence would be exceeded, on average, 1 time in every 100 measurements. Both Hansen [18] and Edgar [13] apply similar statistical methods to the estimation of their worst-case execution time performance of non-adaptive real-time systems, and provide timing bounds with a probability not exceeding 10^{-5}. Since dynamically adaptable systems are not generally required to implement hard real-time guarantees, we have adopted a slightly lower statistical confidence of 10^{-4} in the realisation of our approach. Higher values are possible, but require a greater number of timing measurements, and result in more pessimistic WCET bounds.

Run-time software adaptation allows contingency behaviours to be added as required, rather than the system being deployed encumbered with multiple, infrequently used behaviours. On resource-constrained devices, this allows the functionality to be optimized at run-time for the prevailing operating conditions, as well as better adjusting the software to handle previously unanticipated conditions [22]. In contrast to statically-defined software, dynamically adaptable systems provide a flexible framework in which developers can create malleable code capable of contending with, and exploiting, highly variable operating environments [37]. However, run-time adaptations change the timing behaviour of the software, and introduce uncertainties about timeliness that creates a difficulty statically estimating the worst-case performance of a dynamic system. This means that any statically produced WCET bounds, i.e., those generated offline, are automatically nullified when an adaptation occurs. Should a sufficient number of potential adaptations exist, the set of all configurations for the software would be too large to test exhaustively. To maintain a valid WCET bound, the timing analysis must be performed at run-time, whenever a functional adaptation is triggered.

Multiple different configurations within sets of automotive software components are already being used within the automotive industry [40]. However, providing run-time flexibility to these software configurations once deployed to the target hardware environment will allow a greater scope for functional updates, performance optimizations, and a more cost-efficient means of resolving unexpected software errors. Our previous work predicting the timeliness of similar volatile software systems [6], has shown that highly accurate timing estimates can be generated at run-time for software systems liable to undergo unanticipated run-time software adaptation.

3.4   Predicting Interaction in Dynamic Systems with FeaturePredict

As part of our work towards providing a feature interaction model that can detect and resolve adverse feature interactions dynamically, we have categorised possible causes for adverse feature interactions in embedded service-oriented systems. This has resulted in a classification of feature interaction that captures types of interaction, channels of interaction and user needs [29]. Types of interaction describe how services interact with each other based on their context. Channels of interaction are concerned with identifying the pathway whereby services may interfere with each other. User needs describe behaviour constraints and QoS constraints of a system. Our classification is part of the process of specifying points of interactions, so that a feature interaction model capturing abstractions of resources and user constraints can be built at design time, and then be used to enable detection and resolution of feature interaction at runtime.

We argue that FeaturePredict, a hybrid approach for addressing adverse feature interaction, is promising in service-oriented embedded systems as it combines design-time analysis of feature interaction with runtime detection and resolution techniques. Such an approach is based on a prediction model capturing static and dynamic feature interaction constraints that can then be used to determine appropriate adaptation strategies when deploying services at runtime. Our prediction model includes resource-aware contracts [30] to address feature interactions arising from resource contention. Systems are conceptually decomposed into a collection of interconnected software components and the resource requirements of individual components are expressed in their respective resource-aware contracts. Resource-aware contracts are considered an abstract part of components that can be automatically processed during adaptation time. Resource-aware contracts are used to describe the resource usage patterns of components and component assemblies, as well as inherent constraints of system resources. Adverse feature interaction can be predicted for possible compositions of software components when resource usage patterns of different components compromise each other or when runtime resource constraints are violated.

The result of such feature interaction analysis can then be used by the Adaptation Controller (in combination with results from TimePredict) to determine appropriate adaptation strategies when requesting TimeAdapt to deploy services at runtime. Depending on the adaptation policies of the Reconfiguration Selection, such strategies might prevent the deployment of a low priority service, if its combination with a higher priority service is likely to cause adverse feature interaction, or might result in the replacement of a service with a preferred service if their combination causes undesired behaviour.

4   Related Work

Following the outline of sections 2 and 3, the related work presented in this section is organised according to the previously identified main challenges.

4.1   Design in Modularisation and MDE

There are a number of existing approaches to advanced modularisation in design. Composition Directives [34] is an approach implemented in Kermeta called Kompose [15] that supports composition of both aspect and base UML models. The Atlas Model Weaver (AMW)[1] is a tool based on the Eclipse Modelling Framework that facilitates the creation of links between models [11]. The Motorola WEAVR [10] is a commercial add-in to the Telelogic TAU tool[2], designed for use in telecoms systems engineering, that supports aspect-oriented extensions

---

[1] http://www.eclipse.org/gmt/amw
[2] http://www.telelogic.com

to state machines. XWeave is a model weaver that supports composition of different architectural viewpoints i.e., the weaver facilitates software product-line engineering by allowing for variable parts of architectural models to be woven according to a specific product configuration [17]. Modelling Aspects Using a Transformation Approach (MATA) [21] is a UML aspect-oriented modelling tool that uses graph transformations to specify and compose aspects. Finally, Klein et al. [23] suggest an approach for weaving multiple behavioural aspects using sequence diagrams. The overriding difference between our approach involving Theme/UML and the other approaches surveyed is our support for commonly used/standard tools and techniques and our focus on supporting embedded platforms. Our tool, Model-Driven Theme/UML, purposely supports standard tools and formats in order to ease adoption of our systematic, integrated approach to model-driven separation of concerns in DRE systems.

4.2   Dynamic Reconfiguration of Real-Time Systems

There are application-specific approaches targeting reconfigurable real-time control systems, that support the execution of compositional adaptations in a timely manner, such as the Port-based Object approach [39] or the dynamic reconfiguration on top of the OSA+ middleware platform [36].

Port-based objects are highly independent concurrent components that interact only indirectly with each other via state variables stored in global and local tables. Adaptations are triggered by policies and include the start and shutdown of components. The Osa+ middleware provides an adaptation approach for the dynamic replacement and migration of services. The approach provides a trade-off between reconfiguration and blackout time by using different state transfer protocols. Once the adaptation fits within the given blackout time, it is atomically executed.

All the above approaches fall into the category of transactional reconfiguration execution models, as they either complete a reconfiguration or abort its effects. Reconfigurations can be executed in a time-bounded manner, however, none of the approaches supports a timely pre-emption of the adaptation to incoming events.

Pre-emptive reconfiguration execution models can directly react to incoming events, coinciding with an ongoing reconfiguration. Examples of such systems are Mitchell's reconfiguration model that targets multimedia components [31] or Li's adaptation model [43] that targets more general applications that follow a reconfigurable data flow system model. The downside of these approaches is that they constrain adaptations to either a very specific application scenario or consider only stateless system components.

4.3   Time-Bounded Reconfiguration

Our time-predictive model for adaptive systems builds upon work done within statistical timing analysis [18,13,26] as well as traditional WCET methods, such as aiT [1] and Bound-T [5]. We leverage these approaches as well as other timing analysis methods, to provide a method of evaluating software timeliness at run-time, and to predict the likely impact of functional adaptations on timing behaviour. Current static timing analysis approaches, typically, directly examine the software source code, and create timing estimates by simulating individual instructions on a detailed model of the processor. These approaches require lengthy periods of off-line analysis, Souyris et al. [38] provide an example of an avionics software task that requires upwards of 12 hours of analysis to produce a timing estimate. This, coupled with the requirement for detailed models of the underlying hardware make static approaches entirely unsuitable for dynamically adaptable software running on more advanced general-purpose chipsets.

Hansen et al.[18] and Edgar [13] apply extreme value modelling techniques to the problem of estimating the worst-case execution time behaviour of software. However, their models require a large amount of statically-generated trace data as input before a representative model of software timeliness can be built. Kumar et al. [26] apply statistical models to a call-flow representation of a soft-real time application to estimate the timing variability inherent in the software. They do not extend their discussion towards dynamically adaptable software systems, since some static call-flow analysis is required. Likewise, the WCET tools aiT [1] and Bound-T [5] do not consider dynamically adaptable software, but focus instead on statically implemented embedded software, typically, operating on reduced chipsets such as the ARM7 and ARM9.

Some frameworks, such as Dynamic AspectJ [3], facilitate run-time dynamic adaptation, in this case through dynamic aspect weaving, but do not consider the timing implications of changes made to the software. Other non-aspect component-based software frameworks, such as PACC/PECT [19] provide time-predictable software, but refrain from dynamic adaptation in order to promote predictability within the code.

Sharma et al. [37] describe a system, called QuO, to allow parameter adaptation within component-based systems by modifying the execution flow through specific components. Based on changing QoS requirements, they can adjust the behaviour of the software, but not introduce new behaviours to the systems. Their approach does not support unanticipated adaptation, nor is there any recourse to timing analysis to inform the adaptation process. The total set of software behaviour remains the same once the system is deployed, and no new functionality can be added at runtime.

Other proposals to time-bounded reconfiguration include Rasche and Polze, who describe a framework for supporting runtime reconfiguration of component-based real-time software [33]. Their approach uses a transaction-based consistency mechanism [42] and schedules reconfiguration commands in free CPU slots. However, the approach has some drawbacks, mainly due to the consistency mechanism used. For example, upper bounds for all component interaction times must be given, which assumes a lot of knowledge from the component developer side. Moreover, a service-oriented approach for dynamic software reconfiguration on top of the OSA+ middleware is presented by Brinkschulte et.al. [7]. Possible reconfiguration actions are rather coarse-grained as they deal with the replacement or movement of a given service. The approach provides a trade-off between reconfiguration and blackout time by using different state transfer protocols. However, as the reconfiguration job can be pre-empted, it cannot be guaranteed to be executed within a specific time bound.

4.4   Feature-Consistent Reconfiguration

Amy and Kedar [14] propose to model features as formulas in Linear Temporal Logic (LTL), and then use model checking to identify pairs of specification formulas that are contradictory with system axioms. Calder and Miller [8] use Promela to model base call services and features as communicating finite state automata, and use LTL to specify the properties for both the base service and the added features. Interactions are detected by violation of properties with the model checker SPIN. These two approaches above focus on detecting interaction at design time, and resolution typically involves changing feature specification. However, resolution at design time is not always possible. Reiff-Marganiec [35] proposes an approach to feature interaction at runtime for evolving telecommunication systems. His approach assumes that features are black boxes that receive messages and might respond with messages. Features are embedded in transactional cocoons. This allows experimenting at runtime with different sequences of possible messages. Resolution of interaction is to find a conflict free path in the solution space, which consists of all possible interleaved executions of features. However, this approach is highly dependent upon transactional support for the underlying system. With richer information about features being available, resolution of interaction at design time would be preferable. Many runtime approaches do not consider resource as a potential source of adverse feature interaction. Bisbal and Cheng [4] first proposed to shift the focus of research from behavioural conflicts to resource conflicts. This approach uses relationships of features and resources to define the resource consumption of individual features, and describes the resource constraints of a set of composed features through their objectives.

5   Conclusion

This paper has identified and introduced key challenges in the development of flexible and dependable systems in highly distributed environments. Following from this, we have presented our framework for achieving a service-oriented approach to the design and deployment of flexible and dependable embedded systems that copes with these challenges. The framework enables service-oriented embedded systems to evolve at runtime and thereby to cater for dynamic changes in user requirements, environmental conditions and network topologies to which they are often exposed. The need for a comprehensive service engineering approach supporting the creation of such systems has been addressed by our model-driven development techniques and tools for systematically designing, analysing, and deploying dynamically composed services. Systems have to be flexible in order to achieve dynamic adaptation and dependable in terms of assuring timeliness at runtime and especially, while achieving changes in the composite. Our dynamic software architecture can dynamically link components to other components or dynamically replace deployed components with newer versions. Systems evolve while preserving service integrity and with minimal service disruption during runtime changes. The need to strengthen the dependability of systems has been addressed by techniques for time-bounded and feature-consistent dynamic adaptation based on predicting the temporal nature of unforeseen service assemblies and on predicting adverse feature interactions of composites.

Acknowledgements. This work was supported, in part, by Science Foundation Ireland grant 03/CE2/1303_1 to Lero - the Irish Software Engineering Research Centre (www.lero.ie).

References

1. aiT. AbsInt: aiT tool homepage (2010), http://www.absint.com/ait/
2. Allen, R., Douence, R., Garlan, D.: Specifying and analyzing dynamic software architectures. In: Astesiano, E. (ed.) ETAPS 1998 and FASE 1998. LNCS, vol. 1382, p. 21. Springer, Heidelberg (1998)
3. Assaf, A., Noyé, J.: Dynamic AspectJ. In: Proceedings of the 2008 symposium on Dynamic Languages (DLS 2008), pp. 1–12 (2008)
4. Bisbal, J., Cheng, B.H.C.: Resource-based approach to feature interaction in adaptive software. In. In: Proceedings of the 1st ACM SIGSOFT Workshop on Self-managed Systems, WOSS 2004, pp. 23–27. ACM, New York (2004)
5. Tidorum, B.-T.: Bound-T tool homepage (2009), http://www.tidorum.fi/bound-t
6. Brennan, S., Cahill, V., Clarke, S.: Applying non-constant volatility analysis methods to software timeliness. In: Proceedings of the 12th Euromicro Conference on Real-Time Systems, Work-in-progress Session (2009)
7. Brinkschulte, U., Schneider, E., Picioroaga, F.: Dynamic real-time reconfiguration in distributed systems: Timing issues and solutions. In: ISORC 2005: Proceedings of the Eighth IEEE International Symposium on Object-Oriented Real-Time Distributed Computing, ISORC 2005 (2005)
8. Calder, M., Miller, A.: Using SPIN for feature interaction analysis - A case study. In: Dwyer, M.B. (ed.) SPIN 2001. LNCS, vol. 2057, pp. 143–162. Springer, Heidelberg (2001)
9. Carton, A., Driver, C., Jackson, A., Clarke, S.: Model-driven Theme/UML. Transactions on Aspect-Oriented Software Development, 428–432 (2009)
10. Cottenier, T.: The motorola weavr: Model weaving in a large industrial context. In: Proceedings of the International Conference on Aspect Oriented Software Development, Industry Track (2006)
11. Didonet Del Fabro, M., Bézivin, J., Jouault, F., Breton, E., Gueltas, G.: AMW: a generic model weaver. Journées sur l'Ingénierie Dirigée par les Modèles (IDM 2005), 105–114 (2005), 2-7261-1284-6
12. Driver, C., Reilly, S., Linehan, E., Cahill, V., Clarke, S.: Managing embedded systems complexity with aspect-oriented model-driven engineering. ACM Transactions on Embedded Computing Systems (TECS) (to appear, 2010)
13. Edgar, S.: Estimation of worst-case execution time using statistical analysis, PhD thesis. PhD thesis, Department of Computer Science, University of York (2002)

14. Felty, A.P., Namjoshi, K.S.: Feature specification and automated conflict detection. ACM Transactions on Software Engineering and Methodology 12(1), 3–27 (2003)

15. France, R., Fleurey, F., Reddy, R., Baudry, B., Ghosh, S.: Providing support for model composition in metamodels. In: Proceedings of the 11th IEEE International Enterprise Distributed Object Computing Conference, EDOC 2007, Washington, DC, USA, p. 253. IEEE Computer Society, Los Alamitos (2007)

16. Galpin, D., Driver, C., Clarke, S.: Modelling hardware verification concerns specified in the e language: An experience report. In: Proceedings of the International Conference on Aspect-Oriented Software Development (AOSD), Industry Track, pp. 207–212 (2009)

17. Groher, I., Voelter, M.: XWeave: models and aspects in concert. In: Proceedings of the 10th International Workshop on Aspect-Oriented Modeling, AOM 2007, pp. 35–40. ACM Press, New York (2007)

18. Hansen, J., Hissam, S., Moreno, G.: Statistical-Based WCET Estimation and Validation. In: 9th International Workshop on Worst-Case Execution Time Analysis (WCET 2009), pp. 123–133 (2009)

19. Hissam, S., Ivers, J.: Prediction-Enabled Component Technology (PECT) Infrastructure: A Rough Sketch. Technical Report CMU/SEI-2002-TN-033, Software Engineering Institute, Carnegie-Mellon University (2002)

20. Hovsepyan, A., Baelen, S.V., Vanhooff, B., Joosen, W., Berbers, Y.: Key Research Challenges for Successfully Applying MDD Within Real-Time Embedded Software Development. In: Vassiliadis, S., Wong, S., Hämäläinen, T.D. (eds.) SAMOS 2006. LNCS, vol. 4017, pp. 49–58. Springer, Heidelberg (2006)

21. Jayaraman, P.K., Whittle, J., Elkhodary, A.M., Gomaa, H.: Model composition in product lines and feature interaction detection using critical pair analysis. In: Engels, G., Opdyke, B., Schmidt, D.C., Weil, F. (eds.) MODELS 2007. LNCS, vol. 4735, pp. 151–165. Springer, Heidelberg (2007)

22. Kim, H.-C., Choi, H.-J., Ko, I.-Y.: An Architectural Model to Support Adaptive Software Systems for Sensor Networks. In: Proceedings of the 11th Asia-Pacific Software Engineering Conference (APSEC 2004), pp. 670–677 (2004)

23. Klein, J., Fleurey, F., Jézéquel, J.M.: Weaving multiple aspects in sequence diagrams. In: Rashid, A., Aksit, M. (eds.) Transactions on AOSD III. LNCS, vol. 4620, pp. 167–199. Springer, Heidelberg (2007)

24. Klus, H., Niebuhr, D., Rausch, A.: A component model for dynamic adaptive systems. In: International Workshop on Engineering of Software Services for Pervasive Environments, ESSPE 2007, pp. 21–28. ACM, New York (2007)

25. Krüger, I., Mathew, R.: Systematic development and exploration of service-oriented software architectures. In: Proceedings of Fourth Working IEEE/IFIP Conference on Software Architecture, WICSA 2004. (June 12-15), pp. 177–187 (2004)

26. Kumar, T., Cledat, R., Sreeram, J., Pande, S.: Statistically Analyzing Execution Variance for Soft Real-Time Applications. In: 6th Joint Meeting of the European Software Engineering Conference and the ACM SIGSOFT Symposium (ESEC/FSE 2007), pp. 529–532 (2007)

27. Lampert, A., Koenig, S.: Configuration management in a heterogeneous target environment. In: Proceedings of Third Israel Conference on Computer Systems and Software Engineering, June 6-7, pp. 148–158 (1988)

28. Linehan, E., Clarke, S.: Managing hardware verification complexity with aspect-oriented model-driven engineering. In: Proceedings of the 1st Workshop on Model Based Engineering for Embedded Systems Design (M-BED), pp. 54–60 (2010)

29. Liu, Y., Meier, R.: Feature Interaction in Pervasive Computing Systems. Electronic Communications of the EASST Journal 11, 1–7 (2008)

30. Liu, Y., Meier, R.: Resource-aware contracts for addressing feature interaction in dynamic adaptive systems. In: Proceedings of the 2009 Fifth International Conference on Autonomic and Autonomous Systems, ICAS 2009, Washington, DC, USA, pp. 346–350. IEEE Computer Society, Los Alamitos (2009)
31. Mitchell, S., Naguib, H., Coulouris, G., Kindberg, T.: Dynamically reconfiguring multimedia components: a model-based approach. In: Proceedings of the 8th ACM SIGOPS European workshop on Support for composing distributed applications, EW 1998, pp. 40–47. ACM, New York (1998)
32. I.Object Management Group. Marte specification beta 2 2008), http://www.omgmarte.org/Documents/Specifications/08-06-09.pdf
33. Rasche, A., Polze, A.: Dynamic reconfiguration of component-based real-time software. In: Proceedings of the 10th IEEE International Workshop on Object-Oriented Real-Time Dependable Systems, WORDS 2005 (2005)
34. Reddy, Y.R., Ghosh, S., France, R.B., Straw, G., Bieman, J.M., McEachen, N., Song, E., Georg, G.: Directives for Composing Aspect-Oriented Design Class Models. pp. 75–105 (2006)
35. Reiff-Marganiec, S.: Runtime Resolution of Feature Interactions in Evolving Telecommunications Systems. PhD thesis, University of Glasgow (2002)
36. Schneider, E., Picioroagă, F., Brinkschulte, U.: Dynamic reconfiguration through osa+, a real-time middleware. In: Proceedings of the 1st International Doctoral Symposium on Middleware, DSM 2004, pp. 319–323. ACM, New York (2004)
37. Sharma, P.K., Loyall, J.P., Heineman, G.T., Schantz, R.E., Shapiro, R., Duzan, G.: Component-Based Dynamic QoS Adaptations in Distributed Real-Time and Embedded Systems. In: International Symposium on Distributed Objects and Applications, DOA (2004)
38. Souyris, J., Pavec, E.L., Himbert, G., Jégu, V., Borios, G.: Computing the worst case execution time of an avionics program by abstract interpretation. In: Proceedings of the 5th Intl Workshop on Worst-Case Execution Time Analysis (WCET 2005), pp. 21–24 (2005)
39. Stewart, D., Volpe, R., Khosla, P.: Design of dynamically reconfigurable real-time software using port-based objects. IEEE Trans. Softw. Eng. 23(12), 759–776 (1997)
40. Thiel, S., Hein, A.: Modeling and using product line variability in automotive systems. IEEE Software 19, 66–72 (2002)
41. Wehrmeister, M.A., Freitas, E.P., Pereira, C.E., Wagner, F.R.: An Aspect-Oriented Approach for Dealing with Non-Functional Requirements in a Model-Driven Development of Distributed Embedded Real-Time Systems. In: Proceedings of the 10th IEEE International Symposium on Object and Component-Oriented Real-Time Distributed Computing SORC 007, Washington, DC, USA, pp. 428–432. IEEE Computer Society, Los Alamitos (2007)
42. Wermelinger, M.: A hierarchic architecture model for dynamic reconfiguration. In: Proceedings of the Second International Workshop on Software Engineering for Parallel and Distributed Systems, pp. 243–254. IEEE Computer Society, Los Alamitos (1997)
43. Zhao, Z., Li, W.: Influence control for dynamic reconfiguration. In: Australian Software Engineering Conference, pp. 59–70 (2007)

Architecting Robustness and Timeliness in a New Generation of Aerospace Systems⋆

José Rufino, João Craveiro, and Paulo Verissimo

University of Lisbon, Faculty of Sciences, LaSIGE
Campo Grande, 1749-016 Lisboa, Portugal
ruf@di.fc.ul.pt, jcraveiro@lasige.di.fc.ul.pt, pjv@di.fc.ul.pt

Abstract. Aerospace systems have strict dependability and real-time requirements, as well as a need for flexible resource reallocation and reduced size, weight and power consumption. To cope with these issues, while still maintaining safety and fault containment properties, temporal and spatial partitioning (TSP) principles are employed. In a TSP system, the various onboard functions (avionics, payload) are integrated in a shared computing platform, however being logically separated into partitions. Robust temporal and spatial partitioning means that partitions do not mutually interfere in terms of fulfilment of real-time and addressing space encapsulation requirements. This chapter describes in detail the foundations of an architecture for robust TSP aiming a new generation of spaceborne systems, including advanced dependability and timeliness adaptation control mechanisms. A formal system model which allows verification of integrator-defined system parameters is defined, and a prototype implementation demonstrating the current state of the art is presented.

1 Introduction

Aerospace systems, namely the onboard computing infrastructure, have strict requirements with respect to dependability and real-time, as well as a need for flexible resource reallocation and reduction of size, weight and power consumption (SWaP). A typical spacecraft onboard computer has to host a set of avionics functions and one or more payload subsystems [13]. Relevant examples of avionics functions are the Attitude and Orbit Control Subsystem (AOCS), Onboard Data Handling (OBDH), Telemetry, Tracking, and Command (TTC) subsystem, and Fault Detection, Isolation and Recovery (FDIR).

Traditionally, dedicated hardware resources have been separately allocated to those functions. However, there has been a recent trend in the aerospace industry towards integrating several functions in the same computing platform. This

---

⋆ This work was partially developed within the scope of the ESA (European Space Agency) Innovation Triangle Initiative program, through ESTEC Contract 21217/07/NL/CB, Project AIR-II (ARINC 653 in Space RTOS – Industrial Initiative, http://air.di.fc.ul.pt). This work was partially supported by Fundação para a Ciência e a Tecnologia (Portuguese Foundation for Science and Technology), through the Multiannual Funding and CMU-Portugal Programs and the Individual Doctoral Grant SFRH/BD/60193/2009.

A. Casimiro et al. (Eds.): Architecting Dependable Systems VII, LNCS 6420, pp. 146–170, 2010.

is advantageous in respect to SWaP requirements, but has introduced potential risks, as these functions may have different degrees of criticality and predictability, and originate from multiple providers or development teams [25,30].

In order to mitigate these risks, an architectural principle was proposed whereby onboard applications are functionally separated in logical containers, called partitions. With partitioning we achieve two results: allowing containment of faults in the domain in which they occur; and enabling independent software verification and validation, thus easing the overall certification process. Partitioning in logical containers implies separation of applications' execution in the time domain and usage of dedicated memory and input/output addressing spaces. Robust *temporal and spatial partitioning* (TSP) means that partitions do not interfere with each other in terms of fulfilment of *real-time* and *addressing space encapsulation* requirements.

This chapter describes in detail the foundations and genesis of an *architecture for robust TSP* aiming at a new generation of spaceborne systems. Firstly, the basic architecture is detailed together with the advanced features introduced in its design. A second result described in the chapter is the introduction of a couple of advanced timeliness adaptation and control mechanisms, crucial to the provision of high degrees of dependability in TSP systems: *mode-based partition schedules* (allowing the temporal requirements of the installed functions to vary according to the mission's phase or mode of operation) and *process deadline violation monitoring* (providing fundamental health monitoring services with enhanced diagnostics support). Thirdly, a *formal system model* is defined. This model and associated tools ease the verifiability of systems based on the architecture. It allows for the verification of the integrator-defined system parameters, such as partition scheduling according to the respective temporal requirements, and lays the ground for schedulability analysis and automated aids to the definition of system parameters. Temporal analysis in TSP systems has not been addressed in the literature to the full extent needed to aid design, integration and deployment of modern TSP systems in space [32].

Our research has been motivated by the challenge launched by several space industry partners, such as the National Aeronautics and Space Administration (NASA) [24] and the European Space Agency (ESA) [29], for applying TSP concepts to computing resources onboard spacecrafts, while observing compliance with existing standards such as the ARINC 653 specification [2]. ARINC 653 defines a standard interface for avionics application software to interact with the underlying core software (operating system). This standard is tightly connected to the Integrated Modular Avionics (IMA) concept, which applies the TSP notion to the civil aviation world [1]. The TSP Working Group, comprising space agencies ESA and CNES (the French government space agency) and industry partners Astrium and Thales Alenia Space, has identified the specific requirements for the adoption of IMA concepts in space, and found no technological feasibility impairments to it [32].

In the wake of space agencies' interest, what originally started as a proof of concept for the addition of TSP-capabilities to a free/opensource real-time operating system, the Real-Time Executive for Multiprocessor Systems (RTEMS), evolved into the definition of a more ambitious and innovative architecture in the context of the AIR (ARINC 653 In Space Real-time Operating System) project [11,23,22]. The AIR architecture has been designed to fulfil the requirements for robust TSP, and foresees the use of different operating systems among the partitions, either real-time operating systems (RTOS) or generic non-real-time ones. Temporal partitioning is achieved through the scheduling of partitions in a cyclic sequence of fixed time slices. Inside each partition, processes compete with each other according to the native process scheduler of the partition. In the case of RTOSs, this is usually a dynamic priority-based scheduler.

The chapter is organized as follows. Section 2 describes the AIR system architecture. Then, Sect. 3 contains the formal definition of a generic model for ARINC 653-based systems with regard to their temporal properties and requirements. Sections 4 and 5 describe the principles and implications of introducing, respectively, mode-based schedules and process deadline violation monitoring into AIR. Sect. 6 demonstrates the properties of the system model and the enhancements described in the previous sections by means of a prototype implementation. Section 7 presents related work and Sect. 8 concludes the chapter.

2   AIR System Architecture

The AIR (ARINC 653 in Space RTOS) architecture is currently evolving towards an industrial product definition by improving and completing the key points identified in early proof-of-concept activities [22]. The fundamental idea in the definition of the AIR architecture is a simple solution for providing robust TSP properties, thus guaranteeing the fulfilment of real-time and dedicated memory and input/output addressing space separation requirements. Faults are confined to their domain of occurrence inside each partition. AIR provides the ARINC 653 functionality missing in off-the-shelf (real-time) operating system kernels, as illustrated in the diagram of Fig. 1, encapsulating those functions in special-purpose additional components with well-defined interfaces. In essence, the AIR architecture preserves the hardware and operating system independence defined in the ARINC 653 specification [2]. AIR foresees the possibility that each partition runs a different operating system, henceforth called *Partition Operating System* (POS) [23].

Applications may use a strict ARINC 653 service interface, the *Application Executive* (APEX) interface or, in the case of system partitions, may bypass this standard interface and use additional functions from the POS kernel, as illustrated in Fig. 1. The existence of system partitions with the possibility of bypassing the APEX interface is a requirement of the ARINC 653 specification. It should noted though that these partitions will typically run system administration and management functions, performed by applications which will be subject to increased verification efforts.

A (system) application, and the given APEX interface, POS and *AIR POS Adaptation Layer* (PAL) instances compose the containment domain of each partition.

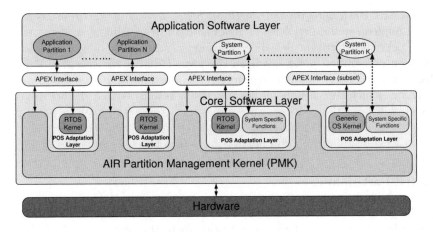

Fig. 1. AIR system architecture

2.1   AIR Partition Management Kernel (PMK)

The *AIR Partition Management Kernel* (PMK) component, transversal to the whole system (see Fig. 1), could be seen as a hypervisor, playing nevertheless a major role in achieving dependability, by ensuring robust TSP.

Temporal Partitioning

Temporal partitioning concerns partitions not interfering with each other's timeliness. In AIR this is guaranteed by a two-level hierarchical scheduling scheme; partitions are scheduled cyclically under a fixed schedule, and processes are scheduled by the native scheduler of the operating system of the partition in which they are executing, as shown in Fig. 2. The partition schedule is repeated cyclically and covers a time interval denominated *major time frame* (MTF).

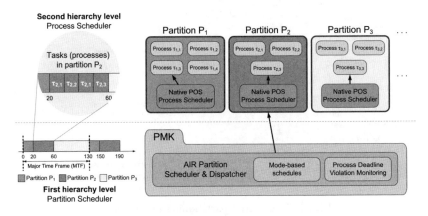

Fig. 2. AIR two-level hierarchical scheduling

The AIR PMK integrates a *Partition Scheduler* and a *Partition Dispatcher* which implement the first level of this hierarchical scheduling scheme. At each clock tick, the Partition Scheduler consults a scheduling table to detect if a partition preemption point has been reached. If that is the case, the Partition Dispatcher is called upon to perform the context switch between the active partition (which currently holds the processing resources) and the heir partition (which will hold the processing resources until the next partition preemption point). The advanced mechanisms represented in Fig. 2 (mode-based schedules and process deadline violation monitoring) are detailed in Sects. 4 and 5.

Spatial Partitioning

Spatial partitioning means that applications running in one partition cannot access addressing spaces outside those belonging to that partition [24,27]. For the support thereto, AIR follows a highly modular design approach illustrated in Fig. 3. Spatial partitioning requirements (specified in AIR and ARINC 653 configuration files with the assistance of development tools support) are described in runtime through a high-level processor-independent abstraction layer. A set of descriptors is provided per partition, primarily corresponding to the several levels of execution (e.g. application, operating system and AIR PMK) and to its different memory sections (e.g. code, data and stack) [22].

The high-level abstract spatial partitioning description needs to be mapped in runtime to the specific processor memory protection mechanisms, exploiting the availability of a hardware Memory Management Unit (MMU), as shown in the lowest layer of Fig. 3. An example of such mapping is the Gaisler SPARC V8 LEON3 three-level page-based MMU core [28].

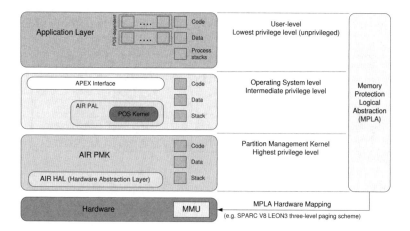

Fig. 3. AIR spatial partitioning mechanisms

Interpartition Communication

Notwithstanding spatial partitioning requirements, typical spacecraft partitioned onboard applications need to exchange data. For example, some payload subsystems may need to read AOCS data or transmit data to FDIR. Thus, AIR PMK provides low-level mechanisms for interpartition communication. Applications access the interpartition communication services through the APEX interface (Sect. 2.3), in a way which is agnostic of whether the partitions are local or remote to one another and how they communicate. The AIR PMK deals with these specifics, being obliged to message delivery guarantees. For physically separated partitions, this implies data transmission through a communication infrastructure. In the case of partitions in the same processing platform, interpartition communication is implemented through memory-to-memory copies not violating spatial separation requirements [22].

2.2   AIR POS Adaptation Layer (PAL)

The AIR POS Adaptation Layer (PAL) plays an important role in the AIR architecture, in the sense it wraps each partition's operating system, hiding its particularities from the AIR architecture components. This allows for a more flexible and homogeneous integration of support to new partition operating systems (or new versions thereof) and a better software development process (supported by separation of concerns and stronger validation and certification processes) [22,8].

2.3   Flexible Portable APEX Interface

The APEX interface provides to the applications a set of services, defined in the ARINC 653 specification [2]. AIR employs an innovative implementation of APEX which consists of two components: the APEX Core Layer and the APEX Layer Interface.

The APEX Core Layer implements the advanced notion of *Portable APEX* intended to ensure portability between the different POSs supported by AIR [26]. The AIR APEX fully exploits the the availability of AIR PAL-related functions, and the POSIX application programming interface currently available on most (RT)OSs [15]. An optimized implementation may invoke directly the native (RT)OS service primitives. The AIR APEX also coordinates, when required, the interactions with the AIR Health Monitor, e.g. upon detection of an error [22].

2.4   AIR Health Monitoring (HM)

The AIR Health Monitor is responsible for handling hardware and software errors (like deadlines missed, memory protection violations, or hardware failures). The aim is to isolate errors within its domain of occurrence: process level errors will cause an application error handler to be invoked, while partition level errors trigger a response action defined at system integration time. Errors detected at system level may lead the entire system to be stopped or reinitialized [22].

2.5 Integration of Generic Operating Systems

The foreseen heterogeneity between POSs is also being extended to include generic non-real-time systems, such as Linux, answering to a recent trend in the aerospace industry. The coexistance of real-time and non-real-time POSs is motivated by the lack of relevant functions in most RTOSs, which are commonly provided by generic non-real-time operating systems. Furthermore, porting these functions (e.g. scripting language interpreters) to RTOSs can be a complicated and error-prone task [16]. An embedded variant of Linux has been approached, and yields a fully functional operating system with a minimal size compatible with the coexistence with other POSs and typical space missions requirements [8,9].

To ensure that a non-real-time kernel as Linux cannot undermine the overall time guarantees of the system by disabling or diverting system clock interrupts, the instructions that could allow this must be wrapped by low-level handlers (paravirtualized) [8].

3 System Model

To allow for formal verification of properties and requirements, the AIR architecture can be modeled as follows. The model presented here focuses on the temporal aspects of the system, which are the most relevant for the contributions of this chapter. This system model is generic enough that it can possibly apply to other TSP systems, especially those based on the ARINC 653 specification [2]. A simplified version of the system model can also apply to hypervisor-based systems in general.

The notation used in this chapter has been chosen so as to follow recent efforts towards a common notation among the research community [10]. To that purpose, symbols to denote the notions of the system model coincide with those used in previous works in the area [10,18]. Symbols for new concepts try, as much as possible, not to conflict with those already widely used in the literature for different concepts. A reference table for this notation, as applicable to the system model resulting from the work presented in this chapter, is presented in the Appendix.

3.1 Partitions

An AIR-based system, or actually a generic ARINC 653-based system, is composed by a set of partitions, P:

$$P = \{P_1, P_2, \ldots, P_{n(P)}\} \ . \tag{1}$$

Each partition P_m is defined as:

$$P_m = \langle \eta_m, d_m, \tau_m, M_m(t) \rangle \tag{2}$$

where η_m is the partition's activation cycle, d_m is its assigned duration (the amount of time to be given to the partition per cycle), and τ_m is the set of processes running inside the partition (these will be covered in detail in Sect. 3.3). $M_m(t)$ is the operating mode of the partition P_m at the instant t, such that:

$$M_m(t) \in \{\mathsf{normal}, \mathsf{idle}, \mathsf{coldStart}, \mathsf{warmStart}\} \ . \tag{3}$$

In the normal mode, the partition is effectively operational, with its process scheduler active, while the idle mode corresponds to a shut-down partition not executing any processes. The coldStart and warmStart modes both indicate that the partition is initializing (with process scheduling disabled), differing from one another regarding the initial context [2].

This model is very flexible, supporting partitions with either an inherently periodic or aperiodic behaviour. As seen in Sect. 2.1, the partition schedule repeats over a major time frame (MTF); thus, a partition which is not by itself periodic can be modeled as having a partition cycle equal to the duration of the MTF. Partitions which do not have strict time requirements, such as those running non-real time operating systems, are also covered, having $d_m = 0$.

3.2   Partition Scheduling

Partitions are scheduled on a fixed cyclic basis in the first of the two levels of the hierarchical scheduling scheme, as illustrated in Fig. 2. The time interval covered by a partition schedule, and over which it repeats, is called the major time frame (MTF). The partition scheduling table (PST) for a system, χ, can be defined as:

$$\chi = \langle MTF, \omega = \{\omega_1, \omega_2, \ldots, \omega_{n(\omega)}\}\rangle \ . \tag{4}$$

ω is a set of time windows, each one defined as:

$$\omega_j = \langle P_j^\omega, O_j, c_j\rangle \qquad P_j^\omega \in P \tag{5}$$

where P_j^ω is the partition scheduled to be active during the jth time window, O_j is the window's offset (relative to the beginning of a major time frame) and c_j is its duration. At this stage, we assume that every partition in P has, at least, one time window, thus $\bigcup_{\omega_j \in \omega} P_j^\omega = P$. Time windows do not intersect and are fully contained within one MTF, so:

$$\begin{cases} O_j + c_j \leq O_{j+1} & \forall j < n(\omega) \\ O_{n(\omega)} + c_{n(\omega)} \leq MTF \ . \end{cases} \tag{6}$$

As a necessary but not sufficient condition for system-wide schedulability, the MTF should be a multiple of the least common multiple (lcm) of all the partitions' cycles:

$$MTF = k \times \operatorname*{lcm}_{\forall P_m \in P} (\eta_m) \qquad k \in \mathbb{N} \ . \tag{7}$$

and the sum of each partition's time windows should account for the duration defined for that partition:

$$\sum_{\{\,\omega_j \in \omega \,|\, P_j^\omega = P_m \,\}} c_j \geq d_m \frac{MTF}{\eta_m} \qquad \forall P_m \in P \;. \tag{8}$$

This is nevertheless not a sufficient condition for compliance with the partitions' temporal requirements. Besides respecting (8), the time windows must guarantee that, if a partition completes more than one cycle inside the MTF, it executes the assigned duration within each of these cycles:

$$\sum_{\substack{\{\,\omega_j \in \omega \,|\, P_j^\omega = P_m \,\wedge \\ O_j \in [k\,\eta_m\,;(k+1)\eta_m]\,\}}} c_j \geq d_m \qquad \forall P_m \in P, \; \forall k \in \left[0..\frac{MTF}{\eta_m} - 1\right] \;. \tag{9}$$

If the condition expressed in (9) holds, each partition P_m has at least d_m time units assigned in each of the $\frac{MTF}{\eta_m}$ cycles completed inside one MTF. Thus (8) will also hold — the sum of all the time windows inside one MTF will be no less than $d_m \frac{MTF}{\eta_m}$.

3.3   Processes

In AIR (and ARINC 653), the scope of process management is restricted to its partition. As defined in (2), each partition $P_m \in P$ contains a set of processes:

$$\tau_m = \{\tau_{m,1}, \tau_{m,2}, \ldots, \tau_{m,n(\tau_m)}\} \;. \tag{10}$$

Each process $\tau_{m,q}$ can be defined as:

$$\tau_{m,q} = \langle T_{m,q}, D_{m,q}, p_{m,q}, C_{m,q}, S_{m,q}(t) \rangle \tag{11}$$

where $T_{m,q}$ is the process's period, $D_{m,q}$ its relative deadline, $p_{m,q}$ its *base* priority, and $S_{m,q}(t)$ represents the status of the process at instant t. If the process $\tau_{m,q}$ is aperiodic or sporadic, $T_{m,q}$ represents the lower bound for the time between consecutive activations. If $D_{m,q} = \infty$, then $\tau_{m,q}$ has no deadlines. The worst case execution time (WCET), $C_{m,q}$, is not originally a process attribute in the ARINC 653 specification. It is though added to the system model, since it is essential for further scheduling analyses.

The status of the process:

$$S_{m,q}(t) = \langle D'_{m,q}(t), p'_{m,q}(t), St_{m,q}(t) \rangle \tag{12}$$

includes the process's absolute deadline time, $D'_{m,q}(t)$, *current* priority, $p'_{m,q}(t)$, and state:

$$St_{m,q}(t) \in \{\mathsf{dormant}, \mathsf{ready}, \mathsf{running}, \mathsf{waiting}\} \;. \tag{13}$$

A **dormant** process is ineligible to receive resources because it either has not been started or has been stopped. A **ready** process is one which is able to be executed, while a **running** process (only one at any time) is the one currently executing.

A waiting process is not eligible to be scheduled until a certain event for which it is waiting has occurred — a delay, a semaphore, a period, etc. — or another process resumes it (if it has been suspended).

Processes inside each partition compete for processing time during the partition's time windows. In RTOSs, this is usually done according to a preemptive priority-driven scheduling algorithm. The convention here is that lower numerical values represent greater priorities. In normal operation with preemption enabled, the heir process in a given partition at a given moment, $heir_m(t)$, is wielded by:

$$heir_m(t) = \tau_{m,h} \in Ready_m(t) \mid (p'_{m,h}(t) < p'_{m,q}(t)) \vee$$
$$(p'_{m,h}(t) = p'_{m,q}(t) \wedge h < q) \qquad \forall \tau_{m,q} \in Ready_m(t), q \neq h \tag{14}$$

where:

$$Ready_m(t) = \{\tau_{m,q} \in \tau_m \mid St_{m,q}(t) \in \{\mathsf{ready, running}\}\} . \tag{15}$$

Processes are assumed to be sorted in decreasing order of antiquity in the ready state. This reads that the process selected to be executed is the highest priority ready (or already running) process in the partition; if more than one process has the highest priority, the oldest one is selected.

4   Mode-Based Schedules

The original AIR Partition Scheduler, integrated in the AIR PMK component (Sect. 2), defines a static scheduling of partitions, cyclically obeying to a Partition Scheduling Table (PST) defined offline, at system integration time (see (4)). The AIR Partition Scheduler verifies whether a partition preemption point has been reached and, in that case, selects the heir partition.

This static scheme is very restricting in terms of configuration flexibility and fault tolerance. The AIR advanced design addresses this issue by introducing support for multiple mode-based partition schedules. Examples of the usefulness of mode-based schedules include the adaptation of partition scheduling to different modes/phases (initialization, operation, etc.) and the accommodation of component failures (e.g., assigning a critical program running in a failed processor to another one). Such a notion is also conveyed in Part 2 of the ARINC 653 specification [3].

The basic mandatory scheduling scheme is extended to allow multiple schedules to be defined at system integration time. At execution time, authorized partitions may request switching between the different PSTs, represented in the rightmost part of Fig. 4.

To this purpose, the system configuration and integration process is extended in two ways:

1. definition of multiple schedules, with different major time frames, partitions, and respective periods and execution time windows;
2. inclusion of restart actions (ScheduleChangeAction) to be performed, on a per-partition and per-schedule basis, when the schedule is changed.

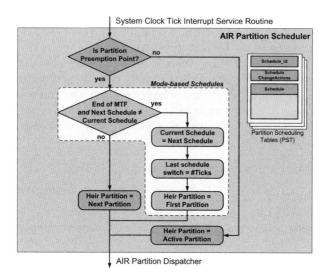

Fig. 4. AIR Partition Scheduler with support for mode-based schedules

The AIR Partition Scheduler has to be modified with the functions highlighted (dotted line) in Fig. 4. These modifications concern the verification, at the end of each MTF, of whether a schedule switch is pending and, if that is the case, make the schedule switch effective.

4.1   Implications on the System Model

The introduction of mode-based schedules imposes a reformulation of the system model presented in Sect. 3. Besides the system now having *a set of* partition scheduling tables, the partitions' timing requirements (period and duration) are no longer attributes of the partition, but rather attributes of the partition *in a given schedule*. Schedules may change on account of the mission's mode/phase changing, and this in turn implies that most likely some processes inside partitions need not be always active. Thus, each partition's timing requirements may change from schedule to schedule; the alternative approach of keeping each partition's time requirements constant throughout the schedules by targeting an extremely pessimistic case would lead to a poorly efficient resource utilization through time.

The system is still composed of a set P of partitions (1), which will now be deprived of timing requirements on their own:

$$P_m = \langle \tau_m, M_m(t) \rangle \ . \tag{16}$$

The system also holds, as mentioned, a set of partition scheduling tables:

$$\chi = \{\chi_1, \chi_2, \ldots, \chi_{n(\chi)}\} \tag{17}$$

which definition should be adjusted from (4):

$$\chi_i = \langle MTF_i, Q_i = \{Q_{i,1}, \ldots, Q_{i,n(Q_i)}\}, \omega_i = \{\omega_{i,1}, \ldots, \omega_{i,n(\omega_i)}\} \rangle \tag{18}$$

where:

$$Q_{i,m} = \langle P^{\chi}_{i,m}, \eta_{i,m}, d_{i,m} \rangle \qquad P^{\chi}_{i,m} \in P . \tag{19}$$

Since now it may be the case that not all partitions will be present in every schedule, the requirements expressed in (7), (8) and (9) are too strong, as they express requirements for each PST in terms of all partitions in the system (regardless of which partitions are present in each PST).

To reflect the changes expressed in (17), (18) and (19), and the concern over the mentioned requirements being too strong, the system model must be enhanced by replacing (5) to (7) with (20) to (22):

$$\omega_{i,j} = \langle P^{\omega}_{i,j}, O_{i,j}, c_{i,j} \rangle \qquad P^{\omega}_{i,j} \in Q_i \tag{20}$$

$$\begin{cases} O_{i,j} + c_{i,j} \leq O_{i,j+1} & \forall j < n(\omega_i) \\ O_{i,n(\omega_i)} + c_{i,n(\omega_i)} \leq MTF_i \end{cases} \tag{21}$$

$$MTF_i = k_i \times \operatorname*{lcm}_{\forall Q_m \in Q_i} (\eta_m) \qquad k_i \in \mathbb{N} . \tag{22}$$

The fundamental timing requirement fulfilment condition expressed in (9) is accordingly updated as can be seen in (23):

$$\sum_{\substack{\{\omega_{i,j} \in \omega_i \mid P^{\omega}_{i,j} = P_m \wedge \\ O_{i,j} \in [k\,\eta_m;(k+1)\eta_m]\}}} c_{i,j} \geq d_m \quad \forall i \leq n(\chi), \forall P_m \in Q_i, \forall k \in \left[0..\frac{MTF_i}{\eta_m} - 1\right] .$$

$$\tag{23}$$

Since (9) implies (8), a replacement for the latter is not provided. The kind of system initially described, with only one statically defined partition scheduling table, can still be modeled, as a special case of a system with $n(\chi) = 1$.

4.2   Implications on the APEX Interface

Support for mode-based schedules requires the provision of additional APEX services. These should allow setting and obtaining the current partition scheduling parameters.

First and foremost, a service which sets the schedule that will start executing at the top of the next MTF must be provided. It must be invoked by an authorized partition, and have the identifier of an existing schedule as its only parameter. The immediate result is only that of storing the identifier of the next schedule.

The effective schedule switch occurs at the start of the next MTF, by having the AIR Partition Scheduler (see Algorithm 1) perform the following steps:

Algorithm 1. AIR Partition Scheduler featuring mode-based schedules

1: $ticks \leftarrow ticks + 1$ ▷ $ticks$ is the global system clock tick counter
2: **if** $schedules_{currentSchedule}.table_{tableIterator}.tick =$
    $(ticks - lastScheduleSwitch)$ mod $schedules_{currentSchedule}.mtf$ **then**
3:      **if** $currentSchedule \neq nextSchedule$ ∧
        $(ticks - lastScheduleSwitch)$ mod $schedules_{currentSchedule}.mtf = 0$ **then**
4:          $currentSchedule \leftarrow nextSchedule$
5:          $lastScheduleSwitch \leftarrow ticks$
6:          $tableIterator \leftarrow 0$
7:      **end if**
8:      $heirPartition \leftarrow schedules_{currentSchedule}.table_{tableIterator}.partition$
9:      $tableIterator \leftarrow (tableIterator + 1)$ mod
        $schedules_{currentSchedule}.numberPartitionPreemptionPoints$
10: **end if**

Line 4: $currentSchedule$ is set to $nextSchedule$, which is the identifier stored in the latest previous call to the service.

Line 5: $lastScheduleSwitch$ is set to the current time.

Also, each partition P_m in the new schedule running in normal mode, i.e. $M_m(t)$ = normal, will have to be restarted according to the value defined for its ScheduleChangeAction (which can indicate that no restart should occur). This action takes place the first time each partition is scheduled/dispatched after the schedule switch (not represented in Algorithm 1). Support for the schedule switch makes up for virtually the whole of the changes made to the original AIR Partition Scheduler.

Another service provided in AIR allows obtaining the full current schedule status information, which (in compliance with ARINC 653 Part 2 [3]) comprises:

− the time of the last schedule switch (0 if none ever occurred);
− the identifier of the current schedule;
− the identifier of the next schedule, which will be the same as the current schedule if no schedule change is pending for the end of the present major time frame.

4.3 Design and Engineering Issues

Since the AIR Partition Scheduler code is invoked at every system clock tick, its code needs to be as efficient as possible. In the AIR implementation presented in Algorithm 1, in the best and most frequent case, only two computations are performed:

Line 1: Increment the number of clock ticks by one.
Line 2: Verify if a partition preemption point has been reached (this best case is also the most frequent one, since this verification will turn out false far more often than true).

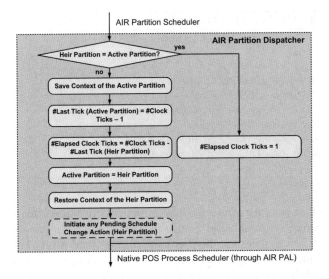

Fig. 5. AIR Partition Dispatcher with support for mode-based schedules

To incorporate the mode-based schedules functionality, the AIR Partition Scheduler computations had to be extended (see Algorithm 1); verifications of the presence of a partition preemption point (line 2) or the end of a MTF (line 3) need to rely on the number of clock ticks elapsed since the last schedule switch, and not solely the number of clock ticks since system initialization.

The AIR Partition Dispatcher is executed after the Partition Scheduler. Its only modification regarding mode-based schedules is the invocation of pending schedule change actions. The mechanism of the AIR Partition Dispatcher, with this modification highlighted (dotted line), is detailed in Fig. 5.

Part 2 of the ARINC 653 specification [3] does not clearly state whether schedule change actions should be performed immediately after effectively changing schedule (i.e., at the beginning of the first MTF under the new schedule, for all partitions) or performed for each partition as it is dispatched for the first time after the schedule switch. It is nevertheless our understanding that the latter approach is more compliant with the fulfilment of temporal separation requirements, since these will only affect its own execution time window. This is specified in Algorithm 2 (line 9). The remaining actions in Algorithm 2 are related to saving and restoring the execution context (lines 4 and 8), and evaluation of the elapsed clock ticks (lines 2 and 6).

5   Process Deadline Violation Monitoring

During the execution of the system, it may be the case that a process exceeds its deadline; this can be caused by a malfunction or because that process's WCET was underestimated at system configuration and integration time. Other factors

---

Algorithm 2. AIR Partition Dispatcher featuring mode-based schedules

1: **if** $heirPartition = activePartition$ **then**
2:     $elapsedTicks \leftarrow 1$
3: **else**
4:     SAVECONTEXT($activePartition.context$)
5:     $activePartition.lastTick \leftarrow ticks - 1$
6:     $elapsedTicks \leftarrow ticks - heirPartition.lastTick$
7:     $activePartition \leftarrow heirPartition$
8:     RESTORECONTEXT($heirPartition.context$)
9:     PENDINGSCHEDULECHANGEACTION($heirPartition$)
10: **end if**

---

related to faulty system planning (such as the time windows not satisfying the partitions' timing requirements) could, in principle, also cause deadline violations; however, such issues can be predicted and avoided using offline tools that verify the fulfilment of the timing requirements as expressed in (23).

In addition, it is also possible that a process exceeds a deadline while the partition in which it executes is inactive, and that will only be detected when the partition is being dispatched, just before invoking the process scheduler. The earliest deadline is checked; following deadlines may subsequently be verified until one has not been missed. This can be computationally optimized with the help of an appropriate data structure with the deadlines in ascending order, allowing for $\mathcal{O}(1)$ retrieval of the earliest deadline. This is extremely relevant given deadline verification is performed inside the system clock interrupt service routine (ISR). Furthermore, this methodology is optimal with respect to deadline violation detection latency.

In the context of Health Monitoring (HM), ARINC 653 classifies process deadline violation as a process level error (an error that impacts one or more processes in the partition, or the entire partition) [2,22]. Possible recovery actions in the event of such an error are:

- ignoring the error (logging it, but taking no action);
- logging the error a certain number of times before acting upon it;
- stopping the faulty process, and reinitializing it from the entry address or starting another process;
- stopping the faulty process, assuming that the partition will detect this and recover;
- restarting or stopping the partition.

The actual action to be performed is defined by the application programmer, through an appropriate error handler [22].

5.1 Implications on the System Model

At instant t, the set of processes having violated their deadlines is given by:

$$
V(t) = \bigcup_{m=1}^{n(P)} \left\{ \tau_{m,q} \in \tau_m \mid D_{m,q} \neq \infty \wedge D'_{m,q}(t) < t \right\} \tag{24}
$$

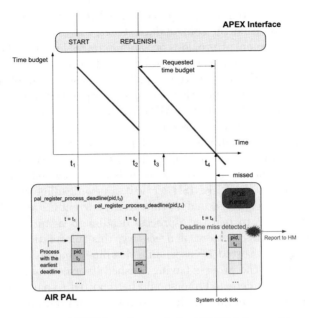

Fig. 6. Integration of the APEX Interface and the AIR PAL to provide process deadline violation detection and reporting

The $D_{m,q} \neq \infty$ condition translates the fact that the notion of deadline violation does not apply to non-real-time processes.

5.2 Implications on the APEX Interface

The information about processes statuses and deadlines is maintained in such a way that it is conveniently kept updated by the relevant APEX primitives which:

- start a process, making it become able to be executed by initializing all its attributes, setting the runtime stack, and placing it in the ready state;
- start a process with a given delay, by placing it in the waiting state until the requested delay is expired;
- suspend the execution of a (periodic) process until the next release point[1];
- postpone a process's deadline time (replenishment);
- perform a partition shutdown or restart.

Each of these primitives will need to insert or update the due processes' deadlines, while the services which stop a process (putting it in the dormant state,

---

[1] A release point of a process is defined in general as the instant the process becomes ready for execution. For a periodic process the consecutive release points will be separated by the respective period.

by its own request or from another process) need to remove the due processes' deadline information from the control data structures.

The AIR PAL component provides private interfaces for these APEX services to register/update and unregister deadlines, and keeps the appropriate data structures containing this information. This is the most reasonable implementation, from the engineering, integrity and spatial separation points of view. An example of how the APEX and the AIR PAL for one given partition integrate to provide this functionality is shown in Fig. 6.

When a process is started, via the START APEX service, its deadline time is set to instant t_3 (obtained by adding the process's time capacity to the current instant), and this value is registered via the AIR PAL-provided interface. Upon a replenishment request (REPLENISH service), a new deadline time, t_4, is calculated (by adding the requested budget time to the current instant). The interface provided by AIR PAL to register a process deadline is again called, to update the information for this process; if necessary, this information will be moved to keep the deadlines sorted by ascending deadline time order. When instant t_4 is reached without the process having finished its execution, a deadline miss has occurred, which is detected and should be reported to partition-wise health monitoring and error handling mechanisms through appropriate primitives.

5.3   Design and Engineering Issues

Figure 7 illustrates the modification to the surrogate clock tick announcement routine provided by the AIR PAL, so as to verify the earliest deadline(s) and report any violations to the health monitoring. Process scheduling and dispatching is ensured by the corresponding native POS mechanisms.

The implementation of process deadline violation monitoring in AIR is shown in Algorithm 3. To keep the computational complexity of the process deadline

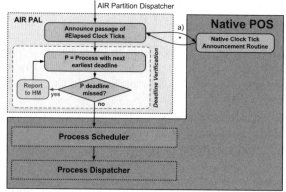

a) Native clock tick announcement routine invoked #Elapsed Clock Ticks times.

Fig. 7. Modifications on the surrogate clock tick announcement routine to accommodate deadline verification features

---

Algorithm 3. Deadline verification at the AIR PAL level

1: *POS_CLOCKTICKANNOUNCE(*elapsedTicks*)
2: **for all** $d \in PAL\_deadlines$ **do**
3:     **if** $d.deadlineTime \geq$ PAL_GETCURRENTTIME( ) **then**
4:         **break**
5:     **end if**
6:     HM_DEADLINEVIOLATED($d.pid$)   ▷ *pid*: process identifier
7:     PAL_REMOVEPROCESSDEADLINE(d)
8: **end for**

---

violation monitoring to a minimum, the information concerning process deadlines is kept at each partition's AIR PAL component, ordered by deadline, and only the earliest deadline is verified by default; this verification (line 3) happens after announcing the passage of the elapsed clock ticks (line 1). The information on the earliest deadline is retrieved in constant time ($\mathcal{O}(1)$). Only in the presence of deadline violations will more deadlines be checked, in ascending order until reaching one that has not been violated.

Currently, the AIR PAL uses a linked list to keep the process deadline information. In the deadline verification process, a violation may be detected (Algorithm 3, line 3), and after reporting its occurrence to Health Monitoring (line 6) the deadline is removed from the control structure (line 7). Since we already have a pointer to the node to be removed, the complexity of the deadline removal from the linked list will effectively be $\mathcal{O}(1)$, as opposed to the generic $\mathcal{O}(n)$ complexity yielded by linked lists.

A point where the use of a self-balancing binary search tree would theoretically outperform a linked list concern the act of inserting, removing or updating nodes, materialized in the register/unregister deadline interfaces provided to the APEX — $\mathcal{O}(\log n)$ vs. $\mathcal{O}(n)$. Nevertheless, since these operations do not happen inside the system clock tick ISR, but rather on a partition's execution time window, and also the number of processes accounted for deadline verification will be typically small, such asymptotic advantage will not correlate to effective and/or significant profit, and certainly not compensate for the more critical downside to operations running during an ISR.

6   Prototype Implementation

To demonstrate the advanced timeliness control features, we developed a prototype implementation of an AIR-based system comprising four partitions. Each partition executes an RTEMS-based [21] mockup application representative of typical functions present in a satellite system. The demonstration was implemented for an Intel IA-32 target, and ran on the QEMU emulator.

This sample system is configured with two PSTs, between which it is possible to alternate through the mode-based schedules service described in Sect. 4. These partition scheduling tables are shown in Fig. 8. Both tables repeat over a MTF of 1300 time units, but this is not a strict requirement — it stems from the partitions'

$P = \{P_1, P_2, P_3, P_4\}$

$Q_1 = Q_2 = \{\langle P_1, 1300, 200\rangle, \langle P_2, 650, 100\rangle, \langle P_3, 650, 100\rangle, \langle P_4, 1300, 100\rangle\}$

$\chi_1 = \langle MTF_1 = 1300, \omega_1 = \{\langle Q_{1,1}, 0, 200\rangle, \langle Q_{1,2}, 200, 100\rangle, \langle Q_{1,3}, 300, 100\rangle, \langle Q_{1,4}, 400, 600\rangle,$
$\qquad\qquad \langle Q_{1,2}, 1000, 100\rangle, \langle Q_{1,3}, 1100, 100\rangle, \langle Q_{1,4}, 1200, 100\rangle\}\rangle$

$\chi_2 = \langle MTF_2 = 1300, \omega_2 = \{\langle Q_{2,1}, 0, 200\rangle, \langle Q_{2,4}, 200, 100\rangle, \langle Q_{2,3}, 300, 100\rangle, \langle Q_{2,2}, 400, 600\rangle,$
$\qquad\qquad \langle Q_{2,4}, 1000, 100\rangle, \langle Q_{2,3}, 1100, 100\rangle, \langle Q_{2,2}, 1200, 100\rangle\}\rangle$

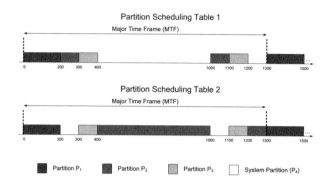

Fig. 8. Partition scheduling tables for the prototype implementation

timing requirements as per (22). Each partition contains one to three mockup processes, which period is a multiple of the respective partition's cycle duration.

We have the possibility to inject a faulty process on P_1, so that a deadline miss occurs even though both PSTs comply with P_1's timing requirements (cf. (23) and (25) for schedule χ_1).

$$\sum_{\{\,\omega_{i,j} \in \omega_i \mid P_{i,j}^\omega = P_m \wedge O_{i,j} \in [k\,\eta_m; (k+1)\eta_m]\,\}} c_{i,j} \geq d_m \qquad i = 1, P_m = Q_{1,1}, k = 0$$

$$\sum_{\{\,\omega_{1,j} \in \omega_1 \mid P_{1,j}^\omega = Q_{1,1} \wedge O_{1,j} \in [0;1300]\,\}} c_{1,j} \geq 200$$

$$\sum_{\{\,\langle Q_{1,1}, 0, 200\rangle\,\}} c_{1,j} \geq 200$$

$$200 \geq 200 \qquad\qquad \Box$$

$$(25)$$

When the faulty process is active, its deadline violation is detected and reported every time (except the first) that P_1 is scheduled and dispatched to execute.

Successive requests to change schedule are correctly handled at the end of the current MTF and do not introduce deadline violations other than the one injected in a process in P_1. This is caused, not by the schedule switch mechanism itself, but by ensuring that the different PSTs comply with the temporal requirements of the partitions therein contained. This is in consonance with the overall tone of

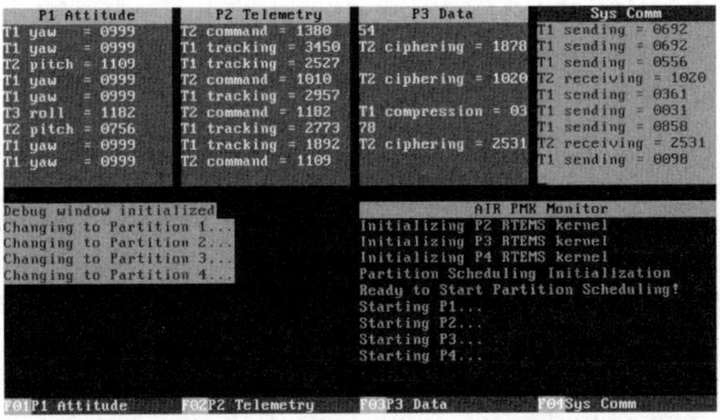

Fig. 9. Prototype implementation demonstration, featuring the VITRAL text-mode windows manager for RTEMS

the ARINC 653 specification, which emphasizes that in many cases the system can only *support* certain properties, and cannot *guarantee* them without proper and careful integration and configuration [2].

To allow for proof of concept visualization and interaction, the prototype includes VITRAL, a text-mode windows manager for RTEMS [7], whose graphical aspect can be seen in Fig. 9. There is one window for each partition, where its output can be seen, and also two more windows which allow observation of the behaviour of AIR components. VITRAL also supports keyboard interaction, which is used, for demonstration purposes, to allow switching to a given partition scheduling table at the end of the present major time frame and activating the faulty process on P_1.

7   Related Work

To the best of our knowledge, the only contemporary approach to flexible scheduling in a TSP system is the mode-based scheduling feature provided by the commercial Wind River VxWorks 653 solution [31]. Previous academic research on TSP solutions [19] and works on scheduling analysis for TSP systems [4,18,12] do not include or foresee mechanisms for timing parameters adaptation.

Mode-based scheduling principles are also employed to communication protocols. In the Time-Triggered Protocol (TTP) [17], the controller state includes an operational mode, repeated at every mode cycle, which controls the sequence, attributes and schedule for nodes to send messages. If a node intends to change mode, it signals the remaining nodes through a frame's control field.

The overall concept of a timing watchdog to detect timing failures in the context of IMA-based systems is mentioned in [5,6]. In order to process deadline violation monitoring, the ARINC 653 specification defines deadline miss as a process level error, but makes no considerations on how or when the error should be detected [2]. In AIR, on the other hand, we propose an efficient implementation of such a mechanism. XtratuM, in its documentation, does not mention any provision of any similar deadline supervision [19]. VxWorks 653 is said to fully implement the ARINC 653 APEX specification, but it is not clear if deadline violation monitoring is addressed [31].

Temporal analysis in TSP systems such as IMA/ARINC 653 as been addressed in some instances in the literature, albeit not to the full extent needed to aid design, integration and deployment of TSP systems in space. In [4] the response time analysis leads to the proposal of abandoning two-level scheduling in favour of a single-level priority preemptive scheduling, and [14] also makes the case for abandoning cyclic partition scheduling, but in favour of reservation-based scheduling.

A theorem for partition schedulability is presented in [18], assuming that each partition is assigned a single continuous execution time window within each iteration of its cycle; this is much of a simplification of the scheduling mechanisms for TSP systems. This fact is also pointed out in [20], which addresses the task and partition scheduling problems with assumptions that differ from those possible when using the IMA and ARINC 653 specifications as a basis. For instance, the authors analyze the schedulability of processes (within a partition) by Earliest Deadline First policies, whereas ARINC 653 mandates a preemptive priority-based algorithm [2].

Finally, [12] models ARINC 653 with two-level scheduling and apply timing analysis techniques to generate partition schedules. This analysis relies on a model with some limiting (and, in some cases, unjustified) assumptions; for instance, the authors ignore aperiodic processes on the grounds that they are scheduled as background workload.

8   Conclusion and Future Work

The strict requirements of modern aerospace systems has brought us to integrating several onboard functions (avionics, payload), traditionally separated in dedicated resources, in the same computing platform. Robust temporal and spatial partitioning (TSP) is introduced to address dependability challenges resulting from this integration. TSP involves onboard applications being separated in logical containers (partitions), implying fault containment. Partitions do not interfere with one another regarding real-time and addressing space separation requirements.

In this chapter we presented the design of the TSP-based AIR architecture, which is compliant with the ARINC 653 specification. Then, we formally modeled AIR, with emphasis on the temporal properties and requirements. The innovative features introduced in the AIR architecture to enforce its dependability with respect to timeliness guarantees (mode-based schedules and process deadline violation monitoring) are then detailed regarding their definition, implementation and implications on the definition of an extended system model. Finally, we presented a prototype implementation, demonstrating the AIR architecture with the newly introduced timeliness adaptation and control features.

Mode-based schedules and process deadline violation monitoring do not, actively and/or by themselves, improve the timeliness of an AIR system. What they do is provide valuable means for system developers, integrators, maintainers and mission controllers to have a much greater control on whether and how this timeliness is achieved. Process deadline violation monitoring can give an almost immediate insight on possible underdimensioning of the execution time given to one or more partitions, which, coupled with mode-based schedules and a system integrated and configured to cope with this kind of event, can allow the problem to be solved in execution time.

As future work, the system model resulting from this chapter, composed of equations:

- (1), (3) and (16)–(23) (partitions, and partition mode-based scheduling);
- (10)–(15) (processes), and;
- (24) (process deadline violations);

will be consolidated and much extended, namely so as to include: *(i)* necessary conditions for process scheduling and deadline fulfilment; *(ii)* spatial separation characteristics, addressing space protection attributes, and fault detection requirements; *(iii)* the implications of unforeseen events on the time model (aperiodic/sporadic processes, event overload, etc.), and; *(iv)* parallelism between partition time windows on a multicore platform [8]. Formal definition of the characteristics and requirements of an ARINC 653-based system, such as those built on the AIR architecture, is of paramount importance for future space missions, since it opens room for system verification and development of timing analysis tools to aid system integration. This also implies deeper studies on schedulability analysis for TSP systems.

Acknowledgments

The authors would like to thank Tobias Schoofs, Sérgio Santos, Cássia Tatibana, Edgar Pascoal, José Neves (GMV Portugal) and James Windsor (ESA–ESTEC) for the joint efforts in the scope of the AIR activities, and Manuel Coutinho, for the extensive work on the VITRAL window manager for RTEMS and on earlier AIR prototyping.

References

1. AEEC: Design guidance for Integrated Modular Avionics. ARINC Report 651-1 (November 1997)
2. AEEC: Avionics application software standard interface, part 1 - required services. ARINC Specification 653P1-2 (March 2006)
3. AEEC: Avionics application software standard interface, part 2 - extended services. ARINC Specification 653P2-1 (December 2008)
4. Audsley, N., Wellings, A.: Analysing APEX applications. In: Proc. 17th IEEE Real-Time Systems Symp., Washington, DC, USA, pp. 39–44 (December 1996)
5. Bate, I., Burns, A.: A dependable distributed architecture for a safety critical hard real-time system. In: IEE Half-Day Colloquium on Hardware Systems for Dependable Applications (Digest No: 1997/335), pp. 1/1–1/6 (1997)

6. Conmy, P., McDermid, J.: High level failure analysis for Integrated Modular Avionics. In: Proc. 6th Australian Workshop on Safety critical systems and software, vol. 3, pp. 13–21. Australian Computer Society, Inc., Brisbane (2001)
7. Coutinho, M., Almeida, C., Rufino, J.: VITRAL - a text mode window manager for real-time embedded kernels. In: Proc. 11th IEEE Int. Conf. on Emerging Technologies and Factory Automation. Prague, Czech Republic (September 2006)
8. Craveiro, J.: Integration of generic operating systems in partitioned architectures. MSc thesis, Faculty of Sciences, University of Lisbon (July 2009)
9. Craveiro, J., Rufino, J., Almeida, C., Covelo, R., Venda, P.: Embedded Linux in a partitioned architecture for aerospace applications. In: Proc. 7th ACS/IEEE Int. Conf. on Computer Systems and Applications, Rabat, Morocco, pp. 132–138 (May 2009)
10. Davis, R., Burns, A.: A survey of hard real-time scheduling algorithms and schedulability analysis techniques for multiprocessor systems. Tech. Rep. YCS-2009-443, University of York, Department of Computer Science (2009)
11. Diniz, N., Rufino, J.: ARINC 653 in space. In: Proc. DASIA 2005 "DAta System. Aerospace" Conf. Edinburgh, Scotland (June 2005)
12. Easwaran, A., Lee, I., Sokolsky, O., Vestal, S.: A compositional scheduling framework for digital avionics systems. In: Proc. 15th IEEE Int. Conf. on Embedded and Real-Time Computing Systems and Applications. Beijing, China (August 2009)
13. Fortescue, P.W., Stark, J.P.W., Swinerd, G. (eds.): Spacecraft Systems Engineering, 3rd edn. Wiley, Chichester (2003)
14. Grigg, A., Audsley, N.: Towards a scheduling and timing analysis solution for integrated modular avionic systems. Microprocessors and Microsystems Journal 22(8), 423–431 (1999)
15. IEEE: 1996 (ISO/IEC) [IEEE/ANSI Std 1003.1, 1996 Edition] Information Technology — Portable Operating System Interface (POSIX) — Part 1: System Application: Program Interface (API) [C Language]. IEEE, New York, USA (1996)
16. Kinnan, L.: Application migration from Linux prototype to deployable IMA platform using ARINC 653 and Open GL. In: Proc. 26th IEEE/AIAA Digital Avionics Systems Conference, Dallas, TX, USA, pp. 6.C.2–1–6.C.2–5 (October 2007)
17. Kopetz, H., Grünsteidl, G.: TTP — a time-triggered protocol for fault-tolerant real-time systems. In: Proc. 23rd Int. Symp. on Fault-Tolerant Computing (1993)
18. Lee, Y., Kim, D., Younis, M., Zhou, J.: Partition scheduling in APEX runtime environment for embedded avionics software. In: Proc. 5th Int. Conf. on Real-Time Computing Systems and Applications, Hiroshima, Japan, pp. 103–109 (1998)
19. Masmano, M., Ripoll, I., Crespo, A.: XtratuM Hypervisor for LEON2: design and implementation overview. Tech. rep., I. U. de Automática e Informática Industrial, Universidad Politécnica de Valencia (January 2009)
20. Mok, A.K., Feng, A.X.: Real-time virtual resource: A timely abstraction for embedded systems. In: Sangiovanni-Vincentelli, A.L., Sifakis, J. (eds.) EMSOFT 2002. LNCS, vol. 2491, pp. 182–196. Springer, Heidelberg (2002)
21. OAR — On-Line Applications Research Corporation: RTEMS C Users Guide, 4.8 edn (February 2008)
22. Rufino, J., Craveiro, J., Schoofs, T., Tatibana, C., Windsor, J.: AIR Technology: a step towards ARINC 653 in space. In: Proc. DASIA 2009 "DAta System. Aerospace" Conf. Istanbul, Turkey (May 2009)
23. Rufino, J., Filipe, S., Coutinho, M., Santos, S., Windsor, J.: ARINC 653 interface in RTEMS. In: Proc. DASIA 2007 "DAta System, Aerospace" Conf. Naples, Italy (June 2007)

24. Rushby, J.: Partitioning in avionics architectures: Requirements, mechanisms and assurance. NASA Contractor Report CR-1999-209347, SRI International, California, USA (June 1999)
25. Sánchez-Puebla, M.A., Carretero, J.: A new approach for distributed computing in avionics systems. In: Proc. 1st Int. Symp. on Information and Communication Technologies, Trinity College Dublin, Dublin, Ireland, pp. 579–584 (2003)
26. Santos, S., Rufino, J., Schoofs, T., Tatibana, C., Windsor, J.: A portable ARINC 653 standard interface. In: Proc. IEEE/AIAA 27th Digital Avionics Systems Conf. St. Paul, MN, USA (October 2008)
27. Seyer, R., Siemers, C., Falsett, R., Ecker, K., Richter, H.: Robust partitioning for reliable real-time systems. In: Proc. 18th Int. Parallel and Distributed Processing Symp., pp. 117–122 (Apr 2004)
28. SPARC International, Inc., Menlo Park, CA, USA: The SPARC Architecture Manual, Version 8 (1992)
29. Terraillon, J.L., Hjortnaes, K.: Technical note on on-board software. European Space Technology Harmonisation, Technical Dossier on Mapping, TOSE-2-DOS-1, ESA (February 2003)
30. Watkins, C., Walter, R.: Transitioning from federated avionics architectures to Integrated Modular Avionics. In: Proc. 26th IEEE/AIAA Digital Avionics Systems Conf. Dallas, TX, USA (October 2007)
31. Wind River: Wind River VxWorks 653 Platform, http://www.windriver.com/products/platforms/safety_critical_arinc_653/ (retrieved on June 17, 2010)
32. Windsor, J., Hjortnaes, K.: Time and space partitioning in spacecraft avionics. In: Proc. 3rd IEEE Int. Conf. on Space Mission Challenges for Information Technology, Pasadena, CA, USA, pp. 13–20 (July 2009)

Appendix: Notation

Symbol	Description
	Convention used
$\mathbb{N}$	Set of natural numbers ($0 \notin \mathbb{N}$)
$n(S)$	(Where S is a set) Equivalent to $\#S$
$a \bmod b$	Modulo operation (remainder of the division of a by b)
	Partitions
P	Set of partitions in the system
$n(P)$	Number of partitions in the system ($n(P) \equiv \#P$)
P_m	Partition m
$M_m(t)$	Operating mode of partition P_m at instant t
	(normal, idle, coldStart, or warmStart)
	Partition scheduling
χ	Set of partition schedules available in the system
$n(\chi)$	Number of partition schedules available ($n(\chi) \equiv \#\chi$)
χ_i	Partition schedule i
MTF_i	Major time frame of schedule χ_i
Q_i	Set of partition time requirements for χ_i
$P_{i,m}^\chi$	Each partition with at least one time window in χ_i
$\eta_{i,m}$	Activation cycle of partition $P_{i,m}^\chi$ under χ_i
$d_{i,m}$	Duration of partition $P_{i,m}^\chi$ under χ_i
ω_i	Set of time windows in schedule χ_i
$n(\omega_i)$	Number of time windows in schedule χ_i ($n(\omega_i) \equiv \#\omega_i$)
$\omega_{i,j}$	Time window j in schedule χ_i
$P_{i,j}^\omega$	Partition active during time window $\omega_{i,j}$
$O_{i,j}$	Offset of time window $\omega_{i,j}$, relative to the beginning of MTF_i
$c_{i,j}$	Duration of time window $\omega_{i,j}$
	Tasks/processes
τ_m	Taskset of partition P_m
$n(\tau_m)$	Number of tasks (processes) in partition P_m ($n(\tau_m) \equiv \#\tau_m$)
$\tau_{m,q}$	Task q of partition P_m
$T_{m,q}$	Period of task $\tau_{m,q}$
$D_{m,q}$	Relative deadline of task $\tau_{m,q}$
$p_{m,q}$	(Base) priority of task $\tau_{m,q}$
$C_{m,q}$	Worst case execution time (WCET) of task $\tau_{m,q}$
$S_{m,q}(t)$	Status of task $\tau_{m,q}$ at instant t
$D'_{m,q}(t)$	(Absolute) deadline time of task $\tau_{m,q}$ at instant t
$p'_{m,q}(t)$	(Current) priority of task $\tau_{m,q}$ at instant t
$St_{m,q}(t)$	State of task $\tau_{m,q}$ at instant t (dormant, ready, running, or waiting)
$Ready_m(t)$	Set of schedulable tasks (ready or running) in partition P_m at instant t
$heir_m(t)$	Heir task in partition P_m at instant t
$V(t)$	Set of tasks which, at instant t, have violated a deadline

Note: This notation, as described in this table, applies to the system model where multiple partition schedules are supported.

Architecting Dependable Systems with Proactive Fault Management

Felix Salfner and Miroslaw Malek

Humboldt-Universität zu Berlin
Institut für Informatik
Unter den Linden 6
10099 Berlin, Germany
{salfner,malek}@informatik.hu-berlin.de

Abstract. Management of an ever-growing complexity of computing systems is an everlasting challenge for computer system engineers. We argue that we need to resort to predictive technologies in order to harness the system's complexity and transform a vision of proactive system and failure management into reality. We describe proactive fault management, provide an overview and taxonomy for online failure prediction methods and present a classification of failure prediction-triggered methods. We present a model to assess the effects of proactive fault management on system reliability and show that overall dependability can significantly be enhanced. After having shown the methods and potential of proactive fault management we describe a blueprint how proactive fault management can be incorporated into a dependable system's architecture.

1 Introduction

With the unstoppable proliferation of computer/communication systems to all domains of human activity, their dependable design, development and operation is and will remain of key importance. Major challenges are posed first and foremost by an ever-increasing system complexity due to growing functional requirements, increasing connectivity, and dynamicity:[1] Growing functional requirements lead to more complex hardware and software designs. For example, today's mobile phones feature graphic acceleration hardware and embedded multi-core processors, they run full-featured multitasking operating systems and are permanently connected to other computer systems via wireless local area networks (WLAN), Bluetooth, or 3G communication networks. Server systems run in virtualized environments where there is no direct link between the resources seen at the operating system level and physical resources. Furthermore, they are

---

[1] We deliberately chose the term *dynamicity* rather than *dynamics*. In our understanding, the latter refers to varying load and usage patterns during runtime whereas *dynamicity* refers to slower processes such as changing configurations, software versions, etc.

A. Casimiro et al. (Eds.): Architecting Dependable Systems VII, LNCS 6420, pp. 171–200, 2010.

built from commercial-off-the-shelf components (COTS) that are dynamically controlled by service-oriented architectures. Although COTS components help to lower cost, suppliers frequently do not reveal their internals, which makes building dependable systems more difficult. Furthermore, current computer systems integrate a non-negligible number of legacy systems, which add significantly to system complexity. And, last but not least, today's systems show an increasing dynamicity: configuration changes, updates, upgrades (sometimes they turn, unintentionally, into downgrades) and patches are the rule rather than the exception. All these factors translate into many degrees of freedom which complicates testing and correctness assurance. One may even conclude that traditional fault tolerance techniques have reached a limit. They are not rendered obsolete, but they need to be accompanied by techniques that are able to handle the dynamicity, complexity, and connectivity of concurrent computer/communication system designs.

One such approach is called *Proactive Fault Management* (PFM). The key notion of PFM is to apply prediction techniques in order to anticipate upcoming failures and to take steps such that the imminent problem can either be avoided or its effects can be alleviated. It differs from traditional fault tolerance techniques in that:

– It proactively takes actions even before an anticipated failure occurs rather than reacting to failures that have already happened.
– It follows an observation-based black-box approach in order to handle hardly comprehensible and understandable system complexity.
– It employs methods that can adapt to changing system behavior, i.e., it can handle system dynamicity. In order to do so, it relies on algorithms from statistical learning theory that allow, e.g., for adjustable classification. These approaches in general allow to handle uncertainty about and within the underlying system.

This chapter gives an overview of proactive fault management. More specifically, we introduce PFM in Sect. 2 and give an overview of online failure prediction techniques in Sect. 3. This also includes a more detailed presentation of two statistical failure prediction approaches, which have been applied to data of a commercial telecommunication platform. In Sect. 4, a coarse-grained classification of failure prediction-driven recovery schemes is provided and an assessment of the effects of PFM on system availability, reliability and hazard rate are described in Sect. 5. After having covered the methods and having pointed out the potential of proactive fault management we provide an architectural blueprint for PFM in Sect. 6.

2   Proactive Fault Management

Proactive Fault Management[2] integrates well into many computing concepts such as *autonomic computing* [38], *trustworthy computing* [55], *adaptive enterprise* [17],

---

[2] In analogy to the term "fault tolerance", we use "proactive fault management" as an umbrella term. It is actually adopted from [14].

recovery-oriented computing [10], and computing with self-* properties where the asterisk can be replaced by any of "configuration", "healing", "optimization", or "protection" (see, e.g., [5]). Most of these terms span a variety of research areas ranging from adaptive storage to advanced security concepts, whereas PFM focuses on faults, respectively failures of such systems.

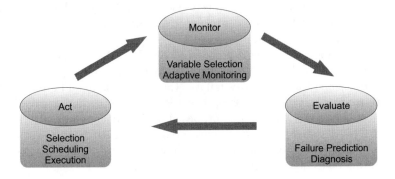

Fig. 1. The MEA cycle of Proactive Fault Management

PFM is based on the *Monitor–Evaluate–Act* (MEA) cycle, which means that the following three steps are continuously repeated during system runtime:

- **Monitor.** PFM is observation-based, which implies that the system is continuously monitored during its entire operation. Although we will not cover all aspects of monitoring, here, a discussion on aspects such as variable selection and adaptive monitoring is included in Sect. 6.
- **Evaluate.** The monitoring data is continuously evaluated in order to check whether the system's current state is failure-prone or not. This is the goal of online failure prediction algorithms. Evaluation might also include diagnosis in order to identify the components that cause the system to be failure-prone[3].
- **Act.** In case of an imminent failure, counteractions are performed in order to do something about the failure. However, there might be several actions available, such that the most effective method needs to be selected. Effectiveness of actions is evaluated based on an objective function taking cost of actions, confidence in the prediction, probability of success and complexity of actions into account. In addition to selecting an appropriate action, its execution needs to be scheduled, e.g., at times of low system utilization, and it needs to be executed.

Our MEA approach is similar to the Monitor, Analyze, Plan, Execute (MAPE) cycle introduced by IBM in the context of autonomic computing and failure prediction [70,40] but we have decided to merge "planning" and "execution"

---

[3] Note that in contrast to traditional diagnosis, in PFM no failure has occurred, yet, posing new challenges for diagnosis algorithms.

into one group since for many environments planning and execution are tightly coupled. For example, planning frequently relies on the action selected (e.g., planning of a (partial) restart probably needs to take other constraints into account than moving computations from one server to another). It should also be noted that both loops in fact are control loops, and the general principles of control theory apply to both of them. More specifically, when designing a dependable system, control loop aspects such as stability and the occurrence of oscillations should be checked for any given approach (see [59] for a good example how this can be done).

Several examples for systems employing proactive fault management have been described in the literature. In [16] a framework called application cluster service is described that facilitates failover (both preventive and after a failure) and state recovery services. FT-Pro, which is a failure prediction-driven adaptive fault management system, was proposed in [50]. It uses false positive error rate and false negative rate of a failure predictor together with cost and expected downtime to choose among the options to migrate processes, to trigger checkpointing or to do nothing.

3   Online Failure Prediction Methods

Predicting the future has fascinated people from beginning of times. World wide, millions work on prediction daily. Experts on prediction range from fortune tellers and meteorologists to pollsters, stock brokers, doctors and scientists. Predictive technologies have been and are used in a variety of areas and in disaster and failure management they cover a wide range from eliminating minor inconveniences to saving human lives.

In a more technical context, failure prediction has a long tradition in mechanical engineering. Especially in the area of preventive maintenance, forecasting a device's failure has been of great interest, which has been accompanied by reliability theory (See, e.g., [29] for an overview). A key input parameter of these models is the distribution of time to failure. Therefore, a lot of work exists providing methods to fit various reliability models to data with failure time occurrences. There were also approaches that tried to incorporate several factors into the distribution. For example, the MIL-book 217 [57] classified, among others, the manufacturing process whereas several software reliability methods incorporated code complexity, fixing of bugs, etc. into their models (see, e.g., [25]). However, these methods are tailored to long-term predictions and do not work appropriately for short-term predictions (i.e., for the next few minutes to hours) as are needed for the PFM. That is why methods for online failure prediction are based on runtime monitoring in order to take into account the current state of the system. Nevertheless, techniques from classical reliability theory can help to improve online failure prediction as well.

A variety of runtime monitoring-based methods have been developed. In this chapter, we describe a classification taxonomy for prediction methods and present two specific approaches from two categories in more detail. The taxonomy and its description is a condensed version of the one described in survey [65].

3.1   Main Categories of Prediction Methods

In order to establish a top-level classification of prediction methods, we first analyze the process of how faults turn into failures.

Several attempts have been made to get to a precise definition of faults, errors, and failures, among which are [54,3,45,18], [67, Page 22], and most recently [4]. Since the latter seems to have broad acceptance, its definitions are used in this article with some additional extensions and interpretations.

- A *failure* is defined as "an event that occurs when the delivered service deviates from correct service". The main point here is that a failure refers to misbehavior that can be observed by the user, which can either be a human or another computer system. Things may go wrong inside the system, but as long as it does not result in incorrect output (including the case that there is no output at all) there is no failure.
- The situation when "things go wrong" in the system can be formalized as the situation when the system's state deviates from the correct state, which is called an *error*. Hence, "an error is the part of the total state of the system that may lead to its subsequent service failure."
- Finally, *faults* are the adjudged or hypothesized cause of an error – the root cause of an error. In most cases, faults remain dormant for some time and once they become active, they cause an incorrect system state, which is an error. That is why errors are also called "manifestation" of faults. Several classifications of faults have been proposed in the literature among which the distinction between transient, intermittent and permanent faults [67, Page 22] and the fault model by Cristian [19], which has later been extended by Laranjeira, et al. [46] and Barborak, et al. [7], are best known.
- The definition of an error implies that the activation of a fault lead to an incorrect state, however, this does not necessarily mean that the system knows about it. In addition to the definitions given by [4], we distinguish between *undetected errors* and *detected errors*: An error remains undetected until an error detector identifies the incorrect state.
- Besides causing a failure, undetected or detected errors may cause out-of-norm behavior of system parameters as a side-effect. We call this out-of-norm behavior a *symptom*[4]. In the context of *software aging*, symptoms are similar to *aging-related errors*, as implicitly introduced in [31] and explicitly named in [30].

Figure 2 visualizes how a fault can evolve into a failure. Note that there can be an m-to-n mapping between faults, errors, symptoms, and failures: For example, several faults may result in one single error or one fault may result in several errors. The same holds for errors and failures: Some errors result in a failure some errors do not, and more complicated, some errors only result in a failure under special conditions. As is also indicated in the figure, an undetected

---

[4] This should not be confused with [41], who use the term *symptom* for the most significant errors within an error group.

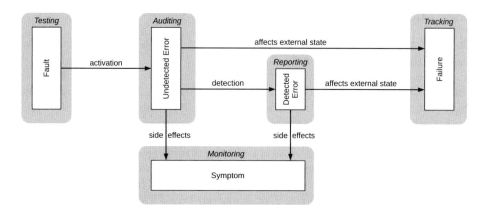

Fig. 2. Interrelations of faults, errors, symptoms, and failures. Encapsulating boxes show the technique by which the corresponding flaw can be made visible.

error may cause a failure directly or might even be non-distinguishable from it. Furthermore, errors do not necessarily show symptoms.

To further clarify the terms fault, error, symptom, and failure, consider a fault-tolerant system with a memory leak in its software. The fault is, e.g., a missing `free` statement in the source code. However, as long as this part of the software is never executed, the fault remains dormant. Once the piece of code that should free memory is executed, the software enters an incorrect state, i.e., it turns into an error (memory is consumed and never freed although it is not needed anymore). If the amount of unnecessarily allocated memory is sufficiently small, this incorrect state will neither be detected nor will it prevent the system from delivering its intended service (no failure is observable from the outside). Nevertheless, if the piece of code with the memory leak is executed many times, the amount of free memory will slowly decrease in the long run. This out-of-norm behavior of the system parameter "free memory" is a symptom of the error. At some point in time, there might not be enough memory for some memory allocation and the error is detected. However, if it is a fault-tolerant system, the failed memory allocation still does not necessarily lead to a service failure. For example, the operation might be completed by some spare unit. Only if the entire system, as observed from the outside, cannot deliver its service correctly, a failure occurs.

Since online failure prediction methods evaluate monitoring data in order to determine whether the current system state is failure-prone or not, the algorithms have to tap observations from the process how a fault evolves into a failure. The gray surrounding boxes in Fig. 2 show the techniques by which each stage can be made visible:

1. In order to identify a fault, *testing* must be performed. The goal of testing is to identify flaws in a system regardless whether the entity under test is actually used by the system or not. For example, in memory testing, the entire memory is examined even though some areas might never be used.

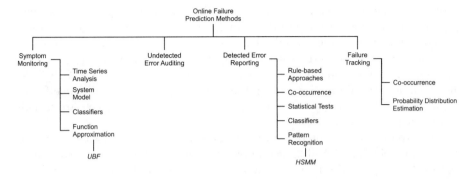

Fig. 3. Coarse-grain classification of online failure prediction techniques. The bottom line represents the exemplary approaches presented in this paper.

2. Undetected errors can be identified by *auditing*. Auditing describes techniques that check whether the entity under audit is in an incorrect state. For example, memory auditing would inspect used data structures by checksumming.
3. Symptoms, which are side-effects of errors, can be identified by *monitoring* system parameters such as memory usage, workload, sequence of function calls, etc. An undetected error can be made visible by identifying out-of-norm behavior of the monitored system variable(s).
4. Once an error detector identifies an incorrect state the detected error may become visible by *reporting*. Reports are written to some logging mechanism such as logfiles or Simple Network Management Protocol (SNMP) messages.
5. Finally, the occurrence of failures can be made visible by *tracking* mechanisms. Tracking is usually performed from outside the system and includes, for example, sending test requests to the system in order to identify service crashes[5].

The taxonomy for online failure prediction algorithms is structured along the five stages of fault capturing. However, fault testing is no option for the purpose of *online* failure prediction and is hence not included in the taxonomy. This taxonomy is discussed in full detail in [65], and we only introduce its main categories here. Figure 3 shows the simplified taxonomy, which also highlights where the two prediction methods that will be discussed in Sect. 3.2 are located.

Failure Prediction Based on Symptom Monitoring. The motivation for analyzing periodically measured system variables such as the amount of free memory in order to identify an imminent failure is the fact that some types of errors affect the system slowly, even before they are detected (this is sometimes referred to as *service degradation*). A prominent example are memory leaks: due to a leak the amount of free memory is slowly decreasing over time, but, as long as there is still memory available, the error is neither detected nor is a failure

---

[5] This is sometimes called *active monitoring*.

observed. When memory is getting scarce, the computer may first slow down (e.g., due to memory swapping) and only if there is no memory left an error is detected and a failure might result. The key notion of failure prediction based on monitoring data is that errors like memory leaks can be grasped by their side-effects on the system (symptoms) such as exceptional memory usage, CPU load, disk I/O, or unusual function calls in the system. Symptom-based online failure prediction methods frequently address non-failstop failures, which are usually more difficult to grasp.

This group of failure prediction methods comprises the majority of existing prediction techniques. Well-known approaches are the Multivariate State Estimation Technique (MSET) [68], trend analysis techniques like the one developed in [28] or function approximation approaches. The Universal Basis Functions (UBF) failure prediction method, which is described in Sect. 3.2, belongs to this category.

Failure Prediction Based on Undetected Error Auditing. Although auditing of undetected errors can be applied offline, the same techniques can be applied during runtime as well. However, we are not aware of any work pursuing this approach, hence the branch has no further subdivisions.

Failure Prediction Based on Detected Error Reporting. When an error is detected, the detection event is usually reported using some logging facility. Hence, failure prediction approaches that use error reports as input data have to deal with event-driven input data. This is one of the major differences to symptom monitoring-based approaches, which in most cases operate on periodic system observations. Furthermore, symptoms are in most cases real-valued while error events mostly are discrete, categorical data such as event IDs, component IDs, etc. The problem statement of detected error failure prediction is shown in Fig. 4. Based on error events that have occurred within a data window prior to present time, online failure prediction has to assess whether a failure will occur at some point of time in the future or not.

Siewiorek and Swarz [66] state that the first approaches to error detection-based failure prediction have been proposed by Nassar et al. [56]. These approaches rely on systematic changes in the distribution of error types and on significant increase of error generation rates between crashes. Another method has been developed by Lin and Siewiorek [52], [51] called Dispersion Frame Technique (DFT). A second group of failure prediction approaches comprises data

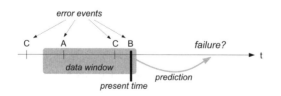

Fig. 4. Event-based failure prediction

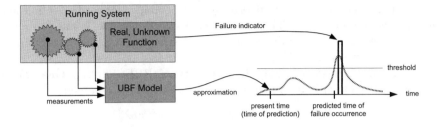

Fig. 5. Failure Prediction using UBF

mining techniques. One of the best-known prediction algorithm of this category has been developed at IBM T.J. Watson by Vilalta et al. (see, e.g., [73]). The authors introduce a concept called event sets and apply data-mining techniques to identify sets of events that are indicative of the occurrence of failures. Further methods have briefly been described by Levy et al. in [49]. We have developed a failure prediction method that is based on pattern recognition. More specifically, the main concept is to use hidden semi-Markov models (HSMM) to identify patterns of errors that are symptomatic for an upcoming failure (see Sect. 3.2).

Failure Prediction Based on Failure Tracking. The basic idea of failure prediction based on failure tracking is to draw conclusions about upcoming failures from the occurrence of previous failures. This may include the time of occurrence as well as the types of failures that have occurred. Failure predictors of this category have been proposed in, e.g., [20] and [61].

3.2   Two Exemplary Methods

Two online failure prediction methods have been developed at Computer Architecture and Communication Group at Humboldt University Berlin: UBF and HSMM. The two methods will be described briefly in order to provide a better understanding of how online failure prediction can be accomplished. Both approaches have been applied to a case study, as is described in Sect. 3.3.

Universal Basis Functions (UBF). UBF [37] is a function approximation method that takes monitoring variables such as workload, number of semaphore operations per second, and memory consumption as input data. It consists of three steps: First, most indicative variables are selected by the Probabilistic Wrapper Approach (PWA). In a subsequent step recorded training data is analyzed in order to identify UBFs that map the monitoring data onto the target function. The target function can be any failure indicator such as service availability, which was the one chosen in the case study (see Fig. 5). The third step consists of applying UBFs to monitoring data during runtime in order to perform online failure prediction. These steps are usually repeated until a sufficient level of failure prediction accuracy is reached (see [35] for details).

PWA is a variable selection algorithm that combines forward selection and backward elimination (c.f., [33]) in a probabilistic framework. It has proven to be very effective, outperforming by far both methods as well as a selection by (human) domain experts [35].

UBF are an extension of Radial Basis Functions (RBF, c.f. [21]). One UBF is a mixture of two kernels used instead of one single Gaussian kernel:

$$k_i(\boldsymbol{x}) = m_i\gamma(\boldsymbol{x}, \boldsymbol{\lambda}_i^\gamma) + (1 - m_i)\delta(\boldsymbol{x}, \boldsymbol{\lambda}_i^\delta) \qquad (1)$$

where k_i denotes the UBF kernel that is a mixture of kernels γ and δ with parameter vectors $\boldsymbol{\lambda}_i^\gamma$ and $\boldsymbol{\lambda}_i^\delta$, respectively. Parameter m_i is the mixture weight and $\boldsymbol{x}$ is the input vector. By including m_i in the optimization, UBF can better adapt to specifics of the data. For example, if a Gaussian and a sigmoid kernel are mixed, either "peaked", "stepping" or mixed behavior can be modeled in various regions of the input space.

Event-based Pattern Recognition using Hidden Semi-Markov Models (HSMM). Taking all errors into account that occur within a time window of length Δt_d, error event timestamps and message IDs form an event-driven temporal sequence, which we called *error sequence*. Based on this notion, the task of failure prediction is turned into a pattern recognition problem where the goal is to identify if the error pattern observed during runtime is indicative for an upcoming failure or not. Hidden semi-Markov models are used as pattern recognition tool and machine learning techniques are applied in order to algorithmically identify characteristic properties indicating whether a given error sequence is failure-prone or not. Of course, error sequences are rarely identical. Therefore, a probabilistic approach is adopted to handle similarity.

More specifically, failure and non-failure error sequences are extracted from training data for which it is known when failures had occurred. Failure sequences are error sequences that have occurred preceding a failure by lead time Δt_l. Non-failure sequences consist of errors appearing in the log when no failures have occurred (see Fig. 6). Two HSMMs are trained: One for failure sequences and the other for non-failure sequences. The main goal of training is that the failure HSMM is specifically tailored towards characteristics of failure sequences, and the non-failure HSMM is mainly needed for sequence classification.

Once the two models have been trained, new unknown sequences that occur during runtime can be evaluated. For this, sequence likelihood (which is a probabilistic measure of similarity to training sequences) is computed for both HSMM models and Bayes decision theory is applied in order to yield a classification. In other words, by training, the failure model has learned what error sequences look like. Hence, if the sequence under consideration is very similar to failure sequences in the training data (the failure sequence HSMM outputs a higher sequence likelihood than the non-failure HSMM), it is assumed that a failure is looming which will occur at time Δt_l ahead.

A thorough analysis of the algorithm's properties such as accuracy of the initial training and complexity aspects together with measurements regarding the computational overhead can be found in [64].

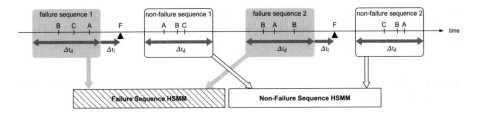

Fig. 6. Training hidden semi-Markov models (HSMM) from recorded training sequences. A,B,C denote error events, ▲ denote the occurrence of failures, Δt_d denotes the length of the data window, Δt_l denotes lead time before failure.

3.3   A Case Study

In order to show how well the failure predictors described in the previous sections work for contemporary complex computer systems, we sketch an extensive case study where we applied the UBF and HSMM failure predictors to data of a commercial telecommunication system. The main purpose of the telecommunication system is to realize a so-called Service Control Point (SCP) in an Intelligent Network (IN). An SCP provides services[6] to handle communication related management data such as billing, number translations or prepaid functionality for various services of mobile communication: Mobile Originated Calls (MOC), Short Message Service (SMS), or General Packet Radio Service (GPRS). The fact that the system is an SCP implies that the system cooperates closely with other telecommunication systems in the Global System for Mobile Communication (GSM), but the system does not switch calls itself. It rather has to respond to a large variety of different service requests regarding accounts, billing, etc. submitted to the system over various protocols such as Remote Authentication Dial In User Interface (RADIUS), Signaling System Number 7 (SS7), or Internet Protocol (IP).

The system's architecture is a multi-tier architecture employing a component-based software design. At the time when measurements were taken the system consisted of more than 1.6 million lines of code, approximately 200 components realized by more than 2000 classes, running simultaneously in several containers, each replicated for fault tolerance.

Failure Definition and Input Data. As discussed in Sect. 3.1, a failure is defined as the event when a system ceases to fulfill its specification. Specifications for the telecommunication system under investigation require that within successive, non-overlapping five minutes intervals, the fraction of calls having response time longer than 250ms must not exceed 0.01%. This definition is equivalent to a required four-nines interval service availability:

$$A_i = \frac{\text{service requests within 5 min. with response time} \leq 250\text{ms}}{\text{total number of service requests within 5 min.}} \geq 99.99\% \quad (2)$$

---

[6] So-called Service Control Functions (SCF).

Hence the failures predicted are performance failures that occur when Eq. 2 does not hold. System error logs and data of the System Activity Reporter (SAR) have been used as input data.

Metrics. The quality (i.e., accuracy) of failure predictors is usually assessed by three metrics that have an intuitive interpretation: precision, recall, and false positive rate:

- *Precision*: fraction of correctly predicted failures in comparison to all failure warnings
- *Recall*: fraction of correctly predicted failures in comparison to the total number of failures. Recall is also called true positive rate.
- *False positive rate*: fraction of false alarms in comparison to all non-failures.

A perfect failure prediction would achieve a one-to-one matching between predicted and actual failures which would result in precision and recall equal to one and a false positive rate equal to zero. If a prediction algorithm achieves, for example, precision of 0.8, the probability is 80% that any generated failure warning is correct (refers to a true failure) and 20% are false warnings. A recall of, say, 0.9 expresses that 90% of all actual failures are predicted and 10% are missed. A false positive rate of 0.1 indicates that 10% of predictions that should not result in a failure warning are falsely classified as failure-prone.

There is often an inverse proportionality between high recall and high precision. Improving recall in most cases lowers precision and vice versa. Many failure predictors (including UBF and HSMM) allow to control this trade-off by use of a threshold. There is also a proportionality between true positive rate (which is equal to recall) and false positive rate: Increasing the true positive rate usually also increases the false positive rate. It is common to visualize this relation by a Receiver-Operating-Characteristic (ROC) [26].

To evaluate and compare failure predictors by a single real number the maximum value of the F-measure (which is the harmonic mean of precision and recall), the value of the point where precision equals recall, or the area under the ROC curve (AUC) can be used.

Results. UBF and HSMM have been applied to data collected from the telecommunication system. We report some of the results here in order to give a rough estimate of the accuracy that can be achieved when failure predictors are applied to complex computer systems. For a threshold value that results in maximum F-measure, the HSMM predictor achieves a precision, recall, and false positive rate of 0.70, 0.62, and 0.016, respectively. This means that failure warnings are correct in 70% of all cases and almost two third of all failures are predicted by HSMM. Area under the ROC curve (AUC) equals 0.873. A detailed analysis of HSMM results can be found in [64, Chap. 9]. The UBF approach has been investigated using ROC analysis and achieved an AUC equal to 0.846. A detailed analysis of properties and results can be found in [36].

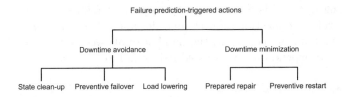

Fig. 7. Classification of actions that can be triggered by failure prediction

4   Prediction-Driven Countermeasures

The third phase in the MEA cycle (c.f. Fig. 1) is to act upon the warning of an upcoming failure. This section gives an overview of the methods that can be triggered by a failure warning.

4.1   Types of Actions

There are five classes of actions that can be performed upon failure prediction, as is shown in the coarse-grained classification in Fig. 7. The two principle goals that prediction-driven actions can target are:

- *Downtime avoidance* (or failure avoidance) aims at circumventing the occurrence of the failure such that the system continues to operate without interruption
- *Downtime minimization* (minimization of the impact of failures) involves downtime, but the goal is to reduce downtime exploiting the knowledge that a failure might be imminent.

Each category of techniques will be discussed separately in the following.

4.2   Downtime Avoidance

Downtime avoidance actions try to prevent the occurrence of an imminent failure that has not yet occurred. Three categories of mechanisms can be identified:

- State clean-up tries to avoid failures by cleaning up resources. Examples include garbage collection, clearance of queues, correction of corrupt data or elimination of "hung" processes.
- Preventive failover techniques perform a preventive switch to some spare hardware or software unit. Several variants of this technique exist, one of which is failure prediction-driven load balancing accomplishing gradual "failover" from a failure-prone to failure-free component. For example, a multiprocessor environment that is able to migrate processes in case of an imminent failure is described in [15]. Current virtualization framework such as XEN[7] offers flexible and easy-to-use interfaces to perform migration from one (virtual) machine to another.

---

[7] http://www.xen.org

- Lowering the load is a common way to prevent failures. For example, web-servers reject connection requests in order not to become overloaded. Within proactive fault management, the number of allowed connections is adaptive and would depend on the assessed risk of failure.

4.3 Downtime Minimization

Repairing the system after failure occurrence is the classical way of failure handling. Detection mechanisms such as coding checks, replication checks, timing checks or plausibility checks trigger the recovery. Within proactive fault management, these actions still incur downtime, but its occurrence is either anticipated or even intended in order to reduce time-to-repair. Two categories exist:

- *Prepared repair* tries to prepare recovery mechanisms for the upcoming failure. Similar to traditional fault tolerance techniques, these methods still react to the occurrence of a failure, but due to preparation, repair time is reduced.
- *Preventive restart* intentionally brings the system down for restart turning unplanned downtime into forced downtime, which is expected to be shorter (fail fast policy).

Prepared Repair. The main objective of reactive downtime minimization is to bring the system into a consistent fault-free state. If the fault-free state is a previous one (a so-called checkpoint), the action applies a roll-backward scheme (see, e.g., [24] for a survey of roll-back recovery in message passing systems). In this case, all computation from the last checkpoint up to the time of failure occurrence has to be repeated. Typical examples are recovery from a checkpoint or the recovery block scheme introduced by [62]. In case of a roll-forward scheme, the system is moved to a new fault-free state (see, e.g., [63]). Both schemes may comprise reconfiguration such as switching to a hardware spare or another version of a software program, changing network routing, etc. Reconfiguration takes place before computations are repeated.

In traditional fault-tolerant computing without proactive fault management, checkpoints are saved independently of upcoming failures, e.g., periodically. When a failure occurs, first, reconfiguration takes place until the system is ready for recomputation / approximation and then all the computations from the last checkpoint up to the time of failure occurrence are repeated. Time-to-repair (TTR) is determined by two factors: time needed to get a fault-free system by hardware repair or reconfiguration, plus the time needed to redo lost computations (in case of roll-backward) or time to get to a new fault-free state (in case of roll-forward). In the case of roll-backward strategies, recomputation time is determined by the length of the time interval between the checkpoint and the time of failure occurrence. This is illustrated in Fig. 8. In the figure, "Checkpoint" denotes the last checkpoint before failure, "Failure" the time of failure occurrence, "Fault-free" the time when a fault-free system is available and "Up" the time when the system is up again (with a consistent state). In some cases recomputation may take less time than originally but the implication still holds. Note that

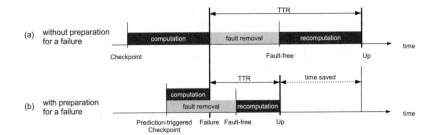

Fig. 8. Improved time-to-repair for prediction-driven repair schemes. (a) classical recovery and (b) improved recovery in case of preparation for an upcoming failure.

specific reactive downtime minimization techniques do not always exhibit both factors contributing to TTR.

Triggering such methods proactively by failure prediction can reduce both factors contributing to TTR:

– Time needed to obtain a fault-free system can be reduced since mechanisms can be prepared for an upcoming failure. Think, for example, of a cold spare: Booting the spare machine can be started right after an upcoming failure has been predicted (and hence before failure occurrence) such that a running fault-free system is available earlier after failure.
– Checkpoints may be saved upon failure prediction close to the failure, which reduces the amount of computation that needs to be repeated. This minimizes time consumed by recomputation. On the other hand, it might not be wise to save a checkpoint at a time when a failure can be anticipated since the system state might already be corrupted. The question whether such scheme is applicable depends on fault isolation between the system that is going to observe the failure and the state that is included in the checkpoint. For example, if the amount of free memory is monitored for failure prediction but the checkpoint comprises database tables of a separate database server, it might be proper to rely on the correctness of the database checkpoint. Additionally, an adaptive checkpointing scheme similar to the one described in [58] could be applied. In [47] predictive checkpointing for a high-availability high performance Linux cluster has been implemented.

Preventive Restart. Parnas [60] has reported on an effect what he called software aging, being a name for effects such as memory leaks, unreleased file locks, accumulated round-off errors, or memory corruption. Based on these observations, Huang et al. introduced a concept that the authors termed rejuvenation. The idea of rejuvenation is to deal with problems related to software aging by restarting the system (or at least parts of it). By this approach, unplanned / unscheduled / unprepared downtime incurred by non-anticipated failures is replaced by forced / scheduled / anticipated downtime. The authors have shown that – under certain assumptions – overall downtime and downtime cost can be reduced by this approach. In [12] the approach is extended by introducing recovery-oriented computing (see, e.g., [10]), where restarting is organized recursively until the problem is solved. In the context of proactive fault management the restart is triggered by failure prediction. Also, a resource consumption trend estimation technique has been implemented into IBM Director Management Software for xSeries servers that can restart parts of the system [14].

5   A Model to Assess the Effect on Reliability

Reliability modeling is an integral part in architecting dependable systems. We have developed a Continuous Time Markov Chain (CTMC) model to assess the effects of proactive fault management on steady-state system availability, reliability and hazard rate. This section introduces the model and lists key results, a full derivation and analysis can be found in [64, Chap. 10].

5.1   Summary of Proactive Fault Management Behavior

Before introducing the CTMC model for reliability assessment, we summarize the behavior of proactive fault management and its effects on mean-time-to-failure (MTTF) and mean-time-to-repair (MTTR). The behavior can be summarized as follows: If the the evaluation step in the MEA cycle (i.e., failure prediction) suggests that the system is running well and no failure is anticipated in the near future (negative prediction), no action is triggered. If the conclusion is that there is a failure comping up (positive prediction) downtime avoidance methods, downtime minimization methods, or both are triggered. From this follows that in case of a false positive prediction (there is no failure coming up although the predictor suggests so, c.f., Sect. 3.3) actions are performed unnecessarily while in case of a false negative prediction (a failure is imminent but the predictor does not warn about it) nothing is done. Table 1 summarizes all four cases.

5.2   Related Work on Models

Proactive fault management is rooted in preventive maintenance, that has been a research issue for several decades (an overview can be found, e.g., in [29]). More specifically, proactive fault management belongs to the category of condition-based preventive maintenance (c.f., e.g., [69]). However, the majority of work

Table 1. Summary of proactive fault management behavior

Prediction	Downtime avoidance	Downtime minimization	
		Prepared repair	Preventive restart
True positive	Try to prevent failure	Prepare repair	Force downtime
False positive	Unneces. action	Unneces. preparation	Unneces. downtime
True negative	No action	No action	No action
False negative	No action	Standard (unprep.) repair (recovery)	No action

has been focused on industrial production systems such as heavy assembly line machines and more recently on computing hardware. With respect to software, preventive maintenance has focused more on long-term software product aging such as software versions and updates rather than short-term execution aging. The only exception is software rejuvenation which has been investigated heavily (c.f., e.g., [42]).

Starting from general preventive maintenance theory, reliability of condition-based preventive maintenance is computed in [44]. However, the approach is based on a graphical analysis of so-called total time on test plots of singleton observation variables such as temperature, etc. rendering the approach not appropriate for application to automatic proactive fault management in software systems. An approach better suited to software has been presented by [1]. They use a continuous-time Markov chain (CTMC) to model system deterioration, periodic inspection, preventive maintenance and repair. However, one of the major disadvantages of their approach is that they assume perfect periodic inspection, which does not reflect failure prediction reality.

A significant body of work has been published addressing software rejuvenation. Initially, the authors of [39] have used a CTMC in order to compute steady-state availability and expected downtime cost. In order to overcome various limitations of the model, e.g., that constant transition rates are not well-suited to model software aging, several variations to the original model of Huang et al. [39] have been published over the years, some of which are briefly discussed here. Dohi et al. have extended the model to a semi-Markov process to deal more appropriately with the deterministic behavior of periodic restarting. Furthermore, they have slightly altered the topology of the model since they assume that there are cases where a repair does not result in a clean state and restart (rejuvenation) has to be performed after repair. The authors have computed steady-state availability [23] and cost [22] using this model. A slightly different model and the use Weibull distributions to characterize state transitions was proposed in [13]. However, due to this choice, the model cannot be solved analytically and an approximate solution from simulated data is presented.

In [27] the authors have used a three state discrete time Markov chain (DTMC) with two subordinated non-homogeneous CTMCs to model rejuvenation in transaction processing systems. One subordinated CTMC models queuing behavior of transaction processing and the second models preventive maintenance. The authors compute steady-state availability, probability of loosing a transaction, and an upper bound on response time for periodic rejuvenation. They model a more complex scheme that starts rejuvenation when the processing queue is empty. The same three-state macro-model has been used in [71], but here, time-to failure is estimated using a monitoring-based subordinated semi-Markov reward model. For model solution, the authors approximate time-to-failure with an increasing failure rate distribution.

A detailed stochastic reward net model of a high availability cluster system in order to model availability was presented in [48]. The model differentiates between servers, clients and network. Furthermore, it distinguishes permanent as well as intermittent failures that are either covered (i.e., eliminated by recon-figuration) or uncovered (i.e., eliminated by rebooting the cluster). Again, the model is too complex to be analyzed analytically and hence simulations are per-formed. An analytical solution for computing the optimal rejuvenation schedule is provided in [2] and uses deterministic function approximation techniques to characterize the relationship between aging factors and work metrics. The op-timal rejuvenation schedule can then be found by an analytical solution to an optimization problem.

The key property of proactive fault management is that it operates upon failure predictions rather than on a purely time-triggered execution of fault-tolerance mechanisms. The authors of [72] propose several stochastic reward nets (SRN), one of which explicitly models prediction-based rejuvenation. However, there are two limitations to this model: first, only one type of wrong predictions is covered, and second, the model is tailored to rejuvenation – downtime avoidance or prepared repair are not included. Furthermore, due to the complexity of the model, no analytical solution for availability is presented. Focusing on service degradation, a CTMC that includes the number of service requests in the system plus the amount of leaked memory was proposed in [6]. An adaptive rejuvenation scheme is analyzed that is based on estimated resource consumption. Later, the model has been combined with the three-state macro model presented in [27] in order to compute availability.

In summary, there is no model that incorporates all four types of predictions (TP, FP, TN, FN) and that accounts for the effects of downtime minimization and downtime avoidance methods. The following sections introduce such a model and show how availability, reliability and hazard rate can be computed from it.

5.3   Computing Availability

The model presented here is based on the CTMC originally published by Huang et. al [39]. It differs from their model in the following ways:

- Proactive fault management actions operate upon failure prediction rather than periodically. However, predictions can be correct or false. Moreover, it makes a difference whether there really is a failure imminent in the system or not. Hence, the single failure probable state S_P in the original model is split into a more fine-grained analysis: According to the four cases of prediction, there is a state for true positive predictions (S_{TP}), false positive predictions (S_{FP}), true negative predictions (S_{TN}) and false negative predictions (S_{FN}).
- In addition to rejuvenation, proactive fault management involves downtime avoidance techniques. That is why there is a transition in our model from the failure probable states S_{TP} and S_{FP} back to the fault-free "up" state S_0.
- With respect to downtime minimization, our model comprises prepared re-pair in addition to preventive restart. In order to account for their effect on time-to-repair, our model has two down states: one for prepared / forced downtime (S_R) and one for unprepared / unplanned downtime (S_F).

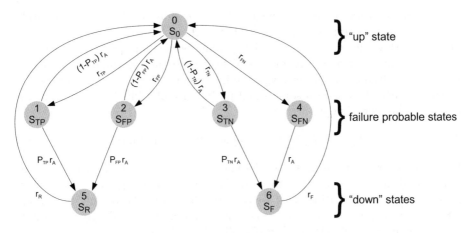

Fig. 9. Availability model for proactive fault management

Our CTMC model is shown in Fig. 9. In order to better explain the model, consider the following scenario: Starting from the up-state S_0 a failure prediction is performed at some point in time. If the predictor comes to the conclusion that a failure is imminent, it is a "positive" prediction and a failure warning is raised. If this is true (something is really going wrong in the system) the prediction is a true positive and a transition into S_{TP} takes place. Due to the warning, some actions are performed in order to either prevent the failure from occurring (downtime avoidance), or to prepare for some forced downtime (downtime minimization). Assuming first that some preventive actions are performed, let

$$P_{TP} := P(\text{failure} \mid \text{true positive prediction}) \tag{3}$$

denote the probability that the failure occurs despite of preventive actions. Hence, with probability P_{TP} a transition into failure state S_R takes place, and with probability $(1 - P_{TP})$ the failure can be avoided and the system returns to state S_0. Due to the fact that a failure warning was raised (the prediction was a positive one), preparatory actions have been performed and repair is quicker (on average), such that state S_0 is entered with rate r_R.

If the failure warning is wrong (in truth the system is doing well) the prediction is a false positive (state S_{FP}). In this case actions are performed unnecessarily. However, although no failure was imminent in the system, there is some risk that a failure is caused by the additional workload for failure prediction and subsequent actions. Hence, let

$$P_{FP} := P(\text{failure} \mid \text{false positive prediction}) \tag{4}$$

denote that an additional failure is induced. Since there was a failure warning, preparation for an upcoming failure has been carried out and hence the system transits into state S_R.

In case of a negative prediction (no failure warning is issued) no action is performed. If the judgment of the current situation to be non failure-prone is correct (there is no failure imminent), the prediction is a true negative (state S_{TN}). In this case, one would expect that nothing happens since no failure is imminent. However, depending on the system, even failure prediction (without subsequent actions) may put additional load onto the system which can lead to a failure although no failure was imminent at the time when the prediction started. Hence there is also some small probability of failure occurrence in the case of a true negative prediction:

$$P_{TN} := P(\text{failure} \mid \text{true negative prediction}) . \tag{5}$$

Since no failure warning has been issued, the system is not prepared for the failure and hence a transition to state S_F rather than S_R, takes place. This implies that the transition back to the fault-free state S_0 occurs at rate r_F, which takes longer (on average). If no additional failure is induced, the system returns to state S_0 directly with probability $(1 - P_{TN})$.

If the predictor does not recognize that something goes wrong in the system but a failure comes up, the prediction is a false negative (state S_{FN}). Since nothing is done about the failure there is no transition back to the up-state and the model transits to the failure state S_F without any preparation. S_{FN} hence represents the state when an unpredicted failure is looming (see [64] for details).

The transition rates of the CTMC can be split into four groups:

- r_{TP}, r_{FP}, r_{TN}, and r_{FN} denote the rate of true/false positive and negative predictions
- r_A denotes the action rate, which is determined by the average time from start of the prediction to downtime or to return to the fault-free state.
- r_R denotes repair rate for forced / prepared downtime
- r_F denotes repair rate for unplanned downtime

Effects of forced downtime / prepared repair on availability, reliability, and hazard rate are gauged by time-to-repair. We hence use a repair time improvement factor k that captures the effectiveness of downtime minimization techniques as mean relative improvement, how much faster the system is up in case of forced downtime / prepared repair in comparison to MTTR after an unanticipated failure:

$$k = \frac{MTTR}{MTTR_p} , \tag{6}$$

which is the ratio of MTTR without preparation to MTTR for the forced / prepared case. Obviously, one would expect that preparation for upcoming failures improves MTTR, thus $k > 1$, but the definition also allows $k < 1$ corresponding to a change for the worse.

All these rates can be determined from precision, recall, false positive rate and a few additional assumptions. Unfortunately, a full derivation of formulas how these rates can be determined goes beyond the scope of this chapter, we refer to [64, Chap. 10].

Steady-state availability is defined as the portion of uptime versus lifetime, which is equivalent to the portion of time, the system is up. In terms of our

CTMC model, availability is the portion of probability mass in steady-state assigned to the non-failed states, which are S_0, S_{TP}, S_{FP}, S_{TN}, and S_{FN}. In order to simplify representation, numbers 0 to 6 (as indicated in Fig. 9) are used to identify the states of the CTMC.

Steady-state availability is determined by the portion of time the stochastic process stays in one of the up-states 0 to 4:

$$A = \sum_{i=0}^{4} \pi_i = 1 - \pi_5 - \pi_6 \tag{7}$$

where π_i denotes the steady-state probability of the process being in state i. π_i can be determined by algebraically solving the global balance equations of the CTMC (see, e.g., [43]). We hence obtain a closed-form solution for steady-state availability of systems with PFM:

$$A = \frac{(r_A + r_p)k\, r_F}{k\, r_F\, (r_A + r_p) + r_A(P_{FP}\, r_{FP} + P_{TP}\, r_{TP} + k\, P_{TN}\, r_{TN} + k\, r_{FN})} . \tag{8}$$

5.4 Computing Reliability and Hazard Rate

Reliability $R(t)$ is defined as the probability of failure occurrence up to time t given that the system is fully operational at $t = 0$. In terms of CTMC modeling this is equivalent to a non-repairable system and computation of the first passage time into a down-state. Therefore the CTMC model shown in Fig.9 can be simplified: the distinction between two down-states (S_R and S_F) is not required anymore and there's no transition back to the up-state.

The distribution of the probability to first reach the down-state S_F yields the cumulative distribution of time-to-failure. In terms of CTMCs this quantity is called first-passage-time distribution $F(t)$. Reliability $R(t)$ and hazard rate $h(t)$ can be computed from $F(t)$ in the following way:

$$R(t) = 1 - F(t) \tag{9}$$

$$h(t) = \frac{f(t)}{1 - F(t)} , \tag{10}$$

where $f(t)$ denotes the corresponding probability density of $F(t)$. In our model $F(t)$ and $f(t)$ are the cumulative and density of a phase-type exponential distribution defined by $\boldsymbol{T}$ and $\boldsymbol{t_0}$ (see, e.g., [43]):

$$F(t) = 1 - \boldsymbol{\alpha} \exp(t\,\boldsymbol{T})\,\boldsymbol{e} \tag{11}$$

$$f(t) = \boldsymbol{\alpha} \exp(t\,\boldsymbol{T})\,\boldsymbol{t_0} , \tag{12}$$

where $\boldsymbol{e}$ is a vector with all ones, $\exp(t\,\boldsymbol{T})$ denotes the exponential of matrix $\boldsymbol{T}$, which is a sub-matrix of the generator matrix, and α is the initial state probability distribution, which is equal to:

$$\alpha = [1 \quad 0 \quad 0 \quad 0 \quad 0] . \tag{13}$$

Closed form expressions exist and can be computed using a symbolic computer algebra tool. However, the solution would fill several pages[8] and will hence not be provided here.

5.5 An Example

In order to give an example, we computed availability and plotted the reliability and hazard rate functions. For the parameters we used the values from HSMM-based failure prediction applied to the telecommunication system (see Sect. 3.3). Since we could not apply countermeasures in the commercial system, we assumed reasonable and moderate values for for P_{TP}, P_{FP}, P_{TN}, and k (see Tab. 2).

Table 2. Parameters assumed in the example

Parameter	precision	recall	fpr	P_{TP}	P_{FP}	P_{TN}	k
Value	0.70	0.62	0.016	0.25	0.1	0.001	2

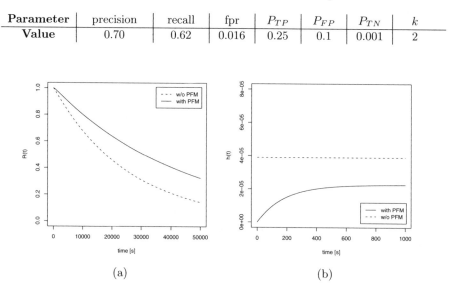

(a)   (b)

Fig. 10. Plots of (a) reliability and (b) hazard rate for the example

The effect on availability can best be seen from the ratio of unavailability with PFM to unavailability without PFM:

$$\frac{1 - A_{PFM}}{1 - A} \approx 0.488 \ . \tag{14}$$

where A_{PFM} denotes steady-state system availability with proactive fault management, computed from Eq. 8, and A denotes steady-state system availability of a system without PFM computed from a simple CTMC with two states (up and down) and the same failure and repair rates as for the case with PFM. The analysis shows that unavailability is roughly cut down by half. Reliability and hazard rate are also significantly improved, as can be seen from Fig. 10.

---

[8] The solution found by Maple™contains approximately 3000 terms.

6   Architectural Blueprint

Incorporating proactive fault management into a system architecture is not a simple task due to various reasons:

- It requires spelled out objectives and constraints, both from a business as well as from a technical perspective.
- It requires input data from all architectural levels.
- It requires domain experts at all architectural levels to identify appropriate failure prediction algorithms as well as available countermeasures.
- It requires thorough modeling and analysis at all levels.
- Maintenance and development of the proactive fault management modules have to be tightly coupled with the development process of the controlled system.

Figure 11 shows an architectural blueprint for a system with proactive fault management. As can be seen, we propose to have separate failure predictors for each system layer. That is, we propose to set up several failure predictors, each analyzing the monitoring data of its specific layer. Such approach enables to develop failure prediction algorithms that are tailored to the specifics of its layer: It allows to select algorithms that are appropriate in terms of specific properties of the input data and allow to handle the amount of data incurred. For example, a predictor on hardware level has to process a large amount of data but failure patterns are not extremely complex, whereas an application level predictor might employ complex pattern recognition algorithms in order to capture failure-prone system states on application level.

System level failure predictors cannot operate independently. For illustration just imagine that both a hardware level failure predictor as well as a Virtual Machine Monitor (VMM) level failure predictor predict an upcoming failure. If the two predictors would operate independently, the VMM failure predictor could trigger the migration of a virtual machine from one physical CPU to another and the hardware level failure predictor would restart the CPU at the same time

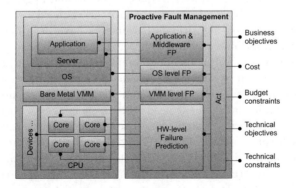

Fig. 11. An architecture for a system with proactive fault management

migration is taking place. For this reason we propose to have the "Act" component of the MEA cycle span all system layers: It incorporates the predictions of
its level predictors in order to select the most appropriate countermeasure. In
order to do so, we propose to apply techniques known as *meta-learning*. A survey on meta-learning can be found in [74]. One of the best-known meta-learning
algorithms is called "stacked generalization" [34], which has successfully been
applied to predict failures for the IBM Blue Gene /L Systems [32].

The decision which countermeasure to apply should not only depend on the
output of the domain failure predictors but has to take other factors into account:

- Treatment of dependent failures. This involves, for example, that a history
  of identified faults and the countermeasures taken need to be kept. Another
  solution might involve the determination of dependencies in the system, such
  as performed in [11].
- Probabilities of success and the costs involved. Depending on the situation,
  some countermeasures are more likely to solve the underlying problem than
  others. The same holds for the costs involved: a slight performance degradation is probably less expensive than a restart of the entire system. The decision, which countermeasure to choose must take these factors into account.
- In addition to the direct costs mentioned before, there might also be boundary business constraints and objectives. For example, if the business has
  service contracts with one company that offers one maintenance operation
  per month for free, it might in some cases be actually cheaper to rely on
  manual repair rather than automated proactive fault management.
- In case of limited budget, tough choices have to be made and we need to find
  out at which level we will achieve the highest payoff in terms of dependability
  gain with minimum performance degradation when PFM methods are used.
  We call such a desirable system property translucency which means that
  we have an insight into dependability and performance at all levels while
  applying specific MEA methods.

We mentioned in the introduction that today's systems are highly dynamic. This
is a challenge for implementing proactive fault management. First, if system
behavior changes frequently (due to frequent updates and upgrades), the failure
prediction approaches have to be adopted to the changed behavior, too. For
example, if the prediction algorithm's parameters have been determined from
training data using machine learning techniques, it might be necessary to repeat
parameter determination. Online change point detection algorithms such as [8]
can be used to determine whether the parameters have to be re-adjusted.

A second critical aspect of system dynamicity is that the capabilities belonging to proactive fault management need to be kept in sync with the functional
capabilities of the servicing system. Since development frequently is driven by
features, the software engineering processes governing proactive fault management have to be adapted accordingly. This also involves thorough modeling and
analysis of the entire MEA cycle. Since the MEA cycle forms a control loop in
the sense of classical control theory, it can be helpful to apply methods from
control theory (such as has been performed in [59]).

Last but not least, dynamicity requires new approaches to monitoring: In an environment where components from various vendors appear and disappear, a robust and flexible monitoring infrastructure is required. Such infrastructure must be pluggable such that new monitoring data sources can be incorporated easily. A second requirement are standardized data formats (such as the Common Base Event Model [9]). Furthermore, monitoring should be adaptable during runtime. Failure predictors performing variable selection during runtime should be able to adapt, e.g., the frequency or precision of the data for a monitored object. For example, if a failure predictor identifies, that simply taking the mean over a fixed time interval is not sufficient for accurate predictions, it should be able to adjust monitoring on-the-fly.

7   Conclusions and Research Issues

As computer and communication systems continue to be more complex, it goes without saying that proactive fault management plays and will continue to play an ever more significant role. Traditional methods already fail to cope with complexity at industrial level and they are inadequate to model the systems' behavior due to dynamicity (frequent changes in configuration, updates, upgrades, extensions and patches) and rapid proliferation in numerous application domains. So the main reasonable approach, in addition to all methods to date, is the use of PFM where with help of predictive technologies downtime can be effectively eliminated by failure avoidance or minimized by efficient preparation for anticipated failures. This can be done by the methods introduced in this paper in combination with effective recovery techniques. System dynamics, changing environments and diverse user preferences will only magnify the usefulness and power of PFM provided a comprehensive system translucency is supported at the design time and architectural trade-offs are well understood at every design layer. Massive redundancy, robust operating systems, composability and self-* (autonomic) computing will effectively complement the PFM methods to further enhance dependability of the future systems. In fact, there is a realistic potential to significantly increase availability as it is predicted from our CTMC model.

There is still a number of requirements and research issues that need to be tackled. First of all more field data for reference and benchmarking purposes is needed but it is very difficult to make it available to the research community. Most companies do not like to share the data and the "anonymization" efforts have not been successful despite interest from various companies [53] . Field data need to be conditioned to be used for effective prediction experiments and it usually takes an enormous amount of effort. Only a concerted effort of industry and academia can solve this issue. Also, bridging the gap between academic approaches and industry will help to assess the use of such methods in widely distributed environments. There are some at cost accessible databases such as RIAC[9] and other sources supported by Reliasoft[10] but they are of little use to

---

[9] http://www.theriac.org/
[10] http://www.reliasoft.com/predict/features2.htm

academic community. Therefore, the academic/industrial efforts such as AMBER (Assessing, Measuring and Benchmarking Resilience)[11] and USENIX[12] to collect failure rates and traces are highly commendable and are gaining critical mass to be useful to a broad research community.

One of the interesting outcomes from the work on the UBF method was that the focus on variable selection has a major impact on model quality. It is important to find out how sensitive are prediction methods to system changes such as reconfiguration, updates, extensions, etc. Adaptive, self-learning methods need to be developed that are able to minimize or even bypass training and tuning and adjust themselves to new system conditions.

The objective function to find out what are the optimal reaction schemes in view of a looming failure is an open research issue. Many practitioners would also like to know the root cause of a looming or actual failure. The research on this topic goes on and some online root cause analysis are under investigation. The trade-offs between workload profile, fault coverage, prediction processing time, prediction horizon and prediction accuracy must also further be researched in order to transfer the PFM methods into engineering practice of architecting dependable systems.

References

1. Amari, S.V., McLaughlin, L.: Optimal design of a condition-based maintenance model. In: Proceedings of Reliability and Maintainability Symposium (RAMS), pp. 528–533 (January 2004)
2. Andrzejak, A., Silva, L.: Deterministic models of software aging and optimal rejuvenation schedules. In: Proceedings of 10th IEEE/IFIP International Symposium on Integrated Network Management (IM 2007), pp. 159–168 (May 2007)
3. Avižienis, A., Laprie, J.-C.: Dependable computing: From concepts to design diversity. Proceedings of the IEEE 74(5), 629–638 (1986)
4. Algirdas Avižienis, J.-C., Laprie, B., Randell, B., Landwehr, C.: Basic concepts and taxonomy of dependable and secure computing. IEEE Transactions on Dependable and Secure Computing 1(1), 11–33 (2004)
5. Babaoglu, O., Jelasity, M., Montresor, A., Fetzer, C., Leonardi, S., van Moorsel, A., van Steen, M. (eds.): SELF-STAR 2004. LNCS, vol. 3460. Springer, Heidelberg (2005)
6. Bao, Y., Sun, X., Trivedi, K.S.: Adaptive software rejuvenation: Degradation model and rejuvenation scheme. In: Proceedings of the 2003 International Conference on Dependable Systems and Networks (DSN 2003). IEEE Computer Society, Los Alamitos (2003)
7. Barborak, M., Dahbura, A., Malek, M.: The Consensus Problem in Fault-Tolerant Computing. Computing Surveys (CSUR) 25(2), 171–220 (1993)
8. Basseville, M., Nikiforov, I.V.: Detection of abrupt changes: theory and application. Prentice Hall, Englewood Cliffs (1993)
9. Bridgewater, D.: Standardize Messages with the Common Base Event Model (2004), http://www-106.ibm.com/developerworks/autonomic/library/ac-cbe1/

---

[11] http://www.amber-project.eu/
[12] http://cfdr.usenix.org/

10. Brown, A., Patterson, D.A.: Embracing failure: A case for recovery-oriented computing (roc). In: High Performance Transaction Processing Symposium (October 2001)
11. Candea, G., Delgado, M., Chen, M., Fox, A.: Automatic Failure-Path Inference: A Generic Introspection Technique for Internet Applications. In: Proceedings of 3rd IEEE Workshop on Internet Applications (WIAPP), San Jose, CA (June 2003)
12. Candea, G., Cutler, J., Fox, A.: Improving availability with recursive microreboots: A soft-state system case study. Performance Evaluation Journal 56(1-3) (March 2004)
13. Cassady, C.R., Maillart, L.M., Bowden, R.O., Smith, B.K.: Characterization of optimal age-replacement policies. In: IEEE Proceedings of Reliability and Maintainability Symposium, pp. 170–175 (January 1998)
14. Castelli, V., Harper, R.E., Heidelberger, P., Hunter, S.W., Trivedi, K.S., Vaidyanathan, K., Zeggert, W.P.: Proactive management of software aging. IBM Journal of Research and Development 45(2), 311–332 (2001)
15. Chakravorty, S., Mendes, C., Kale, L.V.: Proactive fault tolerance in large systems. In: HPCRI Workshop in conjunction with HPCA 2005 (2005)
16. Cheng, F.T., Wu, S.L., Tsai, P.Y., Chung, Y.T., Yang, H.C.: Application cluster service scheme for near-zero-downtime services. In: IEEE Proceedings of the International Conference on Robotics and Automation, pp. 4062–4067 (2005)
17. Coleman, D., Thompson, C.: Model Based Automation and Management for the Adaptive Enterprise. In: Proceedings of 12th Annual Workshop of HP OpenView University Association, pp. 171–184 (2005)
18. International Electrotechnical Commission. Dependability and quality of service. In IEC: International Technical Comission, editor, IEC 60050: International Electrotechnical Vocabulary, IEC, 2 edn. ch. 191 (2002)
19. Cristian, F., Aghili, H., Strong, R., Dolev, D.: Atomic Broadcast: From Simple Message Diffusion to Byzantine Agreement. In: Proceedings of 15th International Symposium on Fault Tolerant Computing (FTCS). IEEE, Los Alamitos (1985)
20. Csenki, A.: Bayes predictive analysis of a fundamental software reliability model. IEEE Transactions on Reliability 39(2), 177–183 (1990)
21. Buhmann, M.D.: Radial basis functions: theory and implementations. Cambridge monographs on applied and computational mathematics, vol. 12. Cambridge University Press, Cambridge (2003)
22. Dohi, T., Goseva-Popstojanova, K., Trivedi, K.S.: Analysis of software cost models with rejuvenation. In: Proceedings of IEEE Intl. Symposium on High Assurance Systems Engineering, HASE 2000 (November 2000)
23. Dohi, T., Goseva-Popstojanova, K., Trivedi, K.S.: Statistical non-parametric algorihms to estimate the optimal software rejuvenation schedule. In: Proceedings of the Pacific Rim International Symposium on Dependable Computing, PRDC 2000 (December 2000)
24. Elnozahy, E.N., Alvisi, L., Wang, Y., Johnson, D.B.: A survey of rollback-recovery protocols in message-passing systems. ACM Computing Surveys 34(3), 375–408 (2002)
25. Farr, W.: Software reliability modeling survey. In: Lyu, M.R. (ed.) Handbook of software reliability engineering, ch. 3, pp. 71–117. McGraw-Hill, New York (1996)
26. Flach, P.A.: The geometry of ROC space: understanding machine learning metrics through ROC isometrics. In: Proceedings of 20th International Conference on Machine Learning (ICML 2003), pp. 194–201. AAAI Press, Menlo Park (2003)
27. Garg, S., Puliafito, A., Telek, M., Trivedi, K.S.: Analysis of preventive maintenance in transactions based software systems. IEEE Trans. Comput. 47(1), 96–107 (1998)

28. Garg, S., van Moorsel, A., Vaidyanathan, K., Trivedi, K.S.: A methodology for detection and estimation of software aging. In: Proceedings of the 9th International Symposium on Software Reliability Engineering, ISSRE (November 1998)

29. Gertsbakh, I.: Reliability Theory: with Applications to Preventive Maintenance. Springer, Berlin (2000)

30. Grottke, M., Matias, R., Trivedi, K.S.: The Fundamentals of Software Aging. In: Proceedings of Workshop on Software Aging and Rejuvenation, in conjunction with ISSRE, Seattle, WA. IEEE, Los Alamitos (2008)

31. Grottke, M., Trivedi, K.S.: Fighting Bugs: Remove, Retry, Replicate, and Rejuvenate. Computer 40(2), 107–109 (2007)

32. Gujrati, P., Li, Y., Lan, Z., Thakur, R., White, J.: A Meta-Learning Failure Predictor for Blue Gene/L Systems. In: Proceedings of International Conference on Parallel Processing (ICPP 2007). IEEE, Los Alamitos (2007)

33. Guyon, I., Elisseeff, A.: An Introduction to Variable and Feature Selection. Journal of Machine Learning Research 3, 1157–1182 (2003); Special Issue on Variable and Feature Selection

34. Wolpert, D.H.: Stacked Generalization. Neural Networks 5(5), 241–259 (1992)

35. Hoffmann, G.A., Trivedi, K.S., Malek, M.: A Best Practice Guide to Resource Forecasting for Computing Systems. IEEE Transactions on Reliability 56(4), 615–628 (2007)

36. Hoffmann, G.A.: Failure Prediction in Complex Computer Systems: A Probabilistic Approach. Shaker, Aachen (2006)

37. Hoffmann, G.A., Malek, M.: Call availability prediction in a telecommunication system: A data driven empirical approach. In: Proceedings of the 25th IEEE Symposium on Reliable Distributed Systems (SRDS 2006), Leeds, United Kingdom (October 2006)

38. Horn, P.: Autonomic Computing: IBM's perspective on the State of Information Technology (October 2001), http://www.research.ibm.com/autonomic/manifesto/autonomic_computing.pdf

39. Huang, Y., Kintala, C., Kolettis, N., Fulton, N.: Software rejuvenation: Analysis, module and applications. In: Proceedings of IEEE Intl. Symposium on Fault Tolerant Computing, FTCS 25 (1995)

40. IBM. An architectural blueprint for autonomic computing. White paper (June 2006), http://www-01.ibm.com/software/tivoli/autonomic/pdfs/AC_Blueprint_White_Paper_4th.pdf

41. Iyer, R.K., Young, L.T., Sridhar, V.: Recognition of error symptoms in large systems. In: Proceedings of 1986 ACM Fall Joint Computer Conference, Dallas, Texas, United States, pp. 797–806. IEEE Computer Society Press, Los Alamitos (1986)

42. Kajko-Mattson, M.: Can we learn anything from hardware preventive maintenance? In: Proceedings of the Seventh International Conference on Engineering of Complex Computer Systems, ICECCS 2001, pp. 106–111. IEEE Computer Society Press, Los Alamitos (2001)

43. Kulkarni, V.G.: Modeling and Analysis of Stochastic Systems, 1st edn. Chapman and Hall, London (1995)

44. Kumar, D., Westberg, U.: Maintenance scheduling under age replacement policy using proportional hazards model and ttt-plotting. European Journal of Operational Research 99(3), 507–515 (1997)

45. Laprie, J.-C., Kanoun, K.: Software Reliability and System Reliability. In: Lyu, M.R. (ed.) Handbook of software reliability engineering, pp. 27–69. McGraw-Hill, New York (1996)

46. Laranjeira, L.A., Malek, M., Jenevein, R.: On tolerating faults in naturally redundant algorithms. In: Proceedings of Tenth Symposium on Reliable Distributed Systems (SRDS), pp. 118–127. IEEE Computer Society Press, Los Alamitos (September 1991)
47. Leangsuksun, C., Liu, T., Rao, T., Scott, S.L., Libby, R.: A failure predictive and policy-based high availability strategy for linux high performance computing cluster. In: The 5th LCI International Conference on Linux Clusters: The HPC Revolution, pp. 18–20 (2004)
48. Leangsuksun, C., Shen, L., Liu, T., Song, H., Scott, S.L.: Availability prediction and modeling of high mobility oscar cluster. In: IEEE Proceedings of International Conference on Cluster Computing, pp. 380–386 (2003)
49. Levy, D., Chillarege, R.: Early warning of failures through alarm analysis - a case study in telecom voice mail systems. In: Proceedings of the 14th International Symposium on Software Reliability Engineering, ISSRE 2003, Washington, DC, USA. IEEE Computer Society, Los Alamitos (2003)
50. Li, Y., Lan, Z.: Exploit failure prediction for adaptive fault-tolerance in cluster computing. In: IEEE Proceedings of the Sixth International Symposium on Cluster Computing and the Grid (CCGRID 2006), pp. 531–538. IEEE Computer Society, Los Alamitos (2006)
51. Linand, T.-T.Y., Siewiorek, D.P.: Error log analysis: statistical modeling and heuristic trend analysis. IEEE Transactions on Reliability 39(4), 419–432 (1990)
52. Lin, T.-T.Y.: Design and evaluation of an on-line predictive diagnostic system. Master's thesis, Department of Electrical and Computer Engineering, Carnegie-Mellon University, Pittsburgh, PA (April 1988)
53. Malek, M., Cotroneo, D., Kalbarczyk, Z., Madeira, H., Penkler, D., Reitenspiess, M.: search of real data on faults, errors and failures,Panel discussion at Sixth European Dependable Computing Conference (EDCC) (October 2006)
54. Melliar-Smith, P.M., Randell, B.: Software reliability: The role of programmed exception handling. SIGPLAN Not. 12(3), 95–100 (1977)
55. Mundie, C., de Vries, P., Haynes, P., Corwine, M.: Trustworthy Computing. Technical report, 10 (2002), http://download.microsoft.com/download/a/f/2/af22fd56-7f19-47aa-8167-4b1d73cd3c57/twc_mundie.doc
56. Nassar, F.A., Andrews, D.M.: A methodology for analysis of failure prediction data. In: IEEE Real-Time Systems Symposium, pp. 160–166 (1985)
57. Department of Defense. MIL-HDBK-217F Reliability Prediction of Electronic Equipment. Washington D.C (1990)
58. Oliner, A., Sahoo, R.: Evaluating cooperative checkpointing for supercomputing systems. In: IEEE Proceedings of 20th International Parallel and Distributed Processing Symposium, IPDPS 2006 (April 2006)
59. Parekh, S., Gandhi, N., Hellerstein, J., Tilbury, D., Jayram, T.S., Bigus, J.: Using Control Theory to Achieve Service Level Objectives In Performance Management. Real-Time Systems 23(1), 127–141 (2002)
60. Parnas, D.L.: Software aging. In: IEEE Proceedings of the 16th International Conference on Software Engineering (ICSE 1994), pp. 279–287. IEEE Computer Society Press, Los Alamitos (1994)
61. Pfefferman, J.D., Cernuschi-Frias, B.: A nonparametric nonstationary procedure for failure prediction. IEEE Transactions on Reliability 51(4), 434–442 (2002)
62. Randell, B.: System structure for software fault tolerance. IEEE Transactions on Software Engineering 1(2), 220–232 (1975)
63. Randell, B., Lee, P., Treleaven, P.C.: Reliability issues in computing system design. ACM Computing Survey 10(2), 123–165 (1978)

64. Salfner, F.: Event-based Failure Prediction: An Extended Hidden Markov Model Approach. Dissertation.de Verlag im Internet, Berlin, Germany (2008)
65. Salfner, F., Lenk, M., Malek, M.: A Survey of Online Failure Prediction Methods. ACM Computing Surveys (CSUR) 42(3), 1–42 (2010)
66. Siewiorek, D.P., Swarz, R.S.: Reliable Computer Systems, 2nd edn. Digital Press, Bedford (1992)
67. Siewiorek, D.P., Swarz, R.S.: Reliable Computer Systems, 3rd edn., p. 908. A. K. Peters, Wellesley (1998)
68. Singer, R.M., Gross, K.C., Herzog, J.P., King, R.W., Wegerich, S.: Model-Based Nuclear Power Plant Monitoring and Fault Detection: Theoretical Foundations. In: Proceedings of Intelligent System Application to Power Systems (ISAP 1997), Seoul, Korea, pp. 60–65 (July 1997)
69. Starr, A.G.: A structured approach to the selection of condition based maintenance. In IEEE Proceedings of Fifth International Conference on Factory 2000 - The Technology Exploitation Process, pages Condition based maintenance (CBM) triggers maintenance activity on a parameter which is indicative of machine health. Regular tasks, which are the staple of planned preventive maintenance become scheduled inspections and measurements rather than repair or (April 1997)
70. Sterritt, R., Parashar, M., Tianfield, H., Unland, R.: A concise introduction to autonomic computing. Advanced Engineering Informatics (AEI) 19(3), 181–187 (2005); Autonomic Computing
71. Vaidyanathan, K., Trivedi, K.S.: A comprehensive model for software rejuvenation. IEEE Transactions on Dependable and Secure Computing 2, 124–137 (2005)
72. Vaidyanathan, K., Harper, R.E., Hunter, S.W., Trivedi, K.S.: Analysis and implementation of software rejuvenation in cluster systems. In: Proceedings of the 2001 ACM SIGMETRICS International Conference on Measurement and Modeling of Computer Systems, pp. 62–71. ACM Press, New York (2001)
73. Vilalta, R., Apte, C.V., Hellerstein, J.L., Ma, S., Weiss, S.M.: Predictive algorithms in the management of computer systems. IBM Systems Journal 41(3), 461–474 (2002)
74. Vilalta, R., Drissi, Y.: A perspective view and survey of meta-learning. Artificial Intelligence Review 18(2), 77–95 (2002)

ASDF: An Automated, Online Framework for Diagnosing Performance Problems[*,**]

Keith Bare[1], Soila P. Kavulya[1], Jiaqi Tan[2], Xinghao Pan[2], Eugene Marinelli[1],
Michael Kasick[1], Rajeev Gandhi[1], and Priya Narasimhan[1]

[1] Carnegie Mellon University, Pittsburgh, PA 15213, USA
{kbare,spertet,emarinel,mkasick}@andrew.cmu.edu,
priya@cs.cmu.edu,rgandhi@ece.cmu.edu
[2] DSO National Laboratories, Singapore, 118230
{tjiaqi,pxinghao}@dso.org.sg

Abstract. Performance problems account for a significant percentage of documented failures in large-scale distributed systems, such as Hadoop. Localizing the source of these performance problems can be frustrating due to the overwhelming amount of monitoring information available. We automate problem localization using ASDF, an online diagnostic framework that transparently monitors and analyzes different time-varying data sources (e.g., OS performance counters, Hadoop logs) and narrows down performance problems to a specific node or a set of nodes. ASDF's flexible architecture allows system administrators to easily customize data sources and analysis modules for their unique operating environments. We demonstrate the effectiveness of ASDF's diagnostics on documented performance problems in Hadoop; our results indicate that ASDF incurs an average monitoring overhead of 0.38% of CPU time and achieves a balanced accuracy of 80% at localizing problems to the culprit node.

1 Introduction

Distributed systems are typically composed of communicating components that are spatially distributed across nodes in the system. Performance problems in such systems can be hard to diagnose and to localize to a specific node or a set of nodes. There are many challenges in problem localization (i.e., tracing the problem back to the original culprit node or nodes) and root-cause analysis (i.e., tracing the problem further to the underlying code-level fault or bug, e.g., memory leak, deadlock). First, performance problems can originate at one node in the system and then start to manifest at other nodes as well, due to the inherent communication across components–this can make it hard to discover the original culprit node. Second, performance problems can change in their manifestation over time–what originally manifests as a memory-exhaustion problem can ultimately escalate to resemble a node crash, making it hard to discover the underlying root-cause of the problem.

Problem-diagnosis techniques tend to gather data about the system and/or the application to develop *a priori* templates of normal, problem-free system behavior; the

---

[*] ASDF stands for Automated System for Diagnosing Failures.
[**] This work is supported by the NSF CAREER Award CCR-0238381, and grant CNS-0326453.

A. Casimiro et al. (Eds.): Architecting Dependable Systems VII, LNCS 6420, pp. 201–226, 2010.
© Springer-Verlag Berlin Heidelberg 2010

techniques then detect performance problems by looking for anomalies in runtime data, as compared to the templates. Typically, these analysis techniques are run offline and post-process the data gathered from the system. The data used to develop the models and to perform the diagnosis can be collected in different ways.

A *white-box* diagnostic approach extracts application-level data directly and requires instrumenting the application and possibly understanding the application's internal structure or semantics. A *black-box* diagnostic approach aims to infer application behavior by extracting data transparently from the operating system or network without needing to instrument the application or to understand its internal structure or semantics. Obviously, it might not be scalable (in effort, time and cost) or even possible to employ a white-box approach in production environments that contain many third-party services, applications and users. A black-box approach also has its drawbacks—while such an approach can infer application behavior to some extent, it might not always be able to pinpoint the root cause of a performance problem. Typically, a black-box approach is more effective at problem localization, while a white-box approach extracts more information to ascertain the underlying root cause of a problem. Hybrid, or *grey-box*, diagnostic approaches leverage the strengths of both *white-box* and *black-box* approaches.

There are two distinct problems that we pursued. First, we sought to address support for problem localization (what we call *fingerpointing*) online, in an automated manner, even as the system under diagnosis is running. Second, we sought to address the problem of automated fingerpointing for Hadoop [1], an open-source implementation of the MapReduce programming paradigm [2] that supports long-running, parallelized, data-intensive computations over a large cluster of nodes.

This chapter describes ASDF, a flexible, online framework for fingerpointing that addresses the two problems outlined above. ASDF has API support to plug in different time-varying data sources, and to plug in various analysis modules to process this data. Both the data-collection and the data-analyses can proceed concurrently, while the system under diagnosis is executing. The data sources can be gathered in either a black-box or white-box manner, and can be diverse, coming from application logs, system-call traces, system logs, performance counters, etc. The analysis modules can be equally diverse, involving time-series analysis, machine learning, etc.

We demonstrate how ASDF automatically fingerpoints some of the performance problems in Hadoop that are documented in Apache's JIRA issue tracker [3]. Manual fingerpointing does not scale in Hadoop environments because of the number of nodes and the number of performance metrics to be analyzed on each node. Our current implementation of ASDF for Hadoop automatically extracts time-varying white-box and black-box data sources and specific white-box data sources on every node in a Hadoop cluster. ASDF then feeds these data sources into different analysis modules (that respectively perform clustering, peer-comparison or Hadoop-log analysis), to identify the culprit node(s), in real time. A unique aspect of our Hadoop-centric fingerpointing is our ability to infer Hadoop states (as we chose to define them) by parsing the logs that are natively auto-generated by Hadoop. We then leverage the information about the states and the time-varying state-transition sequence to localize performance problems.

To the best of our knowledge, ASDF is the first automated, online problem-localization framework that is designed to be flexible in its architecture by supporting the plugging-in of data sources and analysis techniques. Current online problem-localization frameworks, such as IBM Tivoli Enterprise Console [4] and HP Operations Manager [5], allow users to augment rules to their existing analysis techniques but are not geared towards plugging-in new techniques.

2 Online Diagnostic Frameworks

Online diagnostic frameworks provide a unified view of the diverse data sources present in distributed systems, and ease the task of detecting and diagnosing problems. These frameworks are designed to: (i) *flexibly* support new data sources and analysis modules; (ii) *scale* gracefully with the number of nodes in the system; (iii) impose *minimal runtime overheads*; and (iv) *ease maintenance* through the automated deployment of monitoring and analysis scripts.

The key components of an online diagnostic framework, as shown in Figure 1, are:

- Data collectors: Data collectors are daemons that run on each node and collect data from diverse sources such as application logs, and OS performance counters. These data sources can be classified as *time-triggered* sources sampled periodically, *event-triggered* sources collected whenever an event such as an error occurs, and *request-flow* sources tracing the flow of individual requests across nodes. Data collectors may exploit pre-defined schemas [6,7,8] to parse data, or they may forgo the need for schemas and store data in a search index [9]. They impose minimal runtime overheads through data buffering, and sampling.
- Data aggregators: Data aggregators periodically poll a collection of data sources and persist data to file. A primary concern during aggregation is portable transmission of data across heterogeneous nodes. Frameworks achieve portability by using portable data formats such as External Data Representation (XDR) [7], or by leveraging middleware such as ZeroC's ICE (Internet Communications Engine) [10].
- Data analysis: Diagnostic frameworks schedule analysis modules periodically, or upon the occurrence of pre-defined events. Analysis modules may run locally on each node, or globally at a central node. Local analysis modules typically perform simple computations such as data-smoothing, while global analysis modules cross-correlate data from multiple nodes.
- Persistent storage: Archival of historical data becomes increasingly important as the system scales. Popular archival options are data warehouses [4,5], round-robin databases [7,6], and search indices [9]. Companies, such as Google, which process massive amounts of data are opting for distributed databases [11].
- Alarms and visualization: The fingerpointing alarms generated by online diagnostic frameworks range from simple alerts about node crashes and oversubscribed resources [7,6], to process-specific alerts generated by sophisticated event-correlation techniques [4,5]. Visualization of the monitored data allows administrators to spot anomalous trends that might fall outside the scope of the automated diagnosis techniques. For example, developers at Google used vizualization to pinpoint inefficient queries in their AdWords system [11].

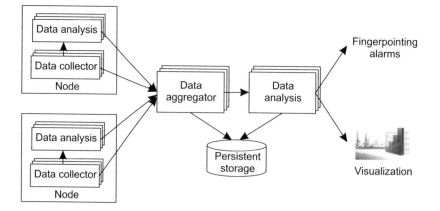

Fig. 1. Key components of online diagnostic frameworks

Table 1. Examples of online diagnostic frameworks

Category	Example frameworks	Data sources	Data analysis
Event/Time-triggered monitors	Ganglia[7], Nagios[6], Splunk[9], Tivoli[4], Operations Manager [5]	OS performance counters, logs, network data	Rule-based [7,6,9], event-correlation [4,5]
Request-flow monitors	Dapper[11], XTrace [12], Magpie [8], Tivoli[4], Operations Manager [5]	RPC traces, application transactions	Clustering [8], Service-level agreement (SLA) violations [4,5]

Current online diagnostic frameworks can be broadly classified as: (i) coarse-grained event/time-triggered monitors at the node, or process-level; and (ii) fine-grained request-flow monitors tracing individual requests. Table 1 presents examples of these frameworks. The event/time-triggered frameworks [7,6,9,4,5] rely on event-correlation and human-generated rules for diagnosis, and are more popular than the request-flow frameworks [11,12,8]. This popularity stems from the easy-to-develop data collection modules, and the simple rule-based abstractions for diagnosis which shield administrators from complex algorithms. Administrators can augment rules to the existing analysis techniques supported by the framework, but these frameworks are typically not geared towards plugging-in new analysis algorithms. ASDF's support for pluggable algorithms can accelerate the testing and deployment of new analysis techniques, and allow administrators to leverage off-the-shelf analysis techniques.

3   Problem Statement

The aim of ASDF is to assist system administrators in identifying the culprit node(s) when the system experiences a performance problem. The research questions center around whether ASDF can localize performance problems quickly, accurately and non-invasively. In addition, performing online fingerpointing in the context of Hadoop presents its own unique challenges. While we choose to demonstrate ASDF 's capabilities for Hadoop in this chapter, we emphasize that (with the appropriate combination of data sources and analysis modules) ASDF is generally applicable to problem localization in any distributed system.

3.1   Goals

We impose the following requirements for ASDF to meet its stated objectives.

Runtime data collection. ASDF should allow system administrators to leverage any available data source (black-box or white-box) in the system. No restrictions should be placed on the rate at which data can be collected from a specific data-source.

Runtime data analysis. ASDF should allow system administrators to leverage custom or off-the-shelf analysis techniques. The data-analysis techniques should process the incoming, real-time data to determine whether the system is experiencing a performance problem, and if so, to produce a list of possible culprit node(s). No restrictions should be placed on the type of analysis technique that can be plugged in.

Performance. ASDF should produce *low false-positive rates*, in the face of a variety of workloads for the system under diagnosis, and more importantly, even in the face of workload changes at runtime[1]. The ASDF framework's data-collection should impose *minimal runtime overheads* on the system under diagnosis. In addition, ASDF 's data-analysis should result in *low fingerpointing latencies* (where we define fingerpointing latency as a measure of how quickly the framework identifies the culprit node(s) at runtime, once the problem is present in the system).

We impose the additional requirements below to make ASDF more practical to use and deploy.

Flexibility. ASDF should have the flexibility to attach or detach any data source (white-box or black-box) that is available in the system, and similarly, the flexibility to incorporate any off-the-shelf or custom analysis module.

Operation in production environments. ASDF should run transparently to, and not require any modifications of, both the hosted applications and any middleware that they might use. ASDF should be deployable in production environments, where administrators might not have the luxury of instrumenting applications but could instead leverage other (black-box) data. In cases where applications are already instrumented to produce logs of white-box data (as in Hadoop's case) even in production environments, ASDF should exploit such data sources.

Offline and online analyses. While our primary goal is to support online automated fingerpointing, ASDF should support offline analyses (for those users wishing to

---

[1] The issue of false positives due to workload changes arises because workload changes can often be mistaken for anomalous behavior, if the system's behavior is characterized in terms of performance data such as CPU usage, network traffic, response times, etc. Without additional semantic information about the application's actual execution or behavior, it can be difficult for a black-box approach, or even a white-box one, to distinguish legitimate workload changes from anomalous behavior.

Analysis modules

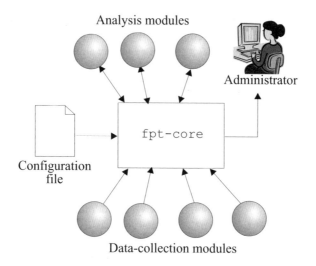

Administrator

fpt-core

Configuration
file

Data-collection modules

Fig. 2. Logical architecture of ASDF

post-process the gathered data), effectively turning itself into a data-collection and data-logging engine in this scenario.

3.2   Non-goals

It is important to delineate the research results in this chapter from possible extensions of this work. In its current incarnation, ASDF is intentionally *not* focused on:

- Root-cause analysis: ASDF currently aims for (coarse-grained) problem localization by identifying the culprit node(s). Clearly, this differs from (fine-grained) root-cause analysis, which would aim to identify the underlying fault or bug, possibly even down to the offending line of code.
- Performance tuning: ASDF does not currently attempt to develop performance models of the system under diagnosis, although ASDF does collect the data that could enable this capability.

4   Approach and Implementation

The central idea behind the ASDF framework is the ability to incorporate any number of different data sources in a distributed system and the ability to use any number of analysis techniques to process these data sources. We encapsulate distinct data sources and analysis techniques into *modules*. Modules can have both inputs and outputs. Most data-collection modules will tend to have only outputs, and no inputs because they collect/sample data and supply it to other modules. On the other hand, analysis modules are likely to have both inputs (the data they are to analyze) and outputs (the fingerpointing outcome).

As an example on the data-collection side, ASDF currently supports a sadc module to collect data through the *sysstat* package [13]. sadc is the system activity data collector in the *sysstat* package that monitors system performance and usage activity, such as CPU, disk and memory usage. There can be multiple *module instances* to handle multiple data sources of the same type. On the analysis side, an example of a currently implemented module is mavgvec, which computes arithmetic mean and variance of a vector input over a sliding window of samples from multiple given input data streams.

4.1 Architecture

The key ASDF component, called the fpt-core (the "fingerpointing core"), serves as a multiplexer and provides a plug-in API for which modules can be easily developed and integrated into the system. fpt-core uses a directed acyclic graph (DAG) to model the flow of data between modules. Figure 2 shows the high-level logical architecture with ASDF's different architectural elements–the fpt-core, its configuration file and its attached data-collection and analysis modules. fpt-core incorporates a scheduler that dispatches events to the various modules that are attached to it.

Effectively, a specific *configuration* of the fpt-core (as defined in its configuration file) represents a specific way of wiring the data-collection modules to the analysis modules to produce a specific online fingerpointing tool. This is advantageous relative to a monolithic data-collection and analysis framework because fpt-core can be easily reconfigured to serve different purposes, e.g., to target the online diagnosis of a specific set of problems, to incorporate a new set of data sources, to leverage a new analysis technique, or to serve purely as a data-collection framework.

As described below, ASDF already incorporates a number of data-collection and analysis modules that we have implemented for reuse in other applications and systems. We believe that some of these modules (e.g., the sadc module) will be useful in many systems. It is possible for an ASDF user to leverage or extend these existing modules to create a version of ASDF to suit his/her system under diagnosis. In addition, ASDF's flexibility allows users to develop, and plug in, custom data-collection or analysis modules, to generate a completely new online fingerpointing tool. For instance, an ASDF user can reconfigure the fpt-core and its modules to produce different instantiations of ASDF, e.g., a black-box version, a white-box version, or even a hybrid version that leverages both black- and white-box data for fingerpointing.

Because ASDF is intended to be deployed to diagnose problems in distributed systems, ASDF needs a way to extract data remotely from the data-collection modules on the nodes in the system and then to route that data to the analysis modules. In the current incarnation of ASDF , we simplify this by running the fpt-core and the analysis modules on a single dedicated machine (called the ASDF control-node). Each data-collection module, abc, has a corresponding abc_rpcd counterpart that runs on the remote node to gather the data that forms that module's output.

4.2 Plug-in API for Implementing Modules

The fpt-core's plug-in API was designed to be simple, yet generic. The API is used to create a module, which, when instantiated, will become a vertex in the DAG mentioned above. All types of modules–data-collection or analysis–use the same plug-in API, simplifying the implementation of the `fpt-core`.

A module's *init()* function is called once each time that an instance of the module is created. This is where a module can perform any necessary per-instance initialization. Typical actions performed in a module's *init()* function include:

– Allocating module-specific instance data
– Reading configuration values from the section for the module instance
– Verifying that the number and type of input connections are appropriate
– Creating output connections for the module instance
– Setting origin information for the output connections
– Adding hooks that allow for the `fpt-core`'s scheduling of that module instance's execution
– Performing any other module-specific initialization that is necessary.

A module's *run()* function is called when the `fpt-core`'s scheduler determines that a module instance should run. One of the arguments to this function describes the reason why the module instance was run. If a module instance has inputs, it should read any data available on the inputs, and perform any necessary processing. If a module instance has outputs, it should perform any necessary processing, and then write data to the outputs.

4.3   Implementation of `fpt-core`

An `ASDF` user, typically a system administrator, would specify instances of modules in the `fpt-core`'s configuration file, along with module-specific configuration parameters (e.g., sampling interval for the data source, threshold value for an analysis module's anomaly-detection algorithm) along with a list of data inputs for each module. The `fpt-core` then uses the information in this configuration file to construct a DAG, with module instances as the graph's vertices, and the graph's edges represent the data flow from a module's outputs to another module's inputs. Effectively, the DAG captures the "wiring diagram" between the modules of the `fpt-core` at runtime.

The `fpt-core`'s runtime consists of two main phases, initialization and execution. As mentioned above, the `fpt-core`'s inialization phase is responsible for parsing the `fpt-core`'s configuration file and constructing the DAG of module instances. The DAG construction is perhaps the most critical aspect of the `ASDF` online fingerpointing framework since it captures how data sources are routed to analysis techniques at runtime.

1. In the first step of the DAG construction, `fpt-core` assigns a vertex in the DAG to each module instance represented in the `fpt-core`'s configuration file.
2. Next, `fpt-core` annotates each module instance with its number of unsatisfied inputs. Those modules with fully satisfied inputs (i.e., output-only modules that specify no inputs) are added to a module-initialization queue.
3. For each module instance on the module-initialization queue, a new thread is spawned and the module's *init()* function is called. The *init()* function verifies the module's inputs, the modules's configuration parameters, and specifies its outputs.

A module's outputs, which are dynamically created at initialization time, are then used to satisfy other module instances' inputs. Whenever a new output causes all of the inputs of some other module instance to be satisfied, that module instance is placed on the queue.

4. The previous step is repeated until all of the modules' inputs are satisfied, all of the threads are created, and all of the module instances are initalized. This should result in a successfully constructed DAG. If this (desirable) outcome is not achieved, then, it is likely that the `fpt-core`'s configuration was incorrectly specified or that the right data-collection or analysis modules were not available. If this occurs, the `fpt-core` (and consequently, the ASDF) terminates.

Once the DAG is successfully constructed, the `fpt-core` enters its execution phase where it frequently calls each of the module instances' *run()* function.

As part of the initialization process, module instances may request to be scheduled periodically, in which case their *run()* functions are called by the `fpt-core`'s scheduler at a fixed frequency. This allows the class of data-collection modules (that typically have no specified inputs) to periodically poll external data sources and import their data values into the `fpt-core`.

For module instances with specified inputs (such as data-analysis modules), `fpt-core` automatically executes their *run()* functions each time that a configurable number of their inputs are updated with new data values. This enables data-analysis modules to perform any analysis immediately when the necessary data is available.

4.4   Configuring the `fpt-core`

Configuration files for the `fpt-core` have two purposes: they define the DAG that is used to perform problem diagnosis and they specify any parameters processing modules may use. The format is straightforward.

A module is instantiated by specifying its name in square brackets. Following the name, parameter values are assigned. The resulting module instance's id can be specified with an assignment of the form "id = *instance-id*". To build the graph, all of a module instance's inputs must be specified as paremeters. This is done with assignments of the form "input[*inputname*] = *instance-id.outputname*" or "input[*inputname*] = @*instance-id*". The former connects a single output, while the latter connects all outputs of the specified module instance. All other assignments are provided to the module instance for its own interpretation. A snippet from the `fpt-core` configuration file that we used in our experiments with Hadoop, along with the corresponding `fpt-core` DAG, are displayed in Figure 3.

4.5   Data-Collection Modules

Given the plug-in API described in Section 4.2, ASDF can support the inclusion of multiple data sources. Currently, ASDF supports the following data-collection modules: `sadc` and `hadoop_log`. We describe the `sadc` module below and the `hadoop_log` module in Section 5.4 (in order to explain its operation in the context of Hadoop).

The `sadc` Module. The *sysstat* package [13] comprises utilities (one of which is `sadc`) to monitor system performance and usage activity. System-wide metrics, such

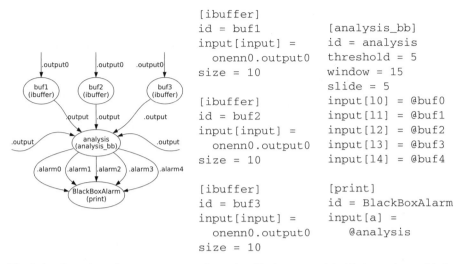

```
                                    [ibuffer]
                                    id = buf1           [analysis_bb]
                                    input[input] =      id = analysis
                                       onenn0.output0   threshold = 5
                                    size = 10           window = 15
                                                        slide = 5
                                    [ibuffer]           input[10] = @buf0
                                    id = buf2           input[11] = @buf1
                                    input[input] =      input[12] = @buf2
                                       onenn0.output0   input[13] = @buf3
                                    size = 10           input[14] = @buf4

                                    [ibuffer]           [print]
                                    id = buf3           id = BlackBoxAlarm
                                    input[input] =      input[a] =
                                       onenn0.output0      @analysis
                                    size = 10
```

Fig. 3. A snippet from the `fpt-core` configuration file that we used for Hadoop, along with the corresponding DAG

as CPU usage, context-switch rate, paging activity, I/O activity, file usage, network activity (for specific protocols), memory usage, etc., are traditionally logged in the /proc pseudo-filesystem and collected by /proc-parsing tools such as `sadc` from the *sysstat* package. ASDF uses a modified version of the *sysstat* code in the form of a library, `libsadc`, which is capable of collecting system-wide and per-process statistics in the form of C data structures.

The ASDF `sadc` data-collection module exposes these /proc black-box metrics as `fpt-core` outputs and makes them available to the `fpt-core`'s analysis modules. We use ZeroC's ICE (Internet Communications Engine) [10] RPC to generate the RPC stubs that facilitate the collection of remote statistics from a `sadc_rpcd` daemon that uses `libsadc` internally. Each node on which we aim to diagnose problems using `sadc` runs an instance of the `sadc_rpcd` daemon. In all, there are 64 node-level metrics, 18 network-interface-specific metrics and 19 process-level metrics that can be gathered via the `sadc` module. Our black-box online fingerpointing strategy leverages the `sadc` module.

4.6 Analysis Modules

White-box and black-box data might reveal very different things about the system–white-box reveals application-level states and the application's behavior, while black-box reveals the performance characteristics of the application on a specific machine. Although ASDF aims to operate in production environments, ASDF allows its user to incorporate any and all (either black-box or white-box) data-sources that are already available in the system. If a data-source can be encapsulated in the form of an `fpt-core` data-collection module, then, it can be made available to the `fpt-core` analysis modules. In this spirit, as we show later, ASDF supports both black-box and white-box fingerpointing for Hadoop.

We discuss some of the basic analysis modules that ASDF supports. Currently, ASDF supports the following analysis modules: knn, mavgvec, and hadoop_log. We describe some of these implemented modules below and the hadoop_log module in Section 5.4 (in order to explain its operation in the context of Hadoop).

The mavgvec module. The mavgvec module calculates the arithmetic mean and variance of a moving window of sample vectors. The sample vector size and window width are configurable, as is the number of samples to slide the window before generating new outputs.

The knn module. The knn (k-nearest neighbors) module is used to match sample points with centroids corresponding to known system states. It takes as configuration parameters k, a list of centroids, and a standard deviation vector with each element of the vector corresponding to each input statistic. For each input sample $\mathbf{s}$, a vector $\mathbf{s}'$ is computed as

$$s'_i = \frac{\log(1 + s_i)}{\sigma_i}$$

and the Euclidean distance between $\mathbf{s}'$ and each centroid is computed. The indices of the k nearest centroids to $\mathbf{s}'$ in the configuration are output.

4.7 Design and Implementation Choices

Throughout the development of ASDF , a number of design choices have been made to bound the complexity of the architecture, but which have resulted in some limitation on the means by which analysis may be performed.

1. Since ASDF uses a directed acyclic graph (DAG) to model the flow of data, data flows are inherently undirectional with no provision for cross-instance data feedback. Such feedback may be useful for certain methods of analysis, for example, if one were to use the output of the black-box analysis to provide hints of anomalous conditions to the white-box analysis, or vice-versa.
2. Although the fpt-core API does have some provisions for propagating alert conditions on inputs, or back-propagating enable/disable state changes on outputs, there is no explicit mechanism for cross-instance data synchronization.
3. Since fpt-core operates in the context of a single node, there is no builtin provision for starting RPC daemons on remote nodes or synchronizing remote clocks. Thus, RPC daemons must be started either manually, or at boot time on all monitored nodes. In addition, clocks on all nodes must be sychronized at all times, as either time skews, or their abrupt correction, may alter the interpretation of cross-node time series data.

We should also note that while the above requirements apply to ASDF as a whole, they don't necessarily apply equally to both the black-box and white-box data collection and analysis components. In general, the black-box instrumentation technique of polling for system metrics in /proc generally requires less cross-node coordination than the white-box technique. For example, since black-box system metrics are polled in realtime, they are timestamped directly on the ASDF control node and passed immediately to the next analysis module—thus, the wallclock time on other nodes is irrelevant to black-box analysis. In contrast, the white-box technique of parsing recently written log files requires clock synchronization across all monitored nodes so that written timestamps in the log files match events as they happen.

Additionally, the white-box technique faces an additional data synchronization issue that is not present in the realtime black-box data collection. Internal buffering in Hadoop results in log data being written at slightly different times on different Hadoop nodes. Additionally, the hadoop-log-parser is unable to compute all statistics in real time, and occasionally needs to delay one or two iterations to resolve values for recent log entries. Since the data analysis must operate on data at the same time points, cross-instance sychronization is needed within the hadoop_log module to ensure that data outputs for each node is updated with Hadoop log data from the same time point.

Since fpt-core has limited control flow, such data synchronization is implemented within the scope of the hadoop_log module itself. Since each module instance shares the same address space, global timestamps are maintained for the most recently seen and most recently outputted timestamps. The hadoop_log module waits for all nodes to reveal data with the same timestamp before updating its outputs, or, if one or more nodes does not contain data for a particular timestamp, this data is dropped.

A more general point concerning online fingerpointing is that data collection may potentially be faster than data analysis. Since some heavyweight analysis algorithms may take many seconds to complete, multiple data collection iterations are likely to occur during ths computation time. Normally, since the analysis algorithms cannot absorb the incoming data flow in a timely fashion, many of these data points are likely to be dropped. To handle this rate mismatch, a buffer module (ibuffer) has been written to collect individual data points from a data collection module output, and present the data as an array of data points to an analysis module, which can then process a larger data set more slowly.

5   Applying ASDF to Hadoop

One of our objectives is to show the ASDF framework in action for Hadoop, effectively demonstrating that we can localize performance problems (that have been reported in Apache's JIRA issue tracker [3]) using both black-box and white-box approaches, for a variety of workloads and even in the face of workload changes. This section provides a brief background of Hadoop, a description of the reported Hadoop problems that we pursued for fingerpointing, the ASDF data and analysis modules that are relevant to Hadoop, and concludes with experimental results for fingerpointing problems in Hadoop.

5.1   Hadoop

Hadoop [1] is an open-source implementation of Google's MapReduce [2] framework. MapReduce eases the task of writing parallel applications by partitioning large blocks of work into smaller chunks that can run in parallel on commodity clusters (effectively, this achieves high performance with brute-force, operating under the assumption that computation is cheap). The main abstractions in MapReduce are (i) Map tasks that process the smaller chunks of the large dataset using key/value pairs to generate a set

Table 2. Injected faults, and the reported failures that they simulate. HADOOP-xxxx represents a Hadoop JIRA entry.

Fault Type	[Source] Reported Failure	[Fault Name] Fault Injected
Resource contention	[Hadoop mailing list, Sep 13 2007] CPU bottleneck from running master and slave daemons on same node.	[CPUHog] Emulate a CPU-intensive task that consumes 70% CPU utilization.
	[Hadoop mailing list, Sep 26 2007] Excessive messages logged to file.	[DiskHog] Sequential disk workload wrote 20GB of data to filesystem.
	[HADOOP-2956] Degraded network connectivity between datanode,s results in long block transfer times.	[PacketLoss] Induce 50% packet loss.
Application bugs	[HADOOP-1036] Infinite loop at slave node due to an unhandled exception from a Hadoop subtask that terminates unexpectedly.	[HADOOP-1036] Manually revert to older version of Hadoop and trigger bug by throwing NullPointerException.
	[HADOOP-1152] Reduce tasks fail while copying map output due to an attempt to rename a deleted file.	[HADOOP-1152] Manually revert to older version of Hadoop and trigger bug by deleting file.
	[HADOOP-2080] Reduce tasks hang due to a miscalculated checksum.	[HADOOP-2080] Simulated by miscomputing checksum to trigger a hang at reducer.

of intermediate results, and (ii) Reduce functions that merge all intermediate values associated with the same intermediate key.

Hadoop uses a master/slave architecture to implement the MapReduce programming paradigm. Each MapReduce job is coordinated by a single jobtracker, that is responsible for scheduling tasks on slave nodes and for tracking the progress of these tasks in conjunction with slave tasktrackers that run on each slave node. Hadoop uses an implementation of the Google Filesystem [14] known as the Hadoop Distributed File System (HDFS) for data storage. HDFS also uses a master/slave architecture that consists of a designated node, the namenode, to manage the file-system namespace and to regulate access to files by clients, along with multiple datanodes to store the data. Due to the large scale of the commodity clusters, Hadoop assumes that failures can be fairly common and incorporates multiple fault-tolerance mechanisms, including heartbeats, re-execution of failed tasks and data replication, to increase the system's resilience to failures.

5.2   Injected Faults

We injected one fault on one node in each cluster to validate the effectiveness of our algorithms at diagnosing each fault. The faults cover various classes of representative real-world Hadoop problems as reported by Hadoop users and developers in: (i) the Hadoop issue tracker [3] from October 1, 2006 to December 1, 2007, and (ii) 40 postings from the Hadoop users' mailing list from September to November 2007. We describe our results for the injection of the six specific faults listed in Table 2.

5.3 ASDF for Hadoop

We deploy ASDF to fingerpoint the performance problems of interest listed in Section 5.2. The Hadoop cluster consists of a master node and a number of slave nodes. In the experiments described in this chapter, we fingerpoint problems only on the slave nodes, as the number of slave nodes in a Hadoop cluster can be arbitrarily many, so it appears most profitable to begin problem diagnosis from the slave nodes. Nonetheless, there is nothing inherently in ASDF 's architecture that would prevent us from finger-pointing problems on the master node as well.

On each slave node, we run two daemons (sadc_rpcd and hadoop_log_rpcd) that interface with the fpt-core running on the ASDF control node shown in the figure. The sadc_rpcd modules on each node support black-box fingerpointing, while the hadoop_log_rpcd modules on each node support white-box fingerpointing. In fact, the ASDF framework supports both the black-box and the white-box analyses in parallel, as shown in the data-flow diagrams in Figure 4.

Each node runs a sadc daemon and/or a hadoop_log daemon, depending on whether black-box and/or white-box analysis is being performed. These RPC daemons expose procedures that return system statistics in the case of sadc and Hadoop state information in the case of the hadoop_log module. A single ASDF instance is run on a dedicated machine (the ASDF control node) in the cluster which runs a small number of ASDF modules for each machine, each of which makes requests to the RPC daemons of a particular slave node.

We decided to collect state data from Hadoop's logs instead of instrumenting Hadoop itself, in keeping with our original goal of supporting problem diagnosis in production

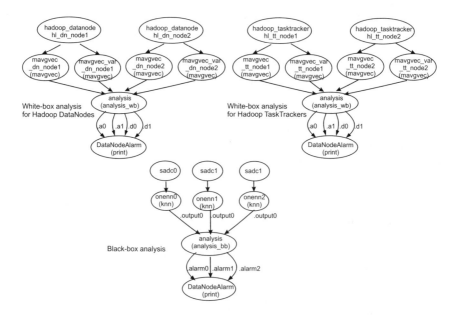

Fig. 4. The DAG constructed by fpt-core to fingerpoint Hadoop

environments. This has the added advantage that we do not need to stay up-to-date with changes to the Hadoop source code and can confine ourselves to the format of the Hadoop logs alone.

The hadoop_log parser provides on-demand, lazy parsing of the logs generated by each of the Hadoop datanode, and tasktracker, instances to generate counts of *event* and *state* occurrences (as defined in Section 5.4). All information from prior log entries is summarized and stored in compact internal representations for just sufficiently long durations to infer the states in Hadoop. We refer interested readers to [15] for further implementation details. The ASDF hadoop_log collection module exposes the log parser counters as FPT outputs for analysis modules. Again, ZeroC's ICE RPC is used to collect remote statistics from a hadoop_log_rpcd daemon which provides an interface to the log parser library.

5.4   Hadoop: White-Box Log Analysis

We have devised a novel method to extract white-box metrics which characterize Hadoop's high-level modes of execution (e.g. Map task, Reduce task taking place) from its textual application logs. Instead of text-mining logs to automatically identify features, we construct an *a priori* view of the relationship between Hadoop's mode of execution and its emitted log entries. This *a priori* view enabled us to produce structured numerical data, in the form of a numerical vector, about Hadoop's mode of execution.

Consider each thread of execution in Hadoop as being approximated by a deterministic finite automaton (DFA), with DFA **states** corresponding to the different modes of execution. Next, we define **events** to be the entrance and exit of states, from which we derive DFA transitions as a composition of one state-entrance and one state-exit event. Since Hadoop is multi-threaded, its aggregate high-level mode of execution comprises multiple DFAs representing the execution modes in simultaneously executing threads. This aggregate mode is represented by a vector of states for each time instance, showing the number of simultaneously executing instances of each state. A full list of states that characterize the high-level behavior of Hadoop is in [15].

Each entry in a Hadoop log corresponds to one event–a state-entrance or state-exit event, or an "instant" event (a special case which denotes the immediate entrance to and subsequent exit from a state for short-lived processing, e.g. a block deletion in the Hadoop datanode). Then, we parse the text entries of the Hadoop logs to extract events. By maintaining a minimal amount of state across log entries, we then infer the vector of states at each time instance by counting the number of entrance and exit events for each state (taking care to include counts of short-lived states, for which entrance and exit events, or instant events, occurred within the same time instance). Some important states for the tasktracker are Map and Reduce tasks, while some important states for the datanode are those for the data-block reads and writes. Details of the log parser implementation and architecture are in [15]. We show, in Figure 5, a snippet of a tasktracker log, and the interpretations that we place on the log entries in order to extract the corresponding Hadoop states, as we have defined them.

We have currently implemented a log-parser library for the logs gathered from the datanode, and the tasktracker. This library maintains state that has constant memory use in the order of the duration for which it is run. In addition, we have

```
2008-04-15 14:23:15,324 INFO org.apache.hadoop.mapred.TaskTracker:
LaunchTaskAction: task_0001_m_000096_0
2008-04-15 14:23:16,375 INFO org.apache.hadoop.mapred.TaskTracker:
LaunchTaskAction: task_0001_r_000003_0
```

Time	...	MapTask	ReduceTask	...	...	...
2008-04-15 14:23:15	...	1	0	...	...	...
2008-04-15 14:23:16	...	1	1	...	...	...

Fig. 5. A snippet from a TaskTracker Hadoop log showing the log entries that trigger the *StateStartEvent* for the *MapTask* and *ReduceTask* states

implemented an RPC daemon that returns a time series of state vectors from each running Hadoop slave, and an ASDF module which harvests state vectors from RPC daemons for use in diagnosis.

To fingerpoint using the white-box metrics, we compute the mean of the samples for a white-box metric *metric* over the window for all the nodes (denoted by $mean\_metric_i$ for node i) and use the mean values for peer comparison. One way to do the peer comparison is to compute the difference (called $diff\_mean\_metric_{i,j}$) of $mean\_metric_i$ at node i with $mean\_metric_j$ at the other nodes. A node i is classified as anomalous if $diff\_mean\_metric_{i,j}$ for $j = 1, 2, \ldots, N$ is greater than a threshold value for more than $\frac{N}{2}$ nodes. This process can be repeated for all the nodes in the system leading to N^2 comparison operations. To reduce the number of comparisons, we use an alternate method: we compute the median of the $mean\_metric_i$ for $i = 1, 2, \ldots, N$ (i.e., across all the nodes in the system). Denote the median value $median\_mean\_metric$. Since more than $\frac{N}{2}$ nodes are fault-free the $median\_mean\_metric$ will correctly represent the metric mean for fault-free nodes. We then compare $mean\_metric_i$ for each node i with $median\_mean\_metric$ value and flag a node as anomalous if the difference is more than a threshold value. A node is fingerpointed during a window if one or more of its white-box metrics show an anomaly. To determine the threshold values for a white-box metric we first compute the standard deviations of the metric for all the slave nodes over the window.

We chose the threshold value for all the metrics to be of the form $max\{1, k \times sigma_{median}\}$ where k is a constant (for all the metrics) whose value is chosen to minimize the false positive rate over fault-free training data (as explained in Section 5.9). The intuition behind the choice of $k \times \sigma_{median}$ in the threshold is that if the metric has a large standard deviation over the window then it is likely that the difference in the mean value of the metric across the peers will be larger requiring a larger threshold value to reduce false positives and vice versa. The reason for choosing the threshold value to be of the form $max 1, k \times \sigma_{median}$ is that several white-box metrics tend to be constant in several nodes and vary by a small amount (typically 1) in one node. The fact that the white-box metric is a constant over the window for a node implies that the standard deviation for that metric will be zero for that node. If several nodes have zero standard deviation, the median standard deviation will also turn out to be zero and will cause significant false positives for the node on which the metric varies by as small as 1.

5.5   Hadoop: Black-Box Analysis

Our hypothesis for fingerpointing slave nodes in the Hadoop system is that we can use peer comparison across the slave nodes to localize the specific node with performance problems. The intuition behind the hypothesis is that on average, the slave nodes will be doing similar processing (map tasks or reduce tasks) and as a result the black-box and white-box metrics would have similar behavior across the nodes in fault free conditions. The black-box and white-box metrics of the slave nodes will behave similarly even if there are changes in the workload since a workload change may cause more (or fewer) maps or reduces to be launched on all the slave nodes. However, when there is a fault in one of the slave nodes, the black-box and white-box metrics of the faulty node will show significant departure from that of the other (non-faulty) slave nodes. We can therefore use peer comparison of averaged metrics to detect faulty nodes in the system. Our hypothesis rests on the following two assumptions: i) all the slave nodes are homogeneous and, ii) more than half of the nodes in the system are fault-free (otherwise, we may end up fingerpointing the non-faulty nodes since their behavior will differ from the faulty nodes).

Our analysis algorithm gathers black-box as well as white-box metrics from all the slave nodes. We collect samples of white-box and black-box metric samples from all the nodes over a window of size *windowSize*. For each node we collect one sample of each white-box and black-box metric per second over the window. Consecutive windows over which the metrics are collected can overlap with each other by an amount equal to *windowOverlap*.

In our black-box fingerpointer, we first characterize the workload perceived at each node by using all the black-box metrics from it. We classify the workload perceived at the node by considering the similarity of its metric vector to a pre-determined set of centroid vectors. Its closest centroid vector is then determined using the one Nearest Neighbor (1-NN) approach. The pre-determined set of centroid vectors are generated by using offline k-Means clustering using fault-free training data.

Instead of using raw metric values to characterize workloads, we use the logarithm of every metric sample (we used $\log(x+1)$ for a metric value, x to ensure positive values for logarithms). We used logarithms to reduce the dynamic range of metric samples since many black-box metrics have a large dynamic range. Furthermore, we scaled the resulting logarithmic metric samples by the standard deviation of the logarithm computed over the fault-free training data. We use these vectors of scaled logarithmic metric values (denoted by X_i for node i) for comparison against the pre-determined centroid vectors using the 1-NN approach. The outcome of the 1-NN is the assignment of a "state" to each X_i (the index of the centroid vector closest to X_i).

For each state we determine the number of vectors X_i that were assigned to it over a window of size *windowSize*. This generates, for a node j, a vector (**StateVector$_j$**) whose dimensions are equal to the number of centroids, and whose k-th component represents the number of times the centroid k was associated with X_i for that node in the window. The **StateVector$_j$** for $j = 1, 2, 3, \ldots, N$ are used for peer comparison to detect the anomalous nodes. This is done by first computing a component-wise median vector (denoted by **medianStateVector**) and then comparing **StateVector$_j$** with

medianStateVector. We use the $\mathcal{L}_1$ distance of **StateVector$_j$ − medianStateVector** for $j = 1, 2, 3, \ldots, N$ and flag a node j as anomalous if the $\mathcal{L}_1$ distance of **StateVector$_j$ − medianStateVector** is greater than a pre-determined threshold.

5.6 Metrics

False-positive rate. A false positive occurs when ASDF wrongly fingerpoints a node as a culprit when there are no faults on that node. Because alarms demand attention, false alarms divert resources that could otherwise be utilized for dealing with actual faults. We measured the false-positive rates of our analyses on data traces where no problems were injected; we can be confident that any alarm raised by ASDF in these traces are false positives. By tuning the threshold values for each of our analysis modules, we were able to observe different average false-positive rates on the problem-free traces.

Fingerpointing latency. An online fingerpointing framework should be able to quickly detect problems in the system. The fingerpointing latency is the amount of time that elapses from the occurrence of a problem to the corresponding alarm identifying the culprit node. It would be relevant to measure the time interval between the first mani-festation of the problem and the raising of the corresponding alarm; however, doing so assumes the ability to tell when the fault first manifested. Since the detection of a fault's manifestation is precisely the problem that we are attempting to solve, we instead mea-sure the time interval between the injection of the problem by us and the raising of the corresponding alarm.

5.7 Empirical Validation

We analyzed system metrics from Hadoop 0.18.3 running on 50-node clusters on Large instances on Amazon's EC2. Each node had the equivalent of 7.5 GB of RAM and two dual-core CPUs, running amd64 Debian/GNU Linux 4.0. Each experiment con-sisted of one run of the GridMix workload, a well-accepted, multi-workload Hadoop benchmark. GridMix models the mixture of jobs seen on a typical shared Hadoop cluster by generating random input data and submitting MapReduce jobs in a manner that mimics observed data-access patterns in actual user jobs in enterprise deployments. The GridMix workload has been used in the real-world to validate performance across different clusters and Hadoop versions. GridMix comprises 5 different job types, rang-ing from an interactive workload that samples a large dataset, to a large sort of uncom-pressed data that access an entire dataset. We scaled down the size of the dataset to 200MB for our 50-node clusters to ensure timely completion of experiments.

ASDF is not dependent on a particular hardware configuration, though the relative overhead of our instrumentation is dependent on the amount of memory and processing power available. Although ASDF assumes the use of Linux and /proc, it is hardware-architecture-agnostic. For our white-box analysis, we make reasonable assumptions about the format of the Hadoop logs, but our Hadoop-log parser was designed so that changes to the log format could be accounted for.

5.8   Performance Impact of ASDF

For data collection, it is preferred that the RPC daemons have minimal CPU time, memory, and network bandwidth overheads so as to minimally alter the runtime performance of the monitored system. In contrast, the cost of analysis on the ASDF control node is of a lesser concern since the fpt-core may run on a dedicated or otherwise idle cycle server. However, the cost of this analysis is still important as it dictates the size of the server needed, or alternatively for a given serrver, determines the number of monitored nodes to which the fingerpointer may scale.

As depicted in Table 3, for our white-box analysis, the hadoop_log_rpcd uses, on average, less than 0.02% of CPU time on a single core on cluster nodes, and less than 2.4 MB of resident memory. For our black-box analysis, the sadc_rpcd uses less than 0.36% of CPU time, and less than 0.77 MB of resident memory. Thus, the ASDF data collection has negligible impact on application performance.

The per-node network bandwidths for both the black-box (sadc) and the white-box (hadoop_log) data-collection are listed in Table 4. Establishing a TCP RPC client connection with each monitored Hadoop slave node incurs a static overhead of 6 kB per-node, and each iteration of data collection costs less than 2 kB/s. Thus, the network bandwith cost of monitoring a single node is negligible, and the aggregate bandwith is on the order of 1 MB/s even when monitoring hundreds of nodes.

Table 3. CPU usage (% CPU time on a single core) and memory usage (RSS) for the data collection processes and the combined black-box & white-box analysis process

Process	% CPU	Memory (MB)
hadoop_log_rpcd	0.0245	2.36
sadc_rpcd	0.3553	0.77
fpt-core	0.8063	5.11

Table 4. RPC bandwidth for TCP transports for the three ASDF RPC types: sadc, hadoop_log-datanode, hadoop_log-tasktracker. Static overheads include per-node traffic to create/destroy connections, and the per-iteration bandwidth includes per-node traffic for each iteration (one second) of data collection.

RPC Type	Static Ovh. (kB)	Per-iter BW (kB/s)
sadc-tcp	1.98	1.22
hl-dn-tcp	2.04	0.31
hl-tt-tcp	2.04	0.32
TCP Sum	6.06	1.85

5.9   Results

Black-box Analysis. We conducted two sets of experiments. In the first set, we ran three iterations of the GridMix workload without injecting any problems. Black-box data was collected by the ASDF for offline analysis. The *windowSize* parameter was set to 60 samples. We varied the threshold value from 0 to 70 for the problem-free traces to assess

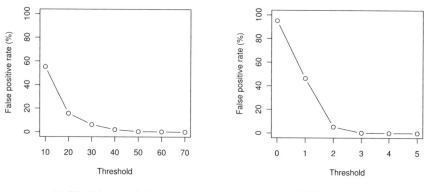

(a) Black-box analysis   (b) White-box analysis

Fig. 6. False-positive rates for black-box and white-box analysis

the false-positive rates, and then used the threshold value to that resulted in a low false-positive rate. In the second set of experiments, we ran the `GridMix` workloads, but unlike the first set of experiments, we injected performance problems from Section 5.2 into the runs. Black-box data was again collected, and the black-box analysis module was used to fingerpointings problems. The *windowSize* parameter was set to 60 samples.

Figure 6a shows the false-positive rates for the different threshold levels. As the threshold is initially increased from 0, false-positive rates drop rapidly. However, beyond a threshold of 60, any further increases in threshold lead to little improvement in the false-positive rates.

Figure 7(a) displays the balanced accuracy of our black-box diagnostic approach. The balanced accuracy ranges from 0 to 100%, and averages the probability of correctly identifying problematic and problem-free windows. A high balanced accuracy indicates a high true-positive rate and a low false-positive rate. The black-box approach was good at detecting resource-contention and hangs in Map tasks (`Hadoop-1036`)– the balanced accuracy ranged from 68% to 84%. The balanced accuracy for the hangs in the reduce tasks (`Hadoop-1152` and `Hadoop-2080`) was low because the fault remained dormant for several minutes from the time we injected the fault to the time the application executed the faulty code. This delay resulted in longer fingerpointing latencies for hangs in Reduce tasks, as shown in Figure 7(b). The fingerpointing latencies for the other problems was about 200 seconds because it took at least 3 consecutive windows to gain confidence in our detection.

White-box Analysis. To validate our white-box analysis module, we ran similar sets of experiments as those for the black-box analysis. We again chose a *windowSize* of 60 samples. We varied the value of k from 0 to 5 for the problem-free traces to assess the false-positive rates, and then used the value of k that resulted in a low false-positive rate. For the second set of experiments, we induced the performance problems listed in Section 5.2, and ran the white-box analysis module on the data collected during the run. The same *windowSize* of 60 samples was chosen, and k was set to 3. Figure 6b shows the false-positive rates for the different values of k. False-positive rates are under 0.2%, and we observe little improvement when the value of k is increased beyond 3.

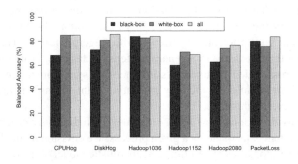

(a) Balanced accuracy. A high balanced accuracy indicates a high true positive rate and low false positive rate.

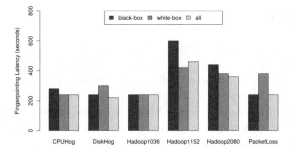

(b) Fingerpointing latency. Delayed manifestation of hangs in reduce tasks (Hadoop1152 and Hadoop2080) led to longer fingerpointing latencies and lower balanced accuracy.

Fig. 7. Fingerpointing results for faults injected

Figures 7(a) and 7(b) show that the white-box diagnostic approach had a higher balanced accuracy, and lower fingerpointing latency than the black-box approach. The difference in the two approaches was most pronounced for hangs in Reduce tasks (Hadoop-1152 and Hadoop-2080) which first manifested as slowdowns in the Reduce tasks, before morphing into decreased activity in the OS performance counters. Combining the outputs of the white-box and black-box analysis yielded a modest improvement in the mean balanced accuracy for the set of problems we injected–the mean balanced accuracy was 71% for the black-box approach, 78% for the white-box approach and 80% for the combined approach.

6 Future Work

In its current implementation, fpt-core provides for unidirectional data flow between data collection and analysis modules with no cycles or data feedback. fpt-core however, does not yet allow module instances to run remotely on different nodes, nor does it allow for explicit data synchronization or other control flow between module instances. We believe these features are necessary to support a robust framework, however, it was unclear until after our experience with fingerpointing in Hadoop exactly how to implement these features in a general, extensible fashion. From our experience in implementing cross-node RPC and cross-instance data synchronization in the context of the hadoop_log module, we are now evaluating plans to implement a cross-node communications layer within fpt-core itself.

We are currently developing new ASDF modules, including a strace module that tracks all of the system calls made by a given process. We envision using this module to detect and diagnose anomalies by building a probabilistic model of the order and timing of system calls and checking for patterns that correspond to problems. We also plan to equip ASDF with the ability to actively mitigate the consequences of a performance problem once it is detected.

7   Related Work

Our previous work focussed on visualization of performance bottlenecks in Hadoop [16,17], and offline diagnosis [18,19,20] of performance problems by comparing the duration of white-box states (Maps and Reduces), and black-box OS performance counters across peers. ASDF presents a framework for online monitoring and diagnosis of problems in distributed systems. Since our work on ASDF involves two complementary aspects–monitoring/instrumentation and problem-diagnosis techniques–we cover the related work in both those aspects.

Monitoring Tools. Numerous tools exist for the performance monitoring of distributed systems of networked computers. Nagios [6] and Ganglia [7] are monitoring systems that coordinate the collection of performance indicators on each networked node in a distributed system. Ganglia focuses on keeping the gathered data compact for storage and visualization, while Nagios, in addition to metric collection, allows rudimentary "state flapping" checks to identify excessively frequent changes in service availability. X-Trace [12] is a network-level tracing tool that aggregates trace messages generated by custom network-level or application-level instrumentation. These tools produce co-ordinated views of a distributed system of communicating components. More recently, X-Trace has been applied to Hadoop [21]. Our work differs from these tools by building an automated, online problem-diagnostic framework that can certainly leverage Ganglia, Nagios and X-Trace output as its data sources, if these data sources are already available in production environments.

Application-Log Analysis. Splunk [9], a commercial log-analyzer, treats logs as searchable text indexes and generates views of system anomalies. Our use of application logs, specifically those of Hadoop, differs from Splunk by converting logs into numerical data sources that then become immediately comparable with other numerical system metrics. Cohen et. al. [22] have also examined application logs, but they used feature selection over text-mining of logs to identify co-occurring error messages, and extracted unstructured data from application logs that limited the extent to which typical machine learning techniques could be used to synthesize the application views from the application logs and system metrics. Xu et. al [23] diagnosed problems in Hadoop by analyzing source code to automatically discover the structure of messages in the `datanode`, logs, and identifying outlier error messages. Our work leverages both application logs and black-box performance counters for diagnosis.

Problem-Diagnosis Techniques. Current problem-diagnosis work [24,25] focuses mostly on collecting traces of system metrics for offline processing, in order to de-termine the location and the root-cause of problems in distributed systems. While var-ious approaches, such as Magpie [8] and Pinpoint [26], have explored the possibility of online implementations (and can arguably be implemented to run in an online man-ner), they have not been used in an online fashion for live problem localization even as the system under diagnosis is executing. Our ASDF framework was intentionally designed for the automated online localization of problems in a distributed system; this required us to address not just the attendant analytic challenges, but also the operational issues posed by the requirement of online problem-diagnosis. Cohen et al.'s [27] work continuously builds ensembles of models in an online fashion and attempts to perform diagnosis online. Our work differs from that of Cohen et al. by building a pluggable ar-chitecture, into which arbitrary data sources can be fed to synthesize information across nodes. This enables us to utilize information from multiple data sources simultaneously to present a unified system view as well as to support automated problem-diagnosis.

In addition, Pinpoint, Magpie, and Cohen et al.'s work rely on large numbers of requests to use as labeled training data *a priori* for characterizing the system's normal behavior via clustering. However, Hadoop has a workload of long-running jobs, with users initiating jobs at a low frequency, rendering these techniques unsuitable. Pip [28], which relies on detecting anomalous execution paths from many possible ones, will also have limited effectiveness at diagnosing problems in Hadoop.

The idea of correlating system behavior across multiple layers of a system is not new. Hauswirth et al's "vertical profiling" [29] aims to understand the behavior of object-oriented applications by correlating metrics collected at various abstraction levels in the system. Vertical profiling was used to diagnose performance problems in applications in a debugging context at development time, requiring access to source code while our approach diagnoses performance problems in production systems without using application knowledge.

Triage [30] uses a check-point/reexecution framework to diagnose software failures on a single machine in a production environment. They leverage an ensemble of pro-gram analysis (white-box) techniques to localize the root-cause of problems. ASDF is designed to flexibly integrate both black-box and white-box data sources, providing the opportunity to diagnose problems both within the application, and due to external factors in the environment. Triage targeted single-host systems whereas ASDF targets distributed systems.

8   Future Research Challenges

In our opinion, most of the future research challenges for online diagnostic frameworks lie in the development of online diagnosis algorithms that leverage the diverse data sources available in large-scale distributed systems for more accurate diagnosis. There has been considerable research in developing robust, monitoring frameworks which impose minimal overhead [11,7,8,12]. While scalability and the incorporation of new data sources, such as those proffered by virtualized environments, will continue to be a challenge for monitoring, we foresee the following key challenges for online diagnosis:

- Complex failure modes: The complex interactions between components in large-scale distributed systems can result in complex failure modes where cascading failures ripple through multiple nodes in the system. The scale of the system also increases the probability of multiple independent failures. Developing tools that can accurately localize the root-cause of these problems is challenging.
- Scalability: Large-scale distributed systems exert pressure on online diagnostic frameworks to analyze massive amounts of data and diagnose problems within minutes. Efficiently processing the monitored data in systems consisting of tens of thousands of nodes will present opportunities for developing new distributed data-analysis algorithms.
- Adaptation: Diagnosis algorithms need to adapt to new workloads, seasonal trends, and environmental changes such as upgrades. Research is needed to determine what interfaces online diagnostic frameworks should expose to data collection and analysis plugins to support adaptation.
- Translating diagnostic outcomes into recovery actions: Diagnosis techniques typically rely on problem signatures [27] to identify root-causes that could trigger automated recovery actions. This approach works well for recurrent problems, but more research is needed for novel problems.

9 Conclusion

In this chapter, we described our experience in designing and implementing the ASDF online problem-localization framework. The architecture is intentionally designed for flexibility in adding or removing multiple, different data-sources and multiple, different data-analysis techniques. This flexibility allows us to attach a number of data-sources for analysis, as needed, and then to detach any specific data-sources if they are no longer needed. We also applied this to Hadoop, effectively demonstrating that we can localize performance problems (that have been reported in Apache's JIRA issue tracker [3]) using both black-box and white-box approaches, for a variety of workloads and even in the face of workload changes. We demonstrate that we can perform online fingerpointing in real time, that our framework incurs reasonable overheads and that our false-positive rates are low.

References

1. Foundation, T.A.S.: Hadoop (2007), http://hadoop.apache.org/core
2. Dean, J., Ghemawat, S.: MapReduce: Simplified data processing on large clusters. In: USENIX Symposium on Operating Systems Design and Implementation, San Francisco, CA, pp. 137–150 (December 2004)

3. Foundation, T.A.S.: Apache's JIRA issue tracker (2006), `https://issues.apache.org/jira`
4. IBM: Tivoli enterprise console (2010), `http://www.ibm.com/software/tivoli/products/enterprise-console`
5. Packard, H.: Hp operations manager (2010), `http://www.managementsoftware.hp.com`
6. LLC., N.E.: Hagios (2008), `http://www.nagios.org`
7. Ganglia: Ganglia monitoring system (2007), `http://ganglia.info`
8. Barham, P., Donnelly, A., Isaacs, R., Mortier, R.: Using Magpie for request extraction and workload modelling. In: USENIX Symposium on Operating Systems Design and Implementation, San Francisco, CA (December 2004)
9. Inc., S.: Splunk: The it search company (2005), `http://www.splunk.com`
10. ZeroC, I.: Internet Communications Engine, ICE (2010), `http://www.zeroc.com/ice.html`
11. Sigelman, B.H., Barroso, L.A., Burrows, M., Stephenson, P., Plakal, M., Beaver, D., Jaspan, S., Shanbhag, C.: Dapper, a large-scale distributed systems tracing infrastructure. Technical Report dapper-2010-1, Google (April 2010)
12. Fonseca, R., Porter, G., Katz, R., Shenker, S., Stoica, I.: X-Trace: A pervasive network tracing framework. In: USENIX Symposium on Networked Systems Design and Implementation, Cambridge, MA (April 2007)
13. Godard, S.: SYSSTAT (2008), `http://pagesperso-orange.fr/sebastien.godard`
14. Ghemawat, S., Gobioff, H., Leung, S.: The Google File System. In: ACM Symposium on Operating Systems Principles, Lake George, NY, pp. 29 – 43 (October 2003)
15. Tan, J., Narasimhan, P.: RAMS and BlackSheep: Inferring white-box application behavior using black-box techniques. Technical Report CMU-PDL-08-103, Carnegie Mellon University PDL (May 2008)
16. Tan, J., Pan, X., Kavulya, S., Gandhi, R., Narasimhan, P.: Mochi: Visual Log-Analysis Based Tools for Debugging Hadoop. In: USENIX Workshop on Hot Topics in Cloud Computing (HotCloud), San Diego, CA (June 2009)
17. Tan, J., Kavulya, S., Gandhi, R., Narasimhan, P.: Visual, log-based causal tracing for performance debugging of MapReduce systems. In: International Conference on Distributed Computing Systems, Genoa, Italy (June 2010)
18. Tan, J., Pan, X., Kavulya, S., Gandhi, R., Narasimhan, P.: SALSA: Analyzing Logs as State Machines. In: USENIX Workshop on Analysis of System Logs, San Diego, CA (December 2008)
19. Pan, X., Tan, J., Kavulya, S., Gandhi, R., Narasimhan, P.: Ganesha: Black-Box Diagnosis of MapReduce Systems. In: Workshop on Hot Topics in Measurement and Modeling of Computer Systems (HotMetrics), Seattle, WA (June 2009)
20. Pan, X., Tan, J., Kavulya, S., Gandhi, R., Narasimhan, P.: Blind Men and the Elephant: Piecing together Hadoop for diagnosis. In: International Symposium on Software Reliability Engineering (ISSRE), Mysuru, India (November 2009)
21. Konwinski, A., Zaharia, M., Katz, R., Stoica, I.: X-tracing Hadoop. Hadoop Summit (March 2008)
22. Cohen, I.: Machine learning for automated diagnosis of distributed systems performance. SF Bay ACM Data Mining SIG (August 2006)
23. Xu, W., Huang, L., Fox, A., Patterson, D.A., Jordan, M.I.: Detecting large-scale system problems by mining console logs. In: ACM Symposium on Operating Systems Principles, Big Sky, Montana, pp. 117–132 (October 2009)

24. Aguilera, M.K., Mogul, J.C., Wiener, J.L., Reynolds, P., Muthitacharoen, A.: Performance debugging for distributed system of black boxes. In: ACM Symposium on Operating Systems Principles, Bolton Landing, NY, 74–89 (October 2003)
25. Kiciman, E., Fox, A.: Detecting application-level failures in component-based internet services. IEEE Trans. on Neural Networks: Special Issue on Adaptive Learning Systems in Communication Networks 16(5), 1027–1041 (2005)
26. Chen, M.Y., Kiciman, E., Fratkin, E., Fox, A., Brewer, E.: Pinpoint: Problem determination in large, dynamic internet services. In: IEEE Conference on Dependable Systems and Networks, Bethesda, MD (June 2002)
27. Cohen, I., Zhang, S., Goldszmidt, M., Symons, J., Kelly, T., Fox, A.: Capturing, indexing, clustering, and retrieving system history. In: ACM Symposium on Operating Systems Principles, Brighton, United Kingdom, pp. 105–118 (October 2005)
28. Kiciman, E., Fox, A.: Detecting application-level failures in component-based internet services. In: USENIX Symposium on Networked Systems Design and Implementation, San Jose, CA, pp. 115–128 (May 2006)
29. Hauswirth, M., Diwan, A., Sweeney, P., Hind, M.: Vertical profiling: Understanding the behavior of object-oriented applications. In: ACM Conference on Object-Oriented Programming, Systems, Languages, and Applications, Vancouver, BC, Canada, pp. 251–269 (October 2004)
30. Tucek, J., Lu, S., Huang, C., Xanthos, S., Zhou, Y.: Triage: diagnosing production run failures at the user's site. In: Symposium on Operating Systems Principles (SOSP), Stevenson, WA, pp. 131–144 (October 2007)

Is Collaborative QoS the Solution to the SOA Dependability Dilemma?

Matti A. Hiltunen and Richard D. Schlichting

AT&T Labs-Research
180 Park Avenue
Florham Park, NJ 07928, USA
hiltunen/rick@research.att.com

Abstract. Service-oriented architectures (SOAs) are an approach to structuring software in which distributed applications are constructed as collections of interacting services. While they promise many benefits including significant cost savings through service reuse and faster application design and implementation, many of the very aspects that make SOAs attractive amplify the dependability challenges faced by distributed applications. This *dependability dilemma* becomes especially pronounced when the services making up an application are owned and managed by different organizations or are executed on resources owned and operated by third parties, such as cloud computing or utility computing providers. This paper reviews the vision of SOAs, and discusses the characteristics that make them particularly challenging for dependability. It then discusses techniques that have been proposed for building dependable SOAs and why a comprehensive solution remains elusive despite these efforts. Finally, we argue that—despite the fact that service independence is often cited as one of the main attractions of SOAs—any successful solution requires collaborative quality of service (QoS) in which services, service providers, and resource providers cooperate to implement dependability. The primary goals of this paper are to highlight the dependability implications of architectures based on decoupled and independent services such as SOAs, and to suggest possible approaches to enhancing dependability by weakening these characteristics in a controlled way.

1 Introduction

In service-oriented computing (SOC), applications or software systems built across machines in a networked environment are structured as interacting and interoperable services in which functionality is exported through well-defined interfaces. Such a service-oriented architecture (SOA) has many potential advantages. For example, the user of a service does not require any knowledge of how the service operates, which programming language is used to implement the service, or on which operating system the service implementation executes. Instead, given the service interface, a user wanting to access the functionality implemented by the service just writes their code to access the service through that interface and then

A. Casimiro et al. (Eds.): Architecting Dependable Systems VII, LNCS 6420, pp. 227–248, 2010.

handles the service output. Another advantage is that binding to a specific service instance (e.g., IP address, port, access protocol) that actually provides the service to the running program can be dynamic and change from one execution to another. Overall, the structure of an application program in a SOA is one in which the program uses one or more services in the architecture, where each service may in turn utilize yet more services. All the services in the architecture may be owned and operated by multiple different organizations.

While SOAs have been promoted as an architectural concept for a number of years, its viability has been accelerated by the recent emergence of cloud computing as an execution medium and business model. Cloud computing offerings can be divided into three distinct categories: "Software as a Service" (SaaS), "Platform as a Service" (PaaS), and "Infrastructure as a Service" (IaaS). In the SaaS model, end users interact with software services over the Internet, typically using a standard web browser. Examples of such services include business applications such as ERP (enterprise resource planning) and CRM (customer relationship management), as well as consumer services such as email. In the PaaS model, the service provider provides an integrated environment (platform) that its customer can use to implement and deploy applications. Examples of PaaS offerings include Windows Azure and Google App Engine. Finally, in the IaaS model, the service provider typically provides the user with a virtual machine (VM) that can be used to run any operating system or application. While these cloud service models can be viewed loosely as examples of service oriented computing in their own right, more concretely, SOA services are increasingly executing in the cloud on IaaS or PaaS platforms. The providers of SaaS also often use SOAs internally to construct their services.

The focus of this paper is on the *dependability* of SOAs [1], and in particular, on the challenges of realizing dependability in such a purposely decoupled structuring methodology. Dependability in this context is an umbrella concept that includes a number of *Quality of Service* (QoS) aspects of the services in the architecture. These include *service availability*, which measures the probability that a service instance is reachable and operational when a service is requested; *service reliability*, which measures the probability that a service provides correct response when invoked; *service timeliness*, which measures the response time of the services; and *service security*, which addresses the privacy and integrity issues of the services and the overall architecture. While SOAs offer the potential for increased dependability, they also introduce numerous dependability challenges. For example, the possibility of dynamic runtime service binding makes it in principle trivial for an application to avoid a failed service instance. However, in practice service bindings tend to be relatively static and there may not be alternative instances of the specific service with an identical interface available for the application to utilize. Privacy concerns may also prevent the use of externally provided service instances for applications that process confidential or business critical data.

This paper elaborates on the unique dependability challenges associated with SOAs and offers possible solutions. In particular, we first suggest that the situation is in reality a *dependability dilemma*, since many of the dependability issues in SOAs are caused by the very same features that make them attractive as a software structuring paradigm in the first place. Indeed, this approach exacerbates the traditional dependability challenges of distributed systems to the point that in [27], we paraphrased Leslie Lamport by defining a SOA as "an architecture in which the failure of a service you didn't even know existed can render your application unusable." To resolve this dilemma, we then argue that—despite the fact that service independence is often cited as one of the main attractions of SOAs—any successful solution requires *collaborative QoS* in which services, service providers, and resource providers cooperate to implement dependability. Thus, the main contributions of this paper are twofold. First, we highlight the dependability implications of software architectures such as SOAs in which applications are structured as decoupled and independent services executing in a distributed environment. Second, we suggest a possible approach to enhancing dependability in such architectures that is based on weakening these characteristics in a careful and controlled way, in essence defining a new type of underlying service abstraction.

This paper is organized as follows. Section 2 gives a more detailed overview of the vision of SOAs, and in particular, what they are and why they are attractive as a structuring methodology for software in networked systems. Section 3 then describes the dependability dilemma and outlines the dependability challenges of SOAs. Section 4 sets the stage for our solution by outlining prior work in the area. Section 5 then presents collaborative QoS as one potential approach for increasing the dependability of SOAs while still maintaining many of their positive properties. Section 6 gives three example projects that address some of the issues associated with the vision of collaborative QoS, and Section 7 offers conclusions.

2   Service-Oriented Architectures

In service-oriented architectures (SOAs), software functionality is structured as collections of interacting services, as illustrated in Figure 1. The services include *infrastructure services*, such as discovery services, monitoring, and authentication and authorization services, as well as *application services* that implement application specific functions. The infrastructure services provide the foundation for building, running, and accessing the application services. The service consumers can interact with services using a traditional request-reply paradigm (solid lines), or the services can be utilized using a workflow paradigm (dashed line) where services are arranged into a logical workflow graph and the data to be processed passes from one service to another as specified by the graph. The implementation details for each service are generally not relevant to the users of a service, but the implementation may itself use a distributed system of multiple machines and databases.

The specific steps needed to make a service available and invoke it are illustrated in Figure 2. First, the service provider publicizes its service by registering it with the discovery service. The registration includes a description of the service

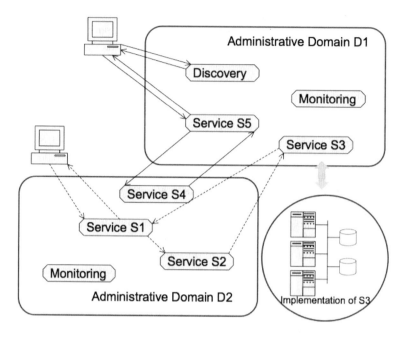

Fig. 1. Example Service-Oriented Architecture

provided—that is, descriptions of the methods including their argument types, etc.—and the address of the service provider. A consumer subsequently uses the discovery service to locate a provider that can provide a service required by the consumer. Finally, using the information from the discovery service, the consumer connects with the provider and constructs service requests based on the method descriptions. Note that while the discovery process may be completely dynamic and happen at runtime, in practice, service discovery is often done by the application designer at system design time.

The term SOA is often used to describe an architecture where all services are owned, operated, and used by one organization, and where there is typically only one instance of each service. In situations such as this, service bindings are static. However, in this paper we consider SOAs in their most general form in order to address the broadest range of issues. Specifically, we consider SOAs owned and operated by multiple organizations with multiple administrative domains, and that are potentially widely geographically distributed, even across continents. We assume that some services may have multiple implementations and that the services can be discovered using one or more discovery services. Such SOAs have numerous users and applications utilizing the services, where the users' access patterns and request rates vary over time.

SOAs are a general concept and there are a number of concrete implementations. For example, Web services [3] are an instantiation of a SOA where services are described using the Web Services Description Language (WSDL) [7] and the

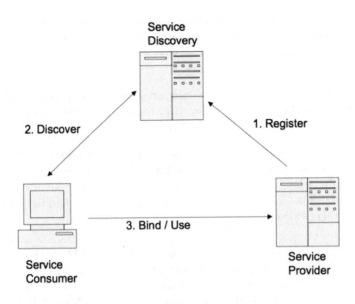

Fig. 2. SOA components and their interactions

messages exchanged between service consumers and providers are specified using SOAP [10]. Many prior distributed architecture proposals such as Java RMI and CORBA can also be viewed as specific instantiations of SOAs.

The attractiveness of SOAs for structuring large-scale software systems results from the fundamental characteristics of the approach, many of which are related to either the *service abstraction* aspect or the *dynamic configuration* aspect. We now elaborate on each of these in turn.

Service Abstraction. By design, services in a SOA are self-contained logical entities in which functionality is exposed only through exported interfaces, as captured in the service description registered with the discovery service. This type of service abstraction is a powerful structuring tool since, for example, the internal logic of the service is hidden from the outside world (*encapsulation*). Other fundamental advantages that follow from this aspect of SOAs include:

- *Independence.* Services are autonomous and have full control over the logic they encapsulate.

- *Reuse.* Services are designed to be used by different consumers in different applications, something only possible because of the way in which services are abstracted.

- *Heterogeneity.* The specific hardware, operating systems, service implementation language, and even the underlying transport protocols are abstracted away, which means they can differ between services or even different instantiations of the same service.

- *Distribution.* Since the location of an executing service is obtained using service discovery, invocations can be done independent of their location. This leads to a model in which services can be distributed across arbitrary collections of networked machines.

- *Decoupled Execution.* Services maintain a relationship that minimizes dependencies and only requires that they maintain an awareness of each other through the service discovery mechanism.

- *Cross-Domain Execution.* A SOA may span multiple administrative domains within an enterprise or even across multiple enterprises. This results from the combination of the location independence of service invocations coupled with provisions for a security infrastructure that can handle authorization and authentication.

Dynamic Configuration. Another key characteristic of SOAs is that services are discovered and bound to at runtime, providing the ability to configure applications or other software functionality from services dynamically and to change that configuration if required as execution proceeds. Such flexibility is useful in a large number of contexts. For example, it allows the way in which services are selected to be optimized based on current response time or other dynamic characteristics. It also enables the use of services as the basis for *adaptive systems* that can change their behavior based on the execution conditions or user demands. Such adaptive changes could include, for example, reconfiguring an application or other software system after one or more services fail in some way, or configuring in additional replicas of a given service to help handle an increased workload using load balancing across replicas. The dynamic aspect of SOAs also makes software built in this way *composable* since collections of services can be selected and assembled together in a structured way using only the service descriptions.

3   SOAs and the Dependability Dilemma

As noted above, a SOA built across a collection of networked computers is a distributed system, and as such, it inherits all the characteristics of such systems. When considering dependability and especially fault tolerance, distributed systems have advantages over centralized systems, such as the fact that machine failures are often independent. However, a distributed organization also introduces dependability challenges, including the difficulties associated with handling the partial failure of an executing program when a machine crashes, the need to deal with data consistency across machines in similar situations, and the possibility of partitioned execution. While progress has been made on addressing these issues in the research community over the past 40 years, the overall goal of a coherent and well-understood collection of techniques for constructing dependable distributed systems remains elusive.

The fundamental characteristics of SOAs are a mixed blessing when it comes to realizing this goal. While some make implementing dependability easier—dynamic configuration capabilities, most notably—others actually introduce new challenges or exacerbate existing ones. The problem is that these features are often exactly those that make SOAs valuable as a structuring methodology when considered in the functional, administrative, or other domains. The dependability dilemma is how to preserve these characteristics while still making progress towards implementing distributed systems that are dependable.

As a starting point, consider the comprehensive taxonomy of SOA faults in [4], many of which are specific to the unique characteristics of SOAs. Here, faults are divided into publishing, discovery, composition, binding, and execution faults. Publishing faults address issues related to service deployment and registration, including faults in service description and service deployment. Discovery faults address issues in a consumer locating a service provider, including no service found, wrong service found, and timeout. Composition faults address issues related to creating new services by composing existing services and include faults such as incompatible components or faulty composition. Binding faults address issues related to consumers connecting with a service provider including binding denied (due to lack of authentication or authorization), binding to wrong service, and timeout. Finally, execution faults address issues related to consumers interacting with the service including service crash, incorrect result, and timeout.

While such faults are one source of poor dependability, in this paper we take a more holistic view of the SOA, its execution environment, and all aspects of dependability. For example, SOAs often span multiple administrative domains even within a single company. This automatically introduces issues with trust between the different services. Furthermore, software upgrades in one administrative domain may interfere with applications spanning multiple domains. Even if the service interfaces are published, and even if they remain the same through the update, the semantics of a service may change unexpectedly resulting in application failures.

The distributed nature of a SOA also exposes it to a variety of security attacks. For example, hackers may introduce rogue services impersonating legitimate ones to steal information or identify users of the service as possible attack targets. Various types of denial of service attacks may also be deployed against the services in a SOA and it may be difficult for a service to determine if it is being attacked or just being used by a lot of other services and applications that have suddenly had their workload increased.

Other dependability attributes such as timeliness and predictable application performance become challenging in a SOA. The performance of a stand alone application executing on dedicated resources depends only on its workload, and long term changes in the workload can often be predicted and the resources provisioned accordingly. However, in a SOA, each service may execute on dedicated resources but the workload of the service depends on the cumulative workloads of all applications and other services that use this service. The workload of the service naturally dictates its response time. As a result, it becomes increasingly difficult to predict the response time of an application since an unrelated application may be suddenly start using, or increase its usage of, a shared service. The fact that new applications are introduced into the system also increases the difficulty of predicting service workload. The possibility of denial of service attacks against one or more service instances makes the problem even harder.

Other dependability challenges result from the dependencies that can arise as a result of the invocation pattern within a SOA. As described above, in a SOA, an application uses one or more services in the architecture, which in turn may use many other services. The services used may potentially be located all over the world, and be owned and operated by various organizations. As a result, the transitive closure of the services and organizations on which the application depends can become large and can in fact change over time due to dynamic binding. Similarly, the provider of a service will generally not know of all the applications and organizations that depend on its service. As a result, failures, maintenance actions, termination, or even updates of a service instance may have unanticipated consequences for multiple upstream and downstream services. Such extensive sets of dependencies also introduce security and trust challenges. Specifically, the information flow from one service to another is not visible to the application designer, who may know what is passed to or from a service, but not whether the service passes the information to other services potentially untrusted by the application designer.

Finally, the computing and networking infrastructure used has an impact on dependability as well. For example, the emergence of cloud computing has the potential to introduce additional dependability challenges for SOAs when some of the services are executed on third-party cloud infrastructures. While cloud computing is often envisioned as a dynamic infrastructure that can automatically flex to accommodate changes in workloads and react to failures, it still introduces yet another entity that the end application will depend on both for uninterrupted operation and for assurance that data passed to and from the services remain private and uncorrupted.

4   Related Work

4.1   Overview

SOAs are distributed systems, so any research done on dependability in distributed systems applies to SOAs as well. However, a number of recent research efforts have focused specifically on dependability in SOAs, and here we outline some of these efforts. In general, we classify the dependability approaches as follows.

- Application-Layer (AL): Each service in the architecture, as well as the applications using the services, attempt independently to ensure their own dependability. For example, an application may dynamically bind to a different service instance when the one it is using fails to reply in time [24]. Similarly, a service implementation may internally use a variety of fault-tolerance techniques to make itself dependable for the users of this service [27].

– Infrastructure-Layer (IL): The infrastructure—middleware, underlying OSes, the cloud—executes services in a dependable manner. For example, the infrastructure may monitor each service for crash failures and restart the service if necessary [15], allocate resources dynamically to a service instance so that it can meet its timeliness requirements even when the workload changes [16], or invoke application specified adaptive actions [25].

– Application plus Infrastructure (A+I): The application and infrastructure layers interact to ensure dependability. For example, the infrastructure may provide services such as monitoring (e.g., for failures as well as to capture performance characteristics of services [26]) that the application then uses to (a) make initial binding decisions, or (b) to rebind to new service instances.

Most of the prior approaches to dependable SOAs fall into the pattern of runtime monitoring combined with dynamic service binding, as illustrated in Figure 3. For example, the Intelligent Accountability Middleware Architecture (Llama) supports dependable SOAs using monitoring, diagnosis, and reconfiguration [19]. Monitoring is implemented by a distributed architecture of agents, each of which monitors a subset of services. An implementation of Llama based on an ESB (Enterprise Service Bus [6]), where service consumers and providers interact through a shared message bus, makes it easy for monitoring agents to intercept messages and thus, to measure the service times of the monitored services.

Monitoring functionality may be embedded in the service consumer as well. For example, the timeout of a service request may trigger the service user to locate a new service provider. As one specific case, [2] proposes a method for monitoring dynamic service compositions with respect to contracts expressed

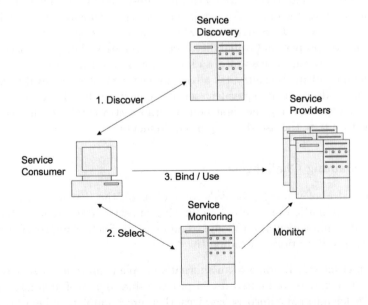

Fig. 3. Monitoring Service

via assertions on services. Dynamic compositions are represented as BPEL [14] processes that can be monitored at run-time to check whether individual services comply with their contracts. Monitors can automatically be defined as additional services and linked to the service composition.

A number of projects focus on dynamic binding and other dependability mechanisms. SOAR (SOA with Reflection) proposes a reflective middleware approach for dependable SOAs [12]. SOAR uses Java reflection to implement dependability mechanisms transparently for the service consumers (re-try and rebinding), service providers (restart), and service brokers (monitoring of service providers). While rebinding typically attempts to locate identical service instances, [8] enables clients to bind to alternative, but not identical, web services that provide compatible functionality through different interaction protocols (i.e., sequences of operations). It uses an infrastructure that traces the successful interactions of the web services, and automatically synthesizes models that approximate the interaction protocols. Various replication strategies and replication patterns for multi-tier implementations of services are surveyed in [13]. A QoS broker architecture is used in [5], where the broker constructs composite services (workflows), monitors the QoS of these composite services, and matches service consumers to the composite services based on their QoS requirements. Liu et al. [20] propose a distributed service discovery mechanism to alleviate the threat of attacks against the discovery service in a military context.

Other projects address the issue of how to compose services in a SOA—either statically or dynamically—given the dependability characteristics of the underlying services and service providers. A comprehensive discussion of the issues and challenges of such self-adaptive SOAs is found in [23]. A QoS-aware service selection algorithm for service composition is presented in [21] and addresses the optimization challenge under a dynamic set of services, time-constrained decision making, and multiple QoS attributes. Zheng and Lyu [28] present a comprehensive list of QoS properties (availability, price, popularity, data-size, success-rate, response time, overall success-rate, and overall response-time) and four standard fault-tolerance strategies (retry, try a backup server, invoke N equivalent services concurrent, and invoke all equivalent services concurrently). They then describe an approach for choosing the right fault-tolerance strategy for each service in a workflow to satisfy the user-level QoS requirements.

4.2   Remaining Challenges

As indicated above, most proposals for increasing the dependability of SOAs involve a combination of external monitoring of services and then rebinding to an alternative implementation should a failure occur. Such an approach, however, has numerous limitations, including the following.

Lack of alternatives. Binding to an alternative implementation of a service works in theory but may be of limited use in practice due to lack of identical services. Especially for internal enterprise services, there may simply not be other implementations that can be trusted. Furthermore, services are often used to provide controlled access to a data source. The data may be proprietary or sensitive to the extent that it is not feasible or advisable to replicate it to independent implementations or deployments of the service.

Application state rollback. A service may maintain state on behalf of the application client. In such situations, rebinding to a different service instance may require a rollback at the client to the point where the state was stored or created. If the client provides interactive service to a human user, such a rollback can cause unintended consequences and possible discontinuities in the user experience. If the service's client is actually another service, a cascading rollback may occur affecting multiple applications and numerous users. Even if the service state is checkpointed periodically, alternative service instances may not be able to interpret the checkpoint and even if they do, a small rollback may still be required.

Monitoring delay. External monitoring only provides historical information about the response time of a service instance. For example, the response time will often increase beyond its recent or historical averages when the instance becomes highly loaded, but the external monitor will not know about the increased workload until the impact is visible. Furthermore, external monitors have to be conservative in the amount of test traffic they submit to the service instance so as not to interfere with the serving of real requests, and multiple measurements are always needed to average over sporadic noise. As a result, there is always a significant lag in the reporting of response time measurements. A delay is also present for status (availability) monitoring since a number of test messages may be required before a service can be declared failed. Having a message interception mechanism, such as the one in the Enterprise Service Bus in [19], alleviates the monitoring delay, but such mechanisms are not universally available.

Other monitoring limitations. External monitoring is fundamentally limited to information that can be extracted by sending and observing test requests, or if an interception mechanism is available, observing real messages sent and received by services. Thus, it cannot report information only known by the service provider (e.g., next scheduled maintenance).

5   Collaborative QoS

The limitations described in Section 4.2 demonstrate that current approaches to enhancing the dependability of SOAs are insufficient and do not completely solve the dependability dilemma. We suggest here that services not only need to take measures to enhance their own dependability, they also need to collaborate with services they use and services that use them to ensure the overall desired level of dependability for applications in a SOA. While service independence is often cited as one of the benefits of SOAs, we argue that the ability to undertake collaboration in a controlled way allows a number of these challenges to be addressed while preserving the characteristics of SOAs that make them an attractive solution in many contexts. Specifically, we consider two types of collaboration: between a service consumer and a service provider, and among all (or many) of the consumers of a service provider (multi-party collaboration.) The tradeoff in all these approaches is that it weakens the SOA abstraction, and as a result, places more responsibility on the service developer by increasing the number of design choices that must be made.

5.1   Producer-Consumer Collaborative QoS

Our proposal is to implement collaboration by means of *translucent QoS interfaces* that are exposed by services in addition to their normal service interfaces, as shown in Figure 4. The QoS interfaces are translucent in the sense that they selectively expose information related to the QoS and QoS mechanisms used by the service instance. These interfaces are an example of the general concept of *translucent APIs* introduced in [11]. In this paper, we apply this concept in the context of SOAs and consider three specific variants of this type of QoS interface: (1) an interface that *reports* current QoS values, (2) an interface that *exposes* QoS mechanisms, and (3) an interface that can be used to *negotiate* QoS requirements. We elaborate on each of these options and their uses below.

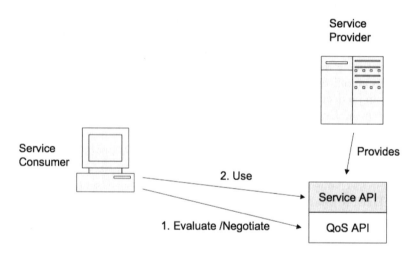

Fig. 4. Services with QoS API

Reporting current QoS values. In this variant, the QoS interface of a service simply reports current locally measured QoS metrics of the service in question. The value of this is based on the observation that the service instance itself inherently has better information about its own state than any external monitoring service. For example, the service instance can measure the response time for each request it processes directly at relatively low cost. It can also predict its response time in the near future by observing its current workload and thereby provide information to other services that they can use to decide whether they should bind to it or some alternative. Similarly, the service instance knows about the fault-tolerance techniques deployed to ensure its availability, the reliability of the underlying execution infrastructure, and any events—reduced redundancy due to failures or scheduled maintenance, for example—that reduce the expected availability at the current time. This information can also be reported through such an interface.

In general, many specific metrics could be included in a reporting interface of this type. Examples include mean response time and variance per operation type, expected availability, and duration until next known downtime (scheduled maintenance). Figure 5 provides a snippet of a WSDL specification for a potential service interface for such a collaborative QoS interface. In this example, the service provides an interface for querying individual attribute values one at a time by specifying the name of the attribute. The basic set of attribute names could be standardized, but services could also support additional attributes where the list of supported attribute names is provided by an additional operation.

```
<message name="QoSRequest">
      <part name="AttributeName" type="xsd:string"/>
</message>
<message name="QoSResponse">
      <part name="AttributeValue" type="xsd:float"/>
</message>

<portType name="QoSQuery">
      <operation name="askValue">
            <input message="tns:QoSRequest"/>
            <output message="tns:QoSResponse"/>
      </operation>
</portType>
```

Fig. 5. Simple QoS interface specification

As an example of how this interface could be used for collaborative QoS, consider the impact of system maintenance (e.g., upgrades) on service availability. System maintenance actions that bring the system down for a period of time may be relatively frequent (e.g., many smaller banks do weekly system maintenance) and their duration may be unpredictably long due to failed software upgrades [9]. In a normal SOA, there is no way for the service provider to communicate to the service consumers about the upcoming maintenance actions. Similarly, any external monitoring service can only detect the outage caused by the maintenance action when the system goes down. Having the QoS interface attached to the service instance makes it trivial to report to any potential users when the service will be going down, and potentially when it is anticipated to be restored and available for service again. As a result, service consumers, knowing how long they require the service to complete their task, can determine if they can use this service provider or if they should look for another provider.

Note that self-reporting in an untrusted environment is prone to abuse. There-fore, in an untrusted environment, additional external monitoring services can provide a point of comparison and thereby allow service users to determine which service instance to use with greater confidence.

Exposing QoS Mechanisms. While reporting only the metrics maintains the encapsulation and isolation of services, exposing details of the dependabil-ity mechanisms used by the service enables more powerful forms of collaborative QoS. For example, a service instance could expose the identity of a backup service with known compatibility, i.e., with both the same syntax and semantics of oper-ations, as well as the same underlying data if the services relies on a data source. For service implementations that use a form of internal replication, the interface could expose the current level of redundancy in the service implementation—i.e, the current number of operational replicas—or the expected recovery time in case of a failure. Specifically, if a replica of the service fails, it may take a period of time for the service to recover given the time to detect and then reconfigure the service. This information can help a service or application using this partic-ular service decide if it should look for an alternative implementation, use the service in degraded mode, or wait for full recovery.

As an example of the use of such an interface, consider *collaborative check-pointing*. Typically, any checkpointing of the service state is done within the implementation without exposing the details to any of the service consumers. In collaborative checkpointing, the service provider exposes the checkpoint of the consumer's session state to the consumer to be stored and used later if necessary.

```
<message name= ..response message to update operation ... >
       .... original response arguments .....
       <part name="CheckpointValue" type="xsd:any"/>
</message>

<message name="RestoreMessage">
       <part name="CheckpointValue" type="xsd:any"/>
</message>

<message name="RestoreResponse">
       <part name="RestoreSuccess" type="xsd:boolean"/>
</message>

<portType name="CheckpointPort">
       <operation name="restoreCheckpoint">
              <input message="tns:RestoreMessage"/>
              <output message="tns:RestoreResponse"/>
       </operation>
</portType>
```

Fig. 6. Collaborative Checkpointing interface specification

Figure 6 provides a snippet of a WSDL specification for a potential service interface for collaborative checkpointing. In this example, the response messages for service requests that modify the session state are enhanced to include a checkpoint of the service session state. Then, an additional operation is provided for the service consumer to restore the service provider with the stored checkpoint. Numerous alternative strategies are naturally possible including providing an explicit operation for requesting a checkpoint.

Negotiating QoS Properties. While exposing more information allows the service consumer to make a better choice among alternative service providers, a true negotiation interface allows the consumer and provider to reach an agreement dynamically on what QoS properties are provided and how. Such an interface would allow, for example, a consumer to take advantage of any service customization features provided by the service provider. That is, the service provider may have multiple fault-tolerance techniques from which to choose, each of which provides a given level of dependability but also with its own cost in terms of increased response time or increased resource usage. Similar tradeoffs are present for security (e.g., cost of cryptographic techniques for data privacy and integrity) and timeliness properties (e.g., cost of reserving dedicated resources to satisfy customer's response time requirements).

Figure 7 illustrates a very simple QoS negotiation interface where the service user presents the required QoS values and the service provider either agrees to provide them or indicates it is not able to comply. A more complex interface would allow the service provider to come up with a counter proposal that the service consumer could accept or reject. The penalty and reward for meeting or missing the agreed QoS level could also be part of the negotiation.

```
<message name="QoSNegotiationRequest">
        <part name="AverageResponseTime" type="xsd:Float"/>
        <part name="Availability" type="xsd:Float"/>
        <part name="Reliability" type="xsd:Float"/>
        . . .
</message>
<message name="QoSNegotiationResponse">
        <part name="QoSResponse" type="xsd:boolean"/>
</message>

<portType name="QoSNegotiation">
        <operation name="Negotiate">
                <input message="tns:QoSNegotiationRequest"/>
                <output message="tns:QoSNegotiationResponse"/>
        </operation>
</portType>
```

Fig. 7. Example of a simple QoS negotiation interface

As an example of the use of the negotiation interface, consider a real-time application that is required to react to an event within a specified time window. The application designer can obviously determine how much time the local code execution takes, but if the application uses external services, their response time is typically unknown. The negotiation interface allows the application to locate service providers that can complete the service requests on time. Upon receiving such a negotiation request, a service provider can attempt to reserve the resources necessary to meet the timeliness requirements.

5.2 Multi-party Collaborative QoS

The idea of QoS collaboration between a service consumer and provider is challenging if the service provider chooses to lie about its QoS metrics or mechanisms. Similarly, the QoS interface does not help with security issues in a SOA because the consumer typically cannot justifiably rely on any security information reported by an unknown service provider. Naturally the application designer may use knowledge about the service providers obtained off-line to determine which service instances the application should use, but unless the list of trusted service providers is encoded in the application program, it is difficult to use the off-line trust evaluation for dynamic runtime service binding.

To address this issue, we propose extending the concept of collaborative QoS from the collaboration between one service consumer and provider to a collaboration between all (or a large number of) service consumers, as illustrated in

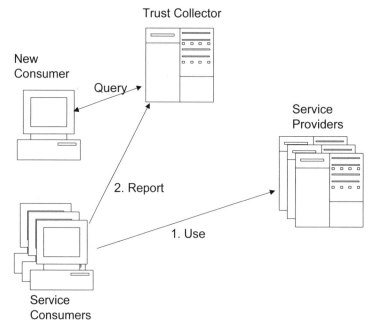

Fig. 8. Trust service

Figure 8. Specifically, we propose a new service—the Trust Collector service—that can be used by service consumers to report any positive or negative service experiences with a provider. The collaboration pattern is analogous to online rating systems such as eBay's seller ratings or Angie's List consumer reviews of real-world service providers such as doctors and contractors. Of course, the trustworthiness of a service provider only becomes apparent after a service has been used for a period time, so the Trust Collector service would most likely get its input after-the-fact from human application or service designers.

6   Towards Collaborative QoS

In this section, we summarize three different projects, each of which addresses one or more issues related to realizing the vision of collaborative QoS.

6.1   Cooperative Fault Tolerance

In [22], we introduced the concept and approach of *cooperative fault tolerance* for improving the availability of web services by taking advantage of similar, but not identical services, potentially owned and operated by separate companies. These services are not identical replicas, but rather provide close to the same functionality. Specifically, our cooperative fault tolerance enables automatic failover between non-identical services by using *transformation web services* that enable a service to use a similar service as its backup.

With cooperative fault tolerance, providers of similar services agree on a common service backup strategy based on their separate services. This could involve, for example, medium or small service providers that do not have enough resources to construct their own backup center using one another's services as failover sites. Or a collection of providers with similar services could contract with a network service provider to construct a shared disaster recovery site, with the transformation mechanism absorbing the difference between each service and the shared backup system. The fundamental idea behind cooperative fault tolerance is to realize enhanced availability at a very high level, essentially doing replication at a *business* level rather than at the service or lower levels.

Our transformation mechanisms focus on the compatibility challenges between the non-identical services as well as between the services and their original consumers. As an example, consider two non-identical services A and B where B is acting as the backup for A. Given the slightly different interfaces, the consumers of service A are typically not able to simply switch to using service B upon the failure of A (e.g., different message formats, code systems, mismatch in parameters). Similarly, the service state can typically not be transferred between A and B (before failure and after recovery) simply using the existing service interfaces. Our solution to these challenges is based on the use of transformation web services. The Client Transformation Web Service (CTWS) transforms the client's request, which uses A's protocol, into the protocol for B. It also controls the failover strategies according to the contents of the request. Similarly, the

Server Transformation Web Service (STWS) transforms the interactions needed between A and B for data sharing.

The transformation services are generated semi-automatically using a code generation tool. To ensure low overhead, we generate the appropriate transformation modules offline rather than relying on runtime composition. The approach is semi-automated in the sense that it requires developers to specify the transformation flow manually, but in a way that is guided based on the WSDL interface descriptions of the original services. Based on these directions, a code generator then generates the transformation web services.

While cooperative fault tolerance is an example of the collaborative QoS concept, it focuses on offline virtual integration of separate services to provide service consumers an improved service. In that sense, it can be viewed as an example of services implementing their own dependability, yet moving in the direction of collaborative QoS.

6.2   Customizable Durability

A key requirement for implementing highly available services is the ability to maintain service state across machine failures and server process crashes. Many techniques exist for protecting service state, including storing the state in a database or maintaining it in replicated processes, and each such technique can be characterized based on its level of protection and its cost in terms of hardware resources required and performance overhead. While many such techniques exist, service developers typically have a very small set of options (e.g., a database or nothing) and the chosen option must be coded in the service implementation (e.g., by denoting objects as session or entity beans in J2EE). Specifically, there is no integrated and transparent way to use different techniques to protect service state. However, different types of service state differ in the degree of protection required; some types such as billing information needs to survive very severe failures, while others might be reconstructed relatively easily should a failure occur. Furthermore, the business or cost requirements associated with the service may change over time, resulting in large code rewrites.

In [27], we introduce an architecture that allows service developers to use different techniques with different tradeoffs to protect service state flexibly and transparently. The service state is stored in one or more *state objects*. We propose to treat *state durability*—that is, the likelihood that the state can survive failures—as an explicit design parameter that is associated with each state object used by a service. Based on this durability attribute, different techniques with different tradeoffs can then be used to ensure the durability of different state objects. For example, the value of one state object can be stored in a database, while another is replicated in-memory on two or more computers. Note that one can view the different techniques as implementations of the stable storage abstraction [18], but with an explicit recognition of and control over the tradeoff between the fidelity of the abstraction and the cost of implementing it.

Our solution is based on *durability proxies* that implement a durability mechanism in a generic state independent manner, a *durability mapping* that specifies which durability mechanism is to be used for each state object, as well as any needed object-specific instructions, and a *durability compiler*. The compiler takes the web service and state object code, the durability mapping, and the necessary durability proxies and generates a web service and the associated state objects where the desired durability mechanisms are used for each state object.

Customizable durability is an example of a technique that allows a service instance to provide different, customized QoS tradeoffs—in this case, performance plus cost versus durability—to service consumers. In that sense, then, it is an example of a technology that provides a starting point for negotiation between consumers and providers about QoS properties and costs.

6.3 SLA-Aware Resource Allocation in Consolidated Server Environments

Virtualization-based server consolidation is gaining popularity in public cloud infrastructures as well as private data centers. The sharing of resources by multiple applications raises new resource allocation challenges such as ensuring responsiveness under dynamically changing workloads and isolating them from demand fluctuations in co-located virtual machines (VMs). In [16,17], we tackle the problem of optimizing resource allocation in consolidated server environments by automatically reconfiguring multitier applications running in virtualized data centers while satisfying response-time-based Service Level Agreements (SLAs) even under rapidly changing workloads. The SLAs specify the required mean response time for the application under different workload conditions, as well as the rewards and penalties for the resource provider for meeting or missing these response time goals.

The resource allocation problem is inherently complicated, especially as the number of hosted applications, available resources, and available distinct management actions increases. The approaches we present use offline model construction, and offline [16] or online [17] solutions to the optimization problem based on heuristic algorithms. While the details of the solution are not relevant here, the model where application owners negotiate with the resource provider for specified execution guarantees is directly related to collaborative QoS. In a general sense, the resource provider can be viewed as a service provider and the application owner as the consumer of this service. However, a more concrete connection to this paper is the fact that such dynamic resource allocation is yet another mechanism for enabling customizable service guarantees and thus, QoS negotiation. Indeed, it would be possible to directly use such a consolidated server environment and its management system to implement customized service instances supporting QoS negotiation. Specifically, when a service user negotiates for a specific QoS, the service provider can use this as the basis for issuing a request to the management system to execute the service with the desired response time guarantees. If the management system accepts the request and can provide the appropriate guarantees, the service provider can then accept the consumer's request for service.

7   Conclusions

SOAs are an attractive approach to structuring software in networked systems, yet features such as service independence that form the basis for much of this value also make ensuring dependability a daunting task. To address this dependability dilemma, we have proposed the idea of collaborative QoS in which controlled sharing of information is used to ease the task of providing fault tolerance, timeliness, and/or security. Specifically, we described how three different types of translucent QoS interfaces could be used either to report current QoS values, to expose QoS mechanisms, or to negotiate QoS requirements. These three variants were all designed for pairwise collaboration between single consumers and single producers. This was then extended to multi-party collaboration, where multiple consumers exchange information about provider services to increase the accuracy of that knowledge. Finally, while a single solution with all these features has yet to be developed, we described three projects that address some of the issues that need to be solved to realize collaborative QoS, and hence, make progress towards the Holy Grail of distributed systems that are truly dependable.

References

1. Avizienis, A., Laprie, J.-C., Randell, B., Landwehr, C.: Basic concepts and taxonomy of dependable and secure computing. IEEE Transactions on Dependable and Secure Computing 1(1), 11–33 (2004)
2. Baresi, L., Ghezzi, C., Guinea, S.: Smart monitors for composed services. In: Proc. International Conference on Service Oriented Computing (ICSOC 2004), pp. 193–202 (2004)
3. Booth, D., Haas, H., McCabe, F., Newcomer, E., Champion, M., Ferris, C., Orchard, D.: Web services architecture, W3C working group note (November 2004), http://www.w3.org/TR/ws-arch/
4. Bruning, S., Weissleder, S., Malek, M.: A fault taxonomy for service-oriented architecture. In: Proc. 10th IEEE High Assurance Systems Engineering Symposium (HASE 2007), pp. 367–374 (2007)
5. Cardellini, V., Casalicchio, E., Grassi, V., Lo Presti, F., Mirandalo, R.: Towards self-adaptation for dependable service-oriented systems. In: de Lemos, R., Fabre, J.-C., Gacek, C., Gadducci, F., ter Beek, M. (eds.) Architecting Dependable Systems VI. LNCS, vol. 5835, pp. 24–48. Springer, Heidelberg (2009)
6. Chappell, D.: Enterprise Service Bus. O'Reilly, Sebastopol, CA (June 2004)
7. Chinnici, R., Moreau, J.-J., Ryman, A., Weerawarana, S.: Web services description language (WSDL) version 2.0 part 1: Core language (June 2007), http://www.w3.org/TR/wsdl20/
8. Denaro, G., Pezzè, M., Tosi, D., Schilling, D.: Towards self-adaptive service-oriented architectures. In: Proc. Workshop on Testing, Analysis, and Verification of Web Services and Applications (TAV-WEB 2006), pp. 10–16 (2006)
9. Dimitras, T., Narasimhan, P.: Why do upgrades fail and what can we do about it. In: Bacon, J.M., Cooper, B.F. (eds.) Middleware 2009. LNCS, vol. 5896, pp. 349–372. Springer, Heidelberg (2009)

10. Gudgin, M., Hadley, M., Mendelsohn, N., Moreau, J.-J., Nielsen, H., Karmarkar, A., Lafon, Y.: SOAP version 1.2 part 1: Messaging framework, 2nd edn. (April 2007), http://www.w3.org/TR/soap12-part1/

11. Hiltunen, M., Schlichting, R.: The lost art of abstraction. In: de Lemos, R., Gacek, C., Romanovsky, A. (eds.) Architecting Dependable Systems III. LNCS, vol. 3549, pp. 331–342. Springer, Heidelberg (2005)

12. Huang, G., Liu, X., Mei, H.: SOAR: Towards dependable service-oriented architecture via reflective middleware. International Journal on Simulation and Process Modeling 3(1/2), 55–65 (2007)

13. Jimenez-Peris, R., Patiño-Martinez, M., Kemme, B., Perez-Sorrosal, F., Serrano, D.: A system of architectural patterns for scaleable, consistent and highly-available multi-tier service-oriented infrastructures. In: de Lemos, R. (ed.) Architecting Dependable Systems VI. LNCS, vol. 5835, pp. 1–23. Springer, Heidelberg (2009)

14. Jordan, D., Evdemon, J., et al.: Web services business process execution language, v. 2 (April 2007), OASIS Standard:
http://docs.oasis-open.org/wsbpel/2.0/OS/wsbpel-v2.0-OS.html

15. Joshi, K., Hiltunen, M., Sanders, W., Schlichting, R.: Automatic model-driven recovery in distributed systems. In: Proc. 24th IEEE Symposium on Reliable Distributed Systems (SRDS 2005), pp. 25–36 (2005)

16. Jung, G., Joshi, K., Hiltunen, M., Schlichting, R., Pu, C.: Generating adaptation policies for multi-tier applications in consolidated server environments. In: Proc. IEEE International Conference on Autonomic Computing (ICAC 2008), pp. 23–32 (2008)

17. Jung, G., Joshi, K., Hiltunen, M., Schlichting, R., Pu, C.: A cost-sensitive adaptation engine for server consolidation of multi-tier applications. In: Bacon, J.M., Cooper, B.F. (eds.) Middleware 2009. LNCS, vol. 5896, pp. 163–183. Springer, Heidelberg (2009)

18. Lampson, B.: Atomic transactions. In: Distributed System-Architecture and Implementation, pp. 246–265. Springer, Heidelberg (1981)

19. Lin, K.-J., Panahi, M., Zhang, Y., Zhang, J., Chang, S.-H.: Building accountability middleware to support dependable SOA. IEEE Internet Computing 13(2), 16–25 (2009)

20. Liu, L., Russell, D., Xu, J., Davies, J., Irvin, K.: Agile properties of service oriented architectures for network enabled capability. In: Proc. Realising Network Enabled Capability, RNEC 2008 (2008)

21. Mabrouk, N., Georgantas, N., Issarny, V.: QoS-aware service-oriented middleware for pervasive environments. In: Bacon, J.M., Cooper, B.F. (eds.) Middleware 2009. LNCS, vol. 5896, pp. 123–142. Springer, Heidelberg (2009)

22. Moritsu, T., Hiltunen, M., Schlichting, R., Toyouchi, J., Namba, Y.: Using web service transformations to implement cooperative fault tolerance. In: Penkler, D., Reitenspiess, M., Tam, F. (eds.) ISAS 2006. LNCS, vol. 4328, pp. 76–91. Springer, Heidelberg (2006)

23. Di Nitto, E., Ghezzi, C., Metzger, A., Papazoglou, M., Pohl, K.: A journey to highly dynamic, self-adaptive service-based applications. Automated Software Engineering 15(3-4), 313–341 (2008)

24. Tsai, W., Weiwei, S., Paul, R., Zhibin, C., Hai, H.: Services-oriented dynamic reconfiguration framework for dependable distributed computing. In: Proc. 28th Annual International Computer Software and Applications Conference (COMPSAC), pp. 554–559 (2004)

25. Wang, G., Wang, C., Chen, A., Wang, H., Fung, C., Uczekaj, S., Chen, Y.-L., Guthmiller, W., Lee, J.: Service level management using QoS monitoring, diagnostics, and adaptation for networked enterprise systems. In: Proc. Ninth IEEE International Enterprise Distributed Object Computing Conference(EDOC 2005), pp. 239–250 (2005)
26. Zeng, L., Lei, H., Chang, H.: Monitoring the QoS for web services. In: Krämer, B.J., Lin, K.-J., Narasimhan, P. (eds.) ICSOC 2007. LNCS, vol. 4749, pp. 132–144. Springer, Heidelberg (2007)
27. Zhang, X., Hiltunen, M., Marzullo, K., Schlichting, R.: Customizable service state durability for service oriented architectures. In: Proc. Sixth European Dependable Computing Conference (EDCC 2006), pp. 119–128 (2006)
28. Zheng, Z., Lyu, M.: A QoS-aware fault tolerant middleware for dependable service composition. In: Proc. IEEE International Conference on Dependable Systems and Networks (DSN), pp. 392 – 397 (June 2009)

Software Assumptions Failure Tolerance: Role, Strategies, and Visions

Vincenzo De Florio

University of Antwerp
Department of Mathematics and Computer Science
Performance Analysis of Telecommunication Systems group
Middelheimlaan 1, 2020 Antwerp, Belgium
Interdisciplinary Institute for Broadband Technology
Gaston Crommenlaan 8, 9050 Ghent-Ledeberg, Belgium

Abstract. At our behest or otherwise, while our software is being executed, a huge variety of design assumptions is continuously matched with the truth of the current condition. While standards and tools exist to express and verify some of these assumptions, in practice most of them end up being either sifted off or hidden between the lines of our codes. Across the system layers, a complex and at times obscure web of assumptions determines the quality of the match of our software with its deployment platforms and run-time environments. Our position is that it becomes increasingly important being able to design software systems with architectural and structuring techniques that allow software to be decomposed to reduce its complexity, but without hiding in the process vital hypotheses and assumptions. In this paper we discuss this problem, introduce three potentially dangerous consequences of its denial, and propose three strategies to facilitate their treatment. Finally we propose our vision towards a new holistic approach to software development to overcome the shortcomings offered by fragmented views to the problem of assumption failures.

1 Introduction

We are living in a society that cannot do without computer systems. Services supplied by computer systems have permeated our environments and deeply changed our societies and the way we live in them. Computers pervade our lives, integrating themselves in all environments. At first confined in large control rooms, now they take the form of tiny embedded systems soon to be "sprayed" on physical entities so as to augment them with advanced processing and communication capabilities. Thus it is very much evident to what extent we depend on computers. What is often overlooked by many is the fact that most of the logics behind computer services supporting and sustaining our societies lies in the software layers. Software has become the point of accumulation of a large amount of complexity [1]. It is ubiquitous, mobile, and has pervaded all aspects of our lives. What is more important for this discussion, software is the main culprit behind the majority of computer failures [2,3,4].

A. Casimiro et al. (Eds.): Architecting Dependable Systems VII, LNCS 6420, pp. 249–272, 2010.

Among the reasons that brought to this state of things we focus our attention here on a particular one. Clever organizations and system structures allowed the visible complexity of software development to be reduced—at first through modules and layers, then by means of objects, and more recently with services, components, aspects, and models. As a result, we have been given tools to compose and orchestrate complex, powerful, and flexible software-intensive systems in a relatively short amount of time. The inherently larger flexibility of software development turned software into the ideal "location" where to store the bulk of the complexity of nowadays' computer-based services. Unfortunately, this very same characteristic of software makes it also considerably *fragile to changes* [1]. In particular software's flexibility also means that most of the assumptions drawn at design-time may get invalidated when the software system is ported, reused, redeployed, or simply when it is executed in a physical environment other than the one originally meant for. This means that truly resilient software systems demand special care to *assumption failures detection, avoidance*, and *recovery*. Despite this fact, no systematic approach allows yet for the expression and verification of hypotheses regarding the expected properties and behaviors of

- the hardware components (e.g. the failure semantics of the memory modules we depend on);
- third-party software (e.g. the reliability of an open-source software library we make use of);
- the execution environment (e.g. the security provisions offered by the Java execution environment we are currently using);
- the physical environment (e.g., the characteristics of the faults experienced in a space-borne vehicle orbiting around the sun).

While several tools exist, in practice most of the above assumptions often end up being either sifted off or "hardwired" in the executable code. As such, those removed or concealed hypotheses cannot be easily inspected, verified, or maintained. Despite the availability of several conceptual and practical tools—a few examples of which are briefly discussed in Sect. 4—still we are lacking methodologies and architectures to tackle this problem in its complex entirety—from design-time to the various aspects of the run-time. As a consequence, our software systems often end up being entities whose structure, properties, and dependencies are not completely known, hence at times deviate from their intended goals.

Across the system layers, a complex and at times obscure "web" of software machines is being executed concurrently by our computers. Their mutual dependencies determine the quality of the match of our software with its deployment platform(s) and run-time environment(s) and, consequently, their performance, cost, and in general their quality of service and experience. At our behest or otherwise, a huge variety of design assumptions is continuously matched with the truth of the current conditions. A hardware component assumed to be available; an expected feature in an OSGi bundle or in a web browser platform; a memory management policy supported by a mobile platform [5], or ranges of operational conditions taken for granted at all times—all are but assumptions and all have a dynamically varying truth value.

Our societies, our very lives, are often entrusted to machines driven by software; weird as it may sound, in some cases this is done without question—as an act of faith as it were. This is clearly unacceptable. The more we rely on computer systems—the more we depend on their correct functioning for our welfare, health, and economy—the more it becomes important to design those systems with architectural and structuring techniques that allow software complexity to be decomposed, but without hiding in the process those hypotheses and assumptions pertaining e.g. the target execution environment and the expected fault- and system models.

Our position is that existing tools will have to be augmented so as to minimize the risks of assumption failures e.g. when porting, deploying, or moving software to a new machine. We envision novel autonomic run-time executives that continuously verify those hypotheses and assumptions by matching them with endogenous knowledge deducted from the processing subsystems as well as exogenous knowledge derived from their execution and physical environments. Mechanisms for propagating such knowledge through all stages of software development would allow the chances of assumptions failures to be considerably reduced. The ultimate result we envisage is the ability to express truly assumption failure-tolerant software systems, i.e., software systems that endorse provisions to efficiently and effectively tackle—to some agreed upon extent—the problem of assumption failures.

This paper makes three main contributions. A first one is exposing our vision of assumption failure-tolerant software systems. Such systems explicitly address three main "hazards" of software development, which we call the Horning syndrome, the Hidden Intelligence syndrome, and the Boulding syndrome. Assumption failures and the three syndromes are presented in Sect. 2. A second contribution is introducing the concept of assumption failure-tolerant software systems and providing three examples of strategies—one for each of the above syndromes. This is done in Sect. 3. A third contribution is our vision of a holistic approach to resilient software development, where the concept of assumption failure plays a pivotal role. Such vision—introduced after a brief overview of related and complementary technologies in Sect. 4—is the subject of Sect. 5. The paper is concluded by Sect. 6 in which we summarize our main lessons learned and provide our conclusions.

2   Three Hazards of Software Development

As mentioned before, assumption failures may have dire consequences on software dependability. In what follows we consider two well known exemplary cases from which we derive a base of three "syndromes" that we deem as the main hazards of assumption failures. We assume the reader to be already familiar with the basic facts of those two cases. Furthermore, we shall focus our attention only on a few aspects and causes—namely those more closely related to the subject at hand.

2.1 Case 1: Ariane 5 Flight 501 Failure

On June 4, 1996, the maiden flight of the Ariane 5 rocket ended in a failure just forty seconds after its lift-off. At an altitude of about 3,700 meters, the launcher veered off its flight path, broke up and exploded. After the failure, the European Space Agency set up an independent Inquiry Board to identify the causes of the failure. The Inquiry Board unravelled several reasons, the most important of which was a failure in the so-called Inertial Reference System (IRS), a key component responsible for flight attitude and movement control in space. Being so critical for the success of the mission, the IRS adopted a simple hardware fault-tolerance design pattern: two identical replicas were operating in parallel (hot standby), executing the same software system. As mentioned before, we shall not focus here on all the design faults of this scheme, e.g. its lack of design diversity [6]. Our focus will be on one of the several concomitant causes, namely a software reuse error in the IRS. The Ariane 5 software included software modules that were originally developed and successfully used in the Ariane 4 program. Such software was written with a specific physical environment as its reference. Such reference environment was characterized by well defined ranges for several flight trajectory parameters. One such parameter was the rocket's maximum horizontal velocity. In the Ariane 4, horizontal velocity could be represented as a 16-bit signed integer. The Ariane 5 was a new generation, thus it was faster. In particular horizontal velocity could not be represented in a signed short integer, which caused an overflow in both IRS replicas. This event triggered a chain of failures that led the rocket to complete loss of guidance and attitude information shortly after the start of the ignition sequence. Now completely blind and unaware, the Ariane 5 committed self destruction as an ultimate means to prevent any further catastrophic failures.

The Ariane 5 failure provides us with several lessons—in the rest of this subsection we shall focus on two of them.

Horning Syndrome. The Ariane 5 failure warns us of the fact that an assumption regarding the target physical environment of a software component may clash with a real life fact. In the case at hand, the target physical environment was assumed to be one where horizontal velocity would not exceed some agreed upon threshold. This assumption clashed with the characteristics of a new target environment.

The term we shall use to describe this event is "assumption failure" or "assumption-versus-context clash". The key lesson in this case is then that the physical environment can play a fundamental role in determining software quality. By paraphrasing a famous quote by Whorf, the environment shapes the way our fault-tolerance software is constructed and determines how dependable it will ultimately be. James Horning described this concept through his well known quote [7]:

> "What is the most often overlooked risk in software engineering?
> That the environment will do something the designer never anticipated."

This is precisely what happened in the case of the failure of the Ariane 5's IRS: new unanticipated environmental conditions violated some design assumptions. For this reason we call this class of assumption failures hazards "the Horning Syndrome", or S_H for brevity. For the same reason we shall use the terms "Horning Assumptions" (A_H) and "Horning Failures" (F_H) respectively to refer to this class of assumptions and of failures.

In what follows we shall use lowercase letters in Italics to denote assumptions. Given a letter representing an assumption, the same letter in bold typeface shall represent the true value for that assumption. As an example, the Ariane-5 failure was caused (among other reasons) by a clash between f: { "Horizontal Velocity can be represented by a short integer" } and $\mathbf{f}$: { "Horizontal velocity is now n" }, where n is larger than the maximum short integer.

Hidden Intelligence Syndrome. The second aspect we deem important to highlight in the context of the failure of the IRS is related to a lack of propagation of knowledge. The Horning Assumption that led to this Horning Failure originated at Ariane 4's design time. On the other hand the software code that implemented the Ariane 4 design did not include any mechanism to store, inspect, or validate such assumption. This vital piece of information was simply lost. This loss of information made it more difficult to verify the inadequacy of the Ariane 4 software to the new environment it had been deployed. We call an accident such as this a case of the Hidden Intelligence Syndrome (S_{HI}). Consequently we use the terms Hidden Intelligence Assumption (A_{HI}) and Hidden Intelligence Failure (F_{HI}).

Unfortunately accidents due to the S_H and the S_{HI} are far from being uncommon—computer history is crowded with examples, with a whole range of consequences. In what follows we highlight this fact in another well known case—the deadly Therac-25 failures.

2.2   Case 2: The Therac-25 Accidents

The Therac-25 accidents have been branded as "the most serious computer-related accidents to date" [8]. Several texts describe and analyze them in detail—including the just cited one. As we did for the Ariane 5, here we shall not provide yet another summary of the case; rather, we shall highlight the reasons why the Therac-25 is also a case of the above assumption hazards and of a third class of hazards.

The Therac-25 was a so-called "linac," that is, a medical linear accelerator that uses accelerated electrons to create high-energy beams to destroy tumors with minimal impact on the surrounding healthy tissue. It was the latest member of a successful family of linacs, which included the Therac-6 and the Therac-20. Compared to its predecessors, model 25 was more compact, cheaper and had more functional features. In particular the cheaper cost was a result of several modifications including a substantial redesign of the embedded hardware-software platform. In the redesign, some expensive hardware services were taken over by the software layer. For instance it was decided to remove hardware interlocks that would shut the machine down in the face of certain exceptions.

There is evidence that several such exceptions had occurred while previous models, e.g. the Therac-20, were operative. Unfortunately, none of these occurrences were reported or fed back to the design process of the Therac-25. Had it been otherwise, they would have revealed that certain rare combinations of events triggered the emission of extraordinary high levels of energy beams—were it not for the safety interlocks present in the old models. History repeated itself with model 25, only this time the killer doses of beams *were* emitted, resulting in the killing or serious injuring of several people.

Another Case of the Horning Syndrome. We observe how the Therac may be considered as a special case of Horning Assumption failure in which the "unanticipated behavior" is due to endogenous causes and Horning's "environment" is the hardware platform. The "culprit" in this case is the clash between two design assumptions and two indisputable facts. Assumptions were fault assumption f: {*"No residual fault exists"*} and hardware component assumption p: {*"All exceptions are caught by the hardware and the execution environment, and result in shutting the machine down"*}. The corresponding facts were **f**: {*"Residual faults still exist"*}, that is $\neg f$, and **p**: {*"Exceptions exist that are not caught"*}—that is, $\neg p$. The unanticipated behavior is in this case the machine still remaining operative in a faulty state, thus the violation of the safety mission requirements.

Another Case of Hidden Intelligence. As mentioned already, because of the failure-free behavior of the Therac-20, its software was considered as fault-free. Reusing that software on the new machine model produced a clash. Thus we could say that, for the Therac family of machines, a hardware fault-masking scheme translated into software hidden intelligence—that is, a case of the S_{HI}. Such hidden intelligence made it more difficult to verify the inadequacy of the new platform to its operational specifications.

Boulding Syndrome. Finally we observe how the Therac-25 software, despite its real-time design goals, was basically structured as a quasi closed-world system. Such systems are among the naivest classes of systems in Kenneth Boulding's famous classification [9]: quoting from the cited article, they belong to the categories of "Clockworks" ("simple dynamic system with predetermined, necessary motions") and "Thermostats" ("control mechanisms in which [...] the system will move to the maintenance of any given equilibrium, *within limits*"). Such systems are characterized by predefined assumptions about their platform, their internal state, and the environment they are meant to be deployed in. They are closed, "blind" entities so to say, built from synchronous assumptions, and designed so as to be plugged in well defined hardware systems and environments whose changes, idiosyncrasies, or fluctuations most of them deliberately ignore. Using a well known English vernacular, they are *"sitting ducks"* to change— they keep on doing their prescribed task, as defined at design time, irrespective of environmental conditions; that is, they lack the ability to detect and respond to deployment- and run-time changes.

Clearly the Therac machines and their software comply to this definition. In particular those machines were missing introspection mechanisms (for instance, self-tests) able to verify whether the target platform did include the expected mechanisms and behaviors.

A case like the Therac's—that is, when a clash exists between a system's Boulding category and the actual characteristics of its operational environment—shall be referred to in what follows as a case of the Boulding Syndrome (S_B). The above mentioned Boulding categories and clashes will also be respectively referred to as Boulding Assumptions (S_B) and Boulding Failures (S_B).

2.3   Preliminary Conclusions

By means of two well known cases we have shown how computer system failures can be the result of software assumption failures. Moreover, in so doing we have introduced three major hazards or syndromes requiring particular attention:

Horning syndrome: mistakenly not considering that the physical environment may change and produce unprecedented or unanticipated conditions;

Hidden Intelligence syndrome: mistakenly concealing or discarding important knowledge for the sake of hiding complexity;

Boulding syndrome: mistakenly designing a system with insufficient context-awareness with respect to the current environments.

In what follows we describe examples of strategies to treat some cases of the three syndromes so as to decrease the risk to trigger assumption failures.

3   Assumption Failure-Tolerant Software Systems

The key strategy we adopt here is to offer the designer the possibility to postpone the choice of one out of multiple alternative design-time assumptions to a proper future time (compile-time, deployment-time, run-time, etc.) In what follows we shall describe how to do so for the following classes of assumptions:

– Assumptions related to the failure semantics of hardware components.
– Assumptions related to the fault-tolerance design patterns to adopt.
– Assumptions related to dimensioning of resources.

3.1   Assumptions on Hardware Components' Failure Semantics

As we have already remarked, software depends on certain behaviors expected from the underlying hardware architecture. Hardware neutrality and the principles of layered design dictate that most of the actual processes and actors in the bare machine are not disclosed. Thus for instance we rarely know (and often care about) the particular technology of the main memory integrated circuits our software is making use of.

This is a case of the Hidden Intelligence syndrome. By not expressing explicitly our requirements concerning the way hardware (e.g., memory modules) should behave we leave the door open to dependability assumption failures.

As an example, while yesterday's software was running atop CMOS chips, today a common choice e.g. for airborne applications is SDRAM—because of speed, cost, weight, power and simplicity of design [10]. But CMOS memories mostly experience single bit errors [11], while SDRAM chips are known to be subjected to several classes of severe faults, including so-called "single-event effects" [10], i.e., a threat that can lead to total loss of a whole chip. Examples include:

1. Single-event latch-up (SEL), a threat that can bring to the loss of all data stored on chip [12].
2. Single-event upset (SEU), leading to frequent soft errors [13,14].
3. Single-event functional interrupt (SFI), i.e. a special case of SEU that places the device into a test mode, halt, or undefined state. The SFI halts normal operations, and requires a power reset to recover [15].

Furthermore [10] remarks how even *from lot to lot* error and failure rates can vary more than one order of magnitude. In other words, the superior performance of the new generation of memories is paid with a higher instability and a trickier failure semantics.

Let us suppose for the time being that the software system at hand needs to be compiled in order to be executed on the target platform. The solution we propose to alleviate this problem is as follows:

- First, we assume memory access is abstracted (for instance through services, libraries, overloaded operators, or aspects). This allows the actual memory access methods to be specified in a second moment.
- Secondly, a number of design-time hypotheses regarding the failure semantics of the hardware memory subsystem are drawn. These may take the form of fault/failure assumptions such as for instance:

  f_0: "Memory is stable and unaffected by failures".

  f_1: "Memory is affected by transient faults and CMOS-like failure behaviors".

  f_2: "Memory is affected by permanent stuck-at faults and CMOS-like failure behaviors".

  f_3: "Memory is affected by transient faults and SDRAM-like failure behaviors, including SEL".

  f_4: "Memory is affected by transient faults and SDRAM-like failure behaviors, including SEL and SEU".

- For each assumption f_i (in this case $0 \leq i \leq 4$) a diverse set of memory access methods, M_i, is designed. With the exception of M_0, each M_i is a fault-tolerant version specifically designed to tolerate the memory modules' failure modes assumed in f_i.

Fig. 1. The Serial Presence Detect (yellow circle) allows information about a computer's memory module, e.g. its manufacturer, model, size, and speed, to be accessed

- To compile the code on the target platform, an Autoconf-like toolset [16] is assumed to be available. Special checking rules are coded in the toolset making use of e.g. Serial Presence Detect (see Fig. 1) to get access to information related to the memory modules on the target computer. For instance, Linux tools such as "lshw" provide higher-level access to information such as the memory modules' manufacturer, models, and characteristics (see an example in Fig. 2). Such rules could access local or remote, shared databases reporting known failure behaviors for models and even specific lots thereof. Once the most probable memory behavior **f** is retrieved, a method M_j is selected to actually access memory on the target computer. Selection is done as follows: first we isolate those methods that are able to tolerate **f**, then we arrange them into a list ordered according to some cost function (e.g. proportional to the expenditure of resources); finally we select the minimum element of that list.

The above strategy allows the designer to postpone the choice between alternative design-time assumptions to the right moment, that it, when the code is compiled on the chosen target action. A similar strategy could be embedded in the execution environment, e.g. a Web browser or a Java Virtual Machine. Such strategy could selectively provide access at deployment time to knowledge necessary to choose which of the design-time alternative assumptions has the highest chance to match reality. Note that our strategy helps avoiding S_{HI} and brings the designer to explicitly deal with the problem of assumption failures. Furthermore this is done with full separation of the design concerns.

Comparison with existing strategy. A somewhat similar strategy is used for performance enhancement. Applications such as the mplayer video player [17] can take advantage of predefined knowledge about the possible target processor and enable optimized methods to perform some of their tasks. Mplayer declares this by displaying messages such as "Using SSE optimized IMDCT transform" or "Using MMX optimized resampler". Our procedure differs considerably from the

```
*-memory
        description: System Memory
        physical id: 1000
        slot: System board or motherboard
        size: 1536MiB
    *-bank:0
        description: DIMM DDR Synchronous 533 MHz (1.9 ns)
        vendor: CE00000000000000
        physical id: 0
        serial: F504F679
        slot: DIMM_A
        size: 1GiB
        width: 64 bits
        clock: 533MHz (1.9ns)
    *-bank:1
        description: DIMM DDR Synchronous 667 MHz (1.5 ns)
        vendor: CE00000000000000
        physical id: 1
        serial: F33DD2FD
        slot: DIMM_B
        size: 512MiB
        width: 64 bits
        clock: 667MHz (1.5ns)
```

Fig. 2. Excerpt from the output of command-line `sudo lshw` on a Dell Inspiron 6000 laptop

mplayer's, as it focuses on non-functional (dependability) enhancements. Furthermore, it is a more general design methodology and makes use of knowledge bases. Meta-object protocols, compiler technology, and aspects could provide alternative way to offer similar services.

3.2   Choice of Fault-Tolerance Design Patterns

The choice of which design pattern to use is known to have a direct influence on a program's overall complexity and performance. What is sometimes overlooked is the fact that fault-tolerance design patterns have a strong influence on a program's actual ability to tolerate faults. For instance, a choice like the **redoing** design pattern [18]—i.e., repeat on failure—*implies* assumption e_1 : { "The physical environment shall exhibit transient faults" }, while a design pattern such as **reconfiguration**—that is, replace on failure—is the natural choice after an assumption such as e_2 : { "The physical environment shall exhibit permanent faults" }. Of course clashes are always possible, which means in this case that there is a non-zero probability of a Horning Assumption failure—that is, a case of the S_H. Let us observe that:

1. A clash of assumption e_1 implies a livelock (endless repetition) as a result of redoing actions in the face of permanent faults.
2. A clash of assumption e_2 implies an unnecessary expenditure of resources as a result of applying reconfiguration in the face of transient faults.

The strategy we suggest to tackle this case is to offer the designer the possibility to postpone the binding of the actual fault-tolerance design pattern and to condition it to the actual behavior of the environment.

In what follows we describe a possible implementation of this run-time strategy.

- First, we assume the software system to be structured in such a way as to allow an easy reconfiguration of its components. Natural choices for this are service-oriented and/or component-oriented architectures. Furthermore we assume that the software architecture can be adapted by changing a reflective meta-structure in the form of a directed acyclic graph (DAG). A middleware supporting this is e.g. ACCADA [19].
- Secondly, the designer draws a number of alternative hypotheses regarding the faults to be experienced in the target environments. A possible choice could be for instance e_0: "No faults shall be experienced" and then e_1 and e_2 from above.
- For each fault-tolerance assumption (in this case e_1 and e_2) a matching fault-tolerant design pattern is designed and exported e.g. in the service or component registry. The corresponding DAG snapshots are stored in data structures D_1 and D_2.
- Through e.g. publish/subscribe, the supporting middleware component receives notifications regarding the faults being detected by the main components of the software system. Such notifications are fed into an Alpha-count filter [20,21], that is, a count-and-threshold mechanism to discriminate between different types of faults.
- Depending on the assessment of the Alpha-count oracle, either D_1 or D_2 are injected on the reflective DAG. This has the effect or reshaping the software architecture as in Fig. 3. Under the hypothesis of a correct oracle, such scheme avoids clashes: always the most appropriate design pattern is used in the face of certain classes of faults.

The above strategy is a second example of a way to postpone the choice among alternative design-time assumptions to the right moment—in this case at run-time, when the physical environment changes its characteristics or when the software is moved to a new and different environment. As a consequence, our strategy has the effect to help avoiding S_H and to force the designer not to neglect the problem of assumption failures.

We have developed a prototypical version of this strategy (see Fig. 4) and we are now designing a full fledged version based on the cited ACCADA and on an Alpha-count framework built with Apache Axis2 [22] and MUSE [23].

Comparison with existing strategies. Also in this case there exist strategies that postpone the choice of the design pattern to execution time, though to the

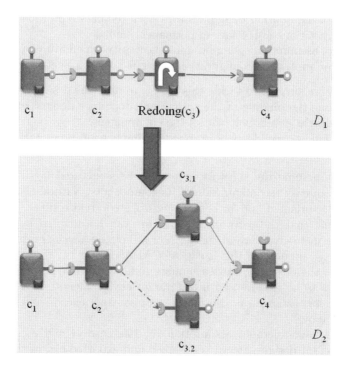

Fig. 3. Transition from a redoing scheme $(D1)$ to a reconfiguration scheme (D_2) is obtained by replacing component c_3, which tolerates transient faults by redoing its computation, with a 2-version scheme where a primary component $(c_{3.1})$ is taken over by a secondary one $(c_{3.2})$ in case of permanent faults

best of our knowledge this has been done only with the design goal of achieving performance improvements. A noteworthy example is FFTW, a code generator for Fast Fourier Transforms that defines and assembles (before compile time) blocks of C code that optimally solve FFT sub-problems on a given machine [24]. Our strategy is clearly different in that it focuses on dependability and makes use of a well-known count-and-threshold mechanism.

3.3   Assumptions Related to Dimensioning Replicated Resources

As well known, a precise characterization of the amount of resources necessary to deal with a certain situation is not always easy or even possible to find out. In some cases, such amount is not to be considered as a static value, fixed once and for all at design-time. Rather, it should be modeled as a dynamic system, i.e. a variable changing over time. When the situation to deal with is a threat to the quality of a software service, then the common approach is to foresee a certain amount of redundancy (time-, physical-, information-, or design-redundancy).

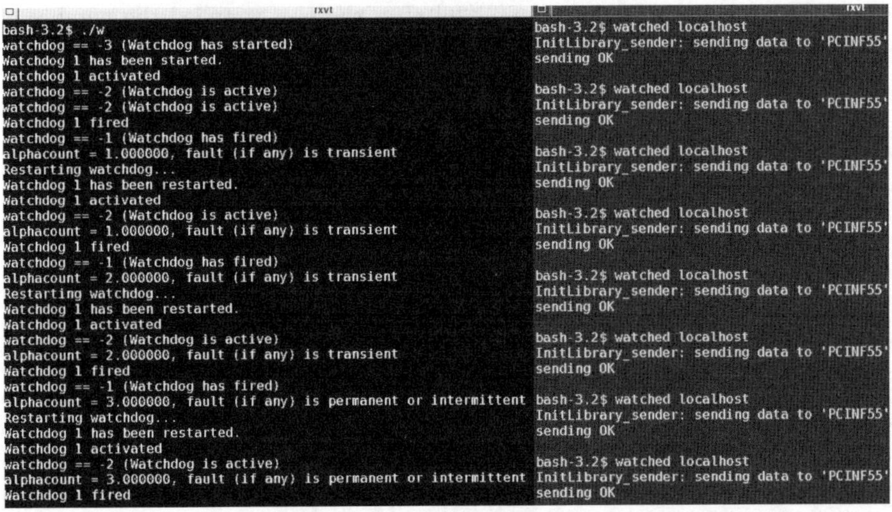

Fig. 4. A scenario involving a watchdog (left-hand window) and a watched task (right-hand). A permanent design fault is repeatedly injected in the watched task. As a consequence, the watchdog "fires" and an alpha-count variable is updated. The value of that variable increases until it overcomes a threshold (3.0) and correspondingly the fault is labeled as "permanent or intermittent."

For instance, replication and voting can be used to tolerate physical faults[1]. An important design problem is redundancy dimensioning. Over-dimensioning redundancy or under-dimensioning it would respectively lead to either a waste of resources or failures. Ideally the replication and voting scheme should work with a number of replicas that closely follows the evolution of the disturbance. In other words, the system should be aware of changes in certain physical variables or at least of the effect they are producing to its internal state. Not doing so—that is, choosing once and for all a certain degree of redundancy—means forcing the designer to take one assumption regarding the expected range of disturbances. It also means that the system will have a predetermined, necessary "motion" that will not be affected by changes, however drastic or sudden. In other words, the system will be a Boulding's *Thermostat*. In what follow we describe a strategy that can be used to enhance the Boulding category of a replication and voting scheme, thus avoiding a case of the S_B.

The strategy we propose is to isolate redundancy management at architectural level, and to use an autonomic computing scheme to adjust it automatically. In what follows we describe a possible implementation for this run-time strategy.

– First, we assume that the replication-and-voting service is available through an interface similar to the one of the Voting Farm [25]. Such service sets

---

[1] Obviously simple replication would not suffice to tolerate design faults, in which case a design diversity scheme such as *N*-Version Programming would be required.

up a so-called "restoring organ" [26] after the user supplied the number of replicas and the method to replicate.

- Secondly, we assume that the number of replicas is not the result of a fixed assumption but rather an initial value possibly subjected to revisions. Revisions are triggered by secure messages that ask to raise or lower the current number of replicas.
- Third, we assume a middleware component such as our Reflective Switchboards [27] to be available. Such middleware deducts and publishes a measure of the current environmental disturbances. In our prototypical implementation, this is done by computing, after each voting, the "distance-to-failure" (dtof), defined as

$$\text{dtof}(n, m) = \lceil \frac{n}{2} \rceil - m,$$

where n is the current number of replicas and m is the amount of votes that differ from the majority, if any such majority exists. If no majority can be found dtof returns 0. As can be easily seen, dtof returns an integer in $[0, \lceil \frac{n}{2} \rceil]$ that represents how close we were to failure at the end of the last voting round. The maximum distance is reached when there is full consensus among the replicas. On the contrary the larger the dissent, the smaller is the value returned by dtof, and the closer we are to the failure of the voting scheme. In other words, a large dissent (that is, small values for dtof) is interpreted as a symptom that the current amount of redundancy employed is not large enough. Figure 5 depicts some examples when the number of replicas is 7.
- When dtof is critically low, the Reflective Switchboards request the replication system to increase the number of redundant replicas.
- When dtof is high for a certain amount of consecutive runs—1000 runs in our experiments—a request to lower the number of replicas is issued. Figure 6 shows how redundancy varies in correspondence of simulated environmental changes.

Function dtof is just one possible example of how to estimate the chance of an impending assumption failure when dimensioning redundant resources. Our experiments [27] show that even such a simplistic scheme allows most if not all dimensioning assumption failures to be avoided. Despite heavy and diversified fault injection, no clashes were observed during our experiments. At the same time, as a side effect of assumption failure avoidance, our autonomic scheme reduces the amount of redundant resources to be allocated and managed. This can be seen for instance in Fig. 7 which plots in logarithmic scale the distribution of the amount of redundancy employed by our scheme during one of our experiments.

The above strategy shows how S_H and S_B may be avoided—in a special case—by creating context-aware, autonomically changing Horning Assumptions. In other words, rather than postponing the decision of the value to bind our assumption to, here we embedded our software system in a very simple autonomic

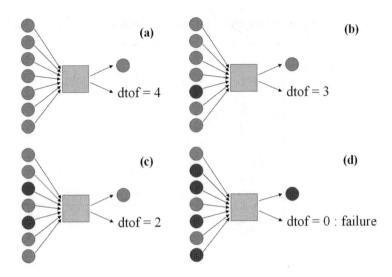

Fig. 5. Distance-to-failure in a replication-and-voting scheme with 7 replicas. In (a), consensus is reached, which corresponds to the farthest "distance" to failure. From (b) to (d), more and more votes dissent from the majority (red circles) and correspondingly the distance shrinks. In (d), no majority can be found—thus, failure is reached.

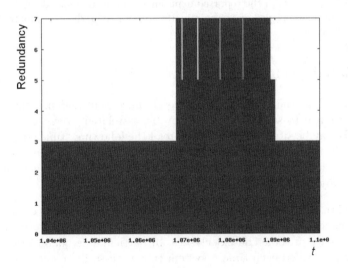

Fig. 6. During a simulated experiment, faults are injected, and consequently distance-to-failure decreases. This triggers an autonomic adaptation of the degree of redundancy.

architecture that dynamically revise dimensioning assumptions. The resulting system complies to Boulding's categories of "Cells" and "Plants", i.e. open software systems with a self-maintaining structure [9].

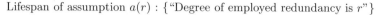

Lifespan of assumption $a(r)$: { "Degree of employed redundancy is r" }

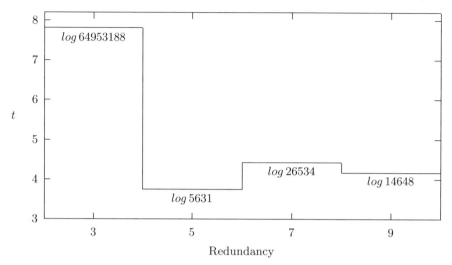

Fig. 7. Histogram of the employed redundancy during an experiment that lasted 65 million simulated time steps. For each degree of redundancy r (in this case $r \in \{3, 5, 7, 9\}$) the graph displays the total amount of time steps the system adopted assumption $a(r)$: { "Degree of employed redundancy is r" }. A logarithmic scale is used for time steps. Despite fault injection, in the reported experiment the system spends 99.92798% of its execution time making use of the minimal degree of redundancy, namely 3, without incurring in failures.

4 Related Technologies

As mentioned in the introduction, several conceptual and practical tools are available to deal to some extent with problems related to assumption failures. Such tools may be situated in one or more of the following "time stages": design-time, verification-time, compile-time, deployment-time, and run-time. In what follows we briefly discuss some families of those tools pointing out their relations with the subjects treated in this paper.

Verification and validation activities, i.e., checking and certification of compliance to specifications, are a fundamental tool to verify and prove the absence of some context clashes. In particular re-qualification is an activity prescribed each time a system (not necessarily a software system) is "relocated" (e.g. reused, or ported); or in case of replacement of some of its parts; or when a system is connected to another system. We observe how, verification and validation being in general off-line activities, assumptions are matched against a reference context information (the hypothized truth) that might differ from the actual context—from "real life", as it were.

Particularly interesting is the family of techniques known as formal verification, which make use of formal (mathematical) methods to assess a system's properties. Properties are described through a formal specification. Formal specification languages, such as the Z notation [28,29], can be used for the non-ambiguous expression of software properties. Compliant tools can then verify the validity of those properties and detect cases of assumption failures. Semantics [30] is another family of techniques that aim at expressing and machine-verifying the meanings of computing systems, their processing and environments.

Unified Modeling Language (UML) is the de-facto modeling language for object-oriented software engineering. A discussion of UML would lead us astray, thus we shall just remark here how UML provides means to describe

- the dependencies among the modeled software parts via component diagrams;
- the mapping of software parts onto the target hardware and execution environment via deployment diagrams;
- assorted knowledge, in the form of annotations;
- rules and constraints, as for instance in the contexts and properties of the Object Constraint Language [31].

UML and related tools situate themselves at design level though can be used to generate implementation artifacts directly from the models. By creating a stronger link between design-time and other "time stages" such tools—when used correctly—make it more difficult to incur in cases of the S_{HI} that are due to model-vs.-code inconsistencies. We observe how the produced artifacts are static entities that strictly follow design-time rules; as such they are not able to self-adapt so as to withstand faults or re-optimize in view of changed conditions. In other words, those implementation artifacts may suffer from the S_B.

Design by Contract [32] is a design approach that systematically deals with the mutual dependences of cooperating software components. Depending on the context, any two software components may find themselves in the role of a client and of a supplier of some service. A well-defined "contract" formally specifies what are the obligations and benefits of the two parties. This is expressed in terms of pre-conditions, post-conditions, and invariants. Design by Contract forces the designer to consider explicitly the mutual dependencies and assumptions among correlated software components. This facilitates assumption failures detection and—to some extent—treatment. The concept of contracts has been recently successfully applied to security of mobile applications [33,5].

Web Services standards provide numerous examples of specifications to expose, manage, and control capabilities and features of web services architectures. It is worth highlighting here a few of these standards:

WSDL (Web Services Description Language) is an XML language that allows a client to query and invoke the services exported by any third-party web service on the Internet. This high degree of flexibility exacerbates the problem of depending on third party software components, i.e., software of unknown characteristics and quality [34]. The need to discipline this potential chaos brought to a number of other specifications, such as WS-Policy.

WS-Policy implements a sort of XML-based run-time version of Design by Contract: using WS-Policy web service suppliers can advertise their pre-conditions (expected requirements, e.g. related to security), post-conditions (expected state evolutions), and invariants (expected stable states).

WSDM (Web Services Distributed Management) and its two complementary specifications MUWS (Management Using Web Services) and MOWS (Management Of Web Services), which respectively expose manageability capabilities and define a monitoring and control model for Web Services resources. This allows for instance quality-of-service monitorings, enforcing a service level agreement, or controlling a task.

XML-based deployment descriptors typical of service-oriented and component-oriented middleware platforms such as J2EE or CORBA are meant to reduce the complexity of deployment especially in large-scale distributed systems. Their main focus is clearly deployment-time. Despite their widely recognized values, some authors observe that they exhibit a "semantic gap" [1] between the design intent and their verbose and visually dense syntax, which in practice risks to conceal the very knowledge they are intended to expose. This is probably not so relevant as the exposed knowledge is meant to be reasoned upon by machines.

Introspection. The idea of introspection is to gain access into the hidden software complexity, to inspect the black-box structure of programs, and to interpret their meaning through semantic processing, the same way the Semantic Web promises to accomplish with the data scattered through the Internet. Quoting [35], "introspection is a means that, when applied correctly, can help crack the code of a software and intercept the hidden and encapsulated meaning of the internals of a program". Introspection is achieved e.g. by instrumenting software with data collectors producing information available in a form allowing semantic processing, such as RDF[36]. This idea is being used in the Introspector project, which aims at instrumenting the GNU programming tool-chain so as to create a sort of semantic web of all software derived from those tools. The ultimate goal is very ambitious: "To create a super large and extremely dense web of information about the outside world extracted automatically from computer language programs" [35]. This would allow the design of software able to reason about the dependability characteristics of other software. Tools based on introspection include:

GASTA (Gcc Abstract Syntax Tree Analysis) [37], which uses introspection to automatically annotate C code to analyze the presence of null pointer design faults),

GCC-XML [38], quite similar to GASTA, and

XOGASTAN (XML-Oriented Gcc Abstract Syntax Tree ANalyzer) [39], which uses the abstract syntax tree produced by the GNU compiler while processing a C file and translates it into XML. Another of the XOGASTAN tools can then read the XML file and analyze it.

In its current form introspection is an off-line technique working at code level.

Aspect orientation logically distinguishes a conventional language to encode the functional logics; an aspect language to define specific interconnections among a program's basic functional units; and a so-called aspect weaver, that is a program that composes a software system from both the functional and the aspect logics. Multiple aspect logics can be defined to address different systemic cross-cutting concerns, e.g. enhancing dependability, minimizing energy expenditure, or increasing performance. This has two consequences particularly important for our treatise: the most obvious one is that aspect oriented languages realize pliable software that can be more easily maintained and adapted. Secondly, aspects encode knowledge that regard specific "viewpoints", and encourage the designers doing so. As such, aspect orientation offers a conceptual and practical framework to deal with the three syndromes of software development.

Model Driven Engineering (MDE) is a relatively new paradigm that combines a number of the above approaches into a set of conceptual and practical tools that address several shortcomings of traditional methods of software development. In particular, MDE recognizes that "models alone are insufficient to develop complex systems" [1]. Contrarily to other approaches, which develop general "languages" to express software models in an abstract way, MDE employs so-called domain-specific modeling languages, which make use of semantics to precisely characterize the relationships between concepts and their associated constraints. The ability to express domain-specific constraints and to apply model checking allows several cases of assumption failures to be detected early in the software life cycle. Furthermore, MDE features transformation engines and generators that synthesize from the models various types of artifacts, e.g. source code and XML deployment descriptions. MDE systematically combines several existing technologies and promises to become soon one of the most important "tools" to tame the ever growing complexity of software. As remarked by Schmidt [1], the elegance and the potential power of MDE brought about many expectations; this notwithstanding, scientific studies about the true potential of MDE are still missing [40,41,1].

5   Lessons Learned and Vision

In previous section we discussed very concisely a few families of approaches that can be effectively used to solve some of the problems we introduced in this paper. Here we first summarize lessons learned while doing so, which then brings us to our vision on future approaches and architectures to deal effectively with assumption failures.

First of all, we can summarize that a number of powerful techniques and tools exist or are in the course of being honed that can effectively help dealing with assumption failures. What is also quite apparent is that each of them only tackles specific aspects of the problem and takes a privileged view to it.

Our position in this context is that we are still lacking methodologies and architectures to tackle this problem in its complex entirety. Fragmented views to this very complex and entangled web are inherently ineffective or at best sub-optimal. Missing one aspect means leaving a backdoor open to the manifestations of the three syndromes introduced in Sect. 2. In other words, a holistic approach is required. Taming the complexity of software systems so as to reach true resilience in the face of assumption failures requires a unitary view to the whole of the "time stages" of software development—what the General Systems Theory calls a *gestalt* [9]. We believe one such gestalt for software systems to be the concept of assumption failure. As Boulding writes in the cited paper, gestalts are "of great value in directing research towards the gaps which they reveal"—in the case at hand, the gaps of each fragmented view offered by the approaches mentioned in Sect. 4 to the problems discussed in this paper[2]. In a sense, most if not all of those approaches may be regarded as the result of an attempt to divide and conquer the complexity of software development by abstracting and specializing (that is, reducing the scope of) methods, tools, and approaches. This specialization ends up in the ultimate case of the Hidden Intelligence syndrome. A better approach would probably be considering the unity of the design intent and using a holistic, "cross layered" approach to share sensible knowledge unraveled in one layer and feed it back into the others. We envision a general systems theory of software development in which the model, compile-, deployment-, and run-time layers feed one another with deductions and control "knobs". The strategies discussed in this paper could provide the designer with useful tools to arrange such cross-layering processes. This would allow knowledge slipping from one layer to be still caught in another, and knowledge gathered in one layer to be fed back into others. As an example, the strategy discussed in Sect. 3.2 could feed an MDE tool whose deductions could in turn be published or reified into a context-aware middleware such as our Reflective Switchboards [27].

One way to achieve this could be to arrange a web of cooperating reactive agents serving different software design concerns (e.g. model-specific, deployment-specific, verification-specific, execution-specific) responding to external stimuli and autonomically adjusting their internal state. Thus a design assumption failure caught by a run-time detector should trigger a request for adaptation at model level, and vice-versa. We believe that such a holistic approach would realize a more complete, unitary vision of a system's behavior and properties with respect to the sum of the detached and fragmented views available so far.

---

[2] In the cited paper Boulding applies this concept to the general system of disciplines and theories: "Each discipline corresponds to a certain segment of the empirical world, and each develops theories which have particular applicability to its own empirical segment. Physics, chemistry, biology, psychology, sociology, economics and so on all carve out for themselves certain elements of the experience of man and develop theories and patterns of activity (research) which yield satisfaction in understanding, and which are appropriate to their special segments." Gestalts, that is meta-theories of systems, "might be of value in directing the attention of theorists toward gaps in theoretical models, and might even be of value in pointing towards methods of filling them."

6   Conclusions

Software systems are characterized by predefined assumptions about their intended platform, their internal state, and the environments they are meant to be deployed in. They are often closed, "blind" systems built from synchronous assumptions and designed so as to be plugged in immutable hardware systems and environments whose changes, idiosyncrasies, or fluctuations most of them deliberately ignore. We believe that this approach to software development is not valid anymore. Software ought to be designed and executed taking into account the inevitable occurrence of potentially significant and sudden changes or failures in their infrastructure and surrounding environments. By analyzing well-known software failures we identified three main threats to effective dependable software engineering, which we called the Hidden Intelligence syndrome, the Horning syndrome, and the Boulding syndrome. In this paper we expressed our thesis that services explicitly addressing those threats and requirements are an important ingredient towards truly resilient software architectures. For each of the above mentioned syndromes we also provided exemplary treatment strategies, which form the core of our current work in the adaptive-and-dependable software systems task force of the PATS research group at the University of Antwerp. The key idea is to provide the designer with the ability to formulate dynamic assumptions (assumption variables) whose boundings get postponed at a later, more appropriate, time: at compile time, when we are dealing with hardware platform assumptions for a stationary code; at deployment time, when the application can be assembled on that stage; and at run-time, e.g. when a change in the physical environment calls for adaptation to new environmental conditions. We believe that an effective way to do this is by means of a web of cooperating autonomic "agents" deducting and sharing knowledge, e.g. the type of faults being experienced or the current values for properties regarding the hardware platform and the execution environment. We developed a number of these agents, e.g. Reflective Switchboards [27], ACCADA [19], and an Apache Axis2/MUSE web service framework. Our future steps include the design of a software architecture for assumptions failure treatment based on the close cooperation of those and other building blocks.

We conclude by observing how our research actually "stands on the shoulders of giants", as its conclusions closely follow those in the now classic 1956 paper of Kenneth Boulding on General Systems Theory [9]: indeed, current software engineering practices often still produce systems belonging to Boulding's categories of "Clockworks" and "Thermostats". The root assumption of such systems is their being closed-world, context-agnostic systems characterized by predefined assumptions about their platform, their internal state, and the environment they are meant to be deployed in, which makes them fragile to change. On the contrary, the unitary approach we envision, based on the proposed role of gestalt for assumption failures, would make it possible to design and maintain actual open software systems with a self-maintaining structure (known as "Cells" and "Plants" according to Boulding's terminology) and pave the way to the design of fully autonomically resilient software systems (Boulding's "Beings").

Acknowledgements

My gratitude goes to Jonas Buys, Ning Gui, and Hong Sun for providing me with their helpful comments, suggestions, and valuable assistance, and to Marc and Mieke Leeman for kindly providing me with the output from the execution of the `lshw` command on several computers.

References

1. Schmidt, D.C.: Model-driven engineering. Computer 39(4), 25–31 (2006)
2. Lyu, M.R.: Design, testing, and evaluation techniques for software reliability engineering. In: Proc. of the 24th Euromicro Conf. on Engineering Systems and Software for the Next Decade (Euromicro'98), Workshop on Dependable Computing Systems, Västerås, Sweden, pp. xxxix–xlvi. IEEE Comp. Soc. Press (August 1998) (Keynote speech).
3. Lyu, M.R.: Reliability-oriented software engineering: Design, testing and evaluation techniques. IEE Proceedings – Software 145(6), 191–197 (1998) (special Issue on Dependable Computing Systems)
4. Laprie, J.C.: Dependability of computer systems: from concepts to limits. In: Proc. of the IFIP International Workshop on Dependable Computing and Its Applications (DCIA 1998), Johannesburg, South Africa (1998)
5. De Win, B., Goovaerts, T., Joosen, W., Philippaerts, P., Piessens, F., Younan, Y.: Security Middleware for Mobile Applications. In: Middleware for Network Eccentric and Mobile Applications, pp. 265–284. Springer, Heidelberg (2009)
6. Avižienis, A.: The N-version approach to fault-tolerant software. IEEE Trans. Software Eng. 11, 1491–1501 (1985)
7. Horning, J.J.: ACM Fellow Profile — James Jay (Jim) Horning. ACM Software Engineering Notes 23(4) (July 1998)
8. Leveson, N.G.: Safeware: Systems Safety and Computers. Addison-Wesley, Reading (1995)
9. Boulding, K.: General systems theory—the skeleton of science. Management Science 2(3) (April 1956)
10. Ladbury, R.: SDRAMs: Can't live without them, but can we live with them? In: Thirteenth Biennial Single Effects Symposium, Manhattan Beach, CA (April 2002)
11. Oey, K.K., Teitelbaum, S.: Highly reliable spaceborne memory subsystem. In: 3rd Computers in Aerospace Conference, American Institute of Aeronautics and Astronautics, San Diego, CA, pp. 66–71 (October 1981)
12. Wikipedia: Latchup, `en.wikipedia.org/wiki/Latchup` (retrieved on February 3, 2010)
13. Wikipedia: Soft error, `en.wikipedia.org/wiki/Soft_error` (retrieved on February 3, 2010)
14. Wikipedia: Single-event upset, `en.wikipedia.org/wiki/Single_event_upset` (retrieved on February 3, 2010)
15. Holbert, K.E.: Single event effects, `www.eas.asu.edu/~sim/holbert/eee460/see.html` (retrieved on February 3, 2010)
16. Calcote, J.: Autotools—A Practioner's Guide to GNU Autoconf, Automake, and Libtool. O'Reilly, Sebastopol (2010)

17. Anonymous: Mplayer — the movie player (2008),
    www.mplayerhq.hu/design7/info.html (retrieved on December 13, 2008)
18. Suzuki, M., Katayama, T., Schlichting, R.D.: FTAG: A functional and attribute
    based model for writing fault-tolerant software. Technical Report TR 96-6, De-
    partment of Computer Science, The University of Arizona (May 1996)
19. Gui, N., De Florio, V., Sun, H., Blondia, C.: ACCADA: A framework for continuous
    context-aware deployment and adaptation. In: Guerraoui, R., Petit, F. (eds.) SSS
    2009. LNCS, vol. 5873, pp. 325–340. Springer, Heidelberg (2009)
20. Bondavalli, A., Chiaradonna, S., Di Giandomenico, F., Grandoni, F.: A mechanism
    for discriminating transient from intermittent/permanent faults. Technical Report
    D1A2/AO/6003a, ESPRIT Project 20716 GUARDS (December 1996)
21. Bondavalli, A., Chiaradonna, S., Di Giandomenico, F., Grandoni, F.: Threshold-
    based mechanisms to discriminate transient from intermittent faults. IEEE Trans.
    on Computers 49(3), 230–245 (2000)
22. Anonymous: Apache Axis2/Java—next generation web services (2010),
    ws.apache.org/axis2 (retrieved on February 11, 2010)
23. Anonymous: Apache Muse—a Java-based implementation of WSRF 1.2, WSN 1.3,
    and WSDM 1.1 (2010), ws.apache.org/muse (retrieved on February 11, 2010)
24. Frigo, M.: A fast fourier transform compiler. SIGPLAN Not. 39(4), 642–655 (2004)
25. De Florio, V., Deconinck, G., Lauwereins, R.: The EFTOS voting farm: a software
    tool for fault masking in message passing parallel environments. In: Proc. of the
    24th Euromicro Conference (Euromicro 1998), Workshop on Dependable Comput-
    ing Systems, Västerås, Sweden, pp. 379–386. IEEE Comp. Soc. Press, Los Alamitos
    (August 1998)
26. Johnson, B.W.: Design and Analysis of Fault-Tolerant Digital Systems. Addison-
    Wesley, New York (1989)
27. De Florio, V.: Cost-effective software reliability through autonomic tuning of sys-
    tem resources. In: Proceedings of the Applied Reliability Symposium, Europe
    (April 2010)
28. Baumann, P., Lermer, K.: A framework for the specification of reactive and con-
    current systems. In: Thiagarajan, P.S. (ed.) FSTTCS 1995. LNCS, vol. 1026, pp.
    62–79. Springer, Heidelberg (1995)
29. Bishop, P.G.: Fault Avoidance. In: Dependability of Critical Computer Systems 3:
    Techniques Directory, pp. 56–140. Elsevier Science Publishers, Amsterdam (1990)
30. Sheth, A.P., Verma, K., Gomadam, K.: Semantics to energize the full services
    spectrum. Commun. ACM 49(7), 55–61 (2006)
31. Anonymous: OMG modeling and metadata specifications—object constraint
    language (OCL) (2010),
    www.omg.org/technology/documents/modeling_spec_catalog.htm#OCL
    (retrieved on February 11, 2010)
32. Meyer, B.: Applying Design by Contract. Computer 25(10), 40–51 (1992)
33. Dragoni, N., Massacci, F., Naliuka, K., Siahaan, I.: Security-by-contract: Toward a
    semantics for digital signatures on mobile code. In: López, J., Samarati, P., Ferrer,
    J.L. (eds.) EuroPKI 2007. LNCS, vol. 4582, pp. 297–312. Springer, Heidelberg
    (2007)
34. Green, P.A.: The art of creating reliable software-based systems using off-the-shelf
    software components. In: Proc. of the 16th Symposium on Reliable Distributed
    Systems (SRDS 1997), Durham, NC (October 1997)

35. DuPont, J.M.: Introspector, `www.introspector.sourceforge.net` (retrieved on February 8, 2010)
36. Anonymous: Resource description framework (RDF) / W3C semantic web activity (2008), `www.w3.org/RDF` (retrieved on December 16, 2008)
37. Thouvenin, G.: Gasta: Gcc abstract syntax tree analysis (2004), Available at `http://gasta.sourceforge.net` (retrieved on December 16, 2008)
38. King, B.: Gcc-xml, the xml output extension to gcc (2004), `http://www.gccxml.org`
39. Antoniol, G., Di Penta, M., Masone, G., Villano, U.: Compiler hacking for source code analysis. Software Quality Journal 12(4), 383–406 (2004)
40. Bézivin, J.: MDA: From hype to hope, and reality. In: Stevens, P., Whittle, J., Booch, G. (eds.) UML 2003. LNCS, vol. 2863, Springer, Heidelberg (2003)
41. Bézivin, J.: On the unification power of models. Software and Systems Modeling 4(2), 171–188 (2005)

Architecting Dependable Systems Using Reflective Computing: Lessons Learnt and Some Challenges

Jean-Charles Fabre

CNRS ; LAAS ; 7 avenue du colonel Roche, F-31077 Toulouse, France
Université de Toulouse ; UPS, INSA, INP, ISAE ; LAAS ;
F-31077 Toulouse, France
Jean-Charles.Fabre@laas.fr

Abstract. The use of the reflection paradigm was motivated by the need of separation of concerns in dependable systems. The separation of the application from its fault tolerance mechanisms for instance was a good way to make the system adaptive, the application and mechanisms reusable. One may ask, however, to which extent this separation of concerns is of interest for practical dependable systems. This depends very much on the mechanisms considered, and on some target objective of the system designer in terms of system properties. The present paper attempts to shed some light on these factors by drawing the lessons gained from several research projects with colleagues in the dependability community and beyond. We also claim that some novel technologies are of high interest and that their use should be based on the experience gained in the field of reflective computing. Finally, we express some of the challenges we feel of interest for the development of dependable systems in general and of adaptive fault tolerant systems in particular.

1 Introduction

In the long history of dependable systems development, practitioners have long debated how functional and dependability concerns should be best integrated. Although it can be efficient to develop built-in dependability mechanisms, such a tight integration between functional and non-functional features tend to be highly problematic, in particular in terms of reuse, maintenance and evolution, just to mention a few issues.

Making a hardware and software component dependable first requires the use of appropriate design methods and development tools to improve its quality. It also typically involves the insertion of mechanisms to insure that, in case of errors, the component signals in a way or another (events, error codes, exceptions) its incorrect behaviour to companion components. For software components, this approach is often called defensive programming: Some additional code is inserted (assertions, pre-post conditions, invariants) to check that the component behaves as expected, or at least conforms to its specification. The resulting error detection and sometimes recovery code (e.g. exception handling) is tightly woven with the functional code. When the coverage of this error-detection code is perfect, the resulting components becomes fail-silent, a property with many merits for dependability. Unfortunately, the tight

A. Casimiro et al. (Eds.): Architecting Dependable Systems VII, LNCS 6420, pp. 273–296, 2010.
© Springer-Verlag Berlin Heidelberg 2010

integration of functional and non-function code hinders reuse, maintenance and evolution. To address this problem, a number of researchers have argued for a higher separation of concerns in dependable systems[1]. For instance, both the handling of replication (distributed replicated components), and the verification of global properties (e.g. notion of safety bag or wrappers) can be externalised outside a functional component. Both approaches, however, present quite different degrees of difficulty. On one hand, replication can be considered as a generic mechanism, i.e. independent of the functional specifications of a component, and therefore particularly easy to factor-out into an external entity. This componentisation brings a number of benefits, and quite notably the ability to select, for instance, the most appropriate replication approach based on the operational context (system configuration, performance, environment, fault assumptions, etc.). This is straightforward for replication schemes that do not need to transfer internal states, e.g. actively replicated deterministic identical replicas. By contrast, the properties verified by a wrapper are usually highly application-dependent, and thus much more intimately linked to the application software they verify. A wrapper may hence appear more difficult to develop in a generic manner, and usually requires additional technologies (domain specific languages, logic-based formulas) to be externalised.

The quest for appropriate technologies to separate functional code from non-functional mechanisms has motivated a huge research activity in the past 15 years. The overall conclusion is that dependable software-based systems require separation of concerns technologies at all level of system design to facilitate their development, adaptation, maintenance and evolution, and foster the reuse of their fault tolerance mechanisms. This claim has been advocated by many researchers in the dependability community over the years [1, 2, 3]. However the separation of functional and dependability code has some limits we would like to clarify in this paper from our experience.

Various technologies can be used to implement separation of concerns between functional code, the application or the service provided to the user, and the non-functional mechanisms that are needed to guaranty some dependability properties. Many works have shown the interest of reflective computing to reach this aim and this approach is well-known today, in particular thanks to Patty Maes [4]. In the dependability community, Gul Agha was among the first to show how reflection could be used to compose dependability protocols [1]. Many works have since then relied on specific reflective languages (such as OpenC++ [5] used in FRIENDS [3]) to illustrate the interest of such technology. Beyond the conventional means to perform the implementation (meta-object protocols, aspect oriented programming – AOP), separation of concerns can also be addressed at the architectural level using *Component-Based Software Engineering* (CBSE). The main benefit of this technology is to make visible the software architecture (components hierarchies and bindings) but also

---

[1] **About separation of concerns, a simple motivating example:** Student and non-experienced programmers often dislike using debuggers to find bugs in their programs. They usually include C-like *printf* statements to get the value of a variable. In a sense debuggers are reflective components providing separation of concerns. Thanks to interception mechanisms the debugging actions are external to the application program. The set of breakpoints can be perceived as a pointcut in Aspect Oriented Programming. The actions performed (i.e. the advice) enable program variable to be modified and the program to be continued. This is a form of reflective system providing thus separation of concerns.

provides the means to manipulate the software. More generally, any language (including low-level ones such as VHDL), any system architecture (multi-layered software systems, service oriented architectures), any process (e.g. compilation) can be made reflective. We can mention reflective middleware [6], real-time operating systems [7], but also fault injection tools [8]. The core principle is to make the target software visible and adaptable through a structural and behavioral model, at various stage of its development, from the design stage to the runtime.

Several languages have been developed to implement these ideas and make reflective programming operational, from Open C++V2 [9] in the 90's to Aspect Oriented Programming [10], AspectJ [11] for instance. Beyond languages, modern CBSE technologies (e.g. OpenCOM [12], Fractal [13]) provide component frameworks with reflective capabilities, i.e. observation/introspection (software sensors) and control mechanisms (software actuators.) From a conceptual standpoint, all these technologies exhibit a structural and/or behavioural model of the software system through which manipulations can be performed. Such manipulations can be done at runtime to adapt the software system to some operational conditions and/or to some evolution of the requirements. Such technologies also enable a better reuse of both functional (i.e. application domain related) and non-functional (i.e. dependability related) software components.

As far as dependability is concerned, the separation of concerns essentially targets fault tolerance mechanisms (e.g. replication strategies of software components, wrappers for error confinement, etc.). One may ask, however, how far and how easily reflective approaches can be used to separate such fault-tolerance mechanisms.

In this paper, we propose to build on our long experience in this field to shed some light on this question, and suggest some promising paths for future research. The objective of this paper is **not** to provide a detailed survey, i.e. we do not dive into technical details and refer to papers in which the interested reader can find more information. We rather provide **a short synthesis** of past and recent experience of the author to improve separation of concerns in dependable systems for better flexibility and adaptation. Based on this historical perspective and the work performed at LAAS-CNRS, we present how we now perceive the use of reflective computing for dependable systems development. This personal view leads us to finally draw some lessons but also identify some key challenges that should be addressed in the future.

This paper is organized as follows. In section 2, we first briefly recall the basic principles of reflective computing. We then discuss in several sections the interest of reflective computing for implementing various fault tolerance mechanisms. In section 3, we discuss the reflective implementation of replication strategies. The use of reflective computing for software fault tolerance techniques is addressed in section 4. How reflection can be used for developing self-checking components using wrapping techniques is discussed in section 5. Section 6 is devoted to the composition of dependability mechanisms using reflection. Dependability being a concept orthogonal to all system layers, we discuss the concept of multi-level reflection in section 7 and briefly show its interest in industrial systems in section 8. We finally summarize the lessons learnt through our experience and identify some challenges in section 9 before concluding this paper.

2 Basic Principles Reminder

2.1 Reflection Principles

Reflection allows a system to apply its own computing capabilities to itself. Reflective systems usually are composed of two levels: *the base level* performs the system's main function (the application functionalities), while the *meta-level* observes and modifies the base level (monitoring, reconfiguration, etc.). The two levels interact through a well-defined *meta-interface*. The meta-interface provides functions to observe (software sensors) and control (software actuators) the system in operation. The metainterface attached to the base level enables the meta-level to introspect and trigger base level actions. Metainterfaces attached to the meta-level enable the base level to provide information to the meta-level (reification), e.g. asynchronous events.

The basic observation and actuation mechanisms enable a software control loop to be implemented. The observation mechanisms may reify events or rely on on-demand request to get internal information. Actuation relies on the interface of the target software but may have access to some special interface. The actuation may be more intrusive and modify the target software. This shows the range of possible actions that can be performed by the control software in the loop from the observations obtained.

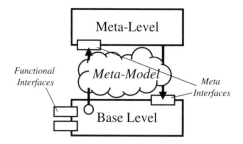

Fig. 1. Basic reflective architecture

The control software running thus at the meta-level manipulates models of the target software describing its organization (structural model) and its execution (behavioral model). A precise definition of such models and their animation at runtime is mandatory for implementing fault tolerance software as an external software layer. This is the key point that is sometimes hidden or ignored, at least not exhibited as a first class concept. *In practice, the meta-level represents a middleware that implements the fault tolerance strategies from the structural and behavioral models described as graph data structures.* Various meta-levels can be stacked together or a single meta-level can be populated with several metaspaces handling different concerns.

To summarize, various technologies can be used to implement a reflective system. For fault tolerant computing, the objective is to provide a reliable connector between the functional code (base level) and the fault tolerance code (meta-level). This component must (i) provide enough information to the metalevel to causally connect fault tolerance actions with the application behavior, i.e. by properly synchronizing the fault tolerance mechanisms with the base level's execution, (ii) enable application state information (including executive support state information) to be delivered to the meta-level to handle replication and cloning for instance, and (iii) provide access to mechanisms to perform recovery actions, i.e. actions and state updates. It is also important to mention that clear confinement areas must be defined between application code and non-functional mechanisms, this being part of the notion of separation of concerns for dependable computing.

It is worth noting that the connector must be reliable, its definition and implementation should ideally be zero-default. This means that some restrictions should be applied to its development as for any critical software. Development processes for critical systems like DO178B [14] or ISO26262 [15], just to name those used in avionics and automotive systems, should be taken into account to improve the testability and the QoS of such software connector. Low-level mechanisms can be used as well to improve the reliability of such connector, like memory protection through OS level features. This shows that pure language-based constructs cannot on their own satisfy all requirements for fault tolerant computing but must be supplemented by appropriate platform mechanisms (error confinement, for instance).

2.2 From Reflection to Components

The initial idea of reflection can be easily combined with *Component-Based Software Engineering* (CBSE) [16] to offer advanced architectural frameworks. Components are reusable software entities that explicitly specify both the services they provide (as *interfaces*), and the services they require (*receptacles*). Components offer three key advantages over more traditional approaches:

1) they decouple functional concerns from non-functional ones by encapsulating each in distinct components;
2) they facilitate development by assembly of existing parts, and support disassembly, thus providing a natural path towards dynamic adaptation, and
3) they encourage reuse, thus lowering cost and raising quality.

A *reflective component-based framework* combines reflection and components to allow a running system to observe its current structure, interfaces, and execution, and to reconfigure, modify, and intercept these at runtime. Components also allow the reconfiguration and interception logic (the meta-level) to be encapsulated in distinct entities, thus clearly, separating the various parts of an adaptable fault-tolerant system: application, fault-tolerance, and adaptation.

As an example, let's give some comments on OpenCOM [12] that is such a reflective component-based system (Fig. 2) and that was used in some of our experiments. It uses *interfaces, receptacles,* and *bindings*. Bindings are components that explicitly link an interface to a receptacle. To adapt a system, OpenCOM supports a process of unbinding, loading/unloading, and rebinding. Each individual OpenCOM component provides three meta-interfaces that enable the detailed examination of a component, and the fine-grained modification of its implementations through various interceptors. Interceptors are mechanisms that are able to intercept interaction among components and reify them. As shown in the Figure 2, they are associated with interfaces (more specifically, local bindings) and enable the insertion of pre- and post-behaviour.

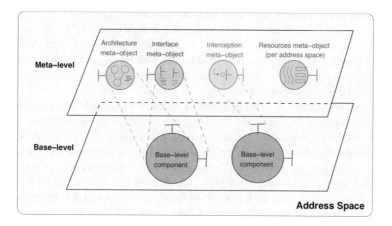

Fig. 2. The architecture of OpenCOM

Figure 2 illustrates the overall organization of the meta-level that enables designers to control the internal organization of a base-level object (*Architecture meta-object*), to access the external representation of a component, i.e. its provided and required interfaces (*Interface meta-object*), to control interactions between components (*Interception metaobject*), and manage base level resources (*Resource Metaobject*).

2.3 Summary and Conclusion

The recent advances in software engineering technologies provide new means to manipulate and control software architectures. Reflection and Component Based Software Engineering are core ingredients of this trend. Reflective component and frameworks are certainly the best approach to develop fault tolerant systems today where reuse, maintenance and evolution are first class objectives. It is also a good way to promote a new generation of COTS components (or reusable subsystems), where observability and controllability are built-in concepts. This is very important to master their behavior in the presence of faults. An interesting analysis of the benefits of reflective component frameworks can be found in [17].

Is separation of concerns and reflection of particular interest for fault tolerance computing? This is the question we want to address in the following sections, covering several fault tolerance techniques (replication, diversification, self-checking components, composition of dependability mechanisms). Indeed, the answer to this question depends very much on the dependencies between the application and the mechanisms (application specific mechanisms, granularity, etc.).

3 Fault Tolerance Using Conventional Replication

In this section, we consider the reflective implementation of conventional replication mechanisms. By conventional replication we consider all replication techniques that are generic and that, to some extent, do not depend tightly on application semantics. We consider both duplex and triple modular redundancy strategies.

For duplex replication strategies, we can first cite primary-backup replication, also named *cold-standby*, that relies on checkpointing either to stable storage or to a backup replica. Semi-active replication, also called *warm-standby*, is a variant where multiple copies are active, only one sends replies to the requester. The fault model in duplex strategies considers crash faults only and such technique assumes that a replica is fail-silent, i.e. it is a self-checking component with high error-detection coverage.

On the other hand, active replication with majority voting (e.g. *Triple Modular Redundancy*), also called hot standby replication, considers more subtle faults like transient faults that may impair the result of the computation.

The strategies mentioned here essentially depend on the fault model, i.e. crash faults or value faults due to hardware defects, but are quite independent from the application semantics.

However, all such replication strategies require access to the state of the computation (of the replica at least, most probably of objects belonging to the lower layers of the system). This is true for passive replication that relies on checkpointing, but it is also true for active replication strategies when cloning a new replica. This is a difficult issue that requires deep access to the internal state of a component (introspection means), but also means to update this internal state. Serialization facilities at the language level and/or OS/middleware level access to components' state are necessary. This means that reflection is required at several levels/layers of the software architecture. We will come back to this issue below and in Section 7.

So, what reflective features are required to implement these strategies?
The first features relate to the synchronization of replicas. Any invocation/request to the application must be reified to the meta-level. The processing of the invocation/request is triggered from the meta-level. When the processing terminates then copies are synchronized (checkpointing, notifications) or the results are validated by vote at the meta-level. For TMR, two options are possible here: *validate-before-propagate* when the validation is done at the server site, *propagate-before-validate* when the validation by vote is performed by the client. The propagation of the various results copies produced by each replica is propagated at the meta-level and the vote as well. A reflective architecture is interesting here to synchronize replicas in various ways and to perform some generic bit-wise voting on the results copies or on message digests. In short, the inter-replica protocols are implemented at the metalevel.

The trickiest issue here is the capture of the internal state of the computation. Is reflection very useful for this? The answer is *Yes* and *No*.

Yes because the description of the state can be done in a separate meta-component and may include data structures of the application and objects belonging to the operating system for instance. This means that any application component must externalize data belonging to its state through the meta-interface or through serialization features [18]. The access to the executive objects belonging to the state can be done in the same way, i.e. additional interface to introspect the operating system for instance. Due to the complexity of the internal state of the executive software, this approach becomes rapidly intractable. A less intrusive solution consists in just intercepting and logging system calls. In reflective terms, the system calls are reified to the meta-level that stores the information in journals[2].

---

[2] For instance, one could use the logs to construct an abstract representation the runtime's state. (e.g. that a socket connection exists with address:port, but not the particular socket ID).

The answer to the above question could be *No* as well if we consider that the developer of the application does the job since he knows better the state of the computation that is required for recovery. Separation of concerns is weak in this case, since the application programmer is involved in the implementation. How to implement this in reflective terms however? The answer is serialization and aspects to capture the state, but also reification of system calls to meta-level components logging the behavior of the computation at a higher level of abstraction.

In conclusion, replication can definitely take advantage of reflective computing for the implementation of inter-replica protocols (IRP). The IRP in itself is independent of the function performed by identical replicas. However, one can see here the limits of reflective computing as soon as the ***independence*** with the application features is not that clear. For instance, any evolution of the application through versioning may have an impact to the state capture. The system designer must make sure that the state capture remains consistent with respect to application versions and releases.

4 Software Fault Tolerance Techniques

In this section we discuss the interest of reflective computing for implementing software fault tolerance techniques. The challenge of software fault tolerance techniques is to prevent design and coding software faults to impair the behavior of an application.

Defensive programming is a way to do so by means of runtime assertions. Such assertions are clearly application dependent and deeply involve data structures of the application program code. They also require synchronization with the computation. All these reasons make such type of mechanisms not easy to externalize. Reflective programming here seems thus limited, although aspect oriented programming may help implementing some sort of separation of concerns.

Well-known software fault tolerance techniques rely on diversification. In a self-checking component [19], the control box ranges from simple runtime assertions to a complete diverse implementation of the function. In recovery blocks [20], the acceptance test can also be considered as a runtime assertion or a diverse implementation of the block. When considering more sophisticated software fault tolerance techniques, like *N-Self-Checking Programming* (NSCP) or *N-Version Programming* (NVP) [21], diversification is the corner stone of the strategy. What is the real benefit of a reflective approach in this context?

The answer is *not much*. The meta-level is here responsible for the scheduling of the versions and the execution of the verification. This means that specific declarations are required to initialize the meta-level. A reference to the interfaces of both the versions and the acceptance test or decision function must be given.

In reflective terms, for the recovery block scheme, the client request is reified to the meta-level that triggers the first block at the base level, capture the results and triggers the acceptance test at the base level. In this case, most of the computation is performed at the base level, provided blocks and acceptance tests are just declared at the meta-level to be triggered. The interest is also limited for NSCP and NVP since decision functions (selection of results among diverse replicas) is definitely application dependent. The interest is however to provide a framework to execute such techniques (RB, NCSP, NVP). Such framework can be provided independently of any reflective computing technology. The insertion of a new diverse replica just corresponds to a declaration to the meta-level, i.e. an initialization of the meta-level software. Only the scheduling of both the replicas and the validation entities are externalized.

In conclusion, the use of pure reflective technologies is of limited interest for conventional software fault tolerance, because of the strong link between software fault tolerance mechanisms (versions) and the application (functional) specifications. A framework of such mechanisms can be provided to control user-defined versions and decision components. The instantiation of such framework can be done at both the base and the meta-level.

5   Wrapping for Error Confinement

In this section, we discuss the interest of reflective computing to develop self-checking software components using wrapping techniques. The notion of self-checking component[3] is of upmost interest for dependability and a corner stone of duplex replication techniques. A self-checking software component can be implemented using wrappers, responsible for the verification of inputs and outputs, but also of some state invariants when observability allows.

Wrapping for error confinement is often used to improve the behavior in the presence of faults of *Off-The-Shelf components* ([C]OTS). The idea here is to develop a software layer that sits around a target component and performs some verification on its behavior. A wrapper can be simple, just capturing input and outputs, preventing thus erroneous input data to corrupt the component and/or preventing output results to be delivered to companion component in the system. Preventing error propagation is this a first objective of such wrappers.

Reflective software technologies can be used to develop the wrappers, since all inputs and outputs can be intercepted at the meta-level. The assertions obviously depend on the semantics of the target component and may require some internal information to perform the verification. This means that a metainterface composed of introspection functions must be added to the component. The assertions can be very application dependant and thus need to be user-defined, so, reflection does not help very much since separation of concerns is difficult to obtain in this case.

However, for standardized services, the development of wrappers can be quite generic and thus based on standard specifications (scheduling, synchronization, etc.) from which properties can be defined whatever the target implementation is. For instance, if the target component is an off-the-shelf operating system kernel, an RTOS, a wrapper can be developed, for instance, to verify of task synchronization by mutexes. The expected property is well identified but requires some information

---

[3] The provision within a component of the required functional processing capability together with concurrent error detection mechanisms leads to the notion of **self-checking component**, either in hardware or in software; one of the important benefits of the self-checking component approach is the ability to give a clear definition of error confinement areas [19]. Roughly speaking, a self-checking component is composed of a function and a controller that validates the outputs of the function or signal an error. Ideally, the controller should provide 100% detection coverage, which is not the case in practice (imperfect error detection).

(e.g. number of waiting threads) computed from target internal data like *mutex queues*. An assertion can thus be developed in a generic manner for all target kernels, provided the metainterface has been implemented for this kernel. The assertion expression remains the same. This shows the interest of reflective computing as a disciplined way to perform error detection. As an external piece of software, the wrapper can be updated, optimized on a case-by-case basis. Its implementation can be based on a formal description of the properties to be verified on-line [22].

The specification of the wrapper may also depend on some fault injection analysis of the failure modes of the target component [23], just to identify the weak part of the implementation of some of the provided services. Indeed, some experiments show that a target RTOS can particularly sensitive to incorrect invocations, i.e. service calls with incorrect parameters [24]. The failure mode in this case can be crash, hang or application failure when corrupted results are delivered. A dedicated wrapper can thus be developed to complement built-in error detection mechanisms and improve error-detection coverage[4].

The notion of wrapper for error confinement can be extended with error recovery mechanisms. In a reflective framework, recovery mechanisms are developed as meta-level software. When an error is detected, some recovery actions can be triggered from the meta-level. They may involve modification of the internal state of the target component, and thus access to some internal data structures. This can be done in a disciplined way using additional functions belonging to the metainterface of the target. These are software actuators that can be developed on purpose or simply based on existing target functions[5].

The crucial issue to develop such error detection and recovery wrappers is the capability of establishing a behavioral model and animating it at runtime. This behavioral model is external to the target component it represents, belongs to the meta-level software but must be animated to be as much as possible conformant to the actual execution. This means that the internal behavior of the target component is at least in

---

[4] **Built-in or external error detection mechanisms?** We observed in our experiments targeting several RTOS by fault injection that the behavior in the presence of faults can be very different. The distribution of the failure modes dramatically exhibits a lack of built-in error detection mechanisms in some cases. The reason is simple and mainly relates to performance issues. From a commercial stand-point it is much better to exhibit good temporal performance than better dependability measures: a small memory footprint for a given set of similar kernel services, a short response time of system calls are good arguments. In addition to this, for safety critical system designers interested by COTS real-time kernels, the need for additional dependability features is not a convincing argument for RTOS providers. The reason is also simple. A robust version of an RTOS has to be developed and maintained for a limited number of copies/customers. Thus, it is not interesting for economic reasons, and then error detection and recovery wrappers are of interest in this case.

[5] **Software sensors and actuators?** Several system calls enable observation to be performed and some action to be done to change the state of the system, or to perform some recovery actions. To do that one can take advantage of existing observation and control features of the base level component. In the case of a system kernel, one can use *getters/setters* functions to read and to manipulate objects belonging to the kernel but also use other function to modify the dynamic configuration of the computation, *kill_task(tid)/create_task()* for instance. When existing mechanisms are insufficient to perform recovery, then additional features must be added to the target, making open source targets very appealing.

part visible to the meta-level software by means of reification (events) and introspection (data) facilities. The definition of the model on top of which error detection and recovery decisions will be made is the corner stone of the reflective architecture. This means that considering a pure black box component is a very limiting factor. When access to the source code is possible either directly (open source component) or thanks to specific agreements with the provider, then the approach has many merits in terms of reuse, flexibility, optimization, maintenance of both the target component and the wrapper.

The limit of the approach relates to the interaction between the target software and the wrapper. The externalization of the dependability software has a price in terms of performance. In some cases, mechanisms identified should be integrated into the target as built-in test mechanisms and then reflection has limited interest. This is something that is often done through successive versions of a given software, it was the case for CORBA middleware packages [25].

In conclusion, reflection is interesting for implementing wrappers when *i)* generic properties can be expressed from the specification of the target, and *ii)* when the metainterface providing introspection facilities remains simple. Regarding recovery actions, it is clear that they must remain at a coarse level (reset, re-initialization of well identified parts of the state, tasks removal and restart, replay of actions – system calls – stored in journals, etc.) Deep fine-grain subtle updates make the reflective approach less interesting, more complicated and probably much less efficient.

6   Composition of Mechanisms

As we have seen in the previous sections, separation of concerns through reflection can help in designing and developing fault tolerance mechanisms independently from the applications. However, the implementation of a dependable application sometimes requires several mechanisms. The composition of dependability mechanisms is this required to comply with non-functional specifications. Separation of concerns should help several mechanisms not only to be designed independently, but also to be glued to a given application on a case-by-case basis.

For instance, one would like to tolerate the crash of a component and at the same time to handle security features like authentication of the requester, integrity of message passing. This implies connecting the target component to a replication strategy, an authentication protocol and a signature handling of message exchange. The use of reflection has some merit when the mechanisms to be composed together are 1) independent of each other and 2) can be activated in sequence. In the above example, the input requests to the component can be intercepted first to perform authentication and signature verification, before executing the replication protocol. This can be done using a stack of reflective levels. The combination of the application and a security reflective level leads to a secure application. The combination of the secure application and a replication reflective level leads to a fault tolerant secure application. Another approach can be to have a single reflective level where a simple scheduler activates several meta-level mechanisms in one way or another.

The difficulty here is when mechanisms have to be mixed together, i.e. when a weaving must be done between several actions performed by several required mechanisms. In this case, a coarse approach is not satisfactory. A fine grain activation of elementary mechanisms is required. This is exactly what could be done using aspect oriented programming, i.e. the weaving of the fine grain mechanisms into the source code. The separation of concerns is again not so clear in this case.

In conclusion, the composition of several dependability mechanisms can thus be considered in two ways:

1) combination of several mechanisms to address several concerns.
2) combination of several mechanisms to solve a single problem.

In the first case, we have to distinguish when *mechanisms are independent or not.* For instance *replication and security* can be viewed as two independent concerns, *orthogonal to each other.* In the second case, several mechanisms are required to solve a single problem, the state capture for instance. To do that, we need to deeply instrument the application code (using AOP for instance) but also get state information from the executive layers. As previously said, the introspection of executive layers might be intractable in complex system, the use of behavioral reflection (interception, logging, and replay of system calls) is preferred since it is less intrusive and more scalable.

7 Multilevel Reflection: From Executive to Application Layers

Dependability is known as a concept orthogonal to system layers, which means that the dependability of the system depends on the dependability of all its software layers, and obviously the underlying hardware. A reflective system, in fact its meta-level software, must take into account information at all layers to implement error detection and recovery. The control software is a safety bag composed of assertions, having parameters from all system layers, and recovery actions using actuators located at several software layers. More generally, high level abstractions in reflective platforms do not allow the implementation of efficient and powerful fault-tolerance mechanisms. They lack too much information about low level layers (hidden states, non deterministic events, detailed implementation choices) that are critical to fault-tolerance mechanisms. To overcome the limitations of mono-level reflection, *multi-level reflection* [26, 27] combines OS-level reflection with information obtained from the middleware and application layers in order to provide a powerful programming model for fault-tolerance computing.

Controlling the non-determinism of application replicas is an interesting example to illustrate this limitation. Multi-level reflection allows the identification of the *mutex* that are truly relevant for the platform's determinism (Figure 3). By only selecting those *mutex*, it tremendously reduces the amount of observation that need to be distributed among the replicated nodes, and allows the approach for the control of non-determinism to scale up to realistic multi-layer platforms.

More generally, multi-level reflection is based on the observation that a multi-layer system contains several overlapping programming logics. These logics offer different

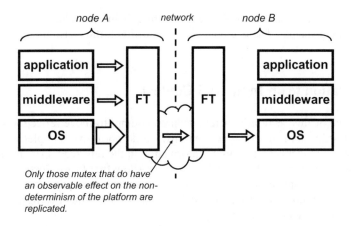

Fig. 3. An example using multi-level reflection

viewpoints on the system that correspond to different abstraction levels. At the OS communication API, for instance, the network activity of a process is viewed as a succession of *socket creations*, *deletions*, *sent* and *received packets*. Inside the middleware implementation, the system is seen in terms of *received requests*, *distributed events*, and *marshaled parameters*. The different viewpoints, corresponding to different programming levels, are related. The reception of a request within the middleware translates into a succession of lower level calls at the OS interface: mutex operations, socket handling, thread management.

Each level of abstraction (OS kernel, system libraries, middleware, application) can be reified into a corresponding meta-model that exports the information that is available at this level. However, as explained with our core example, each of these mono-level meta-models is limited to the information that is available at his corresponding abstraction level: a meta-model that uses an open compiler to reify the language constructs of the application code can not give any information about the thread management if threading is not a first class entity of the considered language. In the same vein, reifying the mutex-activity of the multi-threading library gives no indication of the request currently being processed by the middleware, because the notion of remote method invocation is not included in the programming model of the operating system.

Multi-level reflection builds on the complementary natures of the high and low levels found in a complex system to provide a sound, principled and holistic development framework for fault-tolerance. We refer the interested reader to several paper [26, 27] in which we propose a concrete meta-object protocol that directly supports multi-level reflection on industry-grade platforms.

In conclusion, the use of reflection for dependability implies using this concept at all level of the system architecture. Observation and control features must be available at all software layers to establish and animate models on top of which both detection and recovery software can be developed. The concept of multi-level reflection is thus consistent with dependability that must be addressed at all software layers. In addition, it shows that solving dependability problems requires the combination of information at various levels of abstraction, which is in contradiction with the information hiding principle. The example given in section 8 illustrates the interest of this approach.

8   Application to an Industrial Context

The objective of this section is to report on an attempt to move reflection principles into an industrial domain. For space reasons, we do not provide implementation details; interested readers can find more information in the referred papers mentioned in this section. The objective here is twofold: i) we show first that reflection can be applied to industrial application with significant dependability requirements, and ii) that the principle of multi-level reflection can be implemented without using specific tools devoted to reflective programming.

The example given does not rely on the well-known tools for reflective computing (AOP, open compilers) mentioned earlier in this paper. It shows that reflective computing concepts are of interest to address real-case problems in an industrial context, the development of a *safety-bag* for automotive applications as a multi-level defense software. The good news is that current software frameworks for automotive embedded applications already provide reflective mechanisms!

Our experience in the field of reflective computing for dependability was a key to target robustness of automotive application in complex software architectures. This work was carried out with Renault and Valeo companies within the context of the French Scarlet national project[6].

The Automotive Context

The emerging AUTOSAR software architecture [28] plays an important role today in the development of automotive embedded applications. AUTOSAR is a framework where applications can be developed from software components. In this context, AUTOSAR enables component-based applications to be developed. A middleware (*RunTime Environment, RTE*) is generated from the description of the application in terms of components, tasks and interactions through shared variables. The applications and their communication middleware are executed on top of a basic operating system kernel (essentially a task scheduler) called AUTOSAR OS.

For reasons of scope, we cannot dive into the details of AUTOSAR or into the huge work around development processes like ISO26262 [15] to develop high quality software, but interested readers are referred to the cited literature for more information on these essential topics.

The Objective and Overall Approach

The objective of the work was to design and implement a defense software, a sort of *safety bag*, for multilayered embedded software in automotive applications. The

---

[6] The SCARLET project, funded by ANR (the French National Research Agency, ground transportation research program PREDIT) whose members are: RENAULT (leader), CEA-LIST, INRIA-LORIA, IRCCYN, LAAS-CNRS, TRIALOG, VALEO.

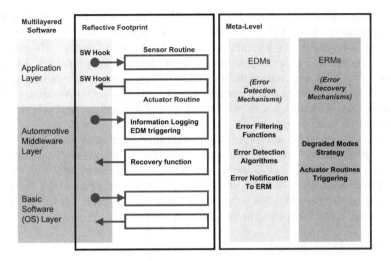

Fig. 4. Wrapping framework principle

defense software must be external to the application and executive software, and should be adjustable to arising needs. It verifies multilevel properties, i.e. properties that concerns the behavior of software objects belonging to several layers.

The whole organization of the target system and its defense software is given in Figure 4. The defense software corresponds to the meta-level box grouping error detection and recovery mechanisms. The notion of reflective footprint corresponds to a set of software sensors and actuators required to implement the error detection and recovery mechanisms. The implementation of this reflective footprint [26] is a connector between the base and the meta-level. As shown in the figure the defense software is orthogonal to all software layers and it collects information at various abstraction levels. In AUTOSAR, the sensors and the actuators can be implemented using the notion of Hook. These hooks can be used to observe and control the behavior of the embedded software[7].

We assume a system may fail in operation due to either physical faults or residual bugs. From the user viewpoint, these faults all result in failures modes. Industrial safety analysis identifies then a list of "unwanted customer events (UCE)" at application software level. These UCE can be potentially safety-critical or not. The hooks are used to (i) observe the computation in progress, (ii) verify the assertions derived from

---

[7] **In AUTOSAR documents, a hook is defined as follows:** A hook function is implemented by the user and invoked by the operating system in case of certain incident. In order to react to these on system or application level, there are two kinds of hook functions.
-   application-specific: hook functions within the scope of an individual OS application;
-   system-specific: hook functions within the scope of complete computing unit (in general provided by the integrator)

These hooks can be use to trace events and read/write access to shared variables. More importantly, they can also be used as error handling means (ErrorHook, ProtectionHook) or mechanisms to control tasks behaviour (preTaskHook, PostTaskHook).

each UCE at *Execution Control Points* (synchronization with the application control flow) according to a pre-defined *Execution Context* (synchronization with the application data), and (iii) finally execute recovery actions. Hook routines are used to log useful information in order to perform the verification of the properties. The precise location of the hook depends on the information to get and on implementation optimization. Actually, we need hooks around service calls that perform critical control or data flow actions. Putting hooks *before* or *after* an interface can be easily realized by automatic code generation.

In the AUTOSAR context, the *RTE* implements a series of hook functions with empty routines that are invoked automatically by the *RTE* when selected events occur (e.g. several OS service calls, application functions invocation, etc.). We use these hooks when they exist in the AUTOSAR RTE specification, and add the missing ones depending on the use case. We refer interested readers to papers describing in detail the use of reflective computing in this context [29].

Summary and Conclusion

Robustness of embedded software is a crucial issue due to the increasing complexity of software functions and their supporting runtime environment. The multiplexing of software components on a given hardware platform, the reuse of existing software components, the flexibility of system configurations and the adaptation to user needs are essential. To this aim, complex multilayer software architectures have been defined in the automotive industry. Improving the robustness of application in this context is a real challenge. The automotive industry is very active to meet this challenge through standardization activities (AUTOSAR, ISO26262).

Our proposal is complementary to built-in mechanisms and relies on multilevel reflection concepts. We have proposed a methodology, done some proof of concepts and showed the feasibility of the approach for automotive software platforms [30]. Our synthetic case studies illustrate as well interesting characteristics for separation of concerns of the multilevel RTE (where most of hooks can be placed even for application or operating system purposes). It shows that such platform already provides basic means for reflective computing. Thanks to reflective computing principles, this experience showed that a defense software can be developed as an external software and customized by a system integrator on a case-by-case basis.

9 Lessons Learnt and Challenges

Is reflection an obsolete concept today? Of course not as it provides fundamental concepts to design adaptive systems regarding various concerns, fault tolerance in particular. Reflection principles lead to a disciplined way of developing systems and makes separation of concerns very effective. Reflective languages including AOP and reflective component based technologies are core ingredients to develop system where dependability is as much as possible independent from the application software. However, as shown in section 8, a reflective architecture can also be developed without dedicated reflective tools. It is a design philosophy that can be implemented with standard languages and system structuring.

Summary and Lessons Learnt

Several fault tolerance techniques can take advantage of separation of concerns using reflective computing. The benefits with respect to maintenance and adaptation compensate performance overhead related to the base-meta-level indirections. Such overhead is in fact very small for distributed implementations of replication protocols, the group communication overhead being several order of magnitude higher that the indirection overhead.

Table 1. Fault tolerance using reflective computing - Summary

Implementing Fault tolerance	At the Meta-level	At the Base level
Replication protocols	Synchronization of replicas according to various strategies	State management for checkpointing based strategies
Software FT strategies	Simple scheduling of application versions and decision	Development of all versions and decisions functions
Wrappers for fault tolerance	Assertions (possibly generic) on the behavior of the target component	Reification of core variable and events to implement assertion verification
Composition of mechanisms	For independent concerns (mechanisms), mechanisms can be implemented and scheduled at the meta-level	For deeply dependent mechanisms, their aggregation remains application dependent.

Nevertheless, separation of concerns does not make things better in some cases, in particular when the mechanisms and the application are too dependent with each other. Table 1 summarizes very briefly some of the insights gained through our experience, i.e. what can be done at the meta-level and what remains dependent on the base level. Such separation means that in some cases the mechanisms can be developed independently from the application, i.e. by a specialist. The application programmer is not involved, the evolution/adaptation of fault tolerance mechanisms according to the context of usage is much better.

Most *Replication Protocols* can be implemented at the meta-level using language or component reflective features. However, the *state handling issue* remains a difficult problem that can either be delegated to the base level developer or implemented using reflective techniques (reflective and aspect oriented languages and serialization features, interception and logging of system calls). In most cases, i.e. complex applications, this cannot be done independently from the application developer. In some other cases, when the independence of the application and its fault tolerance strategy is very strong, reflective computing has limited interest. This is the case for *Software Fault Tolerance* strategies. Design patterns and frameworks can provide the same scheduling facilities to coordinate versions and decisions. The work to be done remains a base level activity.

The development of self-checking components using *Wrapping* is an intermediate case, in particular considering off-the-shelf components. Making visible a core set of variables and the provision of reified events to establish a behavioral model at the meta-level enable wrappers to improve built-in error detection of the target component. When properties can be expressed in generic way from well-defined specifications (scheduling, memory management policy, synchronization mechanism) then an external verification of the properties is possible. Doing the verification externally is interesting because such mechanism may depend of the context of usage and performance tradeoffs to be satisfied (temporal performance vs dependability).

As previously observed, the *composition of dependability mechanism* depends on the dependence with each other. The benefits of reflective computing can be high for independent mechanisms that can be scheduled easily at the meta-level. Otherwise, the work has to be done at the base level.

Handling complexity of application software at various levels of a software architecture is also a difficult issue. The *multi-level reflection* paradigm is certainly a good way to tackle the problem. However, from our experience in the automotive industry, we observed that there is a tradeoff between internal and external mechanisms. Internal mechanisms are necessary to handle highly application-dependent erroneous situations (through error handlers, exceptions handling mechanisms) and cannot be externalized easily. However, as soon as global properties are concerned and when observability is sufficient, reflective computing is of high interest whatever the technique used to implement a reflective framework.

Reflection principles are the basis of AOP, although AOP users seem to ignore such original roots. As a consequence, they do not use sometimes AOP as a very powerful tool to perform separation of concerns but as a fancy compilation facility to glue pieces of code together. It is clear that AOP has many merits regarding fault tolerance computing and dependability architectures, for instance to develop reification and introspection mechanisms, but also to implement state management mechanisms that are highly target software component dependant.

Perspective and Approaches

As far a fault tolerance is concerned, one cannot forget that the first objective is to make systems that are able to tolerate residual internal faults with a high level of coverage and can survive of external faults from the environment. The role of reflection in this context is to help the system designer to separate functional code development from fault tolerance mechanisms as much as possible, when this separation of concerns makes sense. As we have seen before, for safety critical systems implementing software fault tolerance using diversification the benefits of reflection are limited. Other paradigms like design patterns and component frameworks can be used instead to accommodate diverse implementations of a software component.

We distinguish two levels of reflective techniques [31]: 1) *reflection in the small* (from metaobject protocols to aspect oriented programming), and 2) *reflection in the large* (from components to web services).

Reflection in the small using reflective languages including aspect oriented programming is of interest to address internal state access management (serialization of object state) and reify some data belonging to the state for developing external wrappers. The reification of the state can be done at the source code level or at the interpreter level when there is one. The global state of the computation depending also on executive layers objects, the reification of the state must be performed at several abstraction levels. This is exactly what multi-level reflection means. The reification of the state can be done using deep instrumentation (with AOP for instance) or simply using reification of the calls to some meta-level journals management. The result is the provision of (partial) state information to the meta-level though serialization data structures and journals. Such type of reflection helps a software component to be, firstly *self-checking* thanks to complementary error-detection mechanisms and, secondly *recoverable* through state handling mechanisms. This should also lead to a new generation of COTS components, must easier to reuse in dependable systems.

Reflection in the large using Component Based Software Engineering is the most promising. Although detailed semantics of the application is not visible at this level, reflective component frameworks provides means to master the composition and the interaction of a large application, thanks to control mechanisms attached to a reflective component (activation management – *start, stop* –, binding management – *disconnect, connect* –, etc.). In addition, the notion of component can be mapped to error confinement areas using memory protection mechanisms provided by the hardware. This is mandatory to implement techniques to tolerate physical faults but also software faults corrupting memory locations. The main interest of such design approach is certainly the management of fault tolerance strategies at a coarse level of abstraction. Using reflection in the small we have obtained good properties of individual components (*self-checking* and *recoverable*), reflection in the large through reflective components provides the means to defined and adapt the fault tolerance strategies to the environment, the context of usage, the system configuration, but also according to performance tradeoffs.

The above approaches can be applied to a wide range of applications from embedded systems (the automotive context is an example) but also to service oriented architectures (e.g. based on web services and their meta-description supports [32]).

Some Challenges

From a technical standpoint, structural modeling and behavioral modeling is mandatory to control system behavior and perform runtime analysis of the system behavior and reconfiguration actions. Error detection must be based on a detailed knowledge of the application behavior through such models, error recovery must also use this knowledge to perform recovery actions in a consistent manner. Modeling and monitoring of a component-based application is of high interest for dependability, for instance in the temporal domain [33]. This issue has already been investigated for runtime verification and on-the-fly model checking. These works are a source of information and a track of inspiration for reflective component-based software engineering first and separation of concerns for adaptive fault tolerant computing.

The perpetual evolution of systems cannot be ignored, this is also true for dependable systems. Adaptation of fault tolerance mechanisms can be thus imposed by a lack of resources, the insertion of new resources, or new non-functional specifications to be considered (new type of faults, for instance). The fault tolerance software must evolve without stopping the system activity. This implies limiting the number of locks in the system activity and more precisely it requires the identification of adaptable state where the modification of the software configuration can be performed. This is a difficult issue that has been recently addressed at least partially [34]. The evolution of reflective-CBSE should provide mechanisms to tackle this problem, i.e. efficient modeling and monitoring of the system activity.

It is clear that the software engineering community and the dependability community should work more closely together to tackle these problems. They should provide tailored design patterns and reflective component frameworks to solve them for real industrial applications. Last but not least, validation issues of reflective technologies cannot be ignored in this context as well. This has been addressed in the past [35] but there is a long way to follow, validation and complexity being antagonist issues. Separation of concerns should also play a role in this respect.

To speak in more general terms, the evolution of systems in operation is a reality and software engineering technologies do support this trend (service oriented architectures, component-based software engineering, reflective computing and aspect oriented programming, etc.). The evolution can be related to several factors: changes in the system configuration, lack of resources due to failures, upgrades of applications, changes in application specifications, changes in fault assumptions and threats, performance requirements and dependability figures, etc. Many more reasons can be found to justify the fact that evolution may have a strong impact on a system in operation. We do need resilient systems in the future, where resilience can be defined as follows.

« Resilience : persistence of dependability when facing changes » [36]

As far as resilient computing is concerned, the adaptation of systems in operation may have a strong impact on their dependability properties, in particular their fault tolerance capabilities. Clearly, our community can take advantage of novel software engineering technologies, in particular reflective computing, component-based software engineering, model-based code generation, domain specific languages, to address the on-line evolution of dependable systems. In other words, we aim to master the evolution of systems at runtime without impairing their expected dependability properties.

To deal with change, critical computer-based systems of the future need to exhibit a high degree of evolvability and autonomy. To this end, based on the background gained with reflective computing and companion technologies, we need to develop new methods, techniques and tools for describing, designing, analyzing and developing dependable systems for on-line evolvability and autonomy. The problem is complex, several dimensions can be mentioned and must be addressed.

- Designing the system (application and dependability mechanisms) taking on-line adaptation as a first class concept;
- Development of the system through modelling, code generation techniques, frameworks and declarative approaches using domain specific languages;
- Monitoring the system to control its behaviour in both the value and temporal domain, to fulfil real-time properties even in the presence of faults;
- On-line evaluation of dependability measures to trigger adaptation in a proactive manner when the anticipated behaviour violates the dependability objective of the system;
- Validation of the system through software testing of the frameworks instances (including on-line) and fault injection techniques.

The lessons learnt from the work carried out is that several methods and techniques are available today to develop fault tolerant systems benefiting from separation of concerns. However their application to the evolution of dependable systems in operation is still a real big challenge and integrated tools are necessary to help designer of context-aware adaptive dependable systems.

10 Conclusion

This paper tried to summarize a personal understanding of reflective computing and of its implications for architecting dependable systems. It is based on a long experience in the design and the validation of fault tolerant systems. In short, the main lesson is that reflection is a powerful concept for fault tolerant computing, in particular when mechanisms can be independent from the application semantics (replication protocols, authentication, ciphering, etc.). When mechanisms are closely linked to the internal state and behavior of a component/system then the answer must more nuanced. In some cases, the benefits are very small. This is the case for several fault tolerance techniques, essentially those based on diversification. However, the use of reflective computing has some merits for improving the behavior of software components in the presence of faults using wrappers. This is true when the observability is sufficient to develop external assertions in order to verify some properties. The assertions are some time generic enough for several target software components, various implementation of the same OS specification for instance. In addition, it is clear that observability can be very much improved for open source components, giving thus the opportunity to develop more efficient wrappers. The use of such wrappers may depend on the context of integration of the software component. Last but not least the composition of mechanism takes advantage of reflective computing when there are independent concerns from each other.

Independently of which development technique is used, the main objective of architecting a dependable system is clearly its dependability properties. In this respect, one cannot ignore core issues such as, for instance, isolation and error confinement. All techniques improving separation of concerns while guaranteeing error confinement areas are clearly welcome. Another worry is performance: separation of concerns might sometimes be considered too expensive because of the number of indirections triggered during execution. In practice, tradeoffs between performance and separation of concerns have to be analyzed on a case-by-case basis.

Among the challenges, validation is certainly of upmost interest. The typical organization of a reflective system has to be validated by appropriate testing strategies, in particular regarding the "connection" between base and meta-level software. Some attempts have been made [37] but more work has to be done. AOP and CBSE being today the main tools to develop reflective systems, testing strategies targeting these technologies are a very important track of investigation. The success of such research work will decide on the success of reflective-related technologies in general in the context of safety critical systems.

The evolution of dependable systems on-line cannot be bypassed today. I think that runtime adaptation of fault tolerant systems has to be considered, the main question being the following: what is the effect of system evolution with respect to dependability in general and fault tolerance mechanisms in particular? The answer to this question implies precise and scalable structural and behavioral models at runtime. The runtime verification and model checking community should provide inputs to the dependable systems architects to solve this problem. Architecting evolvable dependable systems has already received some attention, and we refer the reader to a book on the subject [38] for a more detailed discussion, but a huge amount of open research questions remains.

As a final word, one can see reflective computing as an help for developers to think about their system's design in a more principled, structured way in order to improve separation of concerns between application and dependability mechanisms. A substantial body of work already exists on these topics, and today's research should clearly take advantage of this past experience. Novel techniques should enforce essential properties of dependable systems, but should also refrain from using fancy and hence often intractable programming tricks. They should focus on some restrictions of use and companion validation techniques in order to find an appropriate balance between separation of concerns and dependability goals.

Acknowledgements

The author wishes to thank colleagues of the dependable computing research group at LAAS who helped me very much understanding core notions of dependable computing and keep them in mind whatever the development technique is, reflective or more conventional. I would also like to warmly thank Brian Randell and Robert Stroud, from the University of Newcastle-upon-Tyne, for the numerous discussions and brainstorming we had on the subject, they have been essential to go around these issues. I would also to thank very much Shigeru Chiba from the University of Tokyo who help us implementing the experiments using OpenC++.

It is my pleasure to warmly thank a long list of my PhD students who contribute to the works and insights reported in this paper: Tanguy Perennou, Marc-Olivier Killijian, Manuel Rodriguez, Juan-Carlos Ruiz, François Taïani, Eric Marsden, Nicolas Salatge, Thomas Pareaud, Thomas Robert, Caroline Lu. Special thanks go to François Taiani for his clever advices on the last version of this paper.

The underlying work reported in this paper has been carried out in particular with the support of CNRS, the European Community through several projects, the Ministry of Research and Education, CNRS-JSPS agreements, France Telecom, the French Defense Research Agency, the French Agency for National Research and Renault.

References

1. Agha, G., et al.: A Linguistic Framework for Dynamic Composition of Dependability Protocols. In: the IFIP Conference on Dependable Computing for Critical Applications (DCCA-3), pp. 197–207. Elsevier, Palermo (1992)
2. Garbinato, B., Guerraoui, R., Mazouni, K.R.: Implementation of the GARF Replicated Objects Platform. Distributed Systems Engineering Journal 2(1), 14–27 (1995)
3. Pérennou, T., Fabre, J.-C.: A Metaobject Architecture for Fault-Tolerant Distributed Systems: the FRIENDS Approach. IEEE Trans. on Computer, Special Issue on Dependability of Computing Systems 47, 78–95 (1998)

4. Maes, P.: Concepts and Experiments in Computational Reflection. In: Conference on Object-Oriented Programming Systems, Languages, and Applications (OOPSLA), Orlando, Florida, pp. 147–155 (1987)
5. Chiba, S.: A Metaobject Protocol for C++. In: Object-Oriented Programming Systems, Languages and Applications (OOPSLA 1995), Austin, Texas, pp. 285–299 (1995)
6. Blair, G.S., Coulson, G., Blair, L., Duran-Limon, H., Grace, P., Moreira, R., Parlavantzas, N.: Reflection, Self-Awareness and Self-Healing in Open ORB. In: Proceedings of the ACM Sigsoft Workshop on Self-Healing Systems, WOSS 2002 (November 2002)
7. Patil, A., Audsley, N.: Implementing Application-Specific RTOS Policies using Reflection. In: Proc. of the 11th IEEE Real-time and Embedded Technology and Applications Symposium, San Francisco, USA, pp. 438–447 (March 2005)
8. Martins, E., Rosa, A.C.A.: A Fault Injection Approach Based on Reflective Programming. In: Proc. of the 2000 International Conference on Dependable Systems and Networks (formerly FTCS-30 and DCCA-8), pp. 407–416 (June 2000)
9. Chiba, S.: A Study on a Compile-time Metaobject Protocol, Phd. Thesis, University of Tokyo, Japan (1996)
10. Kiczales, G., Lamping, J., Mendhekar, A., Maeda, C., Videira Lopes, C., Loingtier, J.-M., Irwin, J.: Aspect-Oriented Programming. In: Aksit, M., Matsuoka, S. (eds.) ECOOP 1997. LNCS, vol. 1241, pp. 220–242. Springer, Heidelberg (1997)
11. Kiczales, G., Hilsdale, E., et al.: An Overview of AspectJ. In: European Conference on ObjectOriented Programming, Springer, London (2001)
12. Coulson, G., Grace, P., et al.: Towards a Component-based Middleware Architecture for Flexible and Reconfigurable Grid Computing. In: International Workshops on Enabling Technologies, Infrastructure for Collaborative Enterprises, 14–16. IEEE Computer Society, Modena (June 2004)
13. Bruneton, E., Coupaye, T., Leclercq, M., Quéma, V., Stefani, J.-B.: The Fractal Component Model and Its Support in Java. Software, Practice and Experience 36(11-12), 29 (2006)
14. RTCA Inc. Document, RTCA/DO-178B dated December 1, – Software Considerations in Airborne Systems and Equipment Certification (1992)
15. ISO/WD 26262-6: Road vehicles, Functional safety, Part 6: Product development: software level (2007)
16. Gorton, I., Heineman, G.T., Crnković, I., Schmidt, H.W., Stafford, J.A., Szyperski, C., Wallnau, K. (eds.): CBSE 2006. LNCS(Programming and Software Engineering), vol. 4063. Springer, Heidelberg (2006)
17. Coulson, G., Blair, G., Grace, P., Taïani, F., Joolia, A., Lee, K., Ueyama, J., Sivaharan, T.: A generic component model for building systems software. ACM Transactions on Computer Systems (TOCS) 26(1), 1–42 (2008)
18. Sun: Interface Serializable, http://java.sun.com/javase/6/docs/api/java/io/Serializable.html
19. Avizienis, A.l., Laprie, J.-C., Randell, B., Landwehr, C.: Basic Concepts and Taxonomy of Dependable and Secure Computing. IEEE Transactions On Dependable And Secure Computing 1(1) (January-March 2004)
20. Randell, B., Xu, J.: The Evolution of the Recovery Block Concept. In: Lyu, M. (ed.) Software Fault Tolerance. Trends in Software series, pp. 1–22. John Wiley & Sons, Chichester (1995)
21. Laprie, J.-C., Arlat, J., Béounes, C., Kanoun, K.: Definition and Analysis of Hardware- and Software-Fault-Tolerant Architectures. Computer 23(7), 39–51 (1990)
22. Rodríguez, M., Fabre, J.-C., Arlat, J.: Wrapping Real-time Systems from Temporal Logic Specifications. In: Bondavalli, A., Thévenod-Fosse, P. (eds.) EDCC 2002. LNCS, vol. 2485, pp. 253–270. Springer, Heidelberg (2002)

23. Rodríguez, M., Salles, F., Fabre, J.-C., Arlat, J.: MAFALDA: Microkernel Assessment by Fault Injection and Design Aid. In: Hlavicka, J., Maehle, E., Pataricza, A. (eds.) EDDC 1999. LNCS, vol. 1667, pp. 143–160. Springer, Heidelberg (1999)

24. Koopman, P., DeVale, J.: Comparing the Robustness of POSIX Operating Systems. In: Proc. 29th IEEE International Symposium on Fault-Tolerant Computing (FTCS-29), Madison, WI, USA, pp. 30–37 (1999)

25. Marsden, E., Fabre, J.-C.: Failure Mode Analysisof CORBA Service Implementations. In: Guerraoui, R. (ed.) Middleware 2001. LNCS, vol. 2218, pp. 216–231. Springer, Heidelberg (2001)

26. Taïani, F., Fabre, F.J.-C., Killijian, M.O.: Towards Implementing Multi-Layer Reflection for Fault-Tolerance. In: Proc. of the IFIP/IEEE Int. Conf on Dependable Systems and Networks (DSN 2003), San Francisco,CA, USA, pp. 435–444 (2003)

27. Taïani, F., Killijian, M.-O., Fabre, J.-C.: A Multi-Level Meta-Object Protocol for Fault-Tolerance in Complex Architectures. In: Proc. of the IFIP/IEEE Int. Conf. on Dependable Systems and Networks (DSN 2005), Yokohama, Japan, pp. 270–279 (2005)

28. AUTomotive Open Standard ARchitecture, http://www.autosar.org

29. Lu, C., Fabre, J.-C., Killijian, M.O.: Robustness of modular multilayered software in the automotive domain: a wrapping-based approach. In: Proc. of the 14th Int. IEEE Conf. on Emergent Technology and Factory Automation (ETFA 2009), Palma-de-Mallorca, Spain (September 2009)

30. Lu, C., Fabre, J.-C., Killijian, M.O.: An approach for improving Fault-Tolerance in Automotive Modular Embedded Software. In: Proc. of the 17th Int. IEEE Conf. on Real-Time and Network Systems (RTNS 2009), Paris, France (October 2009)

31. Cazzola, W., Savigni, A., Sosio, A., Tisato, F.: Rule-Based Strategic Reflection: Observing and Modifying Behaviour at the Architectural Level. In: Proceedings of 14th IEEE International Conference on Automated Software Engineering (ASE 1999), Cocoa Beach, Florida USA, pp. 263–266 (1999)

32. Salatge, N., Fabre, J.-C.: Fault Tolerance Connectors for Unreliable Web Services. In: Proceedings of the 37th Annual IEEE/IFIP International Conference on Dependable Systems and Networks (DSN 2007), pp. 51–60 (2007)

33. Robert, T., Fabre, J.-C., Roy, M.: On-line monitoring of real time applications for early error detection. In: The 14th IEEE Pacific Rim International Symposium on Dependable Computing (PRDC 2008), Taipei, Taiwan, December 15-17 (2008)

34. Fabre, J.-C., Killijian, M.-O., Pareaud, T.: Towards On-Line Adaptation of Fault Tolerance Mechanisms. In: Proc. of the European Dependable Computing Conference (EDCC 2010), Valencia, Spain, pp. 45–54 (2010)

35. Ruiz, J.-C., Fabre, J.-C., Thévenod-Fosse, P.: Testing MetaObject Protocols Generated by Open-Compilers for Safety-Critical Systems. In: Proc. Third Int'l Conf. Metalevel Architectures and Separation of Crosscutting Concerns, pp. 134–152 (2001)

36. Laprie, J.C.: From dependability to resilience. LAAS research report #08001, P 4 (January 2008)

37. Ruiz, J.-C., Killijian, M.-O., Fabre, J.-C., Thévenod-Fosse, P.: Reflective Fault-Tolerant Systems: From Experience to Challenges. IEEE Transactions on Computers 52(12), 237–254 (2003)

38. De Lemos, R., Fabre, J.C., Gacek, C., Gadducci, F., ter Beek, M. (eds.): Architecting Dependable Systems VI. LNCS, vol. 5835, pp. 49–75. Springer, Heidelberg (2009) ISBN: 978-3-642-10247-9

Architecting and Validating Dependable Systems: Experiences and Visions

Andrea Bondavalli, Andrea Ceccarelli, and Paolo Lollini

University of Firenze, Viale Morgagni 65, I-50134, Italy
{bondavalli,andrea.ceccarelli,lollini}@unifi.it

Abstract. The world of computer systems today is composed of very different kind of critical architectures: from embedded safety-critical sensors and safety equipment (e.g., train on-board equipment), to large, highly dependable multi-computers (e.g. plant control systems), to smart resilient components for ubiquitous networks (e.g., biometrics monitoring applications). The common trend for all of them is to become open and part of an integrated cyber world; still, each of them brings specific challenges that need to be addressed for their design and validation, possibly leading to the different architectural and validation solutions. This paper discusses the experiences gained by the authors on architecting and validating dependable systems, considering the activities they carried out during recently ended European FP6 projects, which concerned traditional embedded systems (in the railway domain – SAFEDMI project), large-scale critical infrastructures (in the electric domain – CRUTIAL project), and distributed mobile systems (in the automotive domain – HIDENETS project). The vision on upcoming and future challenges and trends is finally provided considering pervasive/ubiquitous systems in the context of the just started FP7 ALARP project and considering Future Internet scenarios.

Keywords: architectures, validation, dependable systems, SAFEDMI, CRUTIAL, HIDENETS, ALARP.

1 Introduction

In recent years, dependable and resilient services have been required in very different application scenarios and areas. Still acknowledging the importance and usefulness of traditional embedded systems in many scenarios, a continuous trend has been shown towards increased pervasiveness and heterogeneity of systems, where multiplicity of sensors communicate with themselves and to more traditional embedded systems, with the possible support of complex infrastructures [1]. Such systems evolution implies an evolution of the related challenges in architecting and validating critical systems.

The main goal of this paper is to discuss the systems and challenges evolution in architecting and validating critical systems, from traditional embedded systems towards pervasive, dynamic and heterogeneous systems. To concretely instantiate this issue, we will consider three different scenarios addressed by the authors in the context of recently ended European FP6 projects, i.e., SAFEDMI [2], CRUTIAL [3]

A. Casimiro et al. (Eds.): Architecting Dependable Systems VII, LNCS 6420, pp. 297–321, 2010.

and HIDENETS [4], discussing the experiences achieved on architecting and validating critical systems. The focus was on, respectively: i) Centralized embedded system in the safety domain; ii) Highly-reliable large-scale critical infrastructure; iii) Highly-dependable and mobile distributed systems. Each of these scenarios is characterized by different challenges for the architecture design and validation, because of the differences in the required services and in the expected execution environment. Although obviously not exhaustive of all relevant scenarios and systems, they allow defining a trend towards increased system heterogeneity and pervasiveness.

– *Centralized embedded system in the safety domain.* This scenario is the most traditional of those considered. In safety critical systems, a safe fail state is entered whenever a (potentially dangerous) error is detected. Although this approach allows achieving high safety levels, it may result in reduced reliability. Additionally, maintenance is typically on-site, even only to perform upgrade software, because distributed connections on open networks are typically avoided to reduce the risk of potential security attacks. Regarding validation, the environment is usually controlled and traditional V&V techniques successfully apply; however these systems often require certification, so V&V activity must follow very strict rules, often resulting in increased costs due lacks of proper toolset or methodological support. As representative of this class of systems, in Section 2 we will discuss the SAFEDMI project, where a safe on-board Driver Machine Interface for railway trains was developed, aiming to increase reliability using diagnostic self-restarting mechanism and performing distributed maintenance operations through wireless communication.

– *Highly-reliable large-scale critical infrastructure.* Critical Infrastructures (CI) are complex and highly interdependent systems, networks and assets that provide essential services in our daily life. They span a number of key sectors, including energy, finance, authorities, hazardous materials, telecommunications and information technology. Despite their complexity in terms of largeness, multiplicity of interactions, types of interdependencies involved, continuous evolution of the framework conditions under which these infrastructures operate, it is paramount that they be reliable and resilient to continue providing their essential services, so critical infrastructure protection is a priority for most of the countries. Hence, there is the need to: i) build such critical infrastructures following sound engineering design principles, protecting them against both accidental and malicious faults, and ii) to evaluate them to assess their degree of resilience/trustworthiness. In Section 3 we will detail the challenges and main architectural and validation solutions carried out during the CRUTIAL project, focusing on the protection of the electric power grid infrastructure.

– *Highly-dependable and mobile distributed systems.* Traditional distributed systems consist of multiple nodes connected with wired computer networks. Today wireless networking technologies are also available and they facilitate the communication among mobile actors such as vehicles on a highway. Wireless communication technology is flexible for these purposes but the inherent unreliability of links in mobile distributed systems raises the questions of application level unreliability. Since we are dealing with mobile devices, communication link reliability depends on the actual distances between the nodes (nodes may simply be out of each other range), as well as on the presence of obstacles like hills or buildings that may appear between communicating nodes along the route, which may cause temporary loss of connections. Besides unreliable communication links, the hardware and software faults in the application components shall be taken into account as well, especially in safety-critical applications. In Section 4 we will discuss the main challenges and achievements of the HIDENETS project, which concerned the development of resilient system for car-to-car and car-to-infrastructure communication.

To further discuss the evolution of requirements and challenges, in the final part of the paper we consider other two even more challenging scenarios: the first one dealing with pervasive systems in harsh environment, a class of system targeted by a recently started European FP7 project, ALARP [5], in which the authors are directly involved, and the second one providing the vision on future challenges and trends considering in particular the Future Internet of Things and Services.

– *Pervasive systems in harsh environment.* Executing critical services through small, portable devices in harsh environment with uncontrolled system boundaries requires the design of resilient services and networks that are able to react to system evolution and adapt accordingly. Achieving the required dependability, trustability and security levels despite accidental and malicious faults in networks composed by mobile nodes is an architectural challenge due to their intrinsic asynchrony. Additionally, the complexity of the system and the difficulty in identifying all possible relevant factors makes validation a critical task. In Section 5.1 we will outline the challenges and envisioned design and V&V solutions of the just started ALARP project, which proposes the development and validation of wearable equipment for safety of trackside railway workers.

– *Future Internet of Things and Services.* Trends on future systems show an increasing interest towards pervasiveness and heterogeneity, where a multitude of nodes and sensors interact each other and with the infrastructures to execute (possibly resilient) services, and where system boundaries are unknown. Critical architectures in such scenario require i) to be highly resilient to support possible changes in the surrounding, ii) to include autonomic feasibility for self-diagnosis and recovery, and iii) to include on-line self-V&V methods in order to support agile software techniques. Validation can not entirely rely on traditional techniques. First of all, it is extremely difficult to have a complete understanding of the system and of the surrounding, making risk analysis, simulators and prototype less effective in a such dynamic context. Second, the requirements for continuous service and system evolution, paired to the requirements for agile software development, make it necessary to include on-line self-V&V activities, in order to validate the component behavior after changes happened. Such scenario finds its most fitting formulation in the concept of the Future Internet of Things and Service [6]. Architecting and validation challenges in Future Internet are further explored in Section 5.2.

The rest of the paper is organized as follows. Sections 2-4 further discuss the key aspects of the design and validation activities carried out during the SAFEDMI,

CRUTIAL and HIDENETS projects. The three projects are summarized using a structured approach that focus on the architecture definition, architecture validation, and main achievements (by the authors' perspective). In Section 5 the ALARP device and pervasive application scenario is presented, as well as future visions regarding challenges and trends for upcoming computing systems. Conclusions are finally drawn in Section 6, also summarizing the main results achieved within the considered projects.

2 SAFEDMI

Railway Automatic Train Control (ATC) systems are based both on trackside and on-board systems. The ERTMS (European Rail Traffic Management System) train-borne equipment includes, among others, the European Vital Computer (EVC) and the Driver Machine Interface (DMI). The EVC is the core of the on-board ATC system; it supervises the movement of the train by using the information received from the trackside systems (eurobalises) and by the Radio Block Center (RBC). The DMI is the interface between the EVC and the driver; it acquires driver's commands and transforms EVC commands in graphical and audible information according to [7]. The SAFEDMI context and environment is described in Fig. 1.

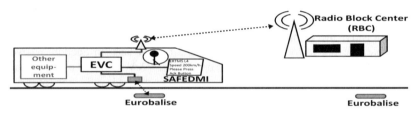

Fig. 1. The SAFEDMI context and environment

The standard ERTMS DMI does not have to fulfill safety requirements although it operates in a critical context. However, many railway operators have begun to require higher safety levels and reduced costs. Moreover, the use of emerging wireless communication technologies is demanded to speed up the DMI configuration and software/firmware upgrade, thus avoiding mechanical operations.

The SAFEDMI project [1] aimed to design and validate a safety-critical Driver Machine Interface, called Safe Driver Machine Interface (SAFEDMI), with no hardware redundancy and using as much as possible hardware and software COTS (Components Off-The-Shelf). SAFEDMI targeted the requirements of Safety Integrity Level 2 (SIL 2 - railway standards propose both qualitative and quantitative classes for the safety of equipments, and SIL 2 quantitatively means that the Tolerable Hazard Rate per hour THR is required to be between $10^{-7} \leq THR \leq 10^{-6}$) according to the railway standards [8]. The main challenges have been: i) the reduction of the hardware complexity and costs by implementing the safety mechanisms in software, and ii) the provision of a safe and secure wireless communication interface to support diagnostics and maintenance. The introduction of emerging wireless communication technologies allows very quick DMI configuration and SW/firmware upgrade, avoiding mechanical operations. In fact a more traditional approach usually requires to extract the DMI itself from the driver desk, open some DMI panel to access an internal communication interface, proceed with the configuration/upgrade, close the DMI, and restore it into the driver desk. Wireless technologies obviously supply a faster way for maintainability. The final achievements of the projects are summarized in [9]. In the following of this section we discuss the SAFEDMI most relevant architectural (Section 2.1) and validation (Section 2.2) solutions and challenges.

2.1 SAFEDMI Architecture

As shown in Fig. 2, the SAFEDMI itself is composed of two components: the Driver Machine Interface (DMI, see [10] for details on its architecture) and the Bridge Device (BD, see [11] for details on its architecture). The DMI is the core of the SAFEDMI: it manages the communication activities with the EVC, with the BD, and with the driver (through a LCD screen and a keyboard). The BD is a wireless access point that allows configuration and diagnostic activities. The internal architecture of the SAFEDMI was designed to address several demands. Here we focus on: i) SIL 2 compliance, and ii) increased system availability.

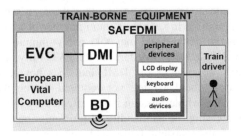

Fig. 2. The SAFEDMI architecture

SIL 2 compliance. The fail-safe fault-tolerant architecture designed in SAFEDMI selected a set of mechanisms according to [12] and [13] on the base of the specific needs of reaching a Safety Integrity Level 2 using hardware COTS components and software-based safety. The proposed solution is compliant with CENELEC standards (such compliance is mandatory for SIL certification). More specifically, it ensures that no single random hardware component failure mode is hazardous by using composite, reactive or inherent fail-safety techniques as suggested in EN 50129 [12]. In SAFEDMI the reactive fail-safety principle was adopted: a safety-related function can be performed by a single item, provided its safe operation is assured by rapid detection and negation of any hazardous fault [12]; as a consequence, efficient error detection plays a crucial role. According to the safety standards [12], [13], the DMI error detection addresses random (permanent and transient) faults and residual systematic faults (mainly software design faults that have not been identified by fault prevention and removal during development). Due to lack of hardware redundancy, active faults in the hardware and residual systematic faults are detected on the basis of their effects on software execution: main implemented mechanisms are i) efficient test procedures with high fault coverage (executed during the DMI start-up and during the normal operative phase of the DMI), ii) data acceptance/credibility checks (executed to verify objects as transmitted files and configuration data), iii) control flow monitoring (applied in the critical functions of the DMI) and iv) multiple computation and comparison (applied in the visualization and keyboard processing functions).

Increased system availability. The safety requirement of the SAFEDMI imposes the presence of a *Safe* mode in the SAFEDMI operational mode, which prevents further operations of the DMI. In *safe* mode the DMI is in an isolated state thus avoiding to propagate errors; whenever the EVC detects that the DMI has entered the Safe mode, it activates the train brakes and stops the train mission. While it is true that this solution provides a safe reaction after error detection, this extreme behavior obviously impacts system availability. The software fault detection mechanism introduced by some design choices carried as a side effect the possibility to increase availability by introducing a further state in the state machine of the overall system, where attempts to recover from some errors are performed before giving up and stopping operations by moving to a safe state. In details, a restart policy is implemented by introducing a *Suspect* mode as fault negation mechanism. Whenever an error is detected, a transition to the *Suspect mode* is forced. Suspect mode is a transitory mode that allows going back to start-up mode, to perform attempts to restart. Using a specific mechanism [14], it is possible to set a maximum number of allowed restart attempts. Moreover, since a re-start of the DMI may take a few minutes, a maximum time to restart the DMI is set. While DMI is restarting, the EVC fully handles the train; EVC tolerates a temporarily absence of the DMI and does not activate brakes only if critical information from the DMI are not required during the restarting period: consequently safety of the whole mission is not affected by this DMI behavior. This mechanism allows increasing the availability of train missions, since SAFEDMI can automatically restart from transient faults and become fully working again, thus avoiding the EVC activates the emergency brakes and interrupts the train mission.

2.2 SAFEDMI Validation

Validation and evaluation tools and techniques are very important components of projects where some rather stringent properties, such as those related to safety, have to be shown *before* the systems goes into operation. The SAFEDMI projects dedicated quite a huge effort to validation activities in order to show that the SIL 2 requirements were satisfied; the selected evaluation methodologies included the solution of analytic models, the application of simulation tools [9] and experimental techniques. The SAFEDMI was evaluated focusing on the safety and availability of the architecture, understanding the behavior and efficiency of its error detection techniques, and analyzing its real-time properties. The communication between the SAFEDMI and its environment was evaluated focusing on the performance and dependability properties of the wireless communication, and the detection properties of the applied safety codes. The most relevant techniques used are summarized in what follows [15].

The *safety and availability of the architecture* were evaluated using a model-based approach. Stochastic Activity Networks (SAN, [16]) was selected as the formalism for the construction of the dependability model since it allows specifying complex conditions and actions for transitions, general firing time distributions, reward functions and easy compositions of sub-models. Since the DMI has a relatively complex architecture including several hardware resources and software tasks, a modular modeling approach was adopted: dependability sub-models were assigned to i) the hardware resources, ii) the software components, iii) the error propagation among them, iv) the error detection mechanisms, and finally v) the system level error handling [15].

The *behavior and efficiency of the error detection techniques* was investigated through software fault injection campaign (i.e., effects or hardware faults were simulated by injecting changes in software). Both qualitative assessment of the correct behavior of the safety mechanism under test (*yes/no verdict* of proper detection and *coverage*), and quantitative evaluation of the error detection techniques were performed. The main measurands identified for quantitative evaluation are two time intervals: i) *detection latency* (time elapsed from the injection of an error and its detection) and ii) *reaction* (after detection, time needed to transit to Suspect mode) [17]. The fault injection campaign allowed to verify that the detection mechanisms of the SAFEDMI satisfies their *real-time properties* (with the exception of one case, where a slight violation of the requirements was observed, analyzed, its caused detected and a simple modification identified to solve the problem [17]); faithfulness in the time measurements collected was provided through a detailed assessment of the measuring system built for the purpose and the results obtained, using principles of metrology (measurement theory) and good practices of fault injection [17].

The *performance and dependability properties* of the wireless communication were investigated using analytical models, simulation (using the NS-2 tool [18]) and experimental approaches (using the prototype). The evaluation of the wireless communication focused on the study of system behavior in terms of commonly used parameters, such as throughput, delay, packet error and packet drops at different layers of the protocol stack [15].

The *detection properties of the applied safety codes*, used in the DMI in communication functions and for the purpose of performing integrity checks of data files or internal data structures (e.g., in ROM), were analyzed through analytical models. Several different solutions were investigated, in order to select the most fitting to the SAFEDMI requirements [15]. Finally, the functional requirements of the SAFEDMI were verified through functional tests executed on the SAFEDMI prototype.

2.3 SAFEDMI Main Achievements

From the point of view of the architecture, the first achievement was the development of a safety-critical architecture with no hardware redundancy and using OTS hw and sw components: the SAFEDMI architecture can be considered a milestone to build highly safety-critical system with reduced costs. Another key achievement was the improvement of the system availability, still without affecting its safety, only through a software solution that introduce a self-restarting mechanism, as alternative to the traditional shutdown implemented in railway system as the safe state. Finally, another key result was the integration of safe wireless communication interfaces within

SAFEDMI, thus moving the DMI from the context of closed system (the actors that communicate with the DMI are known and no intrusion can be expected) to those of open systems, which allows quicker and cheaper maintenance operations while still providing the SIL 2 requirement.

From the point of view of validation, the SAFEDMI was demonstrated to being able to satisfy the SIL 2 requirements. The performed validation activities confirmed us the usefulness of exploiting the cooperation between different evaluation techniques to support the credibility of the provided results, also adopting the basic principles of measuring theory. The trustworthiness of the input parameters (OTS hardware components, error detection coverage of the on-line detection techniques) for the models were assessed through sensitivity analysis to examine whether the range of reasonable values still satisfies the qualitative and quantitative requirements. The resulting models output were confirmed by testing on real prototypes (functional and fault injection campaigns); the measuring instruments and the results achieved were assessed through principles of measuring theory, to guarantee confidence and credibility in the results achieved.

3   CRUTIAL

In this section we discuss the experience on Critical Infrastructure (CI) protection gained during the CRUTIAL [3] project. The project focused on new ICT networked systems for the management of the electric power grid, in which artifacts controlling the physical process of electricity transportation need to be connected with information infrastructures, through corporate networks (intra-nets), which are in turn connected to the Internet. The main challenge for CRUTIAL was to make power control resilient in spite of threats to their information and communication infrastructures. CRUTIAL addressed a number of problems in the field, in particular architectural solutions have been devised to make the Electric Power System (EPS) more resilient to cyber attacks, and testbeds have been implemented to check the proposed solutions on contexts that emulate, on a necessarily small scale, the EPS behavior. Moreover, in order to master the complex mechanisms of global failures, particular focus was put on the study and modeling of the types of failures that are characteristic of interdependent critical infrastructures. The final achievements of the project may be found in [19]. In the following we will discuss the main CRUTIAL achievements concerning both architecture design (Section 3.1) and validation objectives (Section 3.2), especially focusing on aspects directly treated by the authors of this paper.

3.1   CRUTIAL Architecture

In this section we will summarize the main elements of the CRUTIAL architecture. The CRUTIAL project investigated distributed architectures dedicated to the control and management of the power grid, in the perspective of improving the capability of analyzing critical scenarios and designing dependable interconnected power control systems.

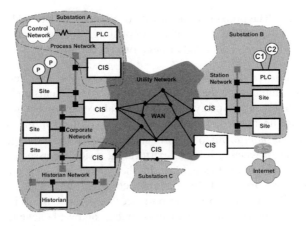

Fig. 3. The CRUTIAL overall architecture (WAN-of-LANs connected by CIS)

As shown if Fig. 3, the system is viewed as a WAN-of-LANs. There is a global interconnection network, the WAN, that switches packets through generic devices called CRUTIAL Information Switches (CIS), which in a simplistic way could be seen as sophisticated circuit or application level firewalls combined with equally sophisticated intrusion detectors, connected by distributed protocols. The architecture addressed requirements coming from the needs of flexible electric power services, characterized by dispersed energy resources, on-demand control and generation/load variations from the market. Each key architecture aspect has been introduced to address specific challenges and objectives identified in the project and characterizing most of the current critical infrastructures. Their main concerns are: i) the achievement of extremely high robustness trusted-trustworthy operation (see [21]), ii) the need to preserve the large legacy composition of CI and keep changes to a minimum, iii) the need to achieve resilience, and iv) the need to control the information flows for implementing global-level security policies. We explore these concerns in what follows [20].

Achieve Extremely High Robustness Trusted-trustworthy Operation. Trusted-trustworthy operation [21] is an architectural paradigm whereby components prevent the occurrence of some failure modes by construction, so that their resistance to faults and attacks can justifiably be trusted. For this purpose, given the severity of threats expected, some key components have been built using *architectural hybridization* methods. In particular, CIS components are trusted to securely switch information flows as a service to edge LANs as clients; LANs trust the services provided by the CIS, but are not necessarily trusted by the latter. In order to be trusted, the CIS itself must be made intrusion-tolerant, prevent resource exhaustion providing perpetual operation (i.e., can not stop), and be resilient against assumption coverage uncertainty, providing survivability.

Preserve the Large Legacy Composition of CI and Keep Changes to a Minimum. For this purpose, *fully-transparent intrusion tolerance* has been adopted aiming at preserving the complete illusion of a standard system to legacy components. It is implemented by innovative replica control and communication algorithms.

Achieve Resilience. The problem of achieving resilience has been addressed through a specialization of intrusion tolerance accounting for critical infrastructures' characteristics. It has been addressed through two paradigms:

- *Proactive-resilience* to achieve exhaustion-safety [22], and ensure perpetual, nonstop operation despite the continuous production of faults and intrusions. This is not a requirement of many intrusion-tolerant systems, but it is definitely of importance for unattended operation, as is desired of the control part of CI.
- *Trustworthiness monitoring* to perform surveillance of the coverage stability of the system, that is, of whether it is still performing inside the assumed fault envelope or beyond assumptions made [23]. In the latter case, dependable adaptation mechanisms are triggered to stabilize coverage and thus, the operational guarantees. This is of extreme importance for situations of instability, either caused by accidental events or malicious attacks, and we believe it can be a key to lower the risk of cascading and/or escalating failures.

Control the Information Flows. It is partly performed through advanced protection mechanisms like the *OrBAC firewall*, which is an adaptation of the classical firewall rule-set operation to enforce an organization-based access control model (OrBAC) [24] for implementing global-level security policies. OrBAC allows the expression of security policy rules as high level abstractions, and it is of importance for homogenizing the diverse security policies of organizations involved in a CI into one policy that controls the global information flow.

3.2 CRUTIAL Validation

Addressing the analysis and evaluation of CI poses a number of challenging issues, among which:

- Complexity and scalability, because of the characteristics of CI in terms of largeness, multiplicity of interactions and types of interdependencies involved. Abstraction layers and modular, hierarchical and compositional approaches are viable directions to cope with these aspects.
- Ability to integrate in the evaluation framework the effects of both accidental and malicious threats.
- Ability to reproduce both structural aspects and temporal behaviors in a context where the studied infrastructures are assembled from many heterogeneous subsystems having different nature, operation phases and regimes with different configurations and behaviors.
- Potential need of combining different formalisms to describe the various components of a system and their dependencies, due to their inherent heterogeneity.
- Potential need of combining discrete and continuous variables into a hybrid modeling approach, e.g., in the case of electric systems encompassing physical electrical infrastructure and the cyber control one.

Major pursued evaluation approaches span both model-based evaluation and experimental techniques. One of the objectives of the CRUTIAL project was to develop comprehensive modeling approaches, supported by measurement based experiments, to analyze critical scenarios in which internal or external faults in a segment of the information infrastructure provoke a serious impact on the controlled electric power infrastructure. The goal was to understand and master such interdependencies to avoid escalating and cascading failures that result in outages and blackouts. Effort was focused on the modeling and analysis of interdependencies, especially considering various types of failures that can occur in the presence of accidental and malicious faults affecting the information and electric power infrastructures.

The modeling framework addressed by CRUTIAL includes both qualitative and quantitative analysis and evaluation methods. Qualitative models have been defined that capture the interaction of the electric infrastructure (EI) and the information infrastructure (II) [25] and that have led to the definition of a new class of automata [26]. To provide a quantitative evaluation of the impact of II failure on the global EPS behavior two main approaches have been followed. The first one is based on an integration of a Stochastic Activity Network model of the EPS with techniques imported from the power engineering field to model and simulate the electrical state of the EPS. This approach allows a rather detailed model of the structure of the EPS, although the model of the control algorithms and of the counter measure that takes place upon a failure are treated at a rather abstract level. The second one is based on Stochastic Well-formed Net (SWN) [27] and is more centered around the protocols addressed by the scenario, so it can represent in some detail the scenarios, but it has to make stochastic assumptions on the EI behavior. The two evaluation approaches have been also integrated in [28], showing the usefulness and effectiveness of their synergic use, one that concentrates more on the structure of the power grid and its physical quantities and one that concentrates on the behavior of the control system supported by the II.

The resulting conceptual modeling framework is well suited: i) to characterize and analyze the interdependencies between the information infrastructure and the controlled power infrastructure, especially the various types of failures that can occur in the presence of accidental and malicious faults, and ii) to assess their impact on the resilience of these infrastructures with respect to the occurrence of critical outages. In addition, two testbeds have been developed which integrate the electric power system and the information infrastructure. A first testbed consists of several power electronic converters, which are interconnected via off-the-shelf communication protocols (TCP/IP); this platform is used to execute different hierarchical and distributed control algorithms. A second testbed builds on environments that are used in industrial automation (SCADA-based) and it is based on a platform for supporting the simulation of attack scenarios. The testbeds and the modeling activities complement each other and provide ways of cross validation and fertilization.

3.3 CRUTIAL Main Achievements

The key idea the CRUTIAL architecture was based on is to encompass a range of mechanisms of incremental effectiveness, to address from the lowest to the highest criticality operations in a CI. Architectural configurations with trusted components in key places induce prevention of some faults, and of certain attack and vulnerability combinations. Middleware software attains automatic tolerance of the remaining faults and intrusions. Trustworthiness enforcing and monitoring mechanisms allow unforeseen adaptation to extremely critical, not predicted situations, beyond the initial assumptions made. Organization-level security policies and access control models allow securing global information flows.

From the validation perspective, we showed that the proposed modeling framework, accounting for both qualitative and quantitative analysis and evaluation methods, can be actually used to build generic models of interdependencies, taking into account the various forms of interactions and coupling the different systems and infrastructures to be considered in the models. Then, it can be used to identify vulnerabilities, inter-dependencies and interoperabilities between systems, to understand what specific assets of the addressed CI are utmost critical and need to be protected the most. Following this analysis, steps can be taken to mitigate the identified vulnerabilities, in an order that reflects the assessed level of criticality.

4 HIDENETS

Recent advances in wireless and portable devices technologies have opened new opportunities for innovative services that can be accessed by mobile users in highly dynamic environments, through a combination of ad-hoc and infrastructure based communication networks. Such services cover a large variety of application domains including information and entertainment (voice and video streaming, online gaming, contextual information services, etc.), as well as safety and dependability critical services (hazard warning, safety and traffic management for transportation systems, assisted living support systems and healthcare monitoring, crisis management, etc.) [29]. This fast growing area poses some significant challenges from the dependability point of view that require the development of innovative approaches to support the design, validation and assessment of such services [30], [31]. In this section we will summarize the experiences on design and validation activities carried out during the HIDENETS project [4]. HIDENETS addressed the provisioning of available and resilient distributed applications and mobile services in highly dynamic environments characterized by unreliable communications and components. The investigations include networking scenarios consisting of ad hoc/wireless (multi-hop) domains as well as infrastructure network domains. Applications and use case scenarios from the automotive domain [29], based on car-to-car communications with additional infrastructure support, have been used to identify the key challenges, threats, and resilience requirements that are relevant in the context of the project. The final achievements of the projects are summarized in [32]. In the following of this section we discuss the HIDENETS most relevant architectural (Section 4.1) and validation (Section 4.2) solutions and challenges, by the authorsÊperspective.

4.1 HIDENETS Architecture

Driven by the challenges and requirements of the use-cases, the HIDENETS project has developed appropriate run-time resilience support via fault-prevention and fault-tolerance mechanisms at the middleware and communication layers. Furthermore, the project adopted appropriate architectural constructs, as well as methodologies to support the design, development, evaluation, and testing of dependable solutions using such mechanisms. The main elements of this architecture are shown in Fig. 4 and are here briefly discussed:

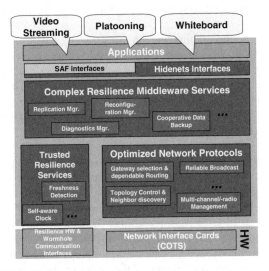

Fig. 4. Simplified HIDENETS node architecture

- *Middleware dependability and resilience services:* These functions enable protection and fault-tolerance for application programs and their data. Functionalities include data replication and efficient access to distributed fault-tolerant storage, error detection and fault diagnosis, as well as recovery actions for different fault scenarios.
- *Enhanced communication protocols:* The geographic mobility of the vehicular nodes leads to rapidly changing ad-hoc network topologies, fluctuating communication link properties, and changing points of attachment to the infrastructure domain. Resilient communication in HIDENETS is achieved via extensions of the Link and Network Layer functionality, including management of multiple interfaces, robust routing and broadcasting schemes, and traffic differentiation.
- *Architectural hybridization:* As certain critical functionalities should remain unaffected by the most frequent fault cases, HIDENETS employs the concept of architectural hybridization [33], which architecturally separates these functionalities. The HIDENETS architecture is divided into two (logical) subsystems:
  - o *Wormhole* subsystem, on which some simple but critical services will reside. We call to these services timeliness and trustworthiness middleware oracles (MW oracles).
  - o *Payload* subsystem, on which complex middleware services, OS services and network services will reside.

MW oracles are trusted components ("more" trusted relative to the Payload subsystem). They offer services useful for applications with strict real-time and/or with strict security requirements. The behavior of these components must be very strict and predictable: to not impact reliability and safety of the whole system their services have to be provided with certain guarantees at the interfaces.

The wormhole part of the architecture provides services with different quality with respect to the payload part. In particular, it assists the execution of fault-tolerant algorithms, offering a minimal set of trusted and timely services, implemented by the MW oracles. In the following we will discuss the challenges related to the timeliness and trustworthiness oracles, forming the wormhole part of the architecture of a HIDENETS node, focusing in particular on the adopted HIDENETS solution to address timeliness needs despite uncertainty.

Addressing timeliness needs despite uncertainty. In distributed, open, dynamic pervasive systems like in HIDENETS, many applications and services may have critical aspects to deal with, in order to provide a dependable (e.g., safe, reliable, available) service. Examples of such aspects are: i) temporal order delivery (for example, the physical time of sensor readings in data fusion process); ii) temporal consistency; iii) reduced and reliable transmission delay. These applications and services are usually time-dependent and use timestamps intensively. Timestamps can be obtained by reading the local clocks of the nodes of the distributed system. Time measurements can be obtained through these timestamps. So, distributed time measurements are performed using clocks of local nodes, and any difference between the clock time views affects the measurement results. Thus, temporal deadlines, distributed estimations, monitoring activities are affected by discrepancies between clocks of involved nodes. As a consequence, it is easy to see that in this kind of systems, the distributed applications and services (especially real-time) require a common view of time.

In order to have a common view of time, it is required that nodes keep their clock synchronized with respect to a global time (it is Temps Atomique International - TAI reference time in HIDENETS): this global time is required to correctly execute a large set of applications and protocols, especially real-time ones. Clock synchronization is thus a fundamental process. However, in complex systems like HIDENETS systems, it is impossible to ensure a-priori that nodes will have a "reasonably good" common view of time: despite the use of synchronization protocols, the time view that a local clock imposes to its node may deviate from global time. Clock synchronization protocols, the clocks themselves and consequently distance from global time are influenced by unpredictability and unreliability factors: distance from global time may vary due to factors related both to the distributed system and network behavior and to the node internal behavior. To overcome these problems, usually systems assume worst-case bounds that are necessary constraints that allow distinguishing unreliable biased data due to poorly-synchronized clocks, from reliable data collected when clock synchronization is good [34]. However these bounds are usually pessimistic values, far from the medium case and are of little practical use.

In HIDENETS we decided to include in the wormhole part of the architecture a new component, the Reliable and Self-Aware Clock (R&SAClock, [35]), which is a specific software component used to obtain time values: instead of a time value composed only by a temporal indicator (i.e., time value $c(t)$ read from local clock), this clock allows obtaining both local clock time value and information on synchronization uncertainty that indicates the quality of the temporal value collected. In this way the components of the system are aware of the quality of the time value, and consequently can use this information when creating timestamps and collecting/using/analyzing timing information.

4.2 HIDENETS Validation

The assessment of the dependability-related attributes of HIDENETS-like systems and applications is a very challenging topic due to their characteristics like heterogeneity of the network domain, large number of components and scenarios, use of OTS components, dynamicity, strong interdependencies between different system parts, variety of threats, and correlated events. A detailed discussion of these system characteristics and their impact on assessment activities is in [36], while in the following we further discuss the heterogeneity and largeness issues.

– *Heterogeneity of the Network Domains.* The HIDENETS networking scenario includes wireless ad-hoc networks, wireless infrastructure-based networks, and also wired networks. The characteristics of these network domains are quite different. For example, the wireless ad-hoc domain (especially in a Car-to-Car environment) shows high dynamicity, caused by changing topologies and changing link properties (varying propagation conditions), while the fixed network has only low dynamicity (mainly due to network traffic fluctuations and congestion). Furthermore, heterogeneity is also caused by different device types, which may differ in capability (processing power, available battery energy), available (wireless) communication interfaces, as well as available middleware functions. The heterogeneity could force the modeler to consider different modeling and solution techniques, each one specifically tailored to capture the behavior of a part of the overall system. In this context several challenging issues arise, like the definition of a proper mapping between subsystems and modeling techniques, as well as the identification of the possible interactions between the different techniques, both at model-level and at solution-level.

– *Large number of components and scenarios.* The set of interacting components involved in a single use-case can be very large, and their number immediately increases if the scale of the system increases as well. The number of components to be considered in the quantitative evaluation process will depend on the level of detail needed to evaluate the quantitative measures under study. Besides the number of components, the complexity of the evaluation also results from the existence of a large number of failure modes and recovery and maintenance scenarios to be taken into account.

In order to tackle such system complexity and analyze the dependability and QoS level as provided by the HIDENETS solutions, adequate holistic evaluation approaches have been developed, which will be discussed in the remaining part of this section. In addition, adequate development tools and subsequently testing methodologies were developed for applications running on top of the HIDENETS framework [37]. A test strategy based on a dedicated testing platform has been devised to support the black-box testing of mobile applications and middleware services in a simulated environment. The feasibility and the practical relevance of the HIDENETS run-time dependability solutions and of the application development approach have been validated in four proof-of-concept test beds [38].

The HIDENETS holistic framework. The properties identified for HIDENETS such as mobility, largeness, dynamicity, variety of threats, together with the necessity of continuous V&V activities during all the design and development stages, call for a composite V&V framework where the synergies and complementarities among several evaluation methods can be fruitfully exploited. In the quantitative assessment of such complex systems, a single evaluation technique (including analytical modeling, simulation and experimental measurement) is not capable of tackling the whole problem, i.e., the dependability evaluation of end-to-end scenarios. To master complexity, the application of the holistic approach allows defining a "common strategy" using different evaluation techniques applied to the different components and sub-systems, thus exploiting their potential interactions. The idea underlying the holistic approach follows a "divide and conquer" philosophy: the original problem is decomposed into simpler sub-problems that can be solved using appropriate evaluation techniques. Then the solution of the original problem is obtained from the partial solutions of the sub-problems, exploiting their interactions. Some of the possible interactions among different evaluation techniques are the following:

- *Cross validation.* A partial solution validates some assumptions introduced to solve another sub-problem, or validates another partial solution (e.g. a simulation model can be used to verify that the duration of an event in an analytic model is exponentially distributed).
- *Solution feedback.* A partial solution (or a part of it) obtained by applying a solution technique to a sub problem is used as input to solve another sub-problem possibly using a different technique (e.g. a critical parameter in an analytic model is obtained using experimental evaluation).
- *Problem refinement.* A partial solution gives some additional knowledge that leads to a problem refinement (e.g. the architecture of a component changes since it is recognized to be a system bottleneck).

It is clear that the system decomposition is not unique, as we can identify different system decompositions corresponding to different levels of abstraction. The higher the level of detail required to capture the system behavior, the higher is the complexity of the system to be modeled and solved. Therefore, a significant effort has been devoted to the identification and implementation of interactions among the different individual methodologies, thus concretizing the holistic philosophy. We moved in two directions.

On one side the goal was to demonstrate how to solve a complex evaluation problem by integrating the results of partial solutions. Based on the hierarchical multilevel modeling and on a multi-phase approach (see [39]), an evaluation workflow was proposed that supports the integration of the results obtained by specific evaluation tasks concerning middleware components and network level characteristics. The workflow does not rely on the presence of a specific partial solution, but it just defines how and where such integration can be realized. Therefore, thanks to its generality, it can be tailored and specified to include different HIDENETS architectural components, thus capturing different system's aspects.

On the other side, we moved from this general context to a more specific one exploring concrete examples of cross-fertilization interaction among different methods, feeding system analytical models with parameter values derived through simulations. For example, as reported in [40], state-based stochastic models and ad-hoc mobility simulators have been integrated in a compositional modeling framework for the analysis of the QoS perceived by the mobile users in a ubiquitous UMTS network scenario, thus allowing to capture more complex and detailed mobility dynamics that may heavily affect the analyzed QoS indicators.

4.3 HIDENETS Main Achievements

From the architectural point of view, we think the key result achieved in HIDENETS was the demonstration of the feasibility and usefulness of the concept of architectural hybridization, which was used as basic idea behind the definition of the HIDENETS node architecture. We showed the benefits that it may bring for achieving improved dependability and the impact on the feasibility of practical systems exhibiting such hybrid nature. Another important achievement concerns the timely detection of timing failures, and in particular the possibility to implement a middleware "trusted" service (the Reliable and Self-Aware Clock discussed in Section 4.1) that provides to the rest of the system a local view of a global distributed time reference, together with information on the quality of the local view of clock. This would be extremely useful for complex systems like HIDENETS, where it is impossible to ensure a-priori that nodes will have a "reasonably good" common view of time.

Focusing on validation activities, we illustrated the feasibility of the holistic approach to perform end-to-end system analysis. We concretely demonstrated that the synergic use of different assessment techniques can actually be an effective mean to mitigate the huge system complexity and provide more trustable results, and we defined an integrated evaluation workflow supporting the integration of the results of external evaluation tasks that consider the precise semantics of the services.

5 Next Challenges and Future Visions

In this section we describe our next challenge and we discuss our vision for main trends and related challenges in architecting and validating future dependable systems. In Section 5.1 the ALARP project for resilient system in dynamic, unpredictable environment is introduced, and the most relevant challenges for architecture design and validation purposes are described. In Section 5.2 we present our vision on trends on systems and network and the most relevant (to our opinion) upcoming challenges: we discuss the Future Internet scenario, where complex, resilient and trusted services are required despite high distributedness, heterogeneity and variability.

5.1 ALARP

Safety of workers in railway scenario is a serious concern, since vehicles are constrained to tracks and therefore drivers have much less margins to react in case of emergencies and therefore trackside workers are exposed to injuries and fatalities [41]. The ALARP project [5] proposes to design, develop and validate an Automatic Track Warning System (ATWS) to improve the safety of trackside workers. The ALARP ATWS will be able to inform the trackside workers about approaching trains on the track, maintenance events on power lines and/or safety equipment in the concerned tracks that may put at risk workers' safety (e.g. being hit by a train or by an electric shock), emergencies on tracks and tunnels nearby the workers (e.g. fires in a tunnel, toxic smoke, etc.), escape routes in case of emergencies. Additionally, it will keep track of the status and position of the workers (to identify those at risk, not responding, or to suggest escape routes).

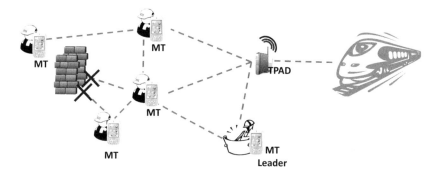

Fig. 5. The ALARP context and environment

ALARP Architecture. The ALARP architecture will be based on the following COTS-based components (see Fig. 5): i) the track-side train presence alert device (TPAD), able to sense an approaching train on the interested track without interfering with the signaling system, using long-range multi-spectral cameras and eaves-dropping the train-network communication, and ii) a set of distributed, low-cost, wearable, context-aware, robust, trustable and highly reliable, wireless Mobile Terminals (MTs) to inform the workers about possible approaching trains and/or other events that could put at risk their safety. The Mobile Terminal (MT) will be able to generate alarms, and to communicate and interact through wireless connections with other MTs and the track-side train presence alert devices together with mechanisms to check validity and trust levels for this ad-hoc communication.

High resilience, security and trustability, despite the possible harsh conditions (e.g. obstacles, high noise and interferences, low light, etc.) are mandatory requirement of the ALARP architecture. Achieving the required dependability and security levels despite accidental and malicious faults in networks composed by mobile nodes is particularly architectural challenge due to their intrinsic asynchrony (unreliable communication, partitioning, mobility, etc.). Several factors induce asynchrony in mobile systems based on wireless communication between them: the unreliability of the communication, the network partitioning, the changes in the network topology and the consequent absence of continuous connectivity to global resources [34]. Furthermore, the threats to resilience and safety are particularly severe: device lifetime and communication are severely limited by scarcity of power; use of wireless links means susceptibility to link attacks ranging from passive eavesdropping to active impersonation, message replay, and message distortion; poor physical protection of mobile devices (especially in a hostile environment like the one considered in ALARP) makes them susceptible to physical damage, and vulnerable to theft or subversion.

ALARP Validation. Concerning validation activities, in ALARP we will advance the state-of-the-art developing modeling construction and solution techniques specifically tailored for the dependability assessment of dynamic, unpredictable, evolvable, safety-critical systems, subject both to accidental and malicious threats. Quantitative evaluation techniques will be used to evaluate the impact of accidental faults on systems dependability, and extensions to qualitative evaluation criteria will be developed to quantify the impact of malicious threats. Therefore, in ALARP we will develop a comprehensive modeling framework that can be used to assess the impact of accidental faults as well as malicious threats in an integrated way.

Additionally, ALARP will take on the challenge of providing a composite V&V framework for dynamic, critical systems and infrastructures where evolution and resiliency/safety are paramount, thus attacking very complex and difficult problems for system evaluation, at the frontier of the state of the art. It is well established and widely recognized that modeling and experimentation complement each other, at least at the conceptual level, but the two approaches have seldom been used in the literature to evaluate real-life systems: the most comprehensive method addressing the construction of analysis models on the basis of measurements performed in a running prototype or in a full deployment has been developed in [42] for performance and performability analysis; a similar approach is recording error propagation traces induced by fault injection experiments [43] to support the construction of error propagation models; other works (e.g., [44]) derive high-level form of behavioral models using experimental measurements obtained from fault injection experiments, while in other papers (e.g., [45]) the values provided from field data are used to setup parameters of analytical models. Other attempts in exploiting the potential interactions among different evaluation approaches were reported in the context of two European projects: DBench [46] and HIDENETS.

The ALARP framework will include both model-based analysis and experimentation (testing), exploiting their potential interactions so as to simplify and increase the possibility of sharing results obtained by the different analysis techniques. Mechanisms will be developed to ensure the cooperation and the integration of these techniques, in order to provide realistic assessments of architectural solutions and of systems in their operational environments. For the analysis of the experimental results, in ALARP we will adopt the approach proposed in [47]. In particular, the authors propose to use OLAP (On-Line Analytical processing) techniques supported by data collected in Data Warehouse that allows: i) to analyze the usually large amount of raw data proposed in evaluation experiments, ii) to compare results from different experiments, and iii) to share experimental results obtained by different research teams.

5.2   Challenges in the Future Internet Scenario

The current situation and the expected evolution of service infrastructures show a clear trend towards dominant characteristics such as extreme complexity, high dynamicity and a very large scale of components/elements and services, high mobility and high scalability needs. In the last few years an increasing attention has been devoted to the natural evolution of ubiquitous computing into new paradigms. The Internet of Things and Service, where multiplicity of heterogeneous sensors, actuators interacts among them and to infrastructure, is enabling one of the most promising and waited vision [48], [1], [6]. There are several factors driving the evolution of Future Internet at all levels from communication commodities to application and service levels, such as, new and upcoming technologies (service oriented approaches, virtualization), as well as market concerns (short time to market, emerging applications). The consequences for architectures and validation purposes must be understood and supported by approaches that improve the resiliency of the elements composing Future Internet, and the trust that can be placed on the services it delivers. This evolution and trends shows the need of new architectures and validation solutions and methodologies/processes.

Architecture. Today, threat detection and failure prediction approaches assume a static system environment and configuration, i.e., it is assumed that system properties are quasi-stationary for the entire period of data collection and operation. However, this assumption does not hold for Future Internet systems which creates several challenges: i) the system changes quicker than a sufficient amount of training data can be obtained, ii) depending on time of recording, training data reflects current system properties to a varying extent, iii) data collection and learning have to be performed in an online manner, i.e., threat detection and failure prediction undergo a permanent update, iv) threats and failures cannot be distinguished anymore and should in general be treated similarly to other faults (furthermore, the specification of what a failure and/or threat is changes over time); v) selecting a minimal yet most indicative set of input variables changes from a singleton task to an ongoing challenge spanning the system's entire lifetime.

It appears extremely difficult, if not impossible, to manage such extremely complex systems relying solely on human intervention. The maintenance costs of such systems are growing so fast that self-management appears to be the most promising solution [49]. The Future Internet, in order to react quickly to changes that may occur, should be able to fully exploit emerging technologies, such as composite framework including a set of mechanisms, policies and processes to ensure the provision of trustworthy services and a resilient Future Internet, where new techniques as the controlled self-stimulation of components/systems in order to enable a more introspective and thus more effective monitoring of its run-time behavior may result a winning solution. Self-stimulation is expected to improve current threat detection and failure prediction algorithms applied to highly dynamic, ever-changing systems.

Validation. Validation methods and methodologies require a deep evolution to adapt to the Future Internet scenario. Traditional V&V approaches that have been applied to embedded critical systems are not adequate for the current and forthcoming large-scale and dynamic service oriented systems. In fact, traditional V&V typically assumes a structured and highly documented development process that allows gathering the required quality evidences, and presumes that the system does not evolve after deployment (i.e., the structure is stable over time). This represents a serious gap, as there are no V&V methods, tools and processes that can cope with the dynamic nature of large-scale service oriented systems, as well as with many other prominent features of these systems such as the use of agile software development methodologies where the requirements evolve during system life cycle. A comprehensive view on research needs and challenges for assessing, measuring and benchmarking of the resilience of information, computer and communication systems can be found in [50]. In the following we discuss some of the challenges specifically related to the Future Internet scenario:

- Predominance of agility in the software development methodologies that brings the need to support traceability to evolving requirements and cope with foremost features of agile software development process that are largely used in the development of service-oriented systems, such as low formalism and sparse documentation.
- Incremental software release development style require to explore the notion of regression in V&V to cope with the development style trend based on successive software releases that characterizes the life cycle of open, service oriented systems. This demands new V&V methods that explore the notion of regression in V&V for open, service oriented systems.
- Dynamic composition of services. The highly dynamic nature of Future Internet systems that require constant adaptation to changes in the environment and demand online reconfiguration through runtime deployment and composition of services makes traditional V&V ineffective, as actually the system structure is changing all the time and has no fixed boundaries. This requires new V&V concepts based on dynamic and evolving system V&V, taking advantage of the service and system monitoring and measurement infrastructure that may be already available in the system for other purposes (e.g., for security and trustworthiness).
- Unavailability of benchmarking and assessment standards. Benchmarking and assessment standards are currently unavailable in many non-safety critical contexts. In Future Internet applications, for example, security and privacy aspects will need to be considered; for these aspects currently no standards exist for benchmarking and for the assessment methods behind them. Research in this direction will need to be performed. Having access to standard benchmark for security and trust (and standard assessment methods) will allow to evaluate in a precise way and to compare results obtained using different systems from the point of view of "quality of service" (in a more general meaning) as perceived by the users. The definition of the standard assessment methods should be based also on the characterization of used tools and methods from a metrological viewpoint.

These observations highlight the urge for new and online dynamic validation methods, tools and techniques capable of assuring the quality of open, large-scale, dynamic service systems without fixed system boundaries, addressing the complete service and software life cycle.

Table 1. Main achievements - overview

Project (system type)	Main achievements – Architecture –	Main achievements – Validation –
SAFEDMI (centralized embedded system in the safety domain)	Development of a safety-critical architecture with no hardware redundancy and using OTS hw and sw components	Demonstration of the achieved safety integrity level
	Improvement of system availability only through a software solution, without affecting its safety	Combined use of different evaluation techniques to provide trustable results, also exploiting the principles of measuring theory
	Integration of safe wireless communication interfaces, still providing the safety requirement but allowing quicker and cheaper maintenance operations	
CRUTIAL (Highly-reliable large-scale critical infrastructure)	Adoption of a range of mechanisms of incremental effectiveness to address from the lowest to the highest criticality operations in a critical infrastructure	Development of a modeling framework accounting for both qualitative and quantitative analysis and evaluation methods, to represent generic models of interdependencies
HIDENETS (Highly-dependable and mobile distributed system)	Application of the architectural hybridization approach for the provision of available and resilient distributed applications and mobile services in highly dynamic environments	Application of the holistic approach to perform end-to-end system analysis, exploiting the synergic use of different assessment techniques to mitigate the huge system complexity and provide more trustable results
	Implementation of a middleware "trusted" service that provides to the rest of the system a local view of a global distributed time reference, together with information on the quality of the local view of clock	Development of model transformations to support an automated evaluation workflow, where outputs of tools are mapped into the inputs of successive tools

6 Conclusions

The goal of this paper was to discuss the evolution of the challenges in architecting and validating critical systems with respect to the systems evolution from traditional embedded systems towards pervasive, dynamic and heterogeneous systems. We made the discussion very concrete considering the problems addressed within recently ended FP6 European projects, whose main achievements are summarized in Table. 1.

Finally, we considered the upcoming challenges for dynamic systems with unpredictable environment and related to the future internet scenarios, also identifying promising research directions that could be taken by the research community in the near future.

Acknowledgments. The authors acknowledge the support given by the European Commission to the research projects SAFEDMI, CRUTIAL and HIDENETS. This work has been partially supported by the European project ALARP, and by the Italian project PRIN [51].

References

1. Satyanarayanan, M.: Pervasive computing: vision and challenges. IEEE Personal Communications 8(4), 10–17 (2001)
2. SAFEDMI – Safe Driver Machine Interface for ERTMS Automatic Train Control, FP6-IST-031413 project, http://www.safedmi.org
3. CRUTIAL - CRitical UTility InfrastructurAL Resilience, FP6-IST-2004-27513, http://crutial.erse-web.it/
4. HIDENETS - HIghly DEpendable ip-basedNETworks and Services – FP6-IST-2004-26979, http://www.hidenets.aau.dk/
5. ALARP - A railway automatic track warning system based on distributed personal mobile terminals – FP7-IST-2010-234088
6. Stuckmann, P., Zimmermann, R.: European research on future Internet design. IEEE Wireless Communications 16(5), 14–22 (2009)
7. ERTMS – Driver Machine Interface Part 1-6, CLC/TS 50459 (2005)
8. EN 50126 – Railway applications - The specification and demonstration of Reliability, Availability, Maintainability and Safety (RAMS) - Part 1: Basic requirements and generic process (2006)
9. SAFEDMI Consortium, D5.3 – Consolidated results and guidelines, EU FP6 IST project SAFEDMI, deliverable D5.3 (August 2008)
10. Ceccarelli, A., Majzik, I., Iovino, D., Caneschi, F., Pinter, G., Bondavalli, A.: A resilient sil 2 driver machine interface for train control systems. In: IEEE Third International Conference on Dependability of Computer Systems (DepCoS-RELCOMEX 2008) (June 2008)
11. Gronbaek, J., Madsen, T.K., Schwefel, H.P.: Safe Wireless Communication Solution for Driver Machine Interface for Train Control Systems. In: Third International Conference on Systems (icons 2008), pp. 208–213 (2008)
12. EN 50129 Railways applications – Communications, signalling and processing systems – Safety related electronic systems for signalling (2000)
13. EN 50128 Railways applications – Communications, signalling and processing systems – Software for railways control and protection system (2001)
14. Serafini, M., Bondavalli, A., Suri, N.: Online diagnosis and recovery: On the choice and impact of tuning parameters. IEEE Trans. on Dependable and Secure Computing 4(4), 295–312 (2007)
15. Bondavalli, A., Ceccarelli, A., Gronbaek, J., Iovino, D., Karna, L., Klapka, S., Madsen, T.K., Magyar, M., Majzik, I., Salzo, A.: Design and evaluation of a safe driver machine interface. IJPE 4(2), 153–166 (2009)
16. Sanders, W.H., Meyer, J.F.: Stochastic activity networks: Formal definitions and concepts. In: Brinksma, E., Hermanns, H., Katoen, J.-P. (eds.) EEF School 2000 and FMPA 2000. LNCS, vol. 2090, pp. 315–343. Springer, Heidelberg (2001)
17. Ceccarelli, A., Bondavalli, A., Iovino, D.: Trustworthy evaluation of a safe driver machine interface through software-implemented fault injection. In: IEEE 15th Pacific Rim International Symposium on Dependable Computing, pp. 234–241 (2009)
18. NS-2 - The Network Simulator (2005), http://www.isi.edu/nsnam/ns/
19. Garrone, F., et al.: CRUTIAL Deliverable D2.2 Analysis of new control applications (2006), http://crutial.erse-web.it

20. Kalam, A.A., Bondavalli, A., Daidone, A.: The CRUTIAL Architecture for Critical Information Infrastructures. In: Lemos, R., Giandomenico, F., Gacek, C., Muccini, H., Vieira, M. (eds.) Architecting Dependable Systems V. LNCS, vol. 5135, pp. 1–27. Springer, Heidelberg (2008)
21. Verissimo, P., Neves, N.F., Cachin, C., Poritz, J., Powell, D., Deswarte, Y., Stroud, R., Welch, I.: Intrusion-tolerant middleware: The road to automatic security. IEEE Security & Privacy 4(4), 54–62 (2006)
22. Sousa, P., Neves, N.F., Verissimo, P.: How resilient are distributed f fault/intrusion tolerant systems? In: Proceedings of the IEEE International Conference on Dependable Systems and Networks (June 2005)
23. Bondavalli, A., Chiaradonna, S., Cotroneo, D., Romano, L.: Effective fault treatment for improving the dependability of COTS- and legacy-based applications. IEEE Transactions on Dependable and Secure Computing 1(4), 223–237 (2004)
24. El Kalam, A.A., Elbaida, R., Balbiani, P., Benferhat, S., Cuppens, F., Deswarte, Y., Miège, A., Saurel, C., Trouessin, G.: Organization-based access control. In: IEEE 4th International Workshop on Policies for Distributed Systems and Networks, pp. 277–288 (June 2003)
25. Laprie, J.-C., Kanoun, K., Kaniche, M.: Modelling interdependencies between the electricity and information infrastructures. In: Saglietti, F., Oster, N. (eds.) SAFECOMP 2007. LNCS, vol. 4680, pp. 54–67. Springer, Heidelberg (2007)
26. Donatelli, S.: Dependent automata for the modelling of dependencies. In: Setola, R., Geretshuber, S. (eds.) CRITIS 2008. LNCS, vol. 5508, pp. 367–374. Springer, Heidelberg (2009)
27. Chiola, G., Dutheillet, C., Franceschinis, G., Haddad, S.: Stochastic Well-formed Coloured nets for symmetric modelling applications. IEEE Transactions on Computers 42(11), 1343–1360 (1993)
28. Beccuti, M., Franceschinis, G., Donatelli, S., Chiaradonna, S., Di Giandomenico, F., Lollini, P., Dondossola, G., Garrone, F.: Quantification of Dependencies in Electrical and Information Infrastructures: the CRUTIAL approach. In: Proc. of the Fourth International CRIS Conference on Critical Infrastructures (CRIS 2009), Linköping, Sweden, April 28-30, pp. 1–8 (2009)
29. Radimirsch, M., et al.: Use-case scenarios and preliminary reference model. EU FP6 IST project HIDENETS, deliverable D1.1 (September 2006),
    http://www.hidenets.aau.dk/Public+Deliverables
30. Basile, C., Killijian, M.O., Powell, D.: A Survey of dependability issues in mobile Wireless networks. LAAS-CNRS research report 02637 (October 2002)
31. Jones, C., Randell, B.: Dependable pervasive systems. University of Newcastle research report CS-TR-839 (2004)
32. Könning, B., et al.: Final evaluation, consolidated results and guidelines. EU FP6 IST project HIDENETS, deliverable D1.3 (January 2009)
33. Veríssimo, P.: Travelling through wormholes: Meeting the grand challenge of distributed systems. In: Proc. Int. Workshop on Future Directions in Distributed Computing, Bertinoro, Italy, pp. 144–151 (June 2002)
34. Verissimo, P., Rodriguez, L.: Distributed Systems for System Architects. Kluwer Academic Publisher, Dordrecht (2001)
35. Bondavalli, A., Ceccarelli, A., Falai, L.: Assuring Resilient Time Synchronization. In: IEEE Symposium on Reliable Distributed Systems (SRDS 2008), October 6-8, pp. 3–12 (2008)
36. Lollini, P., Bondavalli, A., et al.: Evaluation methodologies, techniques and tools (final version). EU FP6 IST project HIDENETS, deliverable D4.1.2 (December 2007)

37. Gábor, H., Waeselynck, H., et al.: Refined design and testing framework, methodology and application results. EU FP6 IST project HIDENETS, deliverable D5.3 (December 2008)

38. Reitenspieß, M., et al.: Experimental proof-of-concept set-up HIDENETS. EU FP6 IST project HIDENETS, deliverable D6.3 (June 2008)

39. Kovacs, M., Lollini, P., Majzik, I., Bondavalli, A.: An integrated framework for the dependability evaluation of distributed mobile applications. In: Proc. of the RISE/EFTS Joint International Workshop on Software Engineering for REsilieNt systEms (SERENE 2008), Newcastle upon Tyne, UK, November 17-19, pp. 29–38 (2008)

40. Bondavalli, A., Lollini, P., Montecchi, L.: QoS Perceived by Users of Ubiquitous UMTS: Compositional Models and Thorough Analysis. Journal of Software, Special Issue: Selected Papers of The 6th IFIP Workshop on Software Technologies for Future Embedded and Ubiquitous Systems (SEUS 2008) 4(7), 675–685 (2009)

41. Office of Rail Regulation, Annual Report on Railway Safety (2005), http://www.rail-reg.gov.uk/upload/pdf/296.pdf

42. Israr, T., Woodside, M., Franks, G.: Interaction Tree Algorithms to Extract Effective Architecture and Layered Performance Models from Traces. Journal of Systems and Software 80(4), 474–492 (2007)

43. Arlat, J., Costes, A., Crouzet, Y., Laprie, J.-C., Powell, D.: Fault Injection and Dependability Evaluation of Fault-Tolerant Systems. IEEE Transactions on Computers 42(8), 913–923 (1993)

44. Arlat, J., Aguera, M., Amat, L., Crouzet, Y., Fabre, J.-C., Laprie, J.-C., Martins, E., Powell, D.: Fault Injection for Dependability Validation - A Methodology and Some Applications. IEEE Transactions on Software Engineering 16(2), 166–182 (1990)

45. Coccoli, A., Urbán, P., Bondavalli, A.: Performance Analysis of a Consensus Algorithm Combining Stochastic Activity Networks and Measurements. In: Proc. Int. Conf. on Dependable Systems and Networks (DSN-2002), pp. 551–560. IEEE CS Press, Los Alamitos (2002)

46. DBench - Dependability Benchmarking (Project IST-2000-25425) (2001), http://www.laas.fr/DBench/

47. Madeira, H., Costa, J., Vieira, M.: The OLAP and Data Warehousing Approaches for Analysis and Sharing of Results from Dependability Evaluation Experiments. In: Proc. Int. Conf. on Dependable Systems and Networks, DSN 2003 (2003)

48. Buckley, J.: From rfid to the internet of things. – Pervasive networked systems – Final Report, Conference organized by DG Information Society and Media, Networks and Communication Technologies Directorate, Brussels (March 6-7, 2006), ftp://ftp.cordis.europa.eu/pub/ist/docs/ka4/ au_conf670306_buckley_en.pdf

49. Kephart, J.O., Chess, D.M.: The Vision of Autonomic Computing. Computer 36(1), 41–50 (2003)

50. Bondavalli, A., Lollini, P., et al.: Final Research Roadmap. EU FP7 AMBER Coordination Action, deliverable D3.2 (December 2009)

51. PRIN, Programmi di ricerca scientifica di rilevante interesse nazionale – Progetto di ricerca DOTS-LCCI: Dependable Off-The-Shelf based middleware systems for Large-scale Complex Critical Infrastructures. Anno (2008)

Author Index

Printing: Mercedes-Druck, Berlin
Binding: Stein+Lehmann, Berlin